The Age of the Arctic: hot conflicts and cold realities

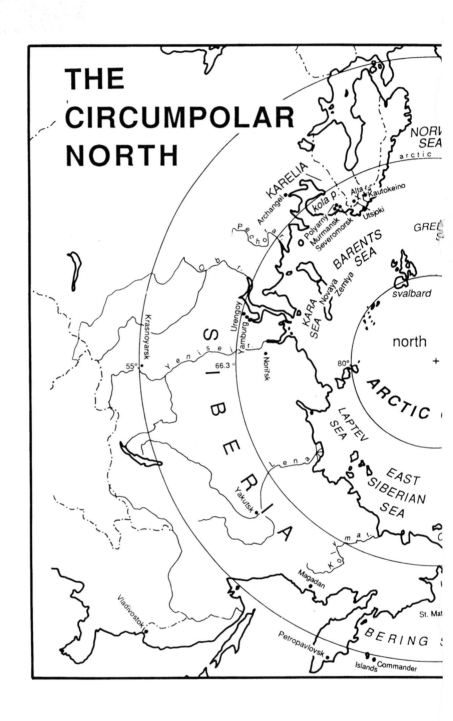

THE CIRCUMPOLAR NORTH

KARELIA
kola p.
Archangel
Pecho
Polyarny
Murmansk
Severomorsk
Alta
Kautokeino
Utsjoki
NOR
SEA
arctic
GRE
BARENTS SEA
Novaya Zemlya
KARA SEA
svalbard
Urengoy
Yamburg
Krasnoyarsk
Yenisei
55°
66.3°
Norilsk
S I B E R I A
Ob
Lena
Yakutsk
north
80°
ARCTIC
LAPTEV SEA
EAST SIBERIAN SEA
Magadan
Kolyma
Vladivostok
Petropavlovsk
Islands
Commander
St. Mat
BERING S

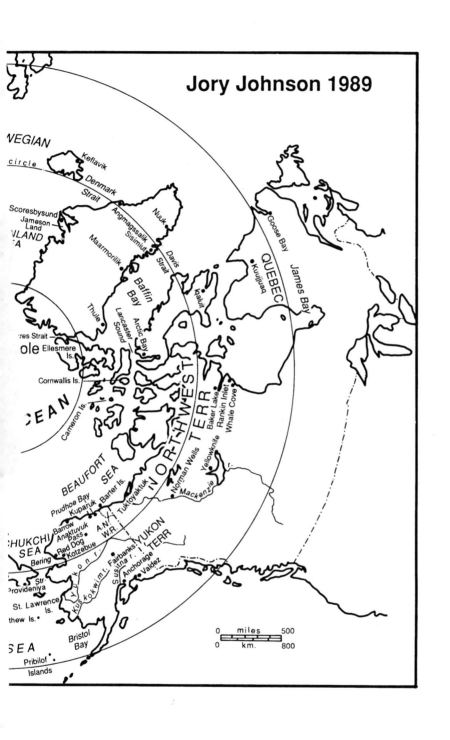

Jory Johnson 1989

Studies in Polar Research
This series of publications reflects the growth of research activity in and about the polar regions, and provides a means of synthesising the results. Coverage is international and interdisciplinary: the books are relatively short and fully illustrated. Most are surveys of the present state of knowledge in a given subject rather than research reports, conference proceedings or collected papers. The scope of the series is wide and includes studies in all the biological, physical and social sciences.

* Also available in paperback

The Age of the Arctic: hot conflicts and cold realities

GAIL OSHERENKO

ORAN R. YOUNG
Institute of Arctic Studies, Dartmouth College

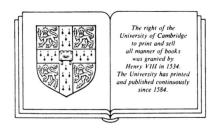

The right of the
University of Cambridge
to print and sell
all manner of books
was granted by
Henry VIII in 1534.
The University has printed
and published continuously
since 1584.

CAMBRIDGE UNIVERSITY PRESS
Cambridge
New York   Port Chester
Melbourne   Sydney

CAMBRIDGE UNIVERSITY PRESS
Cambridge, New York, Melbourne, Madrid, Cape Town, Singapore, São Paulo

Cambridge University Press
The Edinburgh Building, Cambridge CB2 2RU, UK

Published in the United States of America by Cambridge University Press, New York

www.cambridge.org
Information on this title: www.cambridge.org/9780521364515

First published 1989
This digitally printed first paperback version 2005

A catalogue record for this publication is available from the British Library

Library of Congress Cataloguing in Publication data
Osherenko, Gail.
 The Age of the Arctic: hot conflicts and cold realities/Gail Osherenko and
 Oran R. Young.
  p. cm. — (Studies in polar research)
 Includes bibliographies and index.
 ISBN 0 521 36451 5 hardback
 1. Arctic regions—Strategic aspects. 2. Arctic regions–
 –Defenses. 3. Arctic regions—Economic conditions. I. Young, Oran R.
 II. Title. III. Series.
 UA880.074 1989
 355′.033098—dc19   89-562 CIP

ISBN-13 978-0-521-36451-5 hardback
ISBN-10 0-521-36451-5 hardback

ISBN-13 978-0-521-61971-4 paperback
ISBN-10 0-521-61971-8 paperback

Contents

Figures

For Margo Osherenko, who shares our love of the Arctic

Preface

Conflict is a fact of life. Yet many of us seek to avoid conflict whenever possible and, when forced to confront it, treat conflict as an abnormal and generally deplorable state of affairs. Others, purporting to find benefits either for individuals or for society at large flowing from conflict, speak of the functions of social conflict and see no cause for alarm when conflict becomes widespread. Today, there is a rapidly growing field of conflict resolution. Within that field, a growing number of teachers, writers, and other professionals approach conflict simply as a part of everyday life and endeavor to prepare individuals and groups to handle conflict in an informed manner. This latter approach guides our study of the Arctic and is essential to our message. Without judging the costs or benefits of social conflict, we seek to alert people to the pervasiveness of conflict and to provide analytic tools that will help those engaged in conflict not only to improve their comprehension of the circumstances they face but also to enhance their ability to deal with conflict constructively.

Conflict becomes more pervasive in any social setting as the level of human activity rises. Inevitably, actions of specific individuals and groups impinge on the concerns of others. There is nothing mysterious about this. The expansion of human activities forecloses opportunities for parties to avoid conflict by going their separate ways in the hope that an absence of contact will circumvent conflict.

Individuals or groups not organized to promote their interests vigorously are poorly positioned to engage in conflict. Asymmetries with regard to organization serve to suppress conflict since those possessing superior organization are often able to impose their will on poorly organized opponents. As clashes of interest grow, individuals organize to counter opposing interests collectively, the locus of power shifts, and conflict becomes more apparent.

These observations make it easy to understand why conflict analysis constitutes a fruitful approach to circumstances now arising in the Arctic. Prior to the Second World War, the Arctic was a remote frontier capable of offering a safety valve for social conflicts originating in the temperate zones as well as a habitat for subsistence-oriented cultures of indigenous peoples. Rapidly and with little forethought, this situation changed. The Arctic has become a theater for the deployment of strategic weapons systems, a locus of world class oil and gas fields, a prize for those desiring to protect remaining wilderness areas, and an embattled homeland for well-organized groups of Native peoples. Inevitably, these activities clash, giving rise to confrontations within domestic forums and, increasingly, in transnational arenas as well. We neither deplore nor celebrate this state of affairs. Rather, as analysts of conflict, we seek to understand the configuration of interests and issues and offer some guidance to those desiring to handle the emerging array of Arctic conflicts in a constructive manner.

This book is the product of an ongoing collaboration between a husband and wife and a long-running exchange of ideas between a political scientist and a lawyer. We have learned much about conflict not only from team teaching courses on conflict and conflict resolution but also from the process of coming to terms with a variety of conflicts arising from differences in our own temperaments, roles, and professional training. In the process, we have come to believe that everyone should be exposed to some basic ideas about social conflict and about the principal methods of handling conflict. We hope to see the day when courses on conflict and conflict resolution become standard fare in school curriculums. In the meantime, we will rest content if this study of conflict and conflict resolution in the Arctic alerts the major players in this increasingly important region to the circumstances they face and suggests innovative ways for them to come to terms with their conflicts of interest.

Acknowledgements

We wish to acknowledge the role of a number of individuals who helped make this book possible. The faculty, staff, and students of The Center for Northern Studies (CNS) in Wolcott, Vermont, offered us the opportunity to team-teach a course in conflict and conflict resolution that eventually led to this collaboration. In particular, we owe a debt to our CNS colleagues from other disciplines who contributed so much to the development of our way of thinking about the Arctic: Steve Young, George Wenzel, William Osgood, Charlie Cogbill, Randy Hagenstein as well as Nick Flanders, Gail Fondahl, and Gerry Courtin who also read and commented on parts of the draft manuscript. We thank the students at CNS for helping us test our ideas in their classes, and we particularly appreciate the contribution of the northern Native students to our understanding of their homeland. A number of notable northern experts have lectured at CNS and we have learned from them too: Tom Svensson, Thomas Berger, Howard Norman, Ludgar Muller-Wille, Dalee Sambo, Arlene Stairs, Caroline Palliser, Roger Herrera, James Houston, Jack Cram, Barbara Lipton, and Marianne Stenbaek come to mind.

We relied on the prior work of numerous writers and scholars whose work is footnoted in these pages. But accessing the 'gray' literature on the Arctic is frequently difficult, and we wish to thank Walter Slipchenko and others at Circumpolar Affairs in Canada's Department of Indian and Northern Affairs for their assistance in tracking down and providing articles and information including English translations of foreign language materials and photographs. Special thanks to John Merritt and Alan Saunders at the Canadian Arctic Resources Committee (CARC) and to Roy Vontobel at *Caribou News* for assisting our search for illustrations as well as to others who provided photos for the book. CARC's staff has been especially helpful and our contact with two of its Executive Directors,

John Merritt and Peter Burnett, and the competent CARC staff have been helpful in numerous ways.

Terence Armstrong encouraged us to submit a book proposal to the Cambridge University Press series Studies in Polar Research, thus instigating our collaboration. He also assisted by providing a base map of the Arctic which Jory Johnson, a student at Dartmouth College, used to prepare the circumpolar map in this book.

Other friends who read portions of the manuscript and offered their frank comments and suggestions include Elliott Norse, Finn Lynge, Barbara Shapiro, Olav Schramm Stokke, and Linda Young (who also patiently tolerated the conflicts this effort sometimes created in the home we share with her). Cynthia and Cabot Christianson shared their home in Anchorage on numerous occasions and kept us up to date on current information and events in Alaska.

Princeton University's Department of Politics and Center of International Studies provided us both with a quiet yet stimulating work environment in the spring of 1988 that enhanced our ability to complete the manuscript. The John Sloan Dickey Endowment for International Understanding at Dartmouth College encouraged us by activating a process that led to the establishment of an Institute of Arctic Studies, which has become a base for our continuing collaboration.

Maria Murphy, at Cambridge University Press (with whom we developed an extensive relationship by FAX), professionally shepherded this project through the Press, while Audrey Smith provided speedy and thoughtful editing. And finally, our thanks to our neighbor, Lois Eby, who took time away from her own artistic career to prepare the Index.

We wish to thank them all as well as those whom we may have inadvertently left out of these acknowledgements. Despite all this help, we have only ourselves to blame for any remaining deficiencies.

Part 1
The setting

1

Arctic dreams, Arctic realities

We are entering the Age of the Arctic, an era in which Mercator projection maps must give way to polar perspectives in schools, legislative chambers, corporate conference rooms, and military headquarters. Once regarded as an inhospitable wasteland, the Arctic Ocean is now a navigable mediterranean ringed by eight nations. Its partial ice-cover is even an advantage to Soviet and American submarine commanders jockeying beneath the surface for positions from which their missiles could reach key targets in the United States, Europe, and the Soviet Union. Men and women spend months at a time on or under the Arctic Ocean in comfortable quarters aboard icebreakers and submarines. And hundreds of thousands live in Siberian cities or work in mines and oil fields throughout the Circumpolar North.

For almost 500 years, from the fifteenth century to the early twentieth century, a mysterious Arctic lured European and American explorers seeking valuable minerals, a passage to the Orient, answers to the mysteries, and a challenge to the human spirit. The Arctic took the lives of hundreds who possessed neither the wisdom nor the skill to survive there. Today, shippers open two sea routes yearly, one in the northeast passage and one in the northwest passage. Iron, lead, and zinc mines in the Arctic produce valuable ore transported to the South through these once unknown Arctic passages. Nuclear-powered ice breakers and ice-breaking container ships move cargo year round to and from ports that, until recently, were inaccessible for over half the year. The wealth of black gold and its companion natural gas now flows southward through hundreds of miles of pipeline from deposits in northern Alaska and northwestern Siberia. For the military, the Arctic has emerged as one of the world's most important theaters for the deployment and operation of strategic weapons systems. Northern Natives, first treated by white men as semi-savages or barbarians and later regarded with awe for their remarkable ability to survive in a frigid environment, have adapted politically, economically, and socially to assume roles of leadership in international Arctic affairs. The Arctic contains immense tracts of wilderness impelling those who treasure wild places to wage legal and political battles to prevent oil, gas, and mineral development as well as military activities from spoiling their vision of the Arctic. And idealistic saboteurs sink whaling ships in order to close forever the era of Arctic whaling. Taken together, these developments have transformed the Arctic into a region of increasing domestic and international conflicts.

1.1   Arctic realities

We are entering the Age of the Arctic in geopolitical terms. Europe is no longer the principal focal point of global power and international relations. Powerful members of the international community now pursue their interests in arenas previously regarded as peripheries. The Arctic is one such arena. This is not to suggest that 'who rules the Arctic, rules the world', for geopolitical paradigms are also shifting. It would be more accurate to say that 'Who would bring peace and stability to a world of conflict must know and understand the Arctic'. The superpowers are immediate neighbors in the Arctic, and the region is a theater of increasing military activity. Yet, the Arctic may hold the key to stabilizing the nuclear arms race and drastically reducing nuclear weapons.

In America, this vision of the importance of the Arctic to industrialists, policymakers, and military strategists originated in the 1920s with Vilhjalmur Stefansson, who foresaw widespread use of transpolar air routes and predicted that submarine freighters would become economical in the Arctic.[1] He viewed Arctic ice not as an obstacle but as a platform for development. He would not be the least bit surprised by the offshore oil rigs now operating in Arctic coastal waters or by the manmade ice roads and gravel islands used to support drilling equipment in the Beaufort and Barents Seas. The President of ARCO Alaska, Harold Heinze, envisions a network of ice highways across which commercial convoys could cross the Arctic Ocean from Alaska to Northern Europe and the Soviet Union.[2]

In this Age of the Arctic, we are also emerging from a long period of romanticizing the Arctic into an era acknowledging the region's strategic and political importance. The Arctic has become a crucial theater for the deployment and operation of strategic military systems. It is also a major energy frontier which already accounts for 20% of the United States' crude oil production and over 60% of Soviet production. It is the scene of international conflicts over borders, sovereignty, and natural resources – conflicts not only between the superpowers (such as the boundary dispute in the Bering Sea) but also between allies (as in the emotional clash between Canadians and Americans about jurisdiction over the Northwest Passage). The indigenous peoples of the Arctic are leaders in the growing Fourth World movement, the struggle of Native peoples for control over their own destinies. Inuit, Sami, and Dene are at the cutting edge of a movement that links them with aborigines in Australia, Mayans in Central America, and indigenous peoples throughout the globe to awaken the world to the plight and the rights of peoples who occupied these lands before European colonization. The Arctic is also a laboratory for testing ideas about mixed cash/subsistence economies, a setting for efforts to solve pressing economic and social problems that persist in all remote or rural areas whether they are located at the pole or at the equator.

Finally, in this Age of the Arctic, the land of permafrost has become the scene of pitched battles between environmentalists or preservationists and consumptive users of natural resources, be they hunters or oil drillers. The choice between wilderness designation or hydrocarbon development for the coastal plain of the Arctic National Wildlife Refuge in northeastern Alaska has already become one of the most complex and hotly contested decisions of our century. This conflict has pitted a myriad of environmental groups not only against developers, but also against Native residents of the Arctic. The conflicts between preservationists who oppose all consumptive use of wild animals and Native and recreational hunters will be played out most vividly in the Arctic, where Native peoples still depend on wildlife as a critical component of their economy and culture. The resolution or nonresolution of these core value conflicts will not only affect the lives of players in the Arctic arena, but also will teach us more about the nature of conflict and conflict resolution, lessons with global applications.

1.2   The Arctic sublime

Yet there is another reason for calling this the Age of the Arctic, a reason we initially dismissed as a conflicting, distorted vision of the Arctic, but which on closer examination emerges as a powerful force in the world today. This is the Age of the Arctic in philosophical and spiritual terms. We are experiencing a revival of the 19th century vision of the 'Arctic sublime',[3] of an Arctic at once beautiful and terrifying, awesome and exotic, a world apart, a romantic, last frontier offering compelling opportunities and exhilarating risks.

While the heroic, larger-than-life exploits of Kane, Nansen, Peary, Amundsen and others have passed into history, the images set forth in their journals and ships logs remain to inspire us (see Figure 1). The literary works of Robert Service and Jack London and the Arctic seascapes of Sir Edwin Henry Landseer, Frederick Church, and William Bradford impress us. The revival of the Arctic sublime is manifest in glossy picture books (featuring photographs by Fred Bruemmer, Ansel Adams, and others) saturated with Arctic light, ice, and animals as well as in slick magazines promoting tourism or wilderness protection.[4] On television we view specials like '*The Kingdom of the Ice Bear*'. Barely a week goes by without a nature show or children's program offering images of polar bears and Eskimos.

Perhaps the most notable champion in our time of the Arctic sublime, however, is Barry Lopez whose book, *Arctic Dreams*, became a Book of the Month Club selection in 1986.[5] In a series of word portraits of musk oxen, polar bears, and narwhals as well as in his meditations on migration and the lure of the Arctic to European explorers, Lopez depicts an Arctic teeming with wildlife and lavish in the production of spiritual values. Only here or on the African plains, which are already surrounded by a mushrooming and competing human population, can we imagine what life was like in the temperate zones before humans drove whole species to extinction or destroyed their habitats without a second thought. Thus, the Arctic invokes a subconscious nostalgia for a bygone era on earth which we can view today only in particular places in the Arctic at the right moment or vicariously through the works of writers and photographers who have been there.

Even more significant than the whales, walrus, seals, and swarms of seabirds is the landscape they inhabit – a landscape that has become a powerful symbol. It is a magical realm where light and dark, yin and yang, are clearly differentiated. In the Arctic, one cannot ignore darkness, or sleep through it; one must live in it, with it. In the Arctic, the boundaries between day and night, light and dark, are marked in months, not hours. The changes that animals, the land, and especially human beings experience are magnified by the spectacular shifts from summer to winter, from twenty-four hours of light to none. Normal human experiences like mood swings become exaggerated in the Arctic. Perhaps it is the force of both the extraordinary light and the dark of the Arctic which spawned traditional cultures rich in myth. Northern stories and myths, in fact everything about traditional northern cultures, continue to tantalize people steeped in a western culture that is out of touch with its own myths and lacks direct experience with the forces of light and dark. Philo-

Fig. 1. This image of the American explorer, Elisha Kent Kane, painted by Alonso Chappel in 1862, captures the spirit of the 'Arctic sublime', at once beautiful and terrifying, awesome and exotic. *Source*: Stefansson Collection, Dartmouth College.

Fig. 2. Icebergs in Smith Sound between Ellesmere Island and Greenland. *Source*: photo. by G. Osherenko.

sophically and spiritually, Lopez and others have looked north to reestablish contact with missing elements in our own lives and culture. A Jungian analyst and scholar, Dr Marie-Louise von Franz, noted how early Arctic shamans acknowledged the feminine psychological tendencies in a man's psyche (which Jung called the anima), thus enabling them to connect with the unconscious.[6] In physical and psychological terms, both light and lack of light play a critical role in the physical and mental health of Arctic residents who, deprived of vitamin D transmitted to the human body through sunlight, suffer severe mood swings. Studies of Arctic mammals and their patterns of hibernation now suggest that there are more similarities than dissimilarities between humans and other mammals.[7] Problems of obesity and accompanying food disorders may be attributable, in some cases, to latent tendencies to hibernate. The unusual Arctic light upon which Lopez meditates illumines the Age of the Arctic, an age in which the Arctic may unlock some of the physical and psychological mysteries of the human psyche and guide us to appreciate and cultivate renewed connections with the land (see Figure 2).

1.3   The Age of the Arctic

Two perspectives on the importance of the Arctic, one geopolitical and the other philosophical and spiritual, combine to justify the label 'Age of the Arctic'. One perspective, the Arctic sublime, has been well documented; the other, the political and socioeconomic, has not. Thus, this book focuses on the latter. Those who would learn more about the 'Arctic sublime', about the great migrations of animals in the Arctic, about Arctic exploration, about the glaciers and the forces that form and change them, about the cold oceans and the creatures that survive in them, about the grandeur and allure of the Arctic or the traditional life of the indigenous people, have but to amble to the local library. There has been a tremendous outpouring of books, articles, films, and television programs all portraying the Arctic sublime to feed the philosophical and spiritual needs of the Age of the Arctic. And there are numerous texts that describe and analyze the ecology, ornithology, geology, glaciology, and ocean-ography of the Arctic region. Many of these explain carefully and convincingly why the Arctic should be viewed as a distinct geographic region and direct our attention to the physical and biological phenomena that recur throughout the Circumpolar North.[8] But there are remarkably few works elucidating the geopolitical and socioeconomic reasons for viewing the Arctic as a distinct, well-defined geographical region let alone explaining the region's growing importance in national and international affairs. Lopez has written a compelling account of the ecological and philosophical role of the Arctic, which he aptly calls *Arctic Dreams*. We hope to provide an equally compelling counterpoint describing and investigating Arctic realities.

Lopez, like others before him such as John Muir, Robert Marshall, and Margaret Murie, hopes by his evocative depictions of the Arctic to awaken and inspire an attitude of respect, even reverence for the land. He opens and closes *Arctic Dreams* by bowing to the land. We acknowledge the richness of these works and value their contribution to placing the Arctic at the center of our mental maps. But, as students of law and politics, we are not as accustomed to bowing to the land as to probing for a deeper understanding of the conflicts over the land. Unlike Lopez, we are not driven to anger by 'the darkness of politics' but intrigued by conflict, curious to examine the differences among preservationists, environmentalists, and conservationists, struck not by how much of traditional Inuit culture has vanished, but by how much has survived the onslaught of rapid technological change. We embrace what others may see as darkness; we seek to learn from the military strategists and the oil men as well as from the subsistence hunter and the solo kayaker. Awe alone will not solve the growing conflicts in the Arctic. Nor will seeking to escape amidst the ice flows from the human drama in the Arctic. Steeping ourselves in the Arctic sublime will do little to halt the thoughtless destruction of the tundra. That requires the more difficult task of understanding the social, economic, political, and psychological forces now at work in the Arctic. We intend in this book to explain the strategic significance of the Arctic and to provide an interpretive account of the growing conflicts between military, industrial, environmental, and Native interests in the region. In the process, we will explore methods of settlement or resolution of domestic and international Arctic conflicts.

1.4   The plan of the book: a study of conflict

We have chosen to approach our subject in the manner of mediators seeking to know the players and to probe their interests before defining the issues or attempting to find solutions to the conflicts. Thus, the chapters of Part 2 describe the players, their interests, and the concerns of greatest import to them. Chapter 2 addresses security interests in the Arctic focusing initially on the military and strategic calculations of the superpowers, the United States and the Soviet Union. We then discuss the implications of the militarization of the Arctic for the interests of the other Arctic rim states before turning finally to the competing interests of subnational groups (various branches of the military), local, regional, and state governments as well as non-governmental actors (industry, environmental and Native groups). The third chapter deals with industry and commerce, the network of private and governmental enterprises opening mines, exploring for oil and gas, constructing massive hydroelectric facilities, building cities in Siberia, operating hotels in Anchorage, trawling for fish in the Bering Sea. The fourth chapter introduces the indigenous peoples, the original residents of the Arctic – Inuit, Yuit, Sami, Athapaskan, Aleut, Komi, Yakuti, and others – with their internal conflicts of interest as well as their common concerns to preserve traditional ways of life while participating in the growth and development of Arctic industry and commerce. Finally, Chapter 5 introduces those players who would protect the Arctic environment. It explains the significant distinctions among organizations like Greenpeace, Friends of the Earth, and the Canadian Wildlife Federation and canvases the major environmental concerns in the Arctic.

Throughout these chapters we have included information pertinent to all eight Arctic rim nations – the U.S.S.R., Finland, Sweden, Norway, Iceland, Denmark/Greenland, Canada, and the United States. But, we have intentionally avoided the nation-by-nation descriptions available in standard geography texts, choosing instead to offer representative information from each of the nations.

Chapter 6, 'Arctic issues, Arctic conflicts', is our pivotal chapter. It provides the theoretical underpinnings necessary to dissect and analyze political and social conflict, thereby providing a framework for the chapters that follow. It also explains why standard methods of dealing with conflicts are not adequate for responding to conflicts in the Arctic today.

The last three chapters explore appropriate responses to Arctic issues and effective procedures for resolving the resultant conflicts. Chapter 7 identifies and evaluates options available to actors operating in the private sector who have a stake in solving Arctic problems and settling Arctic conflicts. Here the book turns to initiatives open to Native corporations and organizations, environmental groups, industry, and those concerned about war and peace, and discusses prospects for greater cooperation among frequently opposing groups. Chapter 8 examines how public policymakers, especially those located in the United States government, should deal with the Arctic; it makes a case for acquiring greatly enhanced public expertise in Arctic issues. The final chapter discusses potential international responses, focusing on the formation of international regimes as a means of fostering cooperation and ameliorating conflicts between and among Arctic players.

1.5   Drawing an Arctic boundary

As one looks at the polar projection pinned to the wall, it seems difficult to place the southern boundary of this region we call the Arctic. There is a host of definitions to choose from, including those based on average temperatures, on the locus of the treeline, or on the presence of continuous or discontinuous permafrost. We could follow the geographers in using the Arctic Circle (lat. 66° 33′ N.), the latitude beyond which the sun does not appear above the horizon at winter solstice nor set at summer solstice. There are even definitions devised primarily to solve political problems, such as the definition set forth in section 112 of the U.S. Arctic Research and Policy Act of 1984. For our purposes, however, you will not need a thermometer, a permafrost probe, or a statute book. We consider all the lands and seas lying to the north of 60 degrees north latitude to be Arctic. Where areas to the south of 60 degrees encompass tundra biomes inhabitated primarily by Native peoples, as in northern Quebec, and where they do not, as in Anchorage or Fairbanks, we have deviated from this general definition. See map in frontispiece.

1.6   The Arctic: an emerging region

To understand, much less to resolve, conflicts arising in the Arctic, we need to alter our usual perceptions of the region as well as the ways in which private and public actors deal with the region. Above all, we need to dispel simplistic assumptions that the Arctic is a mirror image of its opposite pole and that policies successful in Antarctica will be well-suited to the Arctic. The Arctic differs radically from Antarctica, not only because it is a mediterranean surrounded by land rather than a continent surrounded by water, but more importantly because it is, and has been for centuries, populated by people and not penguins. Unlike the Antarctic, all the northern lands 'belong' to sovereign states. This has led each of the eight Arctic rim nations to develop policies regarding its own part of the Arctic with little regard for other parts of the Arctic region. Thus, the Arctic is seldom perceived as a distinct geographical region. Instead, each piece is seen as a part of a more southerly nation. Until recently, for example, Greenland's economic and political connections have all been with Denmark and the European Community.

It is symbolic that a traveler wishing to journey on scheduled airlines between Alaska and the Canadian Arctic must fly south to Seattle before journeying north again. Communication, transportation, and policy all flow along north/south axes rather than across the northlands. Only within the last few years has scheduled air transportation become available between Nuuk, the capital of Greenland, and the Canadian north (Iqaluit); and even now the flight operates only once a week. This is symptomatic of the way we think about Arctic areas, as economic and political peripheries controlled by governments located in the temperate regions.

Yet the Arctic portions of each of the eight nations that rim the Arctic Ocean have much in common with each other. Throughout the Circumpolar North, we find a remarkably similar climate, nearly identical species of flora and fauna, comparable geologic history, an abundance of comparable renewable and non-renewable resources, and sizable populations of indigenous peoples. The issues each of the Arctic rim nations faces today flow in part from these commonalities of geophysical and human history. All the Arctic rim nations are struggling with questions concerning the appropriate relationship of Native communities to their encompassing nation states. All confront similar conflicts between the extraction of raw materials and the protection of fragile ecosystems. All face the same threats arising from the growing militarization of the Arctic. This is not to say that Arctic areas located within each of the eight nations are identical. Throughout this book, we explore differences as well as commonalities. But, most importantly, we will present the Arctic as an integral, distinct region, a perspective that is highlighted on a polar perspective map and is indispensable to the eventual resolution of many Arctic conflicts.

Notes to Part 1

1. Vilhjalmur Stefansson, *The Northward Course of Empire*, New York: Harcourt, Brace and Co. 1922, 168–202.
2. Heinze presented his visionary megaproject at a 'Global Infrastructure Projects Conference' in Anchorage reported in the *Burlington (Vt.) Free Press*, (14 Sept. 1986), A10.
3. Chauncy Loomis, 'The Arctic Sublime', U. C. Knoepflmacher & G. B. Tennysonin, Eds., *Nature and the Victorian Imagination*, Berkeley: University of California Press, 1977, 95–112. I. S. MacLaren, 'The Aesthetic Map of the North', 1845–1859, 38 *Arctic* (June 1985), 89–103.
4. Good examples are Fred Bruemmer, *The Arctic World*, San Francisco: Sierra Club Books, 1985, and the Wilderness Society's fall 1986 magazine featuring 'Land, Life, and Risk in the Arctic', 50 *Wilderness*, 174.
5. *Arctic Dreams: Imagination and Desire in a Northern Landscape*, New York: Charles Scribner's Sons 1986.
6. See Carl G. Jung *et al.*, *Man and His Symbols*, New York: Doubleday, 1964, 177–8.
7. From a lecture by William Henry Anderson, M.D. Lecturer on Psychiatry, who offers a course in the Harvard Medical School curriculum on psychophysiology of extreme environments.
8. See, for example, Steven B. Young, *To the Arctic: An Introduction to the Far Northern World*, New York: John Wiley 1988, Bernard Stonehouse, *Animals of the Arctic: the Ecology of the Far North*, New York: Holt, Rinehart & Winston, 1971, Carleton Ray and M. G. McCormick-Ray, *Wildlife of the Polar Regions*, New York: H. N. Abrams, 1981, Brian Sage, *The Arctic and Its Wildlife*, New York: Facts on File, 1986.

Part 2
Players and interests

2

The Arctic strategic arena: security interests

The Arctic has possessed an irreducible strategic significance throughout the postwar era. This is partly an outgrowth of geopolitics. The United States and the Soviet Union are immediate neighbors in the Arctic. Western Alaska and eastern Siberia are only 57 miles apart at the Bering Strait, and the Bering Sea is essentially enclosed by Soviet and American territories. Both superpowers front directly on the Arctic Basin; the Soviet Union alone exercises direct control over about half the coastline of the Arctic Ocean. The shortest air route between the homelands of the two superpowers is across the Arctic Basin, a fact of inescapable significance in an age of intercontinental bombers and ballistic missiles. In part, the strategic significance of the Arctic stems from more specific considerations, including western concerns over the exposed northern flank of Europe and Soviet sensitivities regarding the role of the Greenland/Iceland/United Kingdom (GIUK) gap, a natural choke point which consists of the Denmark Strait and the Norwegian Sea and which constitutes the principal outlet to the North Atlantic for vessels of the Soviet Northern Fleet. Because they lie athwart the passage these Soviet vessels must take en route to the open sea, the Norwegian Coast and the Svalbard Archipelago would be obvious Soviet targets in any European war. Yet their physical proximity to the Soviet Union (Norway and the Soviet Union share a common border) makes these areas unusually difficult for NATO to defend.[1] Conversely, there is little likelihood that the GIUK gap will lose its significance as an outlet to the North Atlantic for Soviet vessels based on the Kola Peninsula and, therefore, as a first line of defense for the members of NATO.

Nonetheless, a series of recent developments in military technology have enlarged the role of the Arctic dramatically as a theater of operations for major military systems, transforming the region into a focal point of contemporary strategic thinking.[2] Whereas military planners often dismissed the Arctic as a frozen wasteland over which missiles would fly at high altitudes in the heyday of the land-based intercontinental ballistic missile (ICBM) during the 1960s and 1970s, the Arctic today offers an attractive environment for the operation of ballistic missile nuclear submarines (SSBNs) and high endurance manned bombers equipped with air-launched cruise missiles (ALCMs). Additionally, the region looms large in the thinking of some strategic analysts as an arena for conventional naval warfare. To lend credibility and specificity to these assertions as well as to lay the foundation for a critical examination of the political significance of the militarization of the Arctic, the following sections document the trends in military technology that are fueling the emergence of the Arctic as a strategic arena of vital significance.

2.1   Offensive systems in the Arctic

The increasing vulnerability of land-based ballistic missiles to counterforce strikes has stimulated a surge of interest in the sea and air legs of the strategic triad among those concerned with the stability of the global strategic balance.[3] This has greatly enhanced the prominence of seaborne delivery systems in the strategic calculations of both super-powers. Concomitantly, recent developments in the capabilities of both SSBNs and submarine-launched ballistic missiles (SLBMs) have made the Arctic particularly attractive as an environment for the operation of these systems (see Figure 3). SSBNs deployed in Arctic waters can now command virtually all enemy targets from fixed patrol stations located remarkably close to their respective homelands. There is no need to penetrate dangerous choke points like the GIUK gap or to endure the costs and hazards of using remote and widely scattered patrol stations in the North Atlantic or North Pacific. Already, Soviet SS-N-8 and SS-N-18 missiles mounted on Delta-class submarines can deliver nuclear warheads to military targets both in North America and in Europe from Arctic patrol stations. Similarly, American Trident submarines carrying C-4 missiles are capable of attacking military targets throughout the Soviet Union from Arctic waters. The latest generations of SSBNs, the Soviet Typhoon- and Delta IV-class submarines and the American Ohio-class submarine, are even more effective. The large, ice-reinforced Typhoon is designed specifically for operation in Arctic waters; there are numerous points in the polar pack ice where the Typhoon can punch through to the surface to fire its missiles. But all late model SSBNs are capable of performing well in the Arctic Basin. The pack ice is frequently interrupted by stretches of open water or polynias where any modern submarine can surface. The new SSBNs are or soon will be equipped with the latest delivery vehicles, such as the 6–9 warhead Soviet SS-N-20 or the even newer 10 warhead SS-NX-23 and the American Trident II (also known as the D-5) with 8–10 warheads. These missiles have ranges of more than 8,000 kilometers and are nearly as accurate as land-based ballistic missiles.

Equally important, Arctic waters offer a comparatively safe environment for the operation of SSBNs due to the difficulties of locating submarines, much less tracking them closely or attacking them effectively, under Arctic conditions. The ambient noise of the pack ice and especially the marginal ice zones severely limits the effectiveness of acoustical monitoring devices (for example, sonar systems). The opaqueness of the Arctic Basin's ice makes visual monitoring methods of little use. Similarly,

Fig. 3. U.S. and U.S.S.R. Nuclear-Powered Ballistic Missile Submarines and Submarine-Launched Ballistic Missiles. *Source: Soviet Military Power - 1986.* Washington, D.C.: U.S. Government Printing Office, 1986.

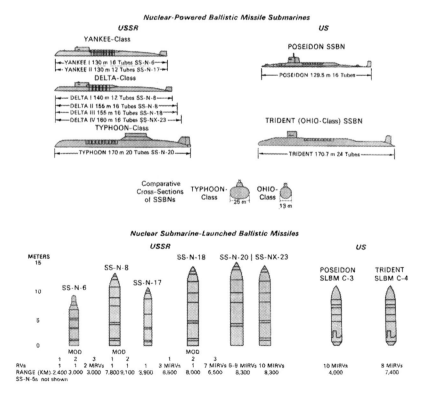

surface vessels cannot maneuver in the pack ice of the Arctic Basin so that they are unable to play a major role in any concerted effort to counter the operation of SSBNs in the Arctic. In sharp contrast to other regions, therefore, responsibility for anti-submarine warfare (ASW) in the Arctic falls primarily to attack submarines (SSNs). As ASW devices become more effective in other environments, the attractions of the Arctic as a secure theater of operations for nuclear submarines will consequently increase.[4] It follows that the Arctic offers a unique combination of ease of operations and comparative safety for seaborne strategic delivery systems.

The Soviet Union has moved vigorously to exploit these military attractions of Arctic waters. Well over half of all Soviet SSBNs are stationed with the Northern Fleet at bases on the Kola Peninsula.[5] These submarines are now active in the Arctic Basin, constituting a virtually invulnerable strategic force that has no need to penetrate NATO defenses stationed along the GIUK gap or even to leave the protected waters of the Soviet Arctic. Additionally, they are capable of repositioning themselves between the Kola Peninsula bases (for example, Polyarny) in the European Arctic and Petropavlovsk in the North Pacific (one of the home ports of the Soviet Pacific fleet) by passing back and forth largely under the cover of Arctic ice.[6] The United States does not have an Arctic base comparable to the Kola bases. Yet American SSBNs based at Bangor, Washington (or at an east coast base now under development) are fully capable of operating in Arctic waters for extended periods. The United States is moving rapidly to build up its fleet of Ohio-class submarines and to fit these submarines with Trident II or D-5 missiles. The ease of operation and comparative safety attainable in the Arctic Basin may also attract American military planners, despite the fact that the United States does not have to contend with problems like penetrating the GIUK gap. Though plans for such operations have not been publicly acknowledged, it seems probable that the United States will follow the Soviet lead in this realm. As a result, the Arctic Basin is well on its way toward becoming a critical theater of operations for seaborne strategic delivery systems.

A similar story emerges from an analysis of air-launched cruise missiles (ALCMs), which are already capable of delivering nuclear warheads to distant targets with great accuracy (see Figure 4). Cruise missiles are, in the words of Charles Mohr of the *New York Times*, '...winged, jet-powered bombs'. They are air-breathing vehicles that fly at comparatively slow speeds and low altitudes, endeavoring to evade conventional air defense systems by means of their maneuverability and their ability to fly in under or confuse ordinary radar scanners. Long-range cruise missiles now in service can travel up to 3,000 kilometers from their launch sites. Cruise missiles mounted on nuclear submarines are currently operational and fully capable of functioning in Arctic waters as well as in the waters of the Atlantic and Pacific Oceans. While some observers regard this as a technological advance of considerable significance,[7] the most fundamental strategic development in this realm arises from the deployment of long-range ALCMs suitable for use in standoff attacks initiated from Arctic airspace.

Fig. 4. A Canadian Forces helicopter recovers an unarmed cruise missile launched from the Canadian Arctic after it landed on Primrose Lake, Alberta. *Source*: U.S. Air Force.

Though interest in manned bombers waned during the 1970s, the growing emphasis on active defenses against ballistic missiles during the 1980s, as exemplified by the American Strategic Defense Initiative (SDI), has given the manned bomber coupled with the ALCM a new lease of life as a strategic delivery system. To the extent that active defense succeeds in providing protection against ballistic missiles, ALCMs, which are not vulnerable to the sort of defense contemplated under SDI, will come to play a role of increasing importance in securing the stability of the strategic balance between the superpowers.[8] Already, the United States has equipped over 130 B-52G bombers with a total of 1,150 long-range cruise missiles and plans to add 600 more ALCMs to its inventory. Work is also proceeding on an Advanced Cruise Missile, which will have both a longer range than the current cruise missile and an enhanced ability to evade detection by ground-based radars. As many as 1,500 air-launched models may be deployed. In contrast to the case of seaborne delivery systems, the Soviet Union is somewhat behind the United States in this field. Yet the Soviets are currently deploying long-range ALCMs on Bear H and Backfire bombers. By the end of the decade, each of the superpowers is expected to have a substantial force of long-range ALCMs mounted on the latest generations of high-endurance bombers (see Figure 5). Prominent among these are the 100 B1-B bombers which have an intercontinental combat radius of 7,500 kilometers and are now entering service in the United States and the Blackjack-A bombers which have a combat radius of 7,300 kilometers and are expected to enter service over the next several years in the Soviet Union. Somewhat farther away, but still within the foreseeable future, is the prospect of deploying Advanced Cruise Missiles on Stealth or B2 bombers whose evasion capabilities will minimize the role of ground-based radars in detecting or tracking these delivery vehicles.

The deployment of long-range ALCMs on the latest generations of manned bombers greatly enhances the role of the Arctic as a theater for military operations.[9] The great circle route over the Arctic Basin remains the shortest air route between North America and the Soviet Union.[10] Long-range ALCMs launched from high-endurance bombers operating in Arctic airspace are capable of reaching most important military targets in North America and Western Europe as well as in the Soviet Union. This makes it possible for each of the superpowers to initiate standoff nuclear strikes against enemy targets from launch sites that are comparatively safe because they are located outside the range of the opponent's detection and intercept capabilities. Additionally, the Arctic itself is a congenial environment for military operations involving cruise missiles mounted on manned bombers. It is a large, sparsely populated region in which military activities are harder to keep track of than in the mid-latitudes. Ionospheric irregularities in the Arctic also interfere with the use of long range over-the-horizon-backscatter (OTH-B) radar systems to detect and monitor the operations of high endurance bombers (especially those equipped with protective devices like the B1-B or designed to minimize their radar profile

Fig. 5. U.S.S.R. and U.S. Bomber Aircraft and Long-Range Cruise Missiles. *Source: Soviet Military Power - 1986.* Washington, D.C.: U.S. Government Printing Office, 1986.

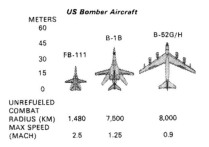

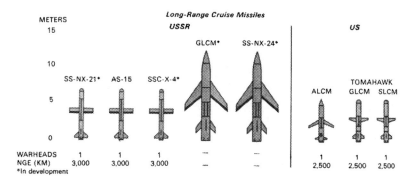

like Stealth).[11] In the calculations of military planners, therefore, the Arctic now ranks as a major theater for the operations of manned bombers equipped with ALCMs as well as for the operations of SSBNs.

2.2   Sea and air defense in the Arctic

Not surprisingly, these developments in offensive systems have triggered a surge of interest on the part of both superpowers in sea and air defense systems suitable for use against SSBNs or manned bombers carrying ALCMs under Arctic conditions. With respect to sea defense, the critical problem arises from the facts that conventional naval vessels are not capable of patrolling ice-infested Arctic waters and that most of the current methods of monitoring the activities of submarines from satellites, aircraft, or sea-bottom mounted acoustical devices are of limited use in tracking the movements of SSBNs operating under the pack ice of the Arctic Ocean or in the marginal ice zones of the Arctic Basin rim. One well-known analyst has gone so far as to assert that '[a]t present, the only method of submarine monitoring that can be used in ice-covered and ice-infested waters is the nuclear-powered attack submarine'.[12] While this statement is perhaps too strong, it does help to explain the interest that both superpowers have shown in the use of attack submarines in the Arctic Basin. Despite serious questions regarding the cost-effectiveness of deploying these systems in the Arctic, over half the Soviet fleet of attack submarines (many equipped with SS-N-15 or SS-N-16 nuclear anti-submarine missiles) is now stationed with the Northern Fleet. This force includes the new Soviet Akula-, Mike-, and Sierra-class attack submarines. Similarly, American Los Angeles-class attack submarines (SSNs) fitted with Harpoon anti-ship missiles, Tomahawk submarine-launched cruise missiles, and the Subroc ASW rocket are increasingly active in the Arctic region. In May 1986, three American nuclear submarines surfaced simultaneously at the North Pole in a test of the Navy's ability to conduct sophisticated submarine operations under Arctic conditions (see Figure 6). Additionally, the U.S. Navy now plans to build a much more advanced attack submarine, the SSN-21 or Seawolf, justified in considerable part by the need to counter Soviet submarine operations in the Arctic region.[13] Given the growing role of the Arctic as a theater for the operation of SSBNs carrying advanced SLBMs, each of the superpowers will experience powerful incentives to devote increasing attention to the problems of sea defense under Arctic conditions.

The deployment of ALCMs has already stimulated a sharp surge of interest in air defense systems for the Arctic region. In North America, the DEW Line, which was built in the 1950s to provide early warning of

Soviet manned bomber attacks but which had been allowed to become obsolete during the 1970s, is now being renovated and modernized. The resultant North Warning System is scheduled for completion in 1992 and will include at least 52 sites strung mainly along the 70th parallel.[14] These sites will contain 13 medium-range, microwave radars and 39 unattended circular phased array short-range radars. Long-range OTH-B radars located on the east and west coasts of the United States will supplement the North Warning System by providing coverage of the eastern and western approaches to the North American Arctic (see Figure 7). Arrangements governing the construction and operation of the North Warning System figure prominently in the military agreement signed by the United States and Canada on 18 March 1985. In a separate, but complementary, arrangement, the United States and Iceland have agreed to construct two radar stations in Iceland to monitor Soviet air and sea traffic in the Arctic. In 1982, the United States and Canada completed work on a new North American Air Defense Master Plan, within the larger framework of the North American Aerospace Defense Command (NORAD), which calls for the dedication of at least six additional Airborne Warning and Control System (AWACS) aircraft to northern defense and the development of Arctic air-intercept capabilities (authorized to use airstrips located in Arctic Canada under emergency conditions) as well as the construction of ground-based early warning systems to counter the emerging threat from Soviet long-range ALCMs in the Arctic region. Today, the United States is making an effort to involve Canada in

Fig. 6. Three nuclear-powered submarines (two American and one British) surfacing at the North Pole, May 1987. *Source*: U.S. Navy.

its Strategic Defense Architecture (SDA) 2000 program, an integrated planning exercise designed to provide a coordinated air and space defense for North America against space-based weapons, ballistic missiles, and cruise missiles mounted on manned bombers.

Given the traditional Soviet emphasis on strategic defense systems, it will come as no surprise that the Soviet Union has devoted enormous resources to defending itself against attacks from manned bombers and air-launched cruise missiles coming in from the North. While military analysts are skeptical regarding their effectiveness against American offensive systems, the Soviets currently maintain 1,200 interceptor aircraft, 9,400 surface-to-air missiles, and 10,000 radars. The available evidence also suggests that the Soviet Union is now engaged in a vigorous effort to upgrade its ground-based radars designed to detect and track air-launched cruise missiles. Under the circumstances, it is accurate to conclude that

Fig. 7. NORAD's modernized warning system. *Source*: 'NORAD 86': Report of the Standing Committee on External Affairs and National Defence.

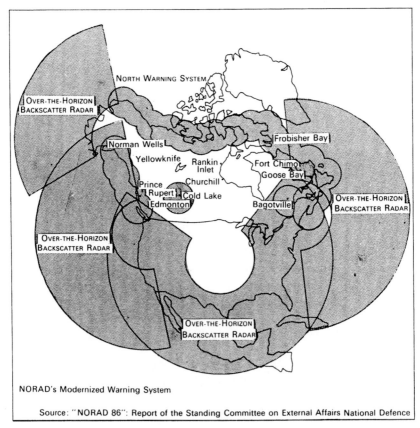

NORAD's Modernized Warning System

Source: "NORAD 86": Report of the Standing Committee on External Affairs National Defence

'...the Soviet Arctic is easily the most heavily militarized part of the [Arctic] littoral'.[15]

2.3   Other military considerations

Several additional observations will help to round out this picture of the emerging role of the Arctic region as a theater for military operations of utmost strategic significance. The European Arctic figures prominently in the maritime strategy that has become a significant component of American strategic doctrine over the last several years.[16] This strategy centers on a plan for the U.S. Navy to attack Soviet forces (including Soviet SSBNs) with conventional weapons in the Barents Sea and on the Kola Peninsula as a response to a Soviet-initiated conventional war in central Europe.[17] It rests on the propositions that horizontal escalation, involving only conventional weapons, is less dangerous than vertical escalation, involving nuclear weapons, and that the threat of horizontal escalation featuring attacks on Soviet forces in the Arctic is likely to be just as effective in deterring Soviet aggression in central Europe as the threat of vertical escalation. Whatever the strategic merit of this maritime strategy,[18] it has certainly come to play an important role in justifying the remarkable American naval buildup that occurred during the Reagan years. In the process, it has made the Arctic a center of attention for those who think about conventional military operations as well as for those who think about nuclear weapons.

As well, the Arctic is characterized by atmospheric phenomena capable of posing serious problems for communications and defense systems. As Johnson, Bradley & Winokur have put it,[19]

> 'Ionospheric irregularities caused by an aurora can modify electromagnetic waves, thereby affecting communications with satellite systems and affecting the utilization of over-the-horizon detection radars for defense against strategic transpolar bomber attack. Additionally, currents induced during large geomagnetic storms in long conductors such as telephone cables, power lines, or pipelines can cause failure or serious damage'.

These features of the Arctic environment may seem advantageous to planners concerned about the ability of strategic delivery systems, such as ALCMs mounted on manned bombers or SLBMs deployed on nuclear submarines stationed in the Arctic basin, to penetrate enemy defenses. But they also pose potential problems for those charged with guiding cruise missiles (in contrast to ballistic missiles) over the Arctic Basin under adverse conditions or maintaining communications with commanders of submarines carrying SLBMs. To the extent that the Arctic continues to emerge as a critical theater for military operations, therefore, we can expect a sharp growth of interest in the unique problems of military communication, command and control (C^3) posed by the atmospheric conditions of the Arctic.

Finally, the construction of industrial facilities of vital economic significance to each of the superpowers has added yet another dimension to the militarization of the Arctic. The Arctic was until recently a remote and frequently ignored region. Even those who now see the Arctic as an important strategic arena tend to assume that the Arctic is not a significant prize in military terms; states might fight *in* the Arctic but not *about* the Arctic. Yet military planners in both the United States and the Soviet Union find themselves thinking increasingly about the security of major industrial installations in the region as well as about the emerging role of the Arctic as a theater for military operations. The Prudhoe Bay/Kuparuk oil fields on the North Slope of Alaska, for example, accounted in 1985 for approximately 19% of the oil produced in the United States and 11% of the oil consumed by the United States. Both the oil fields and the Trans-Alaska Pipeline System (TAPS) used to move the oil to southern markets are highly vulnerable to disruption. Similar observations apply to the burgeoning industrial installations of the Soviet North which now yield over 60% of the oil and natural gas produced in the Soviet Union. Moreover, these facilities are highly concentrated. The supergiant Urengoi natural gas field alone, for example, has come to play a role of vital importance in the Soviet energy equation, and the Soviet Siberian gas pipeline, running 2750 miles from northwestern Siberia to the Czechoslovak border, would be an obvious target in any effort to disrupt the Soviet economy. The dependence of both the American economy and the Soviet economy on secure supplies of energy and other raw materials from the Arctic is virtually certain to increase over the next several decades. Concerns for the security of major industrial installations in the Arctic, therefore, can only add fuel to the continuing militarization of the region during the foreseeable future.

2.4   The Arctic and the strategic balance

Barring highly improbable advances in the realm of strategic or active defense which would render nuclear weapons obsolete or equally improbable advances in the development of hardened or mobile missiles which would restore the preeminence of the land-based ICBM as a secure deterrent or second strike force, the significance of the Arctic as a theater for military operations will continue to grow for some time. It is hardly an exaggeration, therefore, to say that we are entering the age of the Arctic in strategic terms. This trend does not, unfortunately, bode well for sweeping proposals aimed at insulating the Arctic region as a whole from the pressures of East/West competition. Nothing resembling the demilitarization arrangements incorporated in the provisions of Article I of the Antarctic Treaty of 1959, for example, is in the cards for the Arctic. The militarization of the region has proceeded too far already to permit the creation of an Antarctic-type regime for the Arctic region. Ironically, the fact that Arctic militarization is a recent development whose strategic consequences are not yet fully understood only reinforces this conclusion. The superpowers will certainly experience strong incentives to explore the full potential of the Arctic with regard to SSBNs, SLBMs, SLCMs, manned bombers, ALCMs, anti-submarine warfare, air defense systems, and command and control before entering into restrictive arms control agreements covering the region.

The militarization of the Arctic will therefore constitute an international fact of life for the foreseeable future. But is this development fundamentally stabilizing or destabilizing in strategic terms? The available evidence cuts both ways. Manned bombers and, especially, SSBNs operating in the Arctic are remarkably safe from hostile attack. What is more, there is little likelihood of any early or sudden shift in this situation. It follows that the Arctic can play an important role in stabilizing any deterrent system based on the idea of mutual assured destruction (MAD). This is particularly important in the light of growing concerns regarding the vulnerability of land-based strategic missiles (ICBMs) to carefully orchestrated counterforce strikes as well as the capability of strategic defenses designed to counter ICBMs. This suggests that the relative security of the Arctic as an operating environment for strategic weapons is likely to become an increasingly important consideration in stabilizing the overall strategic balance between the superpowers during the foreseeable future. In fact, the emergence of the Arctic as a vital strategic arena may well encourage serious progress toward reducing existing inventories of ICBMs. It seems reasonable to conclude, for instance, that the growing interest of the superpowers in deep reciprocal cuts in existing inventories of increasingly vulnerable, land-based missiles is premised, in part, on the stabilizing role of the Arctic as a theater for the operation of SSBNs and manned bombers equipped with ALCMs.

Yet there is another, less reassuring, side to this picture of the implications of the militarization of the Arctic for the strategic balance. This trend has the inevitable effect of extending the strategic arms race into a new and comparatively unfamiliar region. Already, production schedules for the Typhoon and the Trident II coupled with retrofitting schedules for equipping manned bombers, like the American B-52, with ALCMs have generated irresistible pressures to ignore or set aside the quantitative limitations on strategic delivery vehicles incorporated in the SALT II agreement.[20] In fact, the United States exceeded the overall quantitative ceiling on such vehicles in November 1986, touching off a severe controversy regarding the American attitude toward arms control. There is also considerable potential for an offense/defense arms race in the Arctic as both sides endeavor to develop more sophisticated nuclear attack submarines to track SSBNs together with improved air defense capabilities to counter the threat of ALCMs. Justifiably, knowledgeable observers generally regard offense/defense races as the most dangerous, not to mention the most costly, form of arms race. In this case, moreover, such a race would involve technologies, like cruise missiles and advanced submarines, that are particularly difficult to subject to verifiable restrictions in meaningful arms control arrangements.

We must bear in mind also the facts that the superpowers lie in remarkably close proximity to each other in the Arctic and that atmospheric conditions in the region pose unusual problems for command and control. The margin for error in the Arctic is accordingly small. It would not take much to precipitate an inadvertent clash in the region which could escalate in an uncontrollable fashion. This is one of the reasons why many informed observers are leery about the United States Navy's maritime strategy under which Navy task forces would move to destroy Soviet SSBNs in the Barents and Norwegian Seas during the course of a conventional war in Europe.[21] Under the circumstances, there is no basis for complacency about the strategic consequences of the militarization of the Arctic. We must give serious consideration to proposals designed to regulate this development, even if there is little chance of reaching agreement on any sweeping plan for the demilitarization of the Arctic.

2.5   Interstate relations in the Arctic

How will the militarization of the Arctic affect the national interests and policy calculations of the various states possessing stakes in the Arctic region? What will be the consequences for the pattern of interstate relations in the region?

Because the Soviet Union is unquestionably the paramount Arctic state, let us turn first to the implications of the growing strategic significance of the Arctic region for Soviet policymakers. Roughly half the land area of the Circumpolar North lies within the Soviet Union, and this land area in turn comprises about half the territory of the Soviet Union. The country also exercises direct control over almost half the coastline of the Arctic Basin. Geopolitically, therefore, the Soviet Union is well placed to exploit the military attractions of the Arctic, whether or not it can gain the backing of any of the other Arctic rim states. Additionally, over three quarters of the human population of the entire Circumpolar North is located in the Soviet North. The North American Arctic contains nothing remotely comparable to population centers like Murmansk and Archangel, each of which now has a population of over 300,000. What is more, the Soviets have a long history of industrial, scientific, and military activities in the Far North. These include the development of the world's largest naval complex at Severomorsk on the Kola Peninsula, the construction of several northern airbases designed for use as advanced staging areas, and the use of Novaya Zemlya as a test site for underground nuclear explosions.

Under the circumstances, the Soviet Union will surely seek to maintain its paramount position in the Arctic as the region becomes an increasingly important theater for military operations. This means that the Soviets will endeavor to strengthen their effective control over the portion of the Arctic Basin adjacent to their coastline, applying the international legal concepts of enclosed seas and historic waters to the Kara, Laptev, and East Siberian Seas and exercising strict control over access to the Northern Sea Route on the part of non-Soviet vessels. The effect of this stance will be to create a secure Arctic sanctuary for the operation of Soviet SSBNs as well as for the installation of forward air defense systems designed to counter American ALCMs. Given the emerging role of the Arctic as a theater for military operations, however, the Soviets will also experience clearcut incentives to maintain freedom of movement in the water column and in the airspace of the remainder of the Arctic Basin. Though it may be politically expedient for the Soviets to let the Americans carry the ball with regard to specific issues like access to the Northwest Passage, Soviet interests will often coincide with American interests regarding freedom of movement in the Arctic Basin, and the Soviet Union is likely to oppose initiatives on the part of other Arctic rim states (for example, Norway in the area around the Svalbard archipelago or Canada in the Arctic archipelago) which would have the effect of severely restricting freedom of movement in the Arctic Basin.

The geopolitical position of the Soviet Union in the Arctic makes it possible for the Soviets to operate in this region without regard to the concerns of allies or other ice states. Yet the Soviet Union does have a growing interest in making overtures to the lesser Arctic rim states (for example, Canada, Denmark/Greenland, Norway, and Iceland) in an effort to weaken their alliance ties with the United States. This may well have been one of the considerations underlying occasional Soviet gestures of support for Canadian concerns regarding the transit of the American icebreaker *Polar Sea* through the Northwest Passage in August 1985. It may also have been an important factor in the recent Soviet offer to discontinue work on the Krasnoyarsk ballistic missile detection and tracking radar in central Asia in exchange for an American agreement not to modernize the ballistic missile early warning system (BMEWS) site located at Thule, Greenland. Such considerations may even have played a role in the Soviet suggestion of Iceland as the site for the mini-summit held in October 1986.

Objectively, the militarization of the Arctic reduces the significance of the GIUK gap and the Norwegian flank in Soviet strategic calculations, since Soviet SSBNs can now operate safely and efficiently in the Arctic Basin with no need to move out into the North Atlantic. Given the Soviet propensity to plan for protracted wars, involving efforts to interdict supply lines, even in the nuclear era, however, it may be some time before Soviet planners cease to worry about penetrating NATO defenses stationed along the GIUK gap.[22] At the same time, the geopolitical position of the Soviet Union in the Arctic has some consequences that will inevitably complicate efforts to devise arms control arrangements for this region. Whereas the United States can dispatch both SSBNs and SSNs to the Arctic from east and west coast bases and conduct Arctic operations with ALCMs mounted on bombers based in the lower forty-eight, the Soviet Union has developed large and strategically critical bases (for example, the naval base at Severomorsk) in the Arctic itself. Though the United States may find it tempting to exploit this asymmetry for negotiating purposes, it rests on fundamental geopolitical facts that cannot be ignored in any serious effort to regulate the militarization of the Arctic.

By contrast, the political implications for the United States flowing from the emergence of the Arctic as a strategic arena of vital significance are more complex. The United States has not historically regarded itself as a true Arctic power. The country did not even possess a physical presence in the Far North until the purchase of Alaska in 1867. Though Alaska is about a fifth the size of the lower forty-eight, it contains less than a quarter of 1% of the American population. World War II briefly directed American attention toward the North because of the Aleutian campaign of 1942–1943 and dramatic engineering feats like the construction of the Alcan Highway and the Canol Pipeline.[23] But with the introduction of ICBMs, many Americans reverted to an attitude of benign neglect regarding the Arctic.

Yet the contemporary emergence of the Arctic as a critical theater for military operations makes such attitudes increasingly inappropriate. Whether policymakers like it or not, the United States can no longer avoid taking an interest in developments occurring throughout the Arctic region. Without doubt, the key political implication of this development for the United States centers on the growing importance of relations with northern allies, such as Norway, Iceland, Denmark/Greenland, and Canada.[24] Not surprisingly, the United States is presently stepping up its efforts to collaborate with these lesser Arctic rim states on security issues. American leaders have worked hard to nurture Norway's sometimes ambivalent commitment to NATO as well as to establish good working relations with the Home Rule government in Greenland (the political system established in 1979 in recognition of Greenland's growing autonomy from Denmark). Currently, the United States is seeking actively to maintain the support of Greenlandic leaders for its plan to modernize the ballistic missile early warning system (BMEWS) site located at Thule.[25] After a period of increasing friction during the 1970s, American relations with Iceland are now on a stronger footing. The American airbase at Keflavik seems secure for the moment, and the two countries signed an agreement during 1985 calling for the construction of two radar sites in Iceland, which will contribute to western defenses in the Arctic though they are not formally a component of the North Warning System. It seems likely that the willingness of the United States to accept, at least tacitly, Iceland's desire to be a *de facto* nuclear free zone is a *quid pro quo* for Icelandic acceptance of these radar sites. The triumph of the Progressive Conservative Party in Canada and the emergence of the Mulroney Government in 1984 provided a generally positive environment for Canadian/American collaboration in the Arctic during the mid-1980s. The North Warning System is a fully cooperative venture. Canada will pay about 40% or $600–700 million of the construction cost (this does not include the supplemental OTH-B radars), handle construction of the sites located in Canada, and assume substantial responsibility for the management of the system. Similarly, the two countries have collaborated on the new North American Air Defense Master Plan within the context of the reorganized and expanded North American Aerospace Defense Command (NORAD), and Canada agreed to a 5-year renewal of the basic NORAD agreement in 1986 with no strings attached.[26]

Nonetheless, the militarization of the Arctic carries with it great potential for friction between the United States and its northern allies.

Though there is cause for genuine concern in this realm in dealings with Iceland and Greenland, the problems are particularly severe in connection with Canadian sensitivities relating to the Arctic. In part, this is a consequence of an apparent inability on the part of American leaders to recognize the emotional character and intensity of Canadian feelings about the North. Thus, the American government exerted substantial pressure on Canada to acquiesce in the testing of air-launched cruise missiles (without nuclear armaments) over northern Canada, but the eventual concurrence of the Trudeau government triggered a substantial outpouring of protest on the part of the Canadian public. American icebreakers and nuclear submarines are now active in the waters of the Canadian Arctic archipelago (including the waters of the Northwest Passage). The fact that the American government, as part of its general policy of refusing to acknowledge Canadian sovereignty in the waters of the Arctic archipelago, has not sought explicit permission for transits on the part of these vessels raises hackles in many Canadian quarters regarding the sensitive issue of jurisdiction in the Canadian Arctic. The transit of the American icebreaker *Polar Sea* through the Northwest Passage during the summer of 1985, for example, prompted the Mulroney government (ordinarily disposed to adopt a friendly posture toward the United States) to issue a formal declaration asserting Canadian jurisdiction over all the waters of the Arctic archipelago as internal waters.[27]

Partly, Canadian/American friction in the Arctic arises from the fact, surprising to most Americans, that many Canadians regard the United States as the principal threat to the advancement of Canadian interests in the Far North.[28] Some Canadians have expressed real concern, for example, about the resurgence of interest in air defense in the Arctic because '...the new air-defense system might commit Canada to accept American weapons' stationed on Canadian territory.[29] Many thoughtful Canadians have expressed fears along these lines in conjunction with American efforts to draw Canada into its Strategic Defense Initiative (SDI) as well as its plans to develop an integrated air and space defense system for North America under the terms of Phases 1 and 2 of the Strategic Defense Architecture (SDA) 2000 program.[30] And it is hard to avoid the conclusion that a desire to keep track of American Arctic operations was a significant factor underlying the Canadian decision, articulated in the 1987 Defense White Paper, to purchase a fleet of nuclear-powered submarines capable of patrolling in Arctic waters.[31]

More generally, influential Canadians often react with genuine unease to any pattern of developments leading to an increase in American military activities in the Far North. Though each initiative may take the form of a cooperative Canadian/American venture, Canada does not possess the military capabilities or the resources to participate as an equal partner in such arrangements. Nor is Canada sufficiently confident of its ability to exercise effective occupancy in the Arctic archipelago to respond to a growing American military presence in the area without concern. Such developments are bound to remind many Canadians of the immediate postwar period during which American bases and military personnel dominated the Canadian Arctic.

This brings us directly to the interests and policy calculations of the lesser Arctic rim states. In a general way, the militarization of the Arctic must be a source of concern to these states. They are bound to fear being caught in the middle as the two superpowers deploy larger and larger arsenals of both offensive and defensive weapons in the Arctic region. Such a trend is only too likely to lead to developments that infringe the rights of the lesser states in the region (for example, demands for unrestricted transit of military vehicles) and that subject these states to pressure to cooperate with the military activities of the United States and the Soviet Union (for example, requests for forward basing facilities). The history of lesser states positioned geographically in areas that are attractive to great powers as theaters for military operations is not a happy one. This fact can hardly escape the attention of leaders in Norway, Iceland, Greenland, and Canada as the militarization of the Arctic continues.

Predictably, these states will experience growing incentives to take steps to prevent or to counter the dangers associated with the militarization of the Arctic. They may well become strong advocates of proposals for arms limitations in the region. Already, there is interest in ideas such as extending the notion of a Nordic nuclear-free zone to the Arctic proper, and it seems highly likely that the lesser Arctic rim states will take the lead in exploring ways to prevent a continuing rise in the level of military operations in the Arctic. Similarly, these states may well experience incentives to form a bloc or *de facto* coalition to further their common interests in the Arctic. Among other things, such a bloc could provide mutual support for the jurisdictional claims of the lesser Arctic states (for example, the Norwegian claims in the area around Svalbard or the Canadian claims in the Arctic archipelago) or offer to provide buffer zones to minimize any risks associated with inadvertent confrontations of Soviet and American naval vessels or military aircraft operating in the Arctic. This last point suggests that a bloc of lesser Arctic rim states might find it increasingly expedient to adopt a neutralist posture with respect to the interactions of the superpowers in the Arctic. Given the existing ties between the United States on the one hand and Norway, Denmark, Iceland, and Canada, this may seem politically far-fetched. Yet there are domestic groups in each of these states (for example, the powerful peace movements in the Scandanavian countries and in Greenland) that would respond favorably to developments along these lines, and the continuing militarization of the Arctic could well enhance the attractions of some sort of non-aligned posture for the lesser Arctic rim states. Already, the Home Rule government in Greenland has joined Iceland in seeking to establish the area within its jurisdiction as a nuclear-free zone. It does not take much imagination, moreover, to foresee a situation in which the leftist Inuit Ataqatigiit (IA) party could gain electoral success in Greenland on a platform calling for the elimination of the American military bases located on the island.[32] The Soviet Union would undoubtedly welcome such developments and might well be willing to make political concessions to encourage realignments along these lines.

In many ways, Canada occupies a special place among the lesser Arctic rim states.[33] Geopolitically, Canada is second only to the Soviet Union as an Arctic state. The country fronts on a huge stretch of the Arctic Basin, and about 40% of Canada's land area lies in the Far North. There is also no denying '...the prominent place that the Arctic has in Canadian political consciousness and in a broad range of domestic policies'.[34] Nonetheless, under 100,000 people or only a fraction of 1% of all Canadians live in the Canadian North; the density of human population in this area is lower than anywhere else in the Arctic except Greenland, and Canada lacks the capabilities to initiate largescale activities in the region or, in some cases, even to monitor the activities of states like the United States in its own sector of the Arctic.

The result is a certain ambivalence in Canada's response to the continuing militarization of the Arctic. The country is closely tied to American military planning for the region, as the arrangements for the North Warning System and the North American Air Defense Master Plan, not to mention the more general framework of NORAD which the two countries renewed for an additional five years in March 1986, clearly indicate. But there is also a distinct sense in many Canadian circles that the United States constitutes the principal threat to the country's Arctic interests, and Canada reacts with considerable passion to specific incidents like the voyages of the *Manhattan* in 1969 and the *Polar Sea* in 1985 or the series of cruise missile tests still underway. Under the circumstances, Canada is in need of a coherent Arctic role to complement its northern political consciousness and to allow the country to transcend its awkward and often embarrassing relationship with the United States in the region.[35] One obvious possibility would be for Canada to assume the role of leader of a bloc of lesser Arctic rim states. If such a bloc were to emerge, Canada would certainly be its natural leader. There are indications that such a role is of interest to at least some Canadian leaders. Steps have already been taken to expand ties with the Home Rule government in Greenland. And influential Canadians have proposed upgrading relations with Iceland and taking a stand in support of Norway in its Arctic jurisdictional conflicts with the Soviet Union. Such a redefinition of Canada's role would also be compatible with the suggestions of influential Canadian publicists, like Griffiths, who have called for the articulation of a distinctive northern foreign policy for Canada.[36]

Consider, finally, the implications of the militarization of the Arctic for the interests and policy calculations of all those states that do not belong to the small group of Arctic rim states. While states like Canada and Norway may see this development leading to an acceptance of the Arctic as NATO's new northern flank, other members of NATO are apt to view the growing interest in the Arctic as a distraction from the main arena of East/West concern in central Europe.[37] This undoubtedly accounts for the vigor with which many Atlanticists oppose not only specific initiatives involving the Far North like the United States Navy's forward maritime strategy but also more general arguments regarding the emergence of the Arctic as a strategic arena of vital significance. By contrast, states with highly developed commercial interests, like Japan and Korea, can be expected to react to the militarization of the Arctic primarily in terms of the implications of this trend for the development of commerce in and through the Arctic in the future. They will experience incentives to side with the superpowers on issues regarding freedom of access in the Arctic and to react skeptically to any initiatives on the part of the lesser Arctic rim states that would have the effect of restricting movement in the water column, on the surface of the sea, or in the airspace of the Arctic. Beyond this, the militarization of the Arctic will not have major impacts on the interests of most other members of international society. They may be attracted by the resultant shift of superpower military operations to a remote region, far removed from their domains in geographical terms. But they are not likely to take an active interest in specific aspects of the militarization of the Arctic.

To close this section, we offer some observations regarding the implications of the militarization of the Arctic for the array of international jurisdictional disputes arising in the Arctic.[38] Some of these disputes involve the so-called sector principle, which in its more extreme forms would give individual Arctic rim states complete control over all activities occurring in pie-shaped slices of the region. Others concern transit rights in the various channels of the Northwest Passage and, to a lesser extent, in the Northeast Passage or Northern Sea Route now operated by the Soviet Union. There is also the unique conflict regarding the extent to which the provisions of the Svalbard Convention of 1920, a multilateral agreement awarding sovereignty over Svalbard to Norway but guaranteeing free access to the natural resources of the archipelago to the other signatories, should govern activities occurring on the outer continental shelf adjacent to Svalbard. Beyond this, there are numerous unresolved disputes over the delimitation of maritime boundaries between opposite and adjacent states in the Arctic (for example, the Soviet-American dispute over the Bering Sea Boundary, the Canadian-American dispute over the Beaufort Sea boundary, and the Soviet-Norwegian dispute over the Barents Sea boundary). For decades, most observers treated these conflicts as intriguing oddities rather than as pressing problems requiring a serious search for solutions. So long as the Arctic remained a frozen wasteland of interest only to a handful of indigenous peoples and a small band of explorers or scientists, little depended on the resolution of any of these disputes. But the militarization of the Arctic is rapidly changing this situation. All the Arctic rim states now have well-defined interests in the jurisdictional status of the Arctic as well as increasing incentives to press their claims with vigor.

Not surprisingly, the primary interest of the superpowers is to ensure freedom of movement in the water column and in the airspace of the Arctic region. The American posture in this regard (as expressed officially in National Security Decision Memorandum 144 of 22 December 1971 and reaffirmed in National Security Decision Directive 90 of 14 April 1983) is particularly unambiguous. The United States has no hesitation in rejecting all sector claims in the Arctic, asserting vigorous claims to transit rights in the Northwest Passage and other Arctic straits, and siding with those (like the Soviet Union) desiring to extend the provisions of the Svalbard Convention to the shelf and marine areas surrounding the archipelago. The position of the Soviet Union in this realm is more complex, since the Soviets have a clear interest in exercising effective control over that portion of the Arctic Basin adjacent to their Arctic coast. But given the growing importance of the Arctic as a theater for military operations, the Soviet Union also has good reasons to promote freedom of movement throughout the remainder of the Arctic Basin. Despite some politically motivated Soviet gestures to the contrary, therefore, it is probable that the superpowers will make common cause in responding to

Canadian claims in the Arctic archipelago, Norwegian claims in the Svalbard area, and any Icelandic claims in the waters adjacent to Iceland. What is more, it is safe to assume that the Soviet Union will not advance formal claims in support of Arctic sectors, despite its assertion of *de facto* control over the waters of the Kara, Laptev, and East Siberian Seas.

By contrast, the lesser Arctic rim states will experience growing incentives to assert restrictive claims regarding jurisdictional issues in the Arctic. Success along these lines could serve to hamper the military operations of the superpowers in the region, and it might offer the lesser states some shelter against the predictable intrusions of the superpowers in their Arctic domains. What is more, the lesser Arctic rim states will display a natural tendency to support each other's jurisdictional claims in the Arctic as a means of maximizing international support for their own claims. For example, Canada and Norway have nothing to lose and much to gain from backing each other in advancing expansive claims in the Arctic archipelago and the Svalbard area. Now that Canada and Denmark/Greenland have reached agreement on jurisdictional matters in Baffin Bay and the Davis Strait, there is little to prevent them from joining forces in an effort to surround themselves with buffer zones as a protection against Soviet or American intrusions.[39] And none of these states would stand to lose anything by supporting any jurisdictional claims that Iceland may care to advance. In fact, the emergence of such a mutual support group regarding jurisdictional claims in the Arctic could provide the impetus for the development of a lesser states' bloc in the Arctic as well as offering valuable international support in connection with each of the specific claims.

2.6   Other Arctic interests

Quite apart from the interests of states, the militarization of the Arctic has affected the interests of subnational units and other groups with significant stakes in the region. To complete this picture of the evolving pattern of Arctic security politics, therefore, we must take a look at these interests.

It is always misleading to assume that the interests of subnational units invariably coincide with the national interests of states. The American Navy and the Soviet Navy, for instance, stand to gain from the militarization of the Arctic, since this trend adds greatly to the importance of sea-launched delivery vehicles in the maintenance of deterrent relationships and may even give new offensive roles to naval vessels.[40] Even more specifically, the militarization of the Arctic favors the interests of those committed to submarines rather than surface vessels, because the

Arctic is well-suited to the operation of submarines but poorly suited to the operation of surface vessels. By the same token, there is no reason to expect the American Army or the Soviet Army to react with enthusiasm to the emergence of the Arctic as a strategic arena of vital significance. While navies can expect star roles in the Arctic and there is room for important aerial operations, it is hard to foresee roles of central importance for gound forces in the region. Similarly, we should expect mixed reactions to the militarization of the Arctic from other sectors of government. Agencies supporting Arctic research may respond positively to this development on the grounds that national security needs can be cited as a powerful argument in support of increased funding for research.[41] But influential groups within foreign ministries are more likely to offer vigorous resistance to the idea that the Arctic is emerging as an important strategic arena. Any such idea will seem alien to the Atlanticists who often dominate decision making within the American State Department and who are influential even within the Soviet Foreign Ministry. Though the State Department has teams of experts on each European country, for example, there are only three individuals in the entire Department responsible for following both Arctic and Antarctic affairs.

Turning to regional and local governments, we find a generally negative reaction to the militarization of the Arctic. Some Alaskans may hope that this development will help to shore up the state's economy during slow periods in non-renewable resource industries. But the Home Rule government in Greenland has already taken steps to declare the island a nuclear-free zone. The Legislative Assembly of the Northwest Territories passed a resolution in 1986 declaring the Northwest Territories a 'nuclear weapons free zone'. And 16 individual communities located in the Northwest Territories have now declared themselves nuclear-free zones.[42] It is important not to exaggerate the significance of this regional and local opposition to the militarization of the Arctic. It will certainly not slow down the emergence of the Arctic region as a strategic arena of vital significance or alter the calculations of national interests discussed in the preceding section. But this opposition is worth noting both because it will give rise to serious domestic issues in the Arctic and because it opens up opportunities for interesting transnational coalitions among regional and local groups concerned with the implications of the militarization of the Arctic.

At first glance, the emergence of the Arctic as a vital strategic arena may seem attractive to industrial and corporate interests with substantial stakes in the region. There are, in fact, some real complementarities between corporate interests and national interests in this realm. Politically, industrial and corporate interests have just as much to gain as the military establishments of the superpowers from a policy of maintaining freedom of access throughout the Arctic Basin. Restrictions on access to raw materials and on movement through transportation corridors are always costly to industrial and corporate interests. Moreover, such restrictions imposed in the Arctic could well become unfortunate precedents in industrial as well as military terms in other regions of the world. Technologically, there are obvious points of intersection between the interests of industry and the interests of military planners in the Arctic. Already, navy planners are benefiting from technological developments sponsored by industry in the realm of under-ice detection systems. And there are obvious possibilities for developments of interest to industry in naval research on ice forecasting, Arctic weather, and so forth.

At the same time, there is considerable scope for conflict between industrial and corporate interests on the one hand and the interests of those concerned with military operations in the Arctic on the other. One of the Arctic's principal attractions to industry has been the fact that it is a relatively secure area, free from political turmoil and military tensions.[43] Though the militarization of the Arctic may not alter this situation radically, it will serve to focus public attention on the region and make it more difficult for industrial and corporate interests to carry on their own Arctic operations in an atmosphere of public disinterest. What is more, industries active in the Arctic are apt to find themselves bumping into security zones and veils of secrecy with increasing frequency in the Arctic as the region's significance as a security arena grows. Whereas industries were once free to do almost anything they pleased in the Arctic, they must now face the sensitivities created by military operations in the region as well as the hue and cry raised by Native groups and environmentalists concerned about environmental and socioeconomic impacts.

There is a traditional, somewhat paternalistic, view that treats the expansion of military operations in the Arctic as beneficial to Native interests. On this account, the militarization of the Arctic produces local jobs (both in construction and maintenance) and causes little harm to the natural or social environments. Those who take this view generally cite the construction of the DEW Line during the 1950s as a positive development from the Native point of view. They are apt to regard the proposed NATO Tactical Fighter and Weapons Training Centre at Goose Bay, Labrador in much the same light.

Increasingly, however, the Native peoples of the Arctic have come to oppose the militarization of their homelands in highly vocal terms.[44]

Partly, Native opposition rests on a general antipathy to the use of the Arctic for military operations coupled with a sense that sophisticated weapons systems, especially nuclear weapons, are a cause of disharmony between human beings and the natural environment.[45] This concern certainly underlies the resolutions that the Inuit Circumpolar Conference has passed at each of its triennial General Assemblies expressing profound concern about the militarization of the Arctic. In part, the opposition of Native groups to military operations in the Arctic stems from much more concrete concerns about the impact of these activities on specific Native groups. The older inhabitants of the Pribilof Islands in the Bering Sea remember that they were forcibly removed from their communities and interned in inadequate facilities in southeastern Alaska in 1942 as part of the American war effort.[46] Many of those who live in Kaktovik, a coastal community in northeastern Alaska, recall that their village was moved three times during the 1950s and 1960s to accommodate the demands of the DEW Line site on Barter Island. The residents of Thule in northern Greenland have not forgotten that they were removed from their homes without their consent in 1953 to make way for the construction of an American airbase (and later a BMEWS site). Today, northern Natives are deeply concerned about an array of possible impacts on animals, habitats, socioeconomic patterns, and local health which may flow from expanded military operations in the Arctic.[47] This is what fuels the intense opposition among Native groups to the proposed NATO Tactical Fighter and Weapons Training Centre which would result in a dramatic increase of low-level training flights over Labrador as well as to plans for an enhanced air-defense system for North America which would produce a sizable growth in the presence of interceptors and AWACs in the Far North.[48]

As for the interests of environmental groups, we must start from the premise that the environmental community is suspicious of the operations of military establishments on general principle. Thus, the growth of military operations in any region constitutes an environmental issue in its own right, especially where nuclear weapons and strategic delivery vehicles are involved. This general suspicion is only heightened by the difficulty of obtaining accurate information about military operations and by the tendency of military establishments to ignore procedural requirements designed to safeguard environmental values. If anything, these concerns are particularly strong in the Arctic where distances are great and where there are few people in a position to make first-hand observations regarding the activities of military establishments. The problems environmentalists encountered in conjunction with the decision to construct the North Warning System illustrate this situation dramatically. The United States Air Force made a concerted effort to minimize its response to the procedural requirements of the National Environmental Policy Act (NEPA) with regard to the North Warning System sites in Alaska. The result was a hastily prepared Environmental Assessment that the Air Force used to justify its decision not to prepare a full-scale Environmental Impact Statement for the project. Accordingly, the environmental community lost the opportunity for public participation, despite the fact that one of the North Warning System sites is located in the Arctic National Wildlife Refuge, an area that many environmentalists regard as particularly sensitive in ecological terms.[49] Not surprisingly, the problem is even worse in other parts of the Arctic. The Canadian federal government did not form an environmental assessment and review panel for its part of the North Warning System project. And the Soviet government is not in the habit of letting environmental concerns impinge on its extensive military operations in the Arctic region.

Many environmental groups have come to realize that demilitarization, on the Antarctic model, is no longer on the cards for the Arctic. But we are witnessing the growth of a more focused concern within the environmental community regarding the impact of military activities on ecologically sensitive areas in the Arctic. Plans for the use of nuclear explosives in the Arctic, as in the case of Project Chariot in the 1950s and 1960s, have long been a cause for concern among environmentalists.[50] The testing of systems that could disrupt large animal populations (for example, caribou herds), destroy important habitat, or leave radioactive debris in the Arctic has now become an important issue for some environmental groups. So also has the construction of military installations, such as Arctic airfields and radar sites, some of which may rely on nuclear power as a source of electricity. So far, environmental organizations like Greenpeace and Friends of the Earth have taken the lead in raising these specific concerns stemming from the militarization of the Arctic.[51] But it is likely that other environmental groups will become active in this realm during the foreseeable future.

2.7 Conclusion

More than any other single development, the militarization of the Arctic has the potential to redraw the map of interests and issues in this vast region. As the Arctic's significance as a strategic arena becomes increasingly apparent, policymakers in all the Arctic rim states will find themselves seeking more information about the region and devoting more attention to Arctic affairs. The United States will exhibit a growing interest in the political concerns of its northern allies. The lesser Arctic rim states, such as Canada, Denmark/Greenland, Iceland, and Norway, will experience incentives to form an informal coalition to protect their common interest in limiting the incursions of the superpowers into the Arctic. Canada will find itself tempted to assume a leadership role in a coalition of lesser Arctic rim states, though it will undoubtedly wish to maintain its extensive and cordial relationship with the United States at the same time.

Nor are the implications of the militarization of the Arctic limited to the interests and policy calculations of nation states. We can expect the American Navy and the Soviet Navy to respond enthusiastically to the growing strategic significance of the Arctic. Industrial and corporate interests will react ambivalently, desiring to make common cause with military establishments to maintain freedom of access in the Arctic but concerned about the loss of the Arctic as a secure and obscure hinterland in which to extract non-renewable resources. By contrast, the opposition of Native groups and environmental organizations to the militarization of the Arctic seems certain to grow. While these parties are apt to realize that there is no prospect for a general demilitarization of the Arctic during the foreseeable future, they will almost certainly focus with greater intensity on the negative impacts of specific military activities in the region. As a result, it now seems probable that the militarization of the Arctic will lead to the emergence of effective coalitions between Native groups and environmental organizations who realize that their common interests in the Arctic region far outweigh their differences.

3

The Arctic economic frontier: industrial interests

Though the Arctic may never emerge as a great center of manufacturing industries, the region is destined to become a major source of raw materials of critical importance to advanced industrial societies both in the Arctic rim states and in other Northern Hemisphere states like Japan and Korea.[52] The deposits or reserves of natural resources located in the Arctic are massive. In the case of hydrocarbons alone, responsible estimates of potentially recoverable reserves in the region range between 100 and 200 billion barrels of crude oil and up to 2,000–3,000 trillion cubic feet of natural gas. This is sufficient to make the Arctic a major focus of interest for developers, despite the fact that many of the Arctic's resources will be costly to produce and deliver to consumers due to harsh natural conditions in the region and problems of transporting Arctic resources over long distances to southern markets. What ultimately drives the movement to industrialize the Arctic, however, is that Arctic resources are politically attractive by comparison with similar resources located in countries or regions (for example, the Middle East) subject to internal turmoil or politically inspired disruptions of supply. Because the North American Arctic is controlled by the United States and Canada and the Siberian Arctic is controlled by the Soviet Union, each of the superpowers can proceed with the exploitation of Arctic resources in an atmosphere of relative security and political predictability. It is not surprising, therefore, that the 1970s and 1980s have witnessed a striking trend toward the industrialization of the Arctic, focusing primarily on energy resources but extending to other raw materials as well. (See Figure 8.)

Fig. 8. (a) Oil drilling rig, Endicott Island, Alaska.

3.1   Arctic development

Though the image of a 'great Arctic energy rush' now seems premature, it is undeniable that the exploitation of hydrocarbons has fueled the industrialization of the Arctic.[53] The Prudhoe Bay field located on Alaska's North Slope, discovered only in 1968, originally contained an estimated 9–10 billion barrels of recoverable oil and 26 trillion cubic feet

Fig. 8. (b) Oil processing facility on Alaska's North Slope. *Source*: courtesy of Standard Alaska Production Company.

of recoverable natural gas; it is the largest single field ever discovered in the United States. Today, 1·6 to 1·7 million barrels of oil are produced daily at the Prudhoe Bay field together with the adjoining Kuparuk field and shipped to southern markets through the Trans-Alaska Pipeline System. In 1985, this amounted to about 19% of the crude oil produced in the United States and 11% of the oil consumed in the United States, and these percentages have since risen. Additional recoverable reserves of oil in the North American Arctic run (according to relatively conservative estimates) to 50 or more billion barrels. The recoverable reserves of natural gas in the North American Arctic amount to over 300 trillion cubic feet, though none of this gas is currently exploited commercially because there is no transportation system available to ship Arctic gas to southern markets.

The magnitude of recoverable reserves of oil in the Soviet Arctic is a matter of some controversy. Certainly, the Soviet Union is presently experiencing difficulties in maintaining high levels of production from its western Siberian oil fields.[54] But Soviet Arctic gas reserves are massive. The recoverable reserves of natural gas in northwestern Siberia amount to at least 500 trillion cubic feet and may run over 1,000 trillion cubic feet. The supergiant Urengoy field alone has recoverable reserves of 212 trillion cubic feet; production from this field is now running at a rate of about 9 trillion cubic feet per year. The rapid pace of development of the Urengoy field combined with preparations to produce natural gas from other giant fields located in the lower Ob River Basin (for example, the Yamburg field with 168 trillion cubic feet of recoverable reserves) undoubtedly constitutes a major factor accounting for the inaccuracy of western predictions, made during the late 1970s, to the effect that the Soviet Union would become a net energy importer in the 1980s. Today, over 60 % of both the oil and the natural gas produced in the Soviet Union comes from fields located in northwestern Siberia.[55]

Nor is the energy potential of the Far North confined to oil and natural gas. Estimates of the coal reserves of northern Alaska (mostly located in the western reaches of the Brooks Range) run as high as 4 trillion tons or approximately the magnitude of the coal reserves of the entire lower forty-eight states. The coal reserves of Siberia may well be even larger; some estimates suggest that Siberia contains as much as 7 trillion tons of coal or upwards of half of all the coal reserves in the world. Though much of this Siberian coal is located on the southern edge of the Soviet North in the Kuznetsk Basin, there are large coal deposits in Yakutia and the Soviet Far East.

Recently, the Far North has become a site for large-scale hydroelectric power production to serve the needs of the affluent societies to the South for electricity or to provide cheap power for energy-intensive industries. In the Canadian North, the James Bay Project, initiated in the 1970s, has begun to come on line. Phase 1 of this Project is designed to provide 10,300 megawatts of power, while Phase 2 will add another 3,400 megawatts. By the year 2000, the energy equivalent of 25 to 30 nuclear power plants will flow southward from the generators of the James Bay Project. The return to power in Quebec in 1985 of Robert Bourassa, the principal architect of the James Bay Project, ensures that the theme of 'power from the North' will continue to be politically potent in Canada for the foreseeable future.[56] Most of the northern rivers of Fennoscandia have already been dammed to generate hydroelectric power, and powerful interest groups in Alaska are pushing plans to construct several dams on the Watana/Devil Canyon segment of the Susitna River to provide an ample flow of energy for the industrialization of the Alaskan railbelt region linking Anchorage and Fairbanks. The Soviet Union has outstripped all the other Arctic rim states in promoting the development of hydroelectric power in Siberia. Siberian hydroelectric power stations are now capable of delivering tens of thousands of megawatts and provide Soviet planners with a powerful incentive to locate energy-intensive industries (for example, steel or aluminum plants) in Siberia. While some of the largest of these stations are on the southern edge of the Soviet

North in the Angara-Yenisey region, others are located much farther north in the vicinity of the great nickel/copper mining complex at Norilsk and on the Kolyma River in the Far East. Beyond this, Soviet planners have devoted considerable thought from time to time to proposals to divert massive quantities of water from rivers flowing into the Arctic Basin to stimulate economic development in southern Siberia.[57]

The nonfuel mineral reserves of the Arctic constitute yet another stimulus to the industrialization of the region. The iron ore deposits of Fennoscandia and the Kola Peninsula in the Soviet Union are well-known and have been subject to exploitation for some time. The Norilsk deposit (featuring nickel, copper and platinum-group metals) has become the basis for one of the largest mining complexes in the world. The lure of high-value minerals like gold and diamonds has played a major role in the Soviet drive to develop the Far East (especially the famous Kolyma region). In Alaska, the Red Dog deposit north of Kotzebue is estimated to contain 85 million tons of ore with over 17% zinc, 5% lead, and 2·4 ounces of silver per ton, making it a world-class deposit with an in-the-ground value of over $11 billion at 1983 prices. Cominco, a multinational mining corporation based in Canada, and the NANA regional corporation of northwest Alaska are developing the Red Dog site under the terms of a cooperative agreement, adding a transnational element to the industrialization of the Arctic and raising interesting questions about the role of Native groups in this process.

The extraordinary biological productivity of some northern waters has also given rise to world-class commercial fishing industries in several parts of the Arctic region. In several recent years, the Alaska pollock fishery, centered in the Bering Sea, has ranked as the largest single-species fishery in the world. About 40% of the total American fish harvest comes from Alaskan (mostly Arctic) waters. This harvest produces an annual revenue of $2 billion and offers employment to 50,000 persons. The cod and shrimp fisheries of West Greenland have provided the basis for the socioeconomic transformation of Greenland over the last generation. Issues involving the management of these fisheries led directly to Greenland's decision to withdraw from the European Economic Community (E.E.C.) during the 1980s. Farther to the East, Norway and the Soviet Union share world-class cod and capelin fisheries in the Barents Sea. While the operation of these fisheries does not have the potential of oil and gas development for making headlines, the commercial fisheries under proper management can contribute to the economic development of the Far North long after the recoverable reserves of hydrocarbons are exhausted.

Not surprisingly, these industrial activities have triggered a dramatic expansion of northern transportation systems. The Trans-Alaska Pipeline System (TAPS), constructed at a cost of $8–9 billion in 1974 dollars, carries about 1·7 million barrels of oil a day from Prudhoe Bay to Valdez, an ice-free port over 800 miles to the South on Prince William Sound (see Figure 9). The Soviet Siberian gas pipeline, an $18 billion project, is now operational; it is only one of a network of pipelines constructed to move Siberian hydrocarbons to western consumers both within the Soviet Union and in other parts of Europe. A major issue in the North today concerns the relative merits of alternative pipeline systems designed to transport the natural gas of northern Alaska and the Canadian Arctic to southern consumers. The once favored Alaska Natural Gas Transportation System (ANGTS) now carries an estimated price tag of $40–50 billion and may never be constructed despite the efforts of both the U.S. Federal government and the Canadian Federal government to promote the project. Yet the gas reserves of the North American Arctic are so large that they will inevitably give rise to alternative proposals for transporting them to southern markets.

The Soviet Union is currently able to keep the Northern Sea Route, a commercial artery stretching some 6,140 miles along the Soviet Arctic coast from Murmansk to Vladivostok, open for navigation over 150 days a year with the aid of the world's largest and most powerful fleet of nuclear-powered icebreakers.[58] There is serious interest in opening up all or part of the Northwest Passage for the shipment of natural resources

Fig. 9. Caribou crossing over oil pipelines, Alaska. *Source*: courtesy of Standard Alaska Production Company.

from the Arctic, despite the engineering challenges and environmental hazards associated with the use of this route. The first shipments of crude oil from the Canadian High Arctic, pumped from Panarctic's Bent Horn field on Cameron Island, passed through the Northwest Passage in ice-reinforced tankers in 1985. Gulf Canada Ltd. has tankered several shipments of crude oil westward to Japan from its Amauligak field in the Canadian Beaufort Sea. The Passage is also attractive to those interested in the shipment of goods between Europe and Japan because it is several thousand miles shorter than available alternatives, including the route through the Panama Canal.

The Soviets have pioneered in the construction of rail lines in northern areas underlain by permafrost as well as in the use of ice roads. Some visionaries now foresee the development of an extensive network of ice roads designed for the shipment of commercial goods within the Arctic Basin itself.[59] The Arctic has similarly become a growth area for air traffic, ranging from the operations of commercial airlines taking advantage of great circle routes over the Pole through bush flights intended to take tourists to wilderness areas to airlifts initiated to move excess fish to distant processing facilities. Finally, the construction of high-voltage transmission lines to carry power generated at hydroelectric stations in the Far North to consumers located in southern metropolitan centers has become a major enterprise. The growth of this increasingly dense network of transportation systems together with its associated infrastructure has played a key role in opening up the northern frontier for additional industrial development.

3.2　　The political economy of Arctic development

Despite their abundance in physical terms, the raw materials of the Arctic are costly resources. They are expensive not only in absolute terms but also relative to similar resources located elsewhere. Developers can only overcome the severe climate and harsh natural conditions of the Arctic at great expense. Industries must erect facilities in permafrost, construct gravel islands in offshore areas, and confine their operations to highly restricted periods during the year. An exploratory oil well drilled in the Beaufort Sea can easily cost over $100 million or up to fifty times the cost of a similar well drilled in the Gulf of Mexico. The Arctic is also a frontier region lacking in highly developed infrastructure such as roads, ports, airstrips, communications systems, readily available labor pools, and many cultural amenities. Corporations operating in the Arctic are regularly forced to shoulder extremely high labor costs and to construct self-contained facilities from scratch (for example, the Sohio and ARCO facilities at Prudhoe Bay). Added to this are the facts that there are essentially no local markets for Arctic resources and that it is unusually costly to transport these resources over long distances under Arctic conditions. Arctic oil and gas pipelines, for example, rank among the most complex and expensive civil engineering projects in history. And it is to be expected that these projects will become more complex during the foreseeable future as environmental and Native interests achieve a growing capacity to articulate demands that such projects minimize environmental and socioeconomic impacts.[60]

It is also important to bear in mind that lead times associated with the development of Arctic raw materials are almost always long. The passage of ten years between initial exploratory work and the first delivery of raw materials to southern consumers is average rather than exceptional. Yet the capital costs and the risks incurred during this period are high. There is nothing out of the ordinary about Sohio's experience in paying $227 million to lease a tract in the Beaufort Sea from the U.S. Federal government on which it subsequently drilled a dry hole (the Mukluk well) at a cost of $110 million. Much the same is true of Dome Petroleum's expenditure of several billion dollars on exploratory work in the Canadian Beaufort Sea which has yet to identify recoverable reserves of crude oil large enough to justify the costs of commercial development. In short, the stakes are high in Arctic development. There is little room for developers who either lack access to large reserves of venture capital or hesitate to engage in high risk activities.

The combined effect of these conditions is to create a situation in which developers feel compelled to extract raw materials on an immense scale in the Arctic if they proceed with development at all. Investments in exploration and development are too large to amortize without the prospect of massive revenues when the resources do reach southern markets. And the delays and risks are too great to justify going forward without the prospect of extraordinary returns when largescale deposits of recoverable resources are located. To illustrate, an oil field containing a billion barrels of recoverable crude oil would be classified as a giant field in West Texas and brought into production immediately. In the Canadian Beaufort Sea, by contrast, a billion barrels of proven reserves is about the minimum required to justify commercial development.[61] And even this may seem insufficient as world market prices for crude oil decline. Similar comments are in order regarding other natural resources in the Arctic. The 17% zinc content in Red Dog ore, for example, is exceptional. But it remains to be seen whether this will prove sufficient to make the Red Dog deposit a commercial success during a period of declining prices for many nonfuel minerals (especially in the absence of substantial government subsidies).

These comments suggest as well that the attractions of Arctic resources are highly sensitive to fluctuations in world market prices. There can be no doubt that the softening world market for natural gas has played a determinative role in the inability to put together financing for the construction of the Alaska Natural Gas Transportation System and in the collapse of the Arctic Pilot Project, a plan to move natural gas from the Canadian High Arctic by ice-reinforced tanker. Similar comments are in order concerning recent decisions on the part of several corporations to put the development of oil reserves in the Canadian Beaufort Sea on hold until the world market price for crude oil rises substantially. All the mining operations in Yukon Territory have been shut down from time to time in recent years, not because the deposits themselves are exhausted but because these operations are only marginally profitable at current world market prices for nonfuel minerals.[62] Incentives to purchase the hydroelectric energy produced at James Bay are also highly sensitive to the world market price of crude oil as well as to the fate of alternative sources of electric power, such as nuclear energy. As the price of oil comes down, the willingness of consumers in New York and New England to switch from oil-fired thermal plants to hydroelectric power from northern Quebec is likely to lag as well.

In purely economic terms, therefore, Arctic raw materials often seem marginal, despite the massive size of many Arctic reserves or deposits. Some, like the coal deposits of northern Alaska, probably will not be developed at all during the foreseeable future. It is possible that others, like the Prudhoe Bay gas cap, will meet a similar fate. But this is certainly not true of all the raw materials of the Arctic. Relatively small reserves of oil or gas may prove commercially viable when they can be tied into existing facilities. Thus, several small oil fields along the Beaufort Sea fringe (for example, the Endicott and Lisburne fields) are attractive because the oil can be moved through TAPS, which will have excess capacity as Prudhoe Bay production begins to decline toward the end of this decade. The financial attractions of onshore operations coupled with the prospect of being able to move oil through the TAPS pipeline have undoubtedly played a major role in sparking industry interest in the potential oil reserves located in the coastal plain of the Arctic National Wildlife Refuge (ANWR) of northeast Alaska.[63] Comparatively small recoverable reserves of oil in the Canadian Beaufort Sea now seem more attractive than they did in earlier years as a result of the prospect of extending the small-diameter pipeline that previously ended at Norman

Wells. Similarly, projects like Panarctic's Bent Horn field can succeed because it is possible to move limited quantities of oil by ice-reinforced tanker without making a commitment to a prohibitively expensive pipeline project. In other cases, recoverable reserves or deposits are simply so large that it is hard to ignore them despite the high costs of exploration and development. This may well be true of the Red Dog deposit even in an era of severely depressed world market prices for nonfuel minerals.

Yet this is by no means the whole story regarding the political economy of Arctic resources. For the most part, governments either hold title to Arctic raw materials outright or exercise exclusive management authority over these resources. And governments regularly experience powerful incentives to encourage or discourage Arctic development, incentives that are not based exclusively on world market prices.

Sometimes these incentives are *ad hoc* in nature in the sense that they are not tied to some comprehensive plan or overall industrial policy. Consider the following examples in this light. The State of Alaska has agreed to subsidize the development of the Red Dog deposit by arranging for the construction of the necessary port and haul road on terms favorable to industry because state planners, distressed by the decline in Alaska's petroleum-based economy, believe that the Red Dog mine could become a significant source of employment and tax revenue.[64] The Canadian government adopted a National Energy Program (NEP) in 1981 which subsidized Canadian-owned companies by reimbursing them for up to 80% of their expenditures on Arctic exploratory work. It is debatable whether this Petroleum Incentives Program has had the effect of stimulating or restricting exploratory work in the Canadian Arctic in overall terms. But it undoubtedly encouraged certain companies, like Dome Petroleum, to continue exploratory work in the Beaufort Sea when they would not have done so on the basis of strictly market signals.[65] Much the same can be said of the American effort to encourage the construction of the Alaska Natural Gas Transportation System by providing legislative approval for the procedure of pre-billing on the part of participating corporations. In Greenland, the Home Rule government has offered Greenex A/S substantial tax breaks to operate the Black Angel lead/zinc mine at Maarmorilik in order to provide employment opportunities for Greenlanders and to bolster the poorly developed Greenlandic economy. And the commitment of the Soviet government to the Siberian gas pipeline rests largely on the desire to generate hard currency from sales to western Europe and to obtain advanced western technologies rather than on conventional calculations of economic efficiency in connection with the project.

In other cases, by contrast, Arctic development fits into more comprehensive industrial policies or even broader geopolitical strategies articulated by national governments. It is clear, for example, that persistent Soviet efforts not only to extract the raw materials of Siberia but also to foster the development of heavy industry in the region are part of a much larger program of achieving economic self-sufficiency in a world that frequently seems hostile to Soviet leaders. This undoubtedly has a lot to do with the facts that today over three quarters of the human population of the Arctic resides in the Soviet North and that the major Arctic cities are located in the Soviet Union.[66] Though they do not currently control official policy, some influential Americans favor rapid development of Alaskan resources on the grounds that such a strategy will contribute to energy independence, help to offset burgeoning American balance of payments deficits, and stimulate less political opposition than the exploitation of natural resources in other parts of the country.[67] Others reach precisely the opposite conclusion, citing the importance of protecting large wilderness areas in Alaska and supporting the efforts of Alaskan Natives to maintain the integrity of their traditional cultures. There is a strong vein of political support for Arctic development in Canada on the theory that such development constitutes the most (perhaps the only) effective strategy for achieving effective occupancy and therefore securing Canadian sovereignty in the Arctic. By contrast, some Greenlandic leaders oppose any large-scale exploitation of raw materials in Greenland (for example, the uranium deposit located in southwestern Greenland) on the theory that any such development will prove incompatible with the maintenance of a more traditional socioeconomic system based on the exploitation of renewable resources largely for local use. Those who adopt this view argue that it is either infeasible or undesirable to create a dual system in which a traditional renewable resource-based economy exists side-by-side with large-scale nonrenewable resource extraction largely for export. There are good reasons to believe that the broader Arctic industrial policies that evolve over the next several decades will differ substantially from one Arctic rim state to another. What is not in doubt, however, is that the policies and actions of governments, in contrast to strictly market signals, will play a major role in setting the course of Arctic development.

3.3   Arctic industrial peripheries

For the most part, Arctic industrial development conforms to the classic pattern of core/periphery relationships. The Arctic region consists of a collection of resource-rich hinterlands producing raw materials largely for the benefit of affluent populations located in the metropolitan centers. As Mote puts it in his discussion of the Soviet Union,[68]

> Siberia...is a classic hinterland of the Soviet economy. Its vast expanse includes 57 percent of the Soviet land mass but only 10 percent of the people and less than 10 percent of Soviet manufacturing. Yet, it contains 60 percent of the country's coal resources, 75 percent of its natural gas, 60 percent of its hydroelectric potential, 70 percent of its timber, and probably over half of its strategic minerals.

Mead evokes a similar image in describing Fennoscandia as a '...territory at the margin of the Scandinavian economy'.[69] And the pattern is even more striking throughout the rest of the Circumpolar North. By a large margin, the Soviet North and Fennoscandia constitute the most densely populated and highly industrialized portions of the Arctic region.

In industrial terms, the typical result is a relationship bearing a distinct resemblance to what has become known as dependency or neo-colonialism in other parts of the world. Metropolitan centers and hinterlands are complementary in the sense that core areas provide capital and policy direction while resource-rich peripheries provide a ready source of raw materials to fuel the manufacturing complexes located in the centers. The difference, of course, is that most parts of the Arctic are neither colonies nor newly independent states like the various countries of the third world. Politically, they are simply constituent parts of the advanced industrial systems characteristic of the Arctic rim states. This has led more and more observers to turn to the concept of internal colonialism in seeking to shed light on the circumstances of Arctic peripheries.[70]

Internal colonialism involves a set of tightly linked conditions. To begin with, there is the flow of economic rents (that is, producers' surpluses or monetary returns in excess of normal costs of production) from the exploitation of Arctic resources. Throughout the Arctic, the pattern is the same. The raw materials are physically located in northern areas, but the economic rents arising from the extraction of these resources ultimately benefit corporations, consumers, or governments located in the metropolitan centers. Jellis illustrates this proposition clearly in his study of the Northwest Territories in the 1970s:[71]

> The total value of the rents associated with natural resources projects in the Northwest Territories between 1970 and 1974 approximated $296 million. Of this total, the operating companies retained $106 million (35·9 per cent) in the form of excess profits,

i.e. profits over and above a 15 per cent return on their invested capital; the federal government received $98 million (33·8 percent) mainly from taxes, but also from royalties and a share of Normal Wells production revenue; entities in British Columbia received $15 million (5·1 per cent) in the form of excess transmission charges on Pointed Mountain natural gas; Canadian (mainly corporate) consumers received $25 million (8·6 per cent) in the form of lower prices for Normal Wells refined products; and US consumers received $51 million (17·1 per cent) in the form of undervalued natural gas prices.

And this case is typical. While the exploitation of natural resources in the Arctic does sometimes produce jobs for local residents, northern communities seldom benefit directly from the economic rents associated with such projects.[72]

A second feature of internal colonialism is the prevalence of extreme economic volatility or boom/bust cycles that make it difficult to build stable local economies in the Arctic peripheries. In part, this is attributable to the fact that deposits of nonrenewable resources are finite and subject to (often rapid) exhaustion. The ghost towns associated with the early gold rushes or with copper mining in southcentral Alaska during the 1930s constitute well-known examples. But as Tussing has demonstrated, the same basic problem plagues the petroleum-based economies emerging in the Arctic peripheries today.[73] Partly, boom/bust cycles stem from the striking volatility of world market prices for primary products (including renewable resources) of the sort that are central to Arctic economies. The most spectacular case in point at the present time is crude oil, a commodity whose world market price can change by a factor of two or even four within months. But much the same is true of world market prices for fish, wood products, and many nonfuel minerals. Needless to say, it is hard to build stable economies on the basis of industries that may be here today and gone tomorrow both in physical terms and in financial terms.

To make matters worse, most Arctic peripheries have little ability to influence key decisions regarding matters of political economy and, therefore, to control their own economic destinies in policy terms. For the most part, the fate of the remote communities located in the Arctic is determined by decision makers located in distant metropolitan centers who are motivated by considerations that have little to do with the welfare of Arctic residents. Central governments decide whether to lease oil and gas tracts in the Arctic and whether to issue the necessary permits for the opening of nonfuel mineral deposits in the Far North. Corporations with headquarters in London, New York, Houston, or Vancouver and with a multitude of projects located all over the world ultimately make investment decisions that determine the course of Arctic development. And of course the volatility of world market prices for the raw materials located in the Arctic arises, in considerable measure, from the behavior of consumers and, in some cases, political leaders virtually none of whom live in the Arctic or have any profound concern for the Arctic. Under the circumstances, it is hardly surprising that some groups of Arctic residents are now engaged in a vigorous struggle to break out of this pattern, pushing for arrangements featuring home rule or self-government. But the bonds of internal colonialism are strong and with some notable exceptions (for example, the North Slope Borough in northern Alaska) the remote communities of the Arctic have not been able to assert effective control over their own destiny.[74]

The net effect of these conditions is a pattern featuring regular economic dislocations and extreme dependence on transfer payments from central governments. The wage economy in most Arctic communities is highly unpredictable, and high rates of unemployment are endemic throughout most sectors of the Arctic. Arctic communities typically have miniscule tax bases and few opportunities to generate the revenue needed to provide local services, much less to initiate some alternative pattern of economic development. To be sure, central governments have increasingly filled the gap by making largescale transfer payments to Arctic communities. The Danish government, for example, provides a massive block grant to the Home Rule authorities in Nuuk and covers deficits resulting from the operations of the Royal Greenlandic Trading Company (KGH).[75] The state government in Alaska is certainly correct in its assertions that the State has provided far more aid to remote, largely Native, Alaskan communities than the funds made available under the terms of the Alaska Native Claims Settlement Act of 1971. Yet transfer payments are ultimately a part of the pattern of internal colonialism rather than a harbinger of some emerging alternative. Such payments are controlled from metropolitan centers. They may dry up, sometimes with little warning, for reasons having little or nothing to do with conditions in the remote communities themselves. And in any case, transfer payments typically breed a debilitating psychology of dependence rather than opening up viable alternatives.[76]

There is one sense in which internal colonialism is even more limiting than the neo-colonial relationships characteristic of interactions between advanced industrial societies and resource-rich countries in the third world. Because they are simply components of larger political systems, Arctic peripheries cannot gain bargaining leverage by nationalizing or threatening to expropriate the production of raw materials. To be sure, the Home Rule government in Greenland has gained some leverage through the creation of a Danish/Greenlandic Joint Resources Council as well as through withdrawal from the European Economic Community (E.E.C.).[77] But these developments, which constitute the exception rather than the rule in the Arctic, do not begin to compare with the nationalization of the oil fields of Saudi Arabia or the copper mines of Chile. Those located in the Arctic peripheries are expected to behave as loyal citizens of nations controlled from the metropolitan centers. They are seldom given the option of asserting effective self-determination in economic terms as a basis from which to negotiate mutually satisfactory arrangements governing the exploitation of the raw materials located in the Arctic.

In certain respects, Alaska constitutes an exception to this pattern of internal colonialism in the Arctic peripheries. The Alaska Statehood Act of 1958 transferred title to 104 million acres or over 27% of the land area of Alaska from the Federal government to the state government. Additionally, the state acquired sufficient legal authority to collect substantial economic rents in the form of royalties on raw materials extracted from state-owned lands and of taxes levied on the operations of corporations engaged in the exploitation of natural resources throughout the state. The result has been a bonanza for Alaskan residents, fueled by the development of Prudhoe Bay oil and the high world market price for crude oil that prevailed during the 1970s. In recent years, Alaska has had the highest per capita income of any state in the United States.[78] There is no state income tax or state sales tax. The state has established a Permanent Fund, currently valued at between $8 and $9 billion, with income derived from petroleum development. For several years now, the State of Alaska has even provided each resident of the state with an annual dividend check paid for with income derived from the Permanent Fund's investment portfolio.

The economic success of Alaska is undoubtedly striking. There is nothing remotely comparable to it anywhere else in the Arctic. Yet it is also important to recognize a series of factors that make Alaska's economic success fragile. As Tussing points out, Alaska has developed a petroleum-based economy.[79] Some 85–90% of the state's revenue stems from the exploitation of hydrocarbons, and the private sector is dominated by this industry as well. But oil production at Prudhoe Bay will soon start to decline, and there is no guarantee that large-scale reserves of new oil will be found elsewhere in the state. Any dramatic fall in the world market price for crude oil, such as the one occurring during 1986, can wreak havoc with the economy of Alaska and drastically reduce revenues available to the state government.[80] The Federal government plays a dominant role with respect to many decisions that are critical to the state's economy. Of course, the Federal government exercises exclusive management authority over offshore oil and gas development and offshore fisheries.[81] But it also has sufficient regulatory power to determine whether projects like the Red Dog mine can go forward. Additionally, the corporations that play a dominant role in Alaska (for example, ARCO, Chevron, Exxon, Sohio, Cominco) all have headquarters located in the lower forty-eight states or abroad as well as far-flung economic empires with respect to which their Alaskan operations are small. For the most part, the bargaining strength of these multinational corporations exceeds that of the State of Alaska. Finally, while it is undoubtedly an exaggeration to describe Alaska as an economic colony of Japan, the role of foreign direct investment in Alaska's economy is large and growing rapidly. More and more, the state is perceived as a resource-rich hinterland by those located in the industrialized societies of Asia. Entrepreneurs seeking to initiate new industrial projects in Alaska today generally turn to investors based in Japan and Korea. This need not always be harmful. But it does suggest that it would be a mistake to overemphasize the differences between Alaska and other Arctic peripheries. Overall, though the recent economic success of Alaska is certainly real, this success is fragile and subject to rapid change. It is not sufficient to prove that Alaska has decisively broken out of the pattern of internal colonialism prevailing throughout most of the Arctic.

3.4   Transnational connections

Like other resource frontiers, many parts of the Arctic have become objects of interest to foreign industrialists and investors. There is a natural complementarity between the Arctic with its massive deposits of natural resources and unusually sparse population and highly industrialized areas like Western Europe and Japan, which have large urban populations and concentrations of industry but few local sources of raw materials. The Arctic offers both a secure source of needed raw materials and a variety of interesting investment opportunities to financial planners located in metropolitan centers. For their part, foreign investors can promise capital and advanced technologies for Arctic development as well as providing markets for Arctic resources for which there is no local demand. With a few exceptions (for example, the relationship between Denmark and Greenland prior to 1979), this has not resulted in colonial arrangements or even neo-colonial relationships. But direct investment on the part of foreign corporations or governments is growing rapidly and producing a complex network of transnational connections in the Arctic.

Some observers have come to describe Alaska, only half jokingly, as an economic colony of Japan. One well-known commentator has even characterized the state as the 'Nigeria of the North.'[82] While these images are certainly caricatures, they do serve to highlight the extraordinary role of foreign investment and the export of commodities in Alaska's economy. A multinational corporation based in Britain, British Petroleum, owns a controlling interest in Sohio which, in turn, operates 50·4% of the Prudhoe Bay oil field. Undoubtedly, much of the oil produced in Alaska would be shipped to the Far East if this were not explicitly prohibited by act of Congress.[83] The major hardrock mining project now underway in Alaska, the development of the Red Dog deposit north of Kotzebue, is being carried out by Cominco, a multinational corporation based in Canada. Japan takes virtually all of Alaska's wood products, and Japanese firms have invested heavily in Alaska's timber industry. Similarly, the Japanese not only purchase a large proportion of Alaska's seafood products, they have also come to dominate the fish processing industry in many parts of the state. As Tussing puts it, 'Japan as a net importer of crude materials is a natural partner for Alaska, which exports very little else.'[84]

If anything, the role of foreign investment and raw materials exports is more pronounced in the Canadian Arctic. Traditionally, hydrocarbon development in the Canadian Arctic has been dominated by subsidiaries of American based corporations like Exxon, Mobil, and Gulf. Among the objectives of the Canadian National Energy Program (NEP) adopted in 1981 were '...to boost Canadian ownership of oil and gas production to 50 percent, to increase the share of the oil and gas sector owned by the Canadian government, and to have Canadian control of a significant number of the larger oil and gas companies.'[85] In these terms, the NEP yielded some significant results. The purchase of Gulf Canada Limited in 1985 by a Canadian corporation (Olympia and York Enterprises) '...moved Canadian ownership of the oil and gas industry to 47 percent.'[86] The federal government took vigorous steps to shore up Dome Petroleum, a Canadian corporation which is one of the major operators in the Canadian Beaufort Sea. And Petro-Canada, the national oil company, became an important player in the Canadian Arctic, partly as a result of the back-in provision of the NEP granting the federal government a 25% share of recoverable reserves of oil discovered in frontier areas. Yet the Mulroney government has dismantled many of the provisions of the NEP (without abandoning the Program completely) and come out strongly in favor of free trade and investment between Canada and the United States. As well, the American share of the Canadian oil industry has gone up again with Amoco's purchase of Dome Petroleum.[87] There is no basis, therefore, for predicting any long-term decline in the prominent role of American multinationals in oil and gas development in the Canadian Arctic. Foreign enterprises occupy a similar place with regard to other industrial sectors in the Canadian North. Much of the capital for the James Bay Project originated in New York, and a growing proportion of the electricity generated by the Project is flowing to American consumers in the northeastern states.[88] Moreover, the prospect of exporting relatively inexpensive hydroelectric power produced in northern Quebec to American consumers constitutes the cornerstone of Premier Bourassa's future plans for 'power from the North.' Nor is the Japanese factor absent from the Canadian Arctic. Japanese investors played a major role in some of the efforts to shore up Dome Petroleum in the hope of working toward an agreement under which oil or gas from the Canadian Arctic would find its way to markets in Japan. Gulf Canada has entered into an agreement to ship oil to Japan from the Canadian Beaufort Sea. And commercial interests in Japan have also taken a strong interest in the prospect of opening up the Northwest Passage as a commercial shipping route between Europe and Japan. Should the Passage become commercially significant during the foreseeable future, it is probable that Japanese interests will be the key to the development of Arctic shipping.[89]

Greenland differs somewhat from Alaska and Canada with respect to transnational connections. Prior to the introduction of Home Rule in 1979, Denmark pursued an exclusionary colonial policy in Greenland. The Royal Greenlandic Trading Company (KGH) maintained a monopoly on all trade with Greenland, and the Danish government placed severe restrictions on any foreign investment in the colony. Under the circumstances, it is remarkable how rapidly transnational connections have emerged during the years since the introduction of Home Rule. Greenex A/S, a Danish firm controlled until recently by the Canadian-based Cominco and now controlled by a Swedish corporation, runs the

Black Angel mine, a lead, zinc and silver operation at Maarmorilik on the west coast of Greenland. (See Figure 10.) ARCO has been the lead corporation involved in exploration for oil and gas in the area of Jameson Land located near Scoresbysund on the east coast. Even the Greenlandic fishing industry is destined to experience growing foreign involvement. Whereas KGH once dominated commercial fishing in Greenland, the E.E.C. will (ironically) play an enhanced role in the development of Greenland's fisheries in the future. Under the terms of the agreement governing the termination of Greenland's formal membership in the Common Market, the E.E.C. has undertaken to provide both financial and technical aid for the development of improved commercial fishing operations in Greenlandic waters. As Greenland continues to emerge from its colonial relationship with Denmark, the island will inevitably become involved in a growing web of transnational economic relations. While Greenland has tiny local markets and little modern technology, the Home Rule government faces growing pressure to generate increased revenues. Conversely, the relatively secure raw materials of Greenland are bound to seem attractive to multinational corporations based in North America and Western Europe. What remains to be seen is how successful

Fig. 10. Cominco's Polaris zinc/lead mine located on Little Cornwallis Island in Canada's Northwest Territories. The concentrate storage shed, emblazoned with the Canadian flag, holds nine months of production to be shipped during the ice-free summer months. The mill is to the left. *Source*: Cominco Ltd.

the Home Rule government in Nuuk will be in bargaining with the multinationals regarding the terms of economic development in Greenland.

We are accustomed to employing concepts like self-sufficiency or even autarky in analyzing economic development in the Soviet Union. It may therefore come as a surprise to realize the extent of transnational connections in efforts to develop the Soviet North. In recent years, '... raw-material exports have accounted for more than 50 percent of total Soviet exports and more than 80 percent of hard-currency earnings.'[90] Hydrocarbons from northwestern Siberia constitute the dominant factor in producing these totals. Many observers anticipate that several Western European countries (for example, West Germany, France, Italy) will come to depend on Soviet sources for as much as 25–30% of their natural gas during the foreseeable future.[91] From the Soviet point of view, these exports have become the key to the acquisition of advanced technologies from the West as well as to the availability of hard currencies with which to pay for these technologies. With regard to offshore development in the Barents Sea area, the Soviet Union has displayed growing interest in entering into joint ventures with European corporations.[92] To the East, in East Asian Siberia and the Far East, Soviet planners have turned toward Japan and even the United States as potential markets and as sources of capital for the development of Siberian raw materials. By 1979, Japan had provided $4 billion in credits for Siberian development, despite political difficulties arising from the fact that Japan and the Soviet Union never signed a peace treaty following World War II.[93] Today, there are signs of growing interest on the part of both the Soviet Union and Japan in the formation of an economic partnership for the development of Siberian resources. Interestingly, American corporations, like Occidental Petroleum, El Paso Natural Gas, and Gulf Oil, have taken a definite interest in projects involving the natural resources of the Soviet North.[94] If the political climate between the superpowers should continue to improve, there is no doubt that Soviet planners and American industrialists could find common ground regarding the exploitation of Siberia's raw materials. Some such approach could well offer a solution to the problem of developing resources in disputed areas, like any hydrocarbons discovered in the Navarin Basin in the central Bering Sea. Overall, then, transnational connections are likely to spread through the Soviet North just as quickly as they arise in other parts of the Arctic region. As Whiting puts it, Soviet policymakers '... want to exploit Siberia's natural resources, and the availability of foreign markets provides their main economic justification for the initial investment.'[95]

This survey suggests that the Arctic is destined to become a resource-rich hinterland fueling advanced industrial economies not merely in individual Arctic rim states but also in a whole collection of industrialized societies in the Northern Hemisphere. As such, we should expect to find the region becoming enmeshed in an increasingly complex web of transnational connections. This may seem disturbing to some observers. There are undoubtedly Americans who worry about the prospect of Alaska becoming an economic colony of Japan. Canadian sensitivities regarding foreign (largely American) economic domination are deep-seated, and they may become particularly severe regarding the Arctic, a region of great emotional significance to Canadians accompanied by a remarkably thin Canadian presence.[96] It is easy to foresee the emergence of concerns about foreign economic control in Greenland, even though economic partnerships with foreign multinationals offer the most realistic approach to reducing Greenland's financial dependence on the Danish government. As for Siberia, it seems certain that Soviet leaders will insist on maintaining effective control over resource development even as they enter into deals involving the provision of foreign capital or technology for Siberian projects and the supply of raw materials to markets in Western Europe and Japan. Nonetheless, the effect of the emergence of these transnational connections on the Arctic will be profound. Already, it has become inappropriate to dismiss the region as a frozen wasteland of little interest to anyone but small groups of Native peoples and environmentalists together with a few explorers and scientists. Over the next several decades, these economic developments will integrate the Arctic into the trade and communications networks of the industrialized world. Among other things, this will raise profound questions about the future of the distinctive human cultures and ecosystems of the Arctic region.

3.5   Arctic industrial policies

In capitalist systems, at least, it once seemed sensible to draw a clear distinction between the private sector and the public sector and to assert that decisions about industrial development should flow fundamentally from private initiatives. Today, however, this distinction is no longer tenable. All governments are under pressure to play a major role in articulating industrial policies. There is of course no question about the central role of the state in industrial development in socialist systems. But even in mixed systems, governments have become deeply involved in economic decision making through the evolution of pricing policies, tax and subsidy schemes, and regulatory regimes. Additionally, governments have increasingly taken on the role of protectors of noneconomic values (for example, the maintenance of environmental quality, the protection of cultural integrity), a role that frequently requires intervention in the decision-making processes of actors in the private sector.

The need for clearcut industrial policies is even more apparent in the Arctic than it is in other regions. Throughout the Arctic, governments hold title to the bulk of the region's land and associated natural resources. The U.S. Federal government and the State of Alaska together own about 86% of Alaska. And this is the smallest proportion of public ownership in the Arctic. The Canadian Federal government owns approximately 90% of the Canadian North. The Norwegian government owns 99% of the northern counties of Norway. There is no concept of private ownership in land or natural resources in Greenland. And the Soviet government controls all of the Soviet North. With the development of the legal concept of exclusive economic zones, moreover, governments are now entitled to exercise exclusive management authority over the resources of vast segments of the marine areas of the Arctic region. Though exclusive management authority is not identical to outright ownership, it certainly places governments in a position to play a determinative role regarding all forms of industrial development in the offshore portions of the Arctic. Under the circumstances, governments cannot avoid becoming active in the formulation of Arctic industrial policies. They may or may not choose to articulate such policies in explicit terms, or to formulate these policies comprehensively rather than on a piecemeal basis. But there is no doubt that the actions of governments will go far toward determining the future course of industrial development in the Arctic region.

Arctic industrial policies must address a series of interrelated issues. There is, to begin with, the issue of whether to develop the Arctic at all and if so, at what pace to exploit the natural resources of the region. Some observers view the Arctic as a 'country in reserve', a vast region to be left untouched until other, more easily accessible sources of raw materials are exhausted.[97] Others, by contrast, regard the Arctic as a particularly attractive source of raw materials for the near future both because no price or supply manipulations like those of the Organization of Petroleum Exporting Countries (OPEC) are going to disrupt supplies of Arctic resources and because efforts to develop Arctic resources are unlikely to provoke particularly effective domestic opposition. So far, only the Soviet Union has moved to adopt a definite policy on this issue. Thus, the Soviet government has pursued a persistent program of industrializing the Soviet North over several decades, a program that accounts for the facts that over three quarters of the human population and most of the heavy industry of the entire Arctic region are located within the Soviet Union. But even Soviet policy regarding Arctic development has shifted over the years. What began as a program featuring the creation of large urban centers and heavy industry motivated by '...a strong desire for self-sufficiency'[98] has evolved increasingly toward a program emphasizing the extraction of raw materials by workers who do not become permanent residents of the region and whose efforts are justified by the need to expand exports as a source of hard currency earnings.[99] By comparison, however, none of the other Arctic rim states has articulated any clear policy regarding industrial development in the region. The energy crises of the 1970s triggered a move in the United States to open up Arctic oil and gas provinces at a rapid pace and evoked talk of a 'great Arctic energy rush'. But powerful environmental interests also rallied to the cause of preserving large chunks of Alaska as wilderness areas; Native groups have fought with some success to protect their subsistence lifestyle from the impacts of industrial activities, and the world market price for crude oil has plunged. Under the circumstances, there is no basis for assuming that the United States government will push hard to open up Alaska at a rapid pace during the remaining years of this century. If anything, the situation is even more ambiguous in Canada. Here, a desire to promote Arctic development as a means of buttressing Canadian sovereignty in the Far North is offset by the forces of Canadian nationalism which oppose Arctic development dominated by corporations based in the United States or other foreign countries.

Once efforts to develop the resources of the Arctic get under way, most governments must grapple with a stream of decisions regarding the extent to which they should provide public support or assistance to private developers operating in this realm. In the Soviet Union, of course, such issues do not arise. Instead, state planners must arbitrate among numerous agencies seeking special treatment for their projects. But in the rest of the Arctic rim states, the proper role of government in aiding Arctic development has become a major issue. None of these states has succeeded in articulating a clear policy regarding this issue. The Canadian government, for example, has moved to encourage Arctic development by setting up the Petroleum Incentives Program which subsidizes exploration for hydrocarbons in frontier areas (so long as it is carried out by Canadian corporations), arranging financial bailouts for Dome Petroleum, and encouraging the construction of the Alaska Natural Gas Transportation System. Yet it has also dampened Arctic development from time to time by keeping oil prices artificially low, rejecting proposals for a MacKenzie

Valley Pipeline, and acceding to demands aimed at favoring the production of Albertan hydrocarbons over Arctic hydrocarbons. Much the same is true of the American government. Thus, American policymakers have encouraged Arctic development by holding regular oil and gas lease sales in Alaskan offshore areas as well as by offering legislative sanctions for pre-billing procedures to facilitate financing for the Alaska Natural Gas Transportation System and for the land exchange required to provide access to the Red Dog mine. But the American government has also refused to approve proposals to export Alaskan oil even in the face of gluts in west coast markets and articulated a regulatory regime that environmental and Native groups have been able to exploit to impose severe restrictions on plans to extract the raw materials of the American Arctic.

Given the political attractions of Arctic resources, it is hardly surprising that governments frequently experience powerful incentives to alter the allocations of these resources that would occur if developers were permitted to respond exclusively to the signals provided by market prices. The prohibition on the export of Alaskan oil does not make sense in strictly economic terms. It is motivated by considerations of national security as well as by a desire to protect the interests of the American merchant marine. Similarly, while the financial incentives that the State of Alaska is willing to provide in connection with the construction of a mine in the NANA region or a petroleum refinery in the Valdez area are difficult to justify in terms of economic efficiency, they are easy enough to understand as a political response to pressures to combat high levels of unemployment in the state. Similar examples abound with regard to the Canadian North. The actions of successive Canadian governments in holding energy prices below world market levels have certainly benefited consumers in the urban centers of southern Canada, but they have served to restrict the incentives for developers to produce expensive oil and gas from the Canadian North. It is probable that the net effect of recent Canadian energy policies, as symbolized by the NEP of 1981 and the Western Accord of 1985, has been to favor the production of Albertan hydrocarbons (including those extracted from oil sands) over those located in the Canadian Arctic. The Soviet decision to channel Siberian raw materials into the export trade as a means of increasing hard currency earnings constitutes an even more striking example of the role of public policy in the allocation of Arctic resources. While this decision has hardly slowed down the pace of Soviet northern development, it has certainly been a major factor in shifting the emphasis of Siberian development from a program of integrated industrialization and urbanization to a more classic pattern of 'heartland–hinterland relationships'.

Industrial policies affect the distribution of benefits flowing from Arctic development as well as the allocation of Arctic resources. As the discussion of internal colonialism in an earlier section suggests, the governments of the Arctic rim states have generally played an active role in directing the flow of economic benefits from development away from the Far North. Whether the motivation has been a desire to maximize hard currency earnings as in the case of the Soviet Union, to supply cheap energy to urban consumers as in the case of Canada, or to offer favorable treatment to private corporations as in the case of the United States, the result is the same. The developers and their customers have regularly profited at the expense of those living in the Arctic itself. More recently, almost all the governments of the Arctic rim states have moved to offset this pattern of distribution, at least partially, by introducing systems of transfer payments designed to improve the lot of those residing in Arctic communities. But whether these systems feature block grants like those Denmark provides to the Home Rule government in Greenland, extensive welfare programs like those common to the advanced welfare states of Scandinavia, or a multiplicity of grants and revenue-sharing programs like those characteristic of the United States, they all have severe drawbacks as methods of overcoming the problems associated with internal colonialism. In every case, they tend to reinforce the prevailing psychology of dependence and to detract from efforts to encourage the emergence of self-sufficient communities.[100] While the Arctic rim states have developed relatively clear policies regarding the distribution of benefits from Arctic development, therefore, it is hard to construct a compelling defense of any of these policies.

Finally, all the Arctic rim states must regularly come to terms with values other than economic gain or national security in making policy choices governing Arctic development. For easy reference, we can group these values under the rubrics of nationalism, Natives, and nature.[101] The issues raised by these values are easy enough to identify. To what extent should the Canadian government interfere with efforts to extract raw materials in the Arctic in order to ensure that such efforts are dominated by Canadian corporations? Should Arctic development be postponed in the United States, Canada, or Fennoscandia until all Native claims in the region are definitely settled? Should Native groups be entitled to veto development projects that seem likely to impinge on their subsistence lifestyles? What sorts of restrictions on Arctic development projects are appropriate in order to ensure the preservation of fragile Arctic ecosystems? But the proper responses to such questions are anything but clear. Even in the Soviet Union, there is a growing movement aimed at placing restrictions on Siberian development in the interests of protecting ecosystems and, to a lesser extent, indigenous lifestyles. As for the other Arctic rim states, issues of this sort are rapidly becoming more contentious. The Arctic industrial policies of Canada, for example, are shot through with ambivalences regarding these issues, and successive governments have set up one commission or task force after another without succeeding in articulating anything resembling clear or well-defined Arctic industrial policies. In the United States, litigation over various plans to develop Arctic resources has become a way of life. And there is no reason to believe that recent government initiatives provoked by the concerns of Native groups and environmentalists have succeeded in resolving conflicts over proposed development projects in Fennoscandia (for example, the Alta Dam project in northern Norway).[102]

3.6   Conclusion

Though the deposits or reserves of natural resources located in the Arctic are massive, these resources are typically expensive both to produce and to transport over long distances to southern markets. Yet the raw materials of the Arctic are politically attractive to influential groups in all of the Arctic rim states because they offer the prospect of secure supplies of critical resources (for example, energy) or of large-scale exports capable of providing hard currency or reducing balance of payments problems. Additionally, there is a natural complementarity between the Arctic as a resource-rich but thinly populated hinterland and many metropolitan centers possessing advanced manufacturing complexes but lacking raw materials. Increasingly, this is stimulating the emergence of a complex network of transnational connections in the Arctic as well as a classic pattern of core/periphery relationships or internal colonialism within individual Arctic rim states. Nonetheless, the future of Arctic development is anything but clear at this time. Native groups are rapidly acquiring the resources and the political sophistication to mount effective opposition to Arctic projects that seem inimical to their interests. Environmental groups, even in the Soviet Union, have become a force to be reckoned with on the part of developers. Nationalists are quite capable of provoking serious opposition to Arctic development carried out by multinational corporations based in foreign countries. And all these groups can point to serious questions regarding the economics of many Arctic projects to reinforce their opposition to large-scale economic development in the Far North.

In the final analysis, the actions of the governments of the Arctic rim states will play a determinative role in shaping the course of Arctic development during the foreseeable future. But none of these governments, with the partial exception of the Soviet government, has been able to articulate an unambiguous and well-thought-out set of Arctic industrial policies. If anything, the sound and the fury surrounding the issues underlying Arctic industrial policies are presently increasing as various interest groups become more effective in articulating their concerns in this area. None of this means that the actions of governments will become less important as determinants of Arctic development; far from it. But it does suggest that the path of Arctic development during the foreseeable future will not be straight and that anything but general predictions regarding future occurrences in this realm are hazardous.

4

Arctic homelands: Native interests

They call themselves Inuit, Inupiat, Dene, Iuoravetlan, and other words which, each in their own languages, mean 'the people'. Ethnographers identify them by linguistic groupings such as Athapaskan, Algonqian, Tungus-Manchu, and by cultural groupings such as Eskimo-Aleut, Evenki, Sami, Chukchi. But, by whatever name, they are the indigenous minorities living in seven Arctic rim nations – the United States, Canada, Denmark/Greenland, Norway, Sweden, Finland, and the Soviet Union. (Iceland has no indigenous population.) Social scientists and lawyers often describe them as belonging to a 'Fourth World' composed of 'indigenous peoples who are locked into nations they can never hope to rule...'.[103]

Economically dependent on the core and, in this case, southern society, Arctic communities throughout the Circumpolar North look to areas outside the Arctic for capital, products, markets, and transfer payments. As the preceding chapters illustrate, Arctic communities are experiencing an increasing military and industrial presence. The new occupations – large-scale hardrock mining, hydrocarbon exploration and production, tourism, logging, and fishing – all depend on outside financing, expertise, supplies, and markets. The traditional occupations also rely on external markets – for furs, arts and handicrafts, fish and fish products. Outside interest groups such as environmentalists and animal protection organizations increasingly influence government policies affecting the Arctic, and external market forces deeply affect northern communities. The predominately self-sufficient subsistence economy of an earlier era ended when governments resettled Native people into centralized communities in order to deliver services such as health care and education. (See Figure 11.)

The effects of internal colonialism abound in the Arctic. Unemployment and underemployment are high; dependence on welfare or other types of transfer payments is high; the tax base is low or non-existent in most communities while the demand for services increases; the desire for numerous commodities produced elsewhere is increasing as television and other forms of communication spread throughout the Arctic. A high emigration rate drains northern communities of their most educated individuals, while the overall population of indigenous peoples increases, contributing to a rising demand for transfer payments. Individual pathologies such as alcoholism, suicide, homicide, and depression are prevalent in many northern communities. While these may, in part, be caused by psychological and physical responses to the environment (especially reactions to light and dark cycles), social scientists increasingly trace these pathologies to conditions of anomie and dependency prevalent in remote communities. Traditional cultural norms have been disrupted and not replaced with appropriate new cultural norms.[104]

Indigenous people of the Arctic seeking to overcome internal colonialism have formed powerful, increasingly effective organizations to pursue their aims and voice their views. Three issues dominate their agenda: (1) cultural survival, (2) protection and retention of the land, and (3) self-government. Effective control over natural resources in the homeland underlies each of the agenda items. The absence of economic development (the major aim of assimilationists) as a first priority is no coincidence. Through a brief survey of homelands in each of the Arctic rim nations, we trace the efforts of original peoples in the Arctic to end internal colonialism and take control of their own destiny. We then introduce the new Native organizations, political parties, and leaders who have become powerful players in Arctic conflicts. Finally, we discuss the major issues on the agenda of Native peoples and organizations in the Circumpolar North. Because Natives have become powerful and articulate in moving their agenda, an understanding of their interests is crucial to managing and resolving Arctic conflicts.

4.1   Kalaallit Nunaat[105]: Greenland

Of the over 53,000 inhabitants of Greenland, 82 percent are Inuit.[105] Most of the remainder of the present day population are Danes. Although Inuit (called Greenlanders) are a majority in Greenland, they join the other Arctic peoples as members of the Fourth World because of

Fig. 11. Northern communities.
(a) Ivujivik, northern Quebec; (b) Grise Fjord, NWT.
Source: photos by G. Osherenko.

Fig. 11. (c) Ryktuchi, RSFSR; (d) Qaqortoq, Greenland.
Source: photos by G. Osherenko.

Fig. 11. (e) Sisimiut, Greenland; (f) Yakutsk, RSFSR.
Source: courtesy of DIAND, Canada.

their long history as part of Denmark. Greenland experienced direct colonialism by Denmark from 1721 to 1953, when reform measures replaced colonial status with provincial status and presumably equal civil rights for Greenlanders. Greenland elected two members to the Danish Folketing (Parliament). But the 'reform', instituted to accomplish the assimilationist policies of the era, brought a radical restructuring of society that drastically increased Greenland's economic dependence on Denmark and other western nations.

In 1960, the Danish government decided to bring Greenland into the 20th century by replacing the age-old occupation of hunting with a modern fishing industry. By 1983, a quarter of the population depended on the fishing industry for a livelihood. The desire for economic growth coupled with concerns for providing better health and education led Denmark to relocate most Greenlanders from their scattered camps and settlements into communities along the ice-free southwest coast. A handful of new towns sprouted, with schools, hospitals, fish processing plants, a fleet of ocean-going fishing vessels, large multi-story apartment blocks, and modern central water and waste disposal systems. In the name of self-sufficiency, Greenland came to depend on the world market for fish and fish products. Danes arrived to administer a growing bureaucracy, construct the new cities, teach in the new schools, and provide other skills for which Inuit had not been prepared. The result, a two-class system with higher pay for the Danish workers who came to this 'hardship post', put the original inhabitants clearly on the bottom. While tuberculosis was wiped out and infant mortality became a rarity, unemployment and welfare payments rose along with feelings of alienation and frustration, alcoholism, suicide, and depression.

Now fully an example of internal colonialism, Greenland began to exert political pressure to end two and a half centuries of domination. In 1971, a reform movement led by young Greenlanders educated in Denmark began to call for an end to 'the Danish bulldozer', 'cultural genocide', and discriminatory pay policies.[107] By 1973, the consultative Greenlandic assembly, the *Landsraad*, voted unanimously to recommend Greenlandic home rule. The Danish government responded by appointing a joint Danish-Greenlandic Home Rule Commission which, in 1978, recommended home rule for Greenland following the lines of the Faroe Islands home rule arrangement of 1948. A vast majority of the Greenland population voted in a referendum for home rule, which became a reality in 1979.

Three political parties now shape the debate over relations with Denmark and other nations.[108] The Siumut party, led by Premier

Jonathan Motzfeldt, Lars Emil Johansen, and Moses Olsen, gained a majority in the new Home Rule Parliament (*Landsting*). It is committed to self-determination but not separatism. While Siumut is the centrist party in Greenlandic politics, Nils Orvik describes it as a left of center, social democratic party on the Scandinavian model.[109] In 1984, Siumut championed withdrawal from the European Economic Community (EEC) in order to regain control over its own 200 mile economic zone and, therefore, of the fishery, Greenland's principal industry.

Inuit Ataqatigiit (IA), founded in 1979 by a young radical, Aqqaluk Lynge, opposed the home rule proposal as inadequate because it did not clarify subsurface rights. Originally a Marxist-Leninist party advocating national sovereignty and independence, IA has gradually gained power as the Siumut party has needed it to form a coalition excluding the conservative Atassut party. IA favored withdrawal from the EEC and opposed the ongoing agreement negotiated by Denmark whereby EEC members receive the first right to fishing quotas in Greenlandic waters in exchange for a substantial payment. The payment exceeds the prior subsidies provided to Greenland by the EEC.

Atassut achieved formal party status in 1981. Although its leaders often vote with the social democrats in the Danish Parliament, the party platform includes support for free enterprise, liberalization of trade, increased regional and local authority. Its members favor a form of home rule that does not jeopardize good relations with Denmark, and they favored remaining in the European Economic Community.

All three parties have helped to break the bonds of colonialism, thereby increasing the likelihood of complete independence from Denmark at some future time.[110]

4.2   Alaska

For Alaska's 64,000[111] plus Natives, the Alaska Native Claims Settlement Act (ANCSA) passed in 1971, granting Natives almost 44 million acres of land (almost 12 percent of Alaska lands) and $962.5 million dollars, supposedly ensured the well-being of this and future generations of Alaskan Natives. Congress did not address Native hunting and fishing rights (except to extinguish those based on aboriginal rights) until nine years later when it included provisions protecting non-ethnically based 'subsistence' rights in the Alaska National Interest Lands Conservation Act of 1980 (ANILCA). Despite these two major laws, issues of cultural survival, land protection, and self-government head the agenda of indigenous groups in Alaska today.

The term Alaskan Eskimos is usually used to identify the two major groups of Inuit in Alaska, Inupiat and Yuit. Their combined population numbered well over 34,000 in 1980. Aleuts living on the Pribilof Islands in the Bering Sea and on the Aleutian Chain add another 8,000 natives to Alaska's population, and Athapaskan Indians, residing primarily in Interior Alaska, account for about 9,000. Tlingit, Haida, and Tsimshian tribes living in southeastern Alaska are beyond the geographic scope of this book, though much of the discussion of Alaskan homelands applies to them as well. The Native Alaskan population is increasing rapidly and will soon surpass the high levels recorded in the 18th century before contact with whites brought diseases that decimated the indigenous populations.

Today the non-Native population of Alaska far exceeds the Native population. In 1980, Natives made up less than 16 percent of Alaska's population. City dwellers in Anchorage, Fairbanks, and Juneau have more representation in the state legislature than those in rural Alaska. The new emmigrants looked down on the Natives, and gradually a combination of government policies and neglect undermined traditional ways and left poverty and despair in their wake. The government imposed compulsory education without providing schools in the villages; young children were sent to boarding schools far from home. A generation grew up who could not speak their parents' languages nor engage in the traditional occupations. New technologies – electricity, TV, oil discovery, snowmobiles, satellites – brought waves of cultural shock.

Passage of the Alaska Native Claims Settlement Act (ANCSA) on December 18, 1971 changed the politics and economics of Alaska and the self-image of thousands of Native people. Alaska Natives were no longer second class citizens. They would become (when conveyance of the land was completed) the largest group of private landholders in the state owning some 11·6 percent of the land. But in exchange for what seemed at the time a large amount of land and money, Alaska Natives lost forever the right to base future claims to land on the legal doctrine of aboriginal title. Congress declared that Natives had no ownership or other legal claim to the remaining 88·4 percent of Alaska held by the federal and state governments. In the 1980s, the courts rejected Native claims to aboriginal title to offshore areas and sea ice.[112]

Soon after passage of ANCSA, critics and commentators questioned some of its basic provisions, especially creation of village and regional corporations to receive the land and most of the cash settlement.[113] In time, Alaska Natives realized that they could lose their lands through corporate bankruptcy, takeover, or sale. Shareholder rolls were fixed on 18 December 1971, so that 'new Natives', those born after passage of

ANCSA, would not become shareholders, unless they subsequently inherited shares, and would not be allowed to vote on measures affecting Native land. And finally, there was 'the 1991 problem'. In that year, corporate shares, which were not transferable before 18 December 1991, were to be recalled and reissued as shares which could be purchased by non-Natives. Also, after 1991, Native lands could be subject to a statewide property tax. Since Alaska has no statewide property or income tax today, this appears unlikely. However, statewide property taxes may become a politically palatable way to raise money as oil revenues decline especially since Natives, the single largest group of private property owners, have few representatives in the state legislature.

During the negotiations over ANCSA, the Alaska Federation of Natives (AFN) emerged as a forceful organization for Alaska Natives. Dominated and funded by the Native regional corporations created by ANCSA, AFN successfully lobbied Congress for amendments to ANCSA to remedy some of its most criticized provisions. In 1987, amendments to ANCSA addressed some of these problems. The major provisions (1) retain the existing restraints on alienability of stock in the Native corporations until the shareholders or, in the case of corporations in the Bristol Bay and Aleut regions, the board of directors with shareholder concurrence, vote to remove the restrictions on sale of stock,[114] (2) protect undeveloped Native and Native corporation land from taxation as well as from loss through adverse possession, bankruptcy, and claims of unsecured creditors through an automatic land bank provision,[115] and (3) allow corporations to issue shares to 'new Natives' and additional shares to shareholders over age 65.[116]

By the early 1980s a new movement representing the interests of Native villages in Alaska began to counter the powerful Native corporation interests. These advocates for village interests seek to protect the subsistence economy that provides a crucial base to the economy of small remote communities (with populations under 1,000) and to strengthen Native or 'tribal' governments (as opposed to state chartered local governments) in order to retain control by Natives regardless of demographic changes that are already decreasing the influence of Natives on public government.[117] In 1985, the tribal councils of Akiachak, Akiak, and Tuluksak formed the Yupiit Nation coalition to strengthen tribal government powers at the village level. Joined by a number of other tribal councils primarily in southwest Alaska, they lobbied for far more fundamental changes to ANCSA than the AFN proposals. A larger coalition of tribes and villages in Alaska, the Alaska Native Coalition (ANC), formed in 1986 'to strengthen tribal governments, [to] advocate perpetual protection of Alaska Native lands and land uses, and to monitor the 1991 legislation'.[118] ANC and the Yupiit Nation seek to transfer land from the corporations to tribal ownership where decisions would be made by tribal councils representing their members (all Natives in a community, not only those with voting rights in the corporation) with fewer pressures to make a profit from the land. While officers of the Native corporations and AFN agree with the leaders of the tribal government movement on many of the problems of village Alaska, they part company on the solutions.

4.3   The Canadian Arctic

Over half of Canada's land surface lies north of 60° N, but is populated by fewer than one-third of one percent of Canada's people. Roughly 52,000 are Native.[119] As in Alaska and Greenland, the largest Native group is Inuit with over 18,000 in the Northwest Territories, over 6,000 in Arctic Quebec, and about 3,500 in Labrador. The NWT is also home to over 12,000 Dene (a collective name encompassing a number of Indian tribes) and Metis (people of mixed ancestry). Roughly 5,000 North American Indians and people of mixed Native ancestry live in the Yukon Territory. Eight bands of Cree with a combined population approaching 9,000 reside in The James Bay region of northern Quebec.[119a] Several thousand Naskapi, Montagnais, and members of other Native American tribes span the region from northern Quebec across Labrador. Throughout the Canadian Arctic, birthrates are high. In northern Quebec communities where the population is overwhelmingly Inuit, half the population is under 16, while in the southern part of the province half the population is over 30.

As in Greenland and Alaska, missionaries, whalers, and fur traders left their mark on the Native way of life. Diseases like tuberculosis decimated communities with no immunity. Kinship groups made changes in the traditional hunting lifestyle to trap beaver, fox and other valuable fur animals to sell to the Hudson's Bay Company. Communities grew around the trading posts as the people came to depend on tools, guns, ammunition, and certain foods. A combination of events – drastic declines in some caribou herds which may have been caused in part by greater non-Native hunting pressure and plummeting fur prices during the depression and after World War II – caused severe starvation in many communities. Coastal communities dependent on marine mammals never faced the sweeping starvation experienced by inland communities like Baker Lake though they certainly weathered periods of extreme hardship.

From 1920 to 1950, Canadian government policy aimed to bolster

Canada's claim to sovereignty over the Arctic region. In 1939, the federal government spent $17 per capita for northern police, but only $12·57 per person for health, education, and welfare in the Arctic. After World War II, the policy began to change. In 1953, Inuit officially became wards of the state. As in Greenland, government policies of 'benevolent' paternalism led to the resettlement of families widely spread across the Canadian Arctic into communities of poorly insulated 'matchbox' houses. The need for health care and the desire for some of the comforts of southern society lured the scattered population into the new towns. People continued to hunt and trap for food and furs, but they could no longer reach their traditional hunting grounds without the aid of snowmobiles or motor-boats. The need for cash increased and with it dependency on wage labor as well as welfare. By 1959, half the northern Native population received relief payments.

In the 1970s new objects of southern desire – oil, minerals, hydropower – directed attention to the Native homelands of the Canadian Arctic just as the need for an Alaskan oil pipeline had focused attention on the claims of Alaska Natives. Cree and Inuit inhabitants of northern Quebec filed a lawsuit to halt plans for a massive hydroelectric project damming the great rivers of northern Quebec. The Native residents claimed title to the entire area based on aboriginal use and occupancy. They lost their case in the Quebec Court of Appeals, and, as construction of the hydroproject continued, they settled with the provincial and federal governments. The resulting James Bay and Northern Quebec Agreement signed in 1975 extinguished any claim of the Cree and Inuit of northern Quebec to land based on aboriginal rights in exchange for legal title to a small part of their traditionally used lands, financial compensation, and guaranteed rights to hunt, fish, and trap. This agreement became the model for future settlement of Native claims in Canada.

In 1969, the government released a 'White Paper on Indian Policy' to make Natives 'equal' with other Canadians. The Native community sharply rejected it as an attempt to terminate the rights guaranteed to Natives in the original land grants from the British Crown to Canada and in treaties made with many of the Indian tribes and bands.

In 1973, in a landmark decision involving the Nishga Indians of British Columbia known as the *Calder* case, six out of seven justices of Canada's Supreme Court recognized the existence of Native aboriginal title.[120] The *Calder* case led to a major policy shift in the government's willingness to acknowledge and give meaning to land claims by Canada's Native people. The government began a lengthy process of negotiations with numerous Native groups. Repatriation of the Constitution in 1982 entrenched 'existing aboriginal rights' in the Constitution, though the content of these rights was left to be determined through a series of First Ministers' conferences which failed to produce clarification. Native leaders in Canada, benefiting from the experience of Alaska Natives, are not willing to settle land claims alone. They also seek to reshape the political institutions in the North to gain autonomy for the region and greater control by the indigenous population. In the spring of 1986, a government-appointed 'Task Force to Review Comprehensive Claims Policy' recommended radical changes in the negotiation process to allow for discussion of Native self-government as part of the land claims process. The report *Living Treaties: Lasting Agreements* also recommends avoiding blanket extinguishment of all aboriginal rights as a precondition for settlement and providing flexibility for future changes and amplifications of the settlements.[121]

Ongoing 'comprehensive' Native claims negotiations strengthened existing Native organizations and gave birth to others. Inuit in the western Arctic formed the Committee for Original Peoples' Entitlement (COPE) in January 1970 to defend themselves against environmental damage caused by oil exploration in the MacKenzie Delta and Beaufort Sea. COPE later negotiated a settlement agreement with the federal government.[122] Inuit Taparisat of Canada (ITC) serves as the umbrella organization for six regional Inuit organizations in the Arctic including COPE. With status as parties to the land claims, the regional organizations have become a major force in Canadian politics and a power base for articulate Native leaders.[123]

The Northwest Territories government has limited powers in relation to the federal government. Inuit, Dene, and Metis associations in the NWT boycotted territorial politics until, in 1979, a coalition of newly elected Natives and younger whites gained control of the NWT Legislative Assembly. In 1982, a plebiscite confirmed that a majority of residents of the NWT favored division of the NWT into new territories. The Eastern Arctic communities voted 4 to 1 for creation of Nunavut – a new government in which several years residency would be required to vote, thereby ensuring a continued Inuit majority for many years. The multi-ethnic composition of the western portion of the NWT makes designing new government structures more difficult. Following the referendum, the Legislative Assembly created the Nunavut Constitutional Forum (NCF) and the Western Constitutional Forum (WCF) to study proposals for division of the NWT and new governments. Together, the regional organizations negotiating land claims, NCF, WCF, and other Native organizations are actively pursuing ways to protect northern land and natural resources, gain greater self-government, and ensure cultural survival.

4.4   The Soviet North

The Soviet Union's northern Native populations (totaling about 1 million) dwarf those of other circumpolar nations (which together total roughly 230,000). Despite their numbers, Native peoples in the Soviet North remain minorities in their homeland, comprising only one seventh of the northern population. The bulk of the indigenous population belongs to one of the larger ethnic groups, the Komi and Yakuty, each numbering well over 300,000. Sixteen other distinct ethnic groups vary in number from 200 to 30,000; these are the Khanty, Mansi, Chukchi, Dolgany, Koryaki, Nentsy, Nganasany, Sel'kupy, Yukagiry, Itel'meny, Eskimosy, Aleuty, Saami, Eveny, Evenki, Entsy.[124] They are known as the 'small nationalities'.[125] Among the smallest are those with larger populations outside the USSR; Eskimos numbered 1,500, Aleuts 546, and Saami 1,900 in the 1970 Soviet census. The Soviet Union's northern Natives pursue traditional occupations of hunting, trapping, fishing, and reindeer herding and in most respects parallel indigenous groups elsewhere in the Arctic.

In the Tsarist era, fur trapping, whaling, and missionary activities brought disease and began the disruption of indigenous social systems. After the 1917 revolution, the dominant society viewed the northern half of the USSR with new interest and turned to civilizing the 'semi-savage' tribes. Conflicting government policies touted protection of national (ethnic) identity and assimilation simultaneously. The Soviet Government sought to protect Native minority groups from exploitation, provide them with health care and other essential services, regulate use of hunting and fishing grounds and reindeer pastures, organize a system of administration suitable to the cultural background of the people, and initiate study of the ethnic groups in order to find the best way to introduce them to socialism. As in the North American Arctic, Natives welcomed some of the social services, but government intervention increased dependency and further displaced Native social and political systems.

From 1925 to 1935, a Committee of the North experimented with a variety of administrative models designed to introduce Soviet administration and protect the rights and interests of indigenous peoples. Each band or tribe with more than 100 members elected its own Tribal Council and representatives to a District Native Congress. The experiment was brief; it conflicted with preexisting clan organization and did not effectively serve national goals. As elsewhere in the North, the government imposed a political structure that took power from the village elders. The brief experiment with 'tribal soviets' ended. In their stead, the government created national territorial administrative entities combining a number of minority groups in an area, often with larger non-Native populations. For example, in the Chukotsk District, Chukchis and Eskimos with a combined population of 12,150 are grouped with over 70,000 Russians. Thus, the Russians can easily control the party apparatus and state administration of the autonomous district that bears the name of the dominant indigenous group.[126] Even where ethnic minorities are not outnumbered, Russians retain control through the Moscow-directed hierarchy. Native 'leaders' often hold top posts in local and regional government, but the real power rests with deputy ministers and other higher officials who are usually Russians. Natives may make decisions on matters like establishing a dance troup but have no say in development of a mine. A Native may head the reindeer breeding industry, but Russians hold most of the high level jobs in other industries.[127]

Provision of basic social services came to the Soviet North earlier than in North America as the Soviets established 'cultural bases', consisting of a school, hospital, store, veterinary clinic, social club, and bath house. As in Canada, Alaska, and Greenland, providing such services required nomadic peoples to settle in communities. However, the Soviets found ways to provide services outside of settlements through traveling 'Red Tents' and 'Red Boats', thus encouraging continuation of a nomadic lifestyle. Soviet goals for development of the North entailed large-scale immigration of non-Natives to work at industrial sites and mines in Siberia and depended to some degree on the production of food and clothing by the indigenous population through reindeer herding, hunting, and trapping. Later, the Soviets introduced agriculture and cattle raising to meet the needs of cities growing in the Arctic. In Northeast Siberia, 40 to 60 percent of the meat, milk, and vegetables needed come from local sources.[128]

The Soviets replaced private trading stations with cooperatives and collectivized herding and hunting. They encountered serious resistance that resulted in herd declines. Scarcity of trade goods, foodstuffs, and hunting tools during World War II caused further hardships. Despite the economic importance of Native hunters and herders, construction of a network of natural gas pipelines and natural gas fields in northwestern Siberia destroyed large areas of pasture and hunting blocks. Wild reindeer populations then rose, further ravaging pasturage and spreading diseases among the domesticated herds. Fish stocks important to Native subsistence also declined in areas damaged by mining and industrial development.

As elsewhere in the Arctic, many Native young people educated in government schools have not learned traditional survival skills and traditional occupations. Yet their schooling has failed to prepare them for jobs in industry in the North. In the U.S.S.R., greater numbers of Native people than elsewhere in the Arctic have been trained in institutes to be government administrators and teachers. This may, in some cases, alleviate alienation. Also, the Soviets recognise the value of Native occupations to provide food and furs for an increasing non-Native northern population. The government has tried to improve yields from reindeer herding by providing veterinary technicians, pest and disease control, pasture management, selective breeding, aerial surveying for predator detection and herd monitoring, and sophisticated abattoir facilities.[129] Although this attention to the traditional occupation of reindeer herding may reinforce Native self-esteem, a gap remains in the standard of living between Natives working in traditional fields and those employed in other industries.

4.5   Sami Atnam: the land of the Sami

The aboriginal inhabitants of northern Scandinavia call themselves Sami although until recently outsiders used the term Lapps. Numbering about 50,000,[130] three-fifth (30,000) are Norwegian citizens; 15,500, Swedish; 4,400, Finnish. Fewer than 2,000 Sami live in the Soviet Union, most on the Kola Peninsula east of Finland. Although the Sami population is largely concentrated in northern Scandinavia, Sami remain a minority in most communities. In Norway, Sami compose a majority only in the core communities of the northern county, Finnmark. In Finland in 1970, only about one quarter of the inhabitants of the Sami heartland were Sami, and only in the northernmost community of Utsjoki do they outnumber the Finns.

Best known as a reindeer herding culture, the Sami (designated Lapps by the Swedes) were *not* originally reindeer herders and are *not* predominately herders today. Nonetheless, reindeer husbandry is central to maintenance of the Sami culture. The semi-nomadic Sami once relied on a mix of hunting and fishing, depending on vast herds of wild reindeer, marine mammals, birds and bird eggs, fish and wild herbs. By the 9th century, small domesticated reindeer herds became a part of a mixed hunting, herding economy and only later developed into a monoculture in northern Sweden and Finnmark in Norway requiring long migrations between winter lichen areas and summer grass pastures. Today, only about 30 percent of the Sami in Finland and 16 percent in Sweden list their occupation as reindeer herding. But the majority of the heads of household (61·3 percent in Finland) are engaged in some activity related to the land either in agriculture, foresty, reindeer husbandry, or fishing.[131]

Sami have adapted their lifestyle to the varied terrain and increasing settlement by outsiders. Some lead a settled life, others a more nomadic existence. Much of the Sami homeland lies in the Subarctic forests stretching across northern Sweden and Finland to the Kola peninsula. These lichen rich pine forests offer winter habitat for reindeer. Along the coastline of the Arctic and Atlantic Oceans to the north and west, Sami traditionally depended on marine mammals and still rely on fishing. Between the coastal strip and forest, low hills and wide valleys provide reindeer pasture in spring and autumn. In summer, the herds graze in the high mountain chain in the west. The combination of forest, low hills and lakes, and high alpine pasture enable the Sami to continue reindeer herding.

But this culture has been continually squeezed since the 17th century when the Swedish crown encouraged colonization within Sweden-Finland. Immigrant farmers pushed north using a slash and burn technique to create farmland, destroying reindeer pasture. The Sami, who once inhabited all of Finland, either assimilated or moved north. By the 18th century, competition from settlers led to loss of grazing lands and fishing rights, reducing many Sami to poverty. The Tsar's occupation of Finland in 1809 triggered a massive migration out of Finland into the Sami homelands to the west. Eventually, some Sami applied as settlers for their 'tax lands', lands upon which the Crown levied a sort of property tax and acknowledged rights of individual Sami and Sami communities to the land based on their prior possession from time immemorial.[132] In exchange for a fixed parcel of farmland, a Sami relinquished rights to use a more extensive area for reindeer herding. The arrangement parallels the allotment system in the United States whereby many American Indians lost extensive rights to lands they traditionally used and inhabited. Becoming a settler also often led to loss of identity as a Sami.

By the 17th century, Lutheran missionaries began building churches and converting Swedish subjects in the north.[133] Exceptionally powerful in the Old World where church and state were united, the church, which regarded the nomadic life as an impediment to Christianization, became a major force in assimilation. Fortunately, enlightened clergymen, at times, encouraged the use of native language in churches and schools, demanded that ministers understand Samish, trained Sami for the ministry, and translated the New Testament and other books into Samish.

In the 19th and 20th centuries, industrialization brought new threats to the Sami homelands. Forestry, roads, rail lines, mining, hydropower projects, and, most recently, tourism have cut across reindeer migratory routes, damaged or eliminated reindeer pasture, polluted streams, and shrunk stocks of fish, fowl, and game. Government policies of industrialization and assimilation coerced many Sami into concealing their ethnic identity and obtaining jobs on the railway or in the mines where they were isolated from their own people. Environmental destruction undermined the Native economy based on a combination of hunting, fishing, and herding, and drove many Sami (especially women) to seek wages in southern Scandinavia.

In Norway, dual policies of assimilation and promotion of a national language (Norwegian) undermined the Sami language and culture. These policies were not aimed directly at the Sami but at insuring dominance of Norwegian language and culture over Swedish. Sami lost pride in their own culture as these policies, combined with the ideas of Social Darwinism popular in the 19th century, led the dominant European culture to think it was inevitable and right to overtake the economically less powerful (Sami) culture.

Coloring the past history and current struggles in Samiland is the fact that the homeland is dominated, not by a single southern power, but by three (four, counting the U.S.S.R) national governments. Prior to the modern governments, monarchs in Sweden, Denmark, and Russia fought for control over Scandinavia. Norway and Finland passed among the great powers of the era, always seeking greater autonomy and eventual independence. Each war and treaty produced new political boundaries dividing Samiland between the victors, disrupting the herders' migratory patterns, and separating families.[134] In 1751, the treaty between Denmark-Norway and Sweden-Finland established the boundaries of Samiland in their present form from the western coast to the northern tip of Finland. A famous codicil to this agreement (known as the Sami Magna Carta) prohibited taxation of Sami lands by more than one nation and guaranteed Sami rights to hunt, fish, and herd reindeer throughout former Sami areas without regard to political boundaries. A century later, the Russian government, then in possession of Finland, closed the border between Norway and Finland to reindeer herders. In 1889, the migration routes between Sweden and Finland were also blocked. The political boundaries ignore ecological and cultural realities. Sami children on one side of a political border learn Swedish in school, while their neighbors learn Norwegian or Finnish. Only the few who attend 'Nomad schools' use Samish in the classroom. Political boundaries even affected development of a Sami orthography. Although the written form of Samish is based on the same North Sami dialect, the three Nordic nations only agreed on a common spelling system in 1978.

By this century, when Sami realized the need to organize beyond the community level, they faced, not one, but three national governments and a multiplicity of administrative agencies. With a total Native population only one-fourth greater than that of the Greenlanders (who only had to deal with Denmark), Sami expertise in dealing with administrative bureaucracy was spread thin. In 1904, Sami residing in southern Sweden formed the first association to confront government assimilationist policies. Soon after, Norwegian Sami formed a similar organization in Norway, and in 1906 sent a Sami to the Norwegian Parliament. Although these organizations held Sami national assemblies in 1917 (Norway) and 1918 (Sweden), they made little progress in terminating assimilationist policies until after World War II when successor national Sami organizations in the three countries included representatives from Sami villages and Sami associations developing leadership among the northern Samis. In 1972 the Finnish Sami elected a representative body known as the Sami Parliament which the Finnish Government recognizes as the official Sami advisor to Finland's President and must consult prior to any socioeconomic or political development in the Sami Area.[135]

Not until 1953 did Sami organizations from the three Nordic nations meet to address common issues. That conference led to creation of the Nordic Sami Council (*Nordiska Sameradet*) in 1956 with delegates from three countries meeting every three years and an executive council carrying out the organization's objectives. The Sami Parliament represents Sami in Finland on the Nordic Sami Council while national Sami organizations in Sweden and Norway appoint representatives from their nations.

The Nordic Sami Council deals directly with the powerful transnational organization of the three Nordic nations, the Nordic Council. The Sami Council joined the World Council of Indigenous Peoples (WCIP) in 1976, and uses international organizations to highlight human rights violations by the Nordic nations who purport to champion human rights worldwide. The transnational Sami Nordic Council has been able to achieve aims that were out of reach for Sami organizations operating solely at the national level. Finally, after the 7th Sami Conference in Gallivare, Sweden in 1971, the Nordic Council approved creation of the *Sami Institut'ta* (Nordic Sami Institute) to support and study Sami history, language, culture, law, and economy. The Institute, located in the heart of Samiland in Kautokeino, Norway, is operated and controlled by Sami though funded by all full members of the Nordic Council (Denmark, Finland, Iceland, Norway, and Sweden).[136]

In the post-War period, Sami protest succeeded in changing government policies, effecting a shift toward valuing and protecting Sami culture and language. Nevertheless, Sami have been less successful in establishing ownership of land or veto power over decisions affecting land and natural resources in Samiland. Although each Nordic government has created commitees to study and make recommendations regarding Sami rights, none has enacted laws granting land or financial compensation for loss of land (as the U.S. did in Alaska), nor have any of the nations of Fennoscandia agreed to negotiate directly with Sami to settle Sami land claims (as in Canada).

In the early 1980s, the Sami lost two landmark Supreme Court cases, one over construction of Alta Dam in Norway (1982) and one to establish Sami rights to former 'tax lands' in Sweden (1981). Despite these losses, the conflicts strengthened Sami pride and political awareness. They created a cultural revival, increasing knowledge of and respect for Sami lifeways within and without the Sami community. During the Alta hydropower controversy, Sami joined environmentalists and fishing organizations in non-violent protests; Sami women occupied the office of the Norwegian President; and Sami hunger strikers camped in a traditional Sami tent in front of the Parliament building in Oslo (Figure 12). The media highlighted these protests, and the court cases served as an

Fig. 12. Sami hunger strike in front of the Storting (Norwegian House of Parliament) in October 1979 in protest against the Alta River hydropower dam construction. Note the characteristic Sami tent. The banner reads, "We demand self-determination in Samiland." *Source*: photo. by E. Sletten courtesy of Ethnographic Museum, University of Oslo.

outlet for articulation of Sami views. New and old Sami art forms –
novels, poetry, the traditional Sami song form, *yoik*, paintings and
handicraft – flourished as Sami stepped into the limelight.[137]

4.6   Issues on the Native agenda

Three issues dominate the agendas of Native organizations,
including the Inuit Circumpolar Conference (ICC), Inuit Taparisat of
Canada (ITC), the Nordic Sami Council, the Nunavut Constitutional
Forum, the Dene Nation, COPE, AFN, the Yupiit Nation, the North
Slope Borough, Indigenous Survival International, and many others.
Although there are conflicts among them, the new leaders agree on the
broad goals, if not the methods of achieving these goals. The following
sections describe in some detail Native efforts to (1) ensure cultural
survival, (2) protect and retain Native lands, and (3) attain self-
government. Although we discuss each of these three goals separately,
they are interrelated. Because all northern Native cultures exhibit strong
ties to the land, protection of the land (and water) and control over
decisions affecting it (i.e. self-government) are essential to cultural
survival.

Cultural survival

For peoples of the Fourth World, cultural survival is paramount.
Cultural survival does not mean preservation of cultural artifacts nor does
it mean static resistance to change. Sami writer and poet, Nils-Aslak
Valkeapaa, noted, 'It seems as though the adherents of preservation want
to press our culture the way one presses plants, in order to admire them
later in a herbarium'.[138] Beyond the paramount concern with the land,
three themes pervade discussion of cultural survival: Native control over
education, revitalization of Native languages, and respect for Native
knowledge.

Language and education Languages reflect patterns of thought and ways
of perceiving the world, which are the root of culture. Thus, to pursue
cultural survival, or more aptly, cultural development, it is necessary to
enhance and encourage the distinctly Inuit, Cree, Aleut, Algonquin, Sami,
Chukchi or other Native way of thinking.

Language embodies culture; social norms and rules reinforce culture;
daily activities demonstrate it. While the culture of each of the northern
Native groups is distinct, they share important characteristics disting-
uishing them from non-Native cultures. Native groups value the group
over the individual, cooperation rather than competition, respect for
elders, extended family relations and kinship ties, and communal sharing.

Children must learn and perpetuate the values of their people for the culture to survive. Naturally, therefore, Native peoples are demanding control over education. The Metis Declaration of Rights states, 'we have the right to educate our children in our Native languages, customs, beliefs, music and other art forms'. Yet only in Greenland and northern Quebec have Native people succeeded in asserting control over the schools.

Under the terms of the James Bay and Northern Quebec Agreement of 1975, the Inuit of northern Quebec were able to establish their own schools under the control of the Kativik Regional School Board, representing the Inuit communities in Quebec. While the Province continues to set standards for teacher certification and subjects which must be covered in the schools, Kativik has authority to develop curriculum, make school policy, select and train teachers, and conduct educational research. While elsewhere across the North American Arctic, Native teachers are nearly nonexistant, all kindergarten through grade two teachers in northern Quebec are Inuit except in Kuujjuaq. They are chosen in each settlement by the community and, immediately upon election, assume the role of apprentice teacher.[139] Today, almost all teacher training is conducted in Inuktitut, which is also the language of instruction in the primary school classrooms. Students do not begin a second language in most of the Quebec Inuit communities until age 8 or 9, by which time their cognitive development and reasoning skills are well developed in their Native language and consequently in their Native way of thinking.

Greenland has also made rapid progress since Home Rule in control over education. All teachers in the first and second years of school (children ages 6 to 8) are Greenlandic and instruction is in the Native tongue. Beyond the early years, even in Greenland and Quebec, the number of Native teachers declines rapidly. In 1986, Danes still held half the teaching positions in Greenland.

The Soviets initiated formal schooling in the Arctic earlier than North American governments, and they encouraged learning in the Native languages. In 1918, the People's Commissariat for Information declared that 'all nationalities inhabiting the Russian Soviet Federal Socialist Republic (RSFSR) have the right to be taught in their mother tongue'. This policy carried out Lenin's Declaration of the Rights of the Peoples of Russia in 1917 stating the principle of equality for all people and 'free development of national minorities and ethnic groups'.[140] In the 1930s, the Soviets developed a written form for many northern Native languages. Thousands of Native teachers have been trained at a special Northern section in the University of Leningrad since the 1920s. By 1939, eight teacher's colleges were located in the Soviet Far North.[141]

Today, the Soviets provide a series of twelve textbooks in nine of the languages of the smaller nationalities and basic primers in two additional languages. Where Native language is strong and ethnic groups are not in close contact with Russians, the first three years of schooling are in the Native language with Russian introduced only in the fourth year as a second language. This is true in areas encompassing eight language groups. Where Native people are in closer contact with Russians and have a better command of Russian, only primers and the preparatory classes are in the Native language. For a few Native groups, there is no written language. Where the Native group lives among Russians, it usually adopts the Russian language. Aleut, for example, is disappearing, and is spoken by fewer than 50 elders living on the Commander Islands.

Parents have the right to enroll children in schools using their Native language or in Russian-speaking schools. As in northern Quebec, parents who live in communities with a mixed population where their ethnic group is a minority often select the dominant culture's language for schooling. Overall, the Native language speakers have declined from 86 percent to 77 percent in the last 20 years. Still, this compares favorably to Alaska's 38 percent.

While far ahead of the other circumpolar nations in Native teacher training and Native language education, the Soviet North still lacks sufficient teachers who can speak the vernacular. More importantly, Natives do not control the schools, curriculum, or teacher training. Even when Native language is used, the content of the curriculum and textbooks may not convey the Native culture and way of learning. (See Figure 13.) After all, the Soviets imposed education to further government policies and prepare northern peoples for service in the state and party apparatus.

Western scholars are often skeptical of the Soviet experience as a model for cultural survival. They note the apparent disappearance of certain ethnic groups from recent census reports, a decline in the number of Natives fluent in their mother tongue, and the number of ethnic minorities engulfed by predominately non-Native populations or by larger minority groups. Nevertheless, the long experience of the Soviets in providing education in the mother tongue of ethnic minorities and in training Native teachers is impressive in contrast to the rather short experience of North American and Nordic educators in promoting the retention of Native culture through education.

Fig. 13. (a) Teachers display a book on Khanty writing at the Institute for Teacher's Improvement, Leningrad. (b) Across the North, Native children are schooled in the languages of the dominant culture. Only in pockets of the Soviet North, some communities on Baffin Island, NWT, and in Quebec are children receiving primary education predominately in their Native languages. These children in Nedrasovka on Sakhalin island are studying Russian. *Source*: courtesy of DIAND, Canada.

In Alaska early education in Native languages is rare.[142] In many communities, especially the larger ones, about half the children learn English as a first language and half learn their Native language. Many children grow up speaking neither language well. Members of a whole generation both in Alaska and Canada, who were removed from home and placed in federally run schools where they were forbidden to speak their Native languages, no longer remember their original language. In Fennoscandia, you can hear Sami begin a sentence in Samish and complete it in Swedish. In the more southern and western coastal Sami districts, only the elderly speak Samish fluently. Finnmark, in Norway, remains the stronghold of Sami language, and the Sami Institute located there (discussed previously) carries out work to retain and revitalize the language. Nordic governments are investing more in texts in Samish and offering instruction in Samish at all educational levels. Sweden created a chair of Lappish at the University of Umea. But the Sami themselves are not in control of the school curriculum. Many children do not learn their Native tongue at home, and families feel the need for their children to be educated in the dominant nation's lauguage.

In 1984, the Inuit Institute (*Ilisimatusarfik*) opened in Nuuk, Greenland, the first institute of higher education in the nation and the first Native controlled institute of higher education still in operation in the North.[143] With about 20 students, the Institute focuses on strengthening the Greenlandic language (a variation of Inuktitut) and preserving the Inuit cultural heritage. In Alaska, many university level Native students are learning or relearning their Native languages at the University of Alaska at Fairbanks.

Some regard the loss of Native languages across the North as the most striking threat to cultural survival. Efforts to revitalize some Native languages in Alaska, the Yukon, the Northwest Territories, and Fennoscandia may be too late to do more than preserve them as interesting relics but not as modern languages.

Retention of Native knowledge Just as important as the revitalization of traditional language is the retention of Native knowledge. While the scientific experts convinced the International Whaling Commission (IWC) in the 1970s that the bowhead whale was in imminent danger, its population probably no more than a few hundred, Eskimo hunters in Barrow and the other whaling communities argued ineffectually that the species upon which they had depended for food for centuries was much more abundant. But the scientific community ignored Inupiat knowledge until the State of Alaska, nine oil companies, and the government of the

North Slope Borough funded an aerial count of the migrating whales. The population is now known to be up to 4,000, at least six times earlier reports by 'scientific experts'. The bowhead whale controversy led to establishment of the Alaskan Eskimo Whaling Commission, now an articulate body of Native representatives who use Native knowledge and western scientific methods to protect the whale and ensure a continued Native subsistence hunt. This example is dramatic but no more important than many other forms of Native knowledge which are seldom if every acknowledged by the dominant culture as significant.

The Native movement seeks to place Native knowledge alongside western knowledge as equally valid and vital. The Inuit Circumpolar Conference established the Elder's Conference to give special recognition to the wisdom of elders. In the fall of 1986, the Inuit Studies Association chose 'Facing the Future: What can we learn from the Inuit?' as the theme for its fifth biennial conference. Ecologists, biologists, and wildlife managers have much to learn from Native peoples whose very existence has depended on knowledge of animal behavior, edible plants, migration cycles, snow and ice dynamics, and weather.[144] Inuit warned oil companies of the threat of 'ivu' – the phenomenon of sheets of ice riding up over the pack ice or land with sufficient force to destroy an offshore oil rig. Scientists were skeptical of these reports, discounting the likelihood of such occurrences, until in 1982 an Eskimo family of five that had lived before 1826 was discovered in a perfect state of preservation. Nothing but an ivu would explain the condition of this family caught sleeping and buried alive by a sheet of ice.[145]

Protection of the land

The complex of activities known in the North as 'subsistence' perpetuates northern Native cultures.[146] Protection of northern lands and waters is crucial to continuation of subsistence lifeways. Community life is organized around hunting, fishing, trapping, and gathering activities. 'Country food' is as important culturally as it is nutritionally. For example, store-bought food and cash are not shared, but fruits of the hunt must be distributed communally in accord with strict rules. Consumerism and acquisitiveness are not traditional habits; waiting hours by a seal's breathing hole, stalking a walrus, tracking a snowshoe hare, identifying edible plants and berries are traditional skills. Developing keen powers of observation, learning by imitating, helping each other, making decisions by consensus are skills cultivated in the course of learning to be a hunter as well as traits highly valued in the culture.

Although northern Native people have entered industrial occupations, the mixed economies of the Arctic rely heavily on subsistence activities. Jobs in non-traditional occupations became available earliest in the Soviet North, but even there, the majority of Native people remain in traditional occupations. Three-quarters of the Chukchi, for example, still herd reindeer and/or hunt.[147] Wage labor has been most successfully introduced into Native communities when work schedules at a mine site, oil field, or similar operation are adjusted to allow blocks of time off the job for traditional activities. Wage labor provides the capital to continue traditional occupations – to purchase gasoline, ammunition, ATVs, snowmobiles, or to outfit a whaling boat.

The cultural and economic dependence on subsistence activities fuels the Native movement for both self-determination and secure rights to land and resources. Protection of Sami grazing lands for reindeer, of Alaskan salmon spawning streams, of trap lines in Siberia as well as interior Canada and Alaska, of caribou calving grounds, of whole migration routes, and of ice-covered waters rich with seals and walrus is crucial to those who live off the land. Without control of land and guaranteed rights to hunt, fish, and trap, the social, spiritual, and economic bases of Native village life cannot survive.

Subsistence activities alone, however, cannot sustain the rapidly growing population in northern villages nor will they provide a choice of futures for Native people. Many Natives believe that a secure and independent future depends on Native control over non-renewable resources, especially minerals and hydrocarbons. Ownership or partial ownership of these would place those most directly affected by non-renewable resource development in a position to determine the proper balance between subsistence activities and resource development.

Since northern aboriginal peoples once occupied and used extensive areas of the Arctic, they had a legal basis for claiming all of Alaska, vast regions of Canada, Siberia, Scandinavia, and all the inhabitable coastline of Greenland. What they have been able to retain is only a fraction of that which they originally used and occupied. In the United States, the Tlingit and Haida brought suit under a special jurisdictional act of Congress passed in 1935 permitting the indigenous peoples of southeast Alaska to sue the federal government for compensation for lands illegally taken. The court decided that the Indians were entitled to compensation, but legal battles stalled payment until 1968.[148] That prolonged battle coupled with the need to clarify title to land in preparation for construction of the Alaskan oil pipeline convinced Congress to legislate a 'settlement' of aboriginal claims and extinguish any remaining Native claims to land as well as hunting and fishing rights in Alaska.

The American experience as well as the ambiguities of Canadian law regarding aboriginal rights and Native title probably played a role in the Canadian government's choice of negotiation as a method for settling Native land claims. Together with the Department of Justice, the Comprehensive Claims Branch of the Department of Indian Affairs and Northern Development (DIAND) determines which 'comprehensive' land claims will be accepted for negotiation and conducts the negotiations on behalf of the federal government. Claims to the vast majority of lands in the NWT and Yukon remain to be settled along with claims in Labrador.

One land claims settlement sets a precedent for the next; thus, the percentage of land indigenous peoples retain grows. Under the 1975 Agreement, the James Bay Cree and Inuit of northern Quebec retained ownership amounting to less than three percent of their traditional lands (called Category I lands in the JBNQA).[149] At the time of their negotiations with Quebec and the federal government, a massive hydroproject was already under construction on lands where Natives lived and hunted. The settlement appeared to be the best Natives could get. They received the right to hunt and trap on extensive additional acreage and advisory powers over game management. But future mineral or hydropower development could greatly devalue these limited use rights. In 1971, Congress declared Alaska Native claims to land and water in Alaska void and awarded Native groups ownership rights to 11·6% of Alaska land. Although Natives received only a fraction of the land and water they traditionally used, their landholdings in Alaska make them, as a group, the largest private land owners by a wide margin in a state with little private land. In 1985, the 2,500 Inuvialuit of the northwestern Canadian Arctic were able to secure ownership to roughly 20 percent of the area (land and water) they traditionally used and occupied.

Ongoing negotiations with Natives in the Yukon and the Northwest Territory appear to be closer to completion. On 5 September, Prime Minister Mulroney signed an 'Agreement in Principle' with the Dene and Metis of the NWT and set an agenda for further negotiations. The tentative agreement, when finalized, would secure Native title (in fee simple) to 70,000 square miles of territory, roughly 16 percent of lands originally used and occupied. (Less than 4,000 square miles would include title to the subsurface.) Natives would also have rights to fish and hunt on an additional 386,000 square miles. Negotiations between the Government and the Council of Yukon Indians appear to be reaching a similar stage. That agreement would vest title to roughly 16,000 square miles in Natives of the Yukon territory. Government negotiators hope to sign an agreement in principle on the last and largest land claim with the Tungavik Federation of Nunavut (TFN) in the autumn of 1989. Based on prior settlements, TFN expects to gain title (mostly to the subsurface estate) to 20–25% of lands over which they can document aboriginal use and occupancy, or 350,000–400,000 square miles. Although negotiations are making progress in determining the amounts of land and money to be transferred, difficult issues remain. Major issues are still in contention, including Native political rights and language rights in the eastern Canadian Arctic where Inuktitut is the dominant language. Additionally, the details of ownership as well as the selection of areas to be transferred have yet to be determined. Thus, although there is progress, substantial obstacles to closure remain.[150]

Sami face the toughest uphill battle to regain ownership and control of lands they traditionally used and occupied. Relatively moderate ecological conditions made agriculture and forestry possible in northern Scandinavia. From the 16th century, settlers and industry, encouraged by government, gradually destroyed reindeer pasturage and competed with Sami for fish and game. A fifteen year legal battle, known as the *Skatterfjallsmalet* (Taxed Mountains) Case, ended in 1981 when the Swedish Supreme Court declared the State to be the owner of disputed land used by Sami reindeer herders. The Sami retain use rights which guarantee them compensation for encroachments by individuals, but not protection against expropriation by the State. In most instances, financial compensation is useless since there are no pasturelands and natural reindeer migration routes available for purchase.[151]

In Greenland and Siberia, all land is publicly owned, as are large areas of Samiland. The most that Native peoples in Siberia can hope for is greater local control over land and natural resources. State ownership of land ensures communal ownership, a form of property rights more akin to traditional political systems and one that encourages decisions that benefit the community as a whole, rather than individual owners. However, state ownership of land typically enables the central government to exercise its will on issues of resource extraction, overruling the desires of the local population. All land in Greenland is public, free and open to everyone, including Danes.[152] It is unlawful to fence land without a permit from the local authorities. Private ownership, Alaskan style, would be alien to the Greenlanders. Ownership of natural resources, especially minerals and hydrocarbons both onshore and offshore, has been one of the most controversial issues in Greenland. This is the issue that led the

Inuit Ataqatigiit (IA) party to oppose home rule, and it became a major issue in the June 1984 elections when IA alone called for full control over Greenland's natural resources.

The IA party is likely to push its uncompromising stand for Greenlandic ownership and control of natural resources. Until recently, the party achieved power in the Home Rule Government far in excess of its vote-getting ability. While winning only two seats in the Landsting in 1984, IA gained a third portfolio in the government by joining the Siumut party to form a coalition government. In June 1987, IA won a third seat in the 26 member parliament, and its representatives headed four of the seven cabinet ministries. However, in the spring of 1988 the coalition collapsed leaving Siumut in control. Although Attasut holds no portfolios in the government, it has allowed Siumut to form a minority government that excludes IA. Siumut also called for exclusive Greenlandic rights to the subsurface but was willing to wait to negotiate an agreement with Denmark on this issue until after withdrawal from the EEC. Subsurface mineral rights remain in public ownership controlled by a joint Greenlandic/Danish committee. Both the Home Rule Government and the Government of Denmark have the power to veto proposed mineral and hydrocarbon development, onshore or offshore. In May 1988, the Home Rule Government negotiated a new agreement with Denmark which increases Greenland's share of profits from subsurface development in Greenland.

Although Inuit and Sami living on the coast traditionally depended on the sea and lived in camps on the sea ice as though it were land, nowhere in the Arctic have they gained ownership rights to offshore waters or outer continental shelf lands or resources. A decision in the U.S. courts and the Inuvialuit Final Agreement in Canada both rejected aboriginal claims in the Beaufort Sea. Offshore hydrocarbon development presents a serious threat to subsistence communities dependent on the sea. Questions of control over, as well as a share in revenues from, offshore development remain high on the Native political agenda in the Arctic.

The amount of land and resources to which Natives hold title is not the only indicator of whether Native land is protected. The institutions that hold title to the land and manage it are equally important. The greatest threat to Native land in Alaska is not large-scale resource development but loss of land owned by Native corporations through sale, foreclosure, or bankruptcy. Some village councils seek to transfer corporate land to tribal (Native village) ownership where, they argue, it will be better protected from development, foreclosure, or loss of Native control.

Lawyers for tribal interests argue that tribally owned lands and even some Native corporation lands constitute 'Indian country' subject to the tribal laws.[153] If this interpretation of the definition of Indian country[154] is accepted by the courts, tribal councils could claim sovereign immunity in lawsuits, thereby protecting tribally owned land against unsecured creditors. Furthermore, if corporate lands were transferred to tribal or Native village ownership, the lands might be exempt from state taxes and would be protected from involuntary loss through corporate take-over or bad debts. And finally, proponents of tribal sovereignty argue that all Natives who are members of the Native community (not just shareholders) may seek election as tribal council members and participate in decisions affecting Native lands. The 1987 Amendments to ANCSA substantially reduce the threats to Native corporate lands by providing that all undeveloped Native corporation land is automatically included in the Alaska Land Bank and, thereby, protected from taxation or loss through adverse possession and from being sold or taken as a result of bad debts or bankruptcy. These Amendments also allow Native corporations to transfer certain corporate assets to a Settlement Trust to further protect surface (but not subsurface) lands for the benefit of their Alaska Native shareholders.[155]

Canada has avoided the American example by placing title to Native lands in trust for the Native communities. Under the James Bay Agreement, the small amounts of land granted Cree and Inuit close to the settlements became public lands owned by the individual settlements. The provisions of the Inuvialuit Final Agreement are similar. All members of the community benefit from the land and may participate in the local government controlling it. Eligibility to enjoy the benefits of the Agreement is not limited to a fixed list made at the inception of the settlement, as it was in ANCSA, but is determined by Native ancestry, residency, or recognition by the community as being a member.

Access to and protection of hunting and fishing grounds is as important to cultural survival as land ownership. In Alaska, the State Department of Fish and Game has exclusive jurisdiction over fish and game except where the federal government has extended federal law, as it has over marine mammals and endangered species. The federal government also requires preferential rights for rural subsistence users as a prerequisite for State management of fish and game on federal lands which cover roughly 60 percent of Alaska. Natives have special rights with regard to taking marine mammals, but no ethnically based rights to hunt or fish on land. They play a strictly advisory role to the Alaska Boards of Fish and Game.

As a result, controversies continue over the application of federal and state subsistence laws to Natives. Disputes over the federal and state responsibility to protect Native subsistence rights have led to a multiplicity of lawsuits.

In the James Bay and Northern Quebec Agreement as well as the Western Arctic Accord, detailed provisions acknowledge Natives' exclusive hunting and fishing rights to certain species and preferential rights to other species. The management regimes for hunting and fishing in these agreements allow Natives an advisory role that has resulted, in some cases, in substantial Native power in the decision making process.[156]

The Alaska Native Review Commission recommended exclusive jurisdiction for Natives over fish and wildlife on Native owned lands and shared jurisdiction and management among tribal, state, and federal governments over state and federal lands. Its report also recommends that Native hunting and fishing be regulated only for conservation purposes.[157] The idea of joint management with Native groups would have been anathema to government officials anywhere in the Arctic fifteen years ago. Currently, however, seven wildlife co-management regimes operate in the North American Arctic. These demonstrate the necessity and practicality of public sector officials sharing decision making power with Native user organizations.[158] Non-Native wildlife managers increasingly realize that they cannot achieve Native compliance with wildlife laws without according Native users a significant role in wildlife management decisions.

Self-determination

We the Dene of the Northwest Territories insist on the right to be regarded by ourselves and the world as a nation.

... The Dene find themselves as part of a country. That country is Canada. But the Government of Canada is not the government of the Dene. The Government of the Northwest Territories is not the government of the Dene. These governments were not the choice of the Dene, they were imposed upon the Dene.

... Our plea to the world is to help us in our struggle to find a place in the world community where we can exercise our right to self-determination as a distinct people and as a nation.

What we seek then is independence and self-determination within the country of Canada. This is what we mean when we call for a just land settlement for the Dene Nation.

Excerpts from the Dene Declaration 1975[159]

Indigenous Arctic peoples have realized that the only way to ensure cultural survival and to protect their land and subsistence activities is to gain greater political power and control. In their demands for self-determination and self-government, they use words that frighten non-Native government officials, words like 'tribal sovereignty' and the 'right to recognition as Nations'. Are the Native peoples of Greenland, Canada, Alaska, and Scandinavia moving toward secession from the states in which they live? Are they planning many separate nations or a single new Arctic nation? The answer to both these questions is distinctly no. They are looking for autonomy within the larger states – for greater regional and local government power where Native people compose a majority, for control over decisions affecting land, natural resources, and wildlife, for control over education, domestic relations (marriage, divorce, child welfare, and adoption), dispute resolution, misdemeanor crimes. Greenland may eventually gain total independence from Denmark, but the other indigenous Arctic groups are unlikely to seek separation from the economic and social benefits or military protection provided by their federal governments.

Home rule moved Greenland closer to the goal of self-determination, but the process is not complete. The Home Rule Government, the *Landsstyre*, and the Home Rule legislature, the *Landsting*, gained control over internal affairs – local and regional issues including culture, media, the school system, and most higher education including vocational training. The Home Rule Government also has authority over environmental protection, labor, and most commercial and economic affairs. Together with the local governmental units called boroughs, the legislature may levy taxes. But Denmark retains exclusive jurisdiction over foreign policy, defence, the judiciary, the monetary system, and fiscal matters. In these affairs, Greenland has only a consultative role.

Too many years of economic dependence have made it impossible for any of the Native Arctic peoples to risk total independence from the larger nations to which they belong. They wish to retain and claim the rights and privileges common to all citizens in their respective nations, and they demand more. They demand greater political autonomy than other groups within their nations. They believe their status as original peoples entitles them to be free from certain federal, state, or provincial laws to which other groups are subject.

Native claims and Native governments are not based on apartheid or on affirmative action to right ancient wrongs done to minorities, but on principles of international and domestic law. Like other Fourth World peoples such as the Ainu of Japan, the Aborigines of Australia and South

America, the Maori of New Zealand, all the indigenous peoples of the Arctic are minorities in nations dominated by peoples who arrived later. Indigenous peoples once used and occupied almost the whole of the Arctic. They can document their ancestors' and their own use of vast areas of land, water, and sea ice. These lands and waters were never conquered or purchased in a way recognized as lawful by international law. Today, Native peoples still seek acknowledgement of an aboriginal title predating discovery by Europeans. They reject the notion that governments may extinguish aboriginal rights and titles without a fair exchange of land and money plus the recognition of certain inherent political rights.

Native organizations turn increasingly to principles of international law and seek political and human rights in international fora.[160] Inuit and Yuit of Alaska, Canada, and Greenland have formed an international organization, the Inuit Circumpolar Conference (ICC) to pursue their common goals (see Figure 14), and many northern Native organizations have joined the World Council of Indigenous Peoples (WCIP). Both ICC and WCIP have formal status as non-governmental organizations (NGOs) with the United Nations which gives their spokespersons access to many United Nations' meetings and activities where they are becoming leaders of the Fourth World movement.[161]

Fig. 14. General Assembly of the Inuit Circumpolar Conference, Iqaluit, 1983. *Source*: courtesy of *Caribou News*.

Native organizations are acutely aware that new and more powerful political structures for Native people in the Arctic will be meaningless without the means to finance them. Greenland remains financially dependent on Denmark and the European Economic Community (EEC). Denmark subsidizes roughly half the cost of the Home Rule Government in the form of a block grant. When the Home Rule Government convinced Denmark to withdraw Greenland from the EEC in January 1985, Greenland lost substantial aid grants from the EEC. To replace these, the EEC pays a sizable 'rent' (26·5 million ECUs annually) for first priority for European fishing rights in Greenland's 200 mile fishing zone. This transition from direct payments and foreign aid to block grants and rents gives the Home Rule Government substantial control over revenues but not economic independence. On 1 January 1985, the Home Rule Government assumed control of the KGH (Royal Greenlandic Trade Company) which owns and operates the fishing fleet, fish processing plants, sheep slaughter houses, a domestic airline, supply and passenger ships, and other industrial concerns in Greenland. These businesses provide a substantial base from which to develop an independent economy.

In the Alaska Native Claims Settlement Act (ANCSA), the U.S. Congress tried to provide an economic base for Native peoples within the western institutional framework of the capitalist system. In the view of some critics of ANCSA, the Act failed to secure a sound financial basis for the Native economy and, at the same time, imposed an institutional colonialism that undermined indigenous social institutions. Congress placed what seemed at the time to be generous land and money assets in the hands of Native regional and village corporations, corporations formed to make a profit. Ignoring more traditional forms of control and decision making, Congress assumed in 1971 that most Natives would be assimilated into the dominant political and economic system.

Today, many Natives seriously question the utility of for-profit corporations, especially at the village level. The village corporations must succeed where no business is likely to succeed, where markets do not exist, and where capitalist institutions run counter to traditional community values.[162] For the most part, the Native village corporations were undercapitalized from the start, and fees for legal and corporate advisors whittled away most of the initial capital. Only a few have succeeded; most have languished. In 1986, Haida Corporation (the village corporation for Hydaburg) became the first to face bankruptcy.[163] The regional corporations show more mixed results. While the shareholders of Ahtna

Corporation in the Copper River region of south-central Alaska and Cook Inlet Regional Corporation in Anchorage hold stock which has significantly increased in value since 1971, Bering Straits Native Corporation in the Nome area filed for reorganization under Chapter 11 of the bankruptcy laws in 1986. The Native corporations have not, for the most part, increased the income of Native Alaskans appreciably, nor have they provided many jobs. Improvements in health, housing, education and employment are attributable largely to state and federally funded programs and oil revenues received by the state (sharply declining by 1986). Thus, Native peoples remain dependent on the dominant institutions to the south.

Two Native regional governments provide some hope for breaking the cycle of dependence: the North Slope Borough and the Kativik Regional Government. For residents of the North Slope of Alaska, vast improvements in services and jobs have come from the North Slope Borough (NSB), the regional government formed in 1972 to take advantage of the power to levy a property tax on the Prudhoe Bay and Kuparuk oil field developments. The Borough is not an ethnically defined regional government; its authority, like that of other boroughs in Alaska, comes from the state. Nevertheless, since the population of the North Slope is overwhelmingly Inupiat, it is a Native-run government. The NSB has built schools, sewage treatment plants, and community facilities using its tax base to borrow the capital and incurring huge debts that will take years to repay. It has no more powers than any other borough government in the state, and it fights frequent battles with the federal and state governments, often in court, over the extent, location and timing of offshore oil development which threatens to harm critical marine resources. The NSB has been the prime source of funding for the Inuit Circumpolar Conference and has spawned and supported numerous efforts to promote Native self-determination throughout the Arctic. Its success has been the envy of other regions and the model for the NANA Region, which has formed the Northwest Arctic Borough to be financed by taxes on the Red Dog lead and zinc mine.

Quebec's Inuit have a similar regional governmental entity. Known as the Kativik Regional Government, it exercises governmental power for the Inuit communities of Northern Quebec. A creation of the James Bay and Northern Quebec Agreement of 1975 (JBNQA), it is incorporated under the laws of and receives money through the Province. Its budget is subject to the approval of the Province. Its autonomy is hampered by control from the Province, and its operations curtailed by insufficient funds.[164]

Both in Alaska under ANCSA and in northern Quebec under the JBNQA, a multiplicity of new institutions, corporations, and governments with structures that are 'foreign' to Native communities have created administrative inefficiency, perpetuated dependency on costly outside advisors, and diverted the most educated and acculturated Natives from the villages to the regional governments and corporations. Local institutions are poorly funded and often poorly run. Power has become centralized, radically departing from traditional institutional structures wherein decisions were made by consensus in small kinship groups. Furthermore, leadership qualities essential to direct western political institutions or corporations would have been inappropriate behavior in a traditional subsistence community.

Recognizing ANCSA's failure to provide a framework for assuring cultural survival and protection of Native land, some Native leaders have sought to revive languishing tribal governments. Over 70 tribal governments still exist in Alaska. Many were created in accord with the Indian Reorganization Act (IRA) of 1934, as amended in 1936 to apply to Alaska. These are often referred to as IRA councils. Owning little or no land and having little or no steady source of revenue, the main function of these tribal governments has been to supply services to the communities using state and, especially, federal grants and contracts. Many villages with IRA Councils also have municipal governments as well as village and regional corporations. Tribal governments in the lower 48 states have considerable powers over local affairs including their own tribal courts and authority over domestic matters such as divorce, marriage, and adoption. Some Alaska Natives see tribal government as a way to counter the authority of the Alaska Department of Fish and Game as well as other encroachments of state and federal power on indigenous political rights. In 1985, the Association of Village Council Presidents (AVCP), a regional non-profit organization composed of representatives of the 56 tribal councils in southwest Alaska, lobbied successfully for more representation for villages in the Alaska Federation of Natives. Still unable to garner AFN support for its proposed changes to ANCSA, the 'Yupiit Nation' coalition lobbied Congress in 1986 and 1987 for amendments to ANCSA which would have recognized tribal council authority over Native land, Native power to manage fish and game on Native land, and transfer of municipally owned land conveyed under ANCSA to tribal governments. While they did not succeed in passing amendments to strengthen tribal government, the tribal sovereignty advocates convinced Congress not to further weaken tribal government in Alaska.[165]

In the Canadian Arctic, indigenous peoples are pursuing self-government through three avenues: (1) creation of joint government/ Native decision making bodies through land claims settlements (such as the proposed Nunavut Lands Authority and Nunavut Wildlife Board); (2) entrenchment of aboriginal rights in the Canadian Constitution; and (3) creation of new public governments in the NWT. In the eastern and central Arctic, Inuit have proposed a new government for an area called Nunavut ('Our Land'). Its powers would be similar to those of a province (which are considerable by comparison with an American state) minus full ownership of natural resources.[166] Inuktitut would become the official language. As proposed, Nunavut would receive a share of federal resource revenues and gain limited powers over coastal and ocean management. The great challenge to advocates of Nunavut is to create institutions that ensure Inuit a dominant role in decisions affecting their land and livelihood in an era in which a few major development projects could change the demographic makeup of the region so radically that its current overwhelming Native majority would become a minority. The future of the western Canadian Arctic is more complex due to its current multi-ethnic composition. Proposals envision local control and decentralized authority that would protect the several ethnic minorities. Nunavut proposals, in contrast, would divide the eastern and central Arctic into four regions with a strong centralized government.

4.7   Conclusion

The original peoples of the Arctic have gained unexpected political and economic power in the 1970s and 1980s. Engaged in a struggle to shed the bonds of internal colonialism, they have a record of success in legislative, judicial, and administrative arenas of three nations – Denmark, Canada, and the United States. In Fennoscandia, their legal battles have served to mobilize a new movement for Sami rights, to inform and influence the larger public, and to place their issues on national agendas. In Greenland, an awakened indigenous population won home rule, withdrawal from the European Economic Community, and veto power over as well as partnership in natural resource exploration and exploitation. In the United States, Alaska Natives gained ownership of nearly 12 percent of their state making them the single largest group of private landowners. Alaska Natives have gained substantial economic power in the North Slope and NANA regions through power to tax hydrocarbon and mineral development.

Because of their status as original people, Natives have had something to trade, something the dominant society needed. Their aboriginal rights entitled them, at best, to ownership and control of land, water, and valuable natural resources in the Arctic. At least, their claims clouded title to land, water, and natural resources making exploitation by outsiders risky prior to land claims settlements. By forming national coalitions throughout northern North America, Natives have gained title to land and money or are in the process of negotiating to secure land, water, a steady source of revenue, and political rights. Their success is evident in passage of the Alaska Native Claims Settlement Act in 1971, the ANCSA Amendments of 1987, the James Bay and Northern Quebec Agreement in 1975, the Northeastern Quebec Agreement in 1978, Title VIII (the subsistence provisions) of the Alaska National Interest Lands Conservation Act in 1980, and the Inuvialuit Final Agreement in 1984. Imperfect as these agreements may be, they are testaments to increasing Native power in the Arctic.

An extraordinary change has occurred in North America and Fennoscandia in the last 20 years. The once popular notion that all citizens are the same and should be treated the same has yielded to a new vision of the value to society of distinct cultures. Now, national policies attempt to accommodate the preferences of individual ethnic groups and, especially, Native peoples because of their unique status as the original people of the North. National attitudes have shifted away from Social Darwinism which assumed that it was natural, hence acceptable, for Native cultures to die out in the battle for survival of the fittest. Despite the assumption that northern Native cultures would not survive, they have. Despite government policies promoting assimilation, indigenous Arctic peoples have not assimilated. Now, the world is awakening to a new philosophy that values and protects cultural distinctiveness and diversity.

5

Arctic ecosystems: environmental interests

'...a land of seemingly indestructible majesty'.[167]

'The mountains made an unearthly beautiful frieze against the blue...The place, the scene, the breeze, the birdsong, the fragrance of myriad brave burgeoning mosses and flowers – all blend into one clear entity, one jewel. It is the arctic in its unbelievably accelerated summer life. It is also the personal well-being purchased by striving, by lifting and setting down your legs, over and over, through the muskeg, up the slopes, gaining the summit – man using himself.'[168]

A few fortunate travelers from the temperate regions carry the banner of the Arctic sublime. They seek untrammeled wilderness, adventure, challenge. They hope to see the legendary herds of caribou or spy the spout of a bowhead whale, to photograph a polar bear, to hear the raucus racket of a million murres and kittiwakes on a bird cliff. They return with tales and pictures that inspire millions of other would-be travelers who will never set foot in the Arctic, but who, like those who have hiked the Brooks Range, sailed the Northwest Passage, or paddled any of the great northern rivers, want to see this majestic land protected from all the ravages so evident in less remote spots on earth.

Environmental magazines feature photographs and evocative word pictures of a pristine Arctic. But the message is that the Arctic is endangered by industrial development, transboundary pollution, military activity, and the slaughter of wild animals. This chapter is about organizations, worldwide, engaged in a battle to protect Arctic lands, waters, and wildlife. They are often well-funded and frequently effective players in Arctic conflicts.

We begin this chapter by describing what makes Arctic ecosystems susceptible to disturbance. We then introduce the principal organizations active on Arctic environmental, conservation, and preservation issues and examine differences among them which shape the causes they choose and the strategies they employ. Finally, we focus on a few specific issues most critical to the region or most likely to erupt into serious resource conflicts.

5.1   Arctic ecosystems: are they fragile?

The early Arctic explorers conjured images of a land resistant to man's incursions, its promised passageway to Asia choked with ice, a frozen wasteland, a vast expanse of wilderness, miles of glaciers cutting valleys into jagged, unclimbed mountain ranges. It was a harsh land, unwelcoming and unforgiving. But today's visitors describe this same terrain as delicate – the fragile tundra easily scarred by a single truck's passage. They tell us, 'It can take decades for damaged areas to return to normal, and sometimes the fragile tundra vegetation never does recover'.[169] Perhaps the Arctic is no more fragile and no less indestructible than the tropical forests of South America, but its fragility is different. Careless developers who ignore or misunderstand Arctic ecosystems destroy its renewable resources, pollute its waters, decimate its wildlife.

Arctic ecosystems earn their reputation for being unusually susceptible to disturbance by humans for several reasons unique to the polar regions.[170]

(1) Low temperatures retard the decomposition of natural and manmade substances and the breakdown of pollutants. (See Figure 15a, b.) Oil drums rust but take centuries to rot and vanish if not removed. The Arctic is littered with World War II debris, an unsightly and unhealthy reminder that human garbage takes centuries to decompose in this environment. A massive clean-up campaign in Canada in the 1970s greatly improved the situation there, but the Arctic still contains numerous physical reminders of military activity, mining, and even scientific research expeditions occurring throughout the last century. At low temperatures, oil degrades more slowly and is more toxic to plants and animals. Organic pollutants dumped in a river which would disappear after a few hundred kilometers in the temperate zone, may be transported over a thousand kilometers in an Arctic river before being purified.

(2) Regeneration is a protracted process because of the short growing season. The low temperatures not only affect the breakdown of pollutants,

Fig. 15. (a) Military debris left at Delight Harbor, Padloping Island, NWT. *Source*: photo. by G. Osherenko, 1982.

they slow the release of nutrients available to spur new growth. And cold air temperatures, cold soils, and limited sunlight reduce the growing season to a short, intense summer period. In some years there is little or no thaw in parts of the Arctic. Willow 'trees' only a foot high may be hundreds of years old. When Arctic vegetation is disturbed or transition zone forests cut, regrowth can take centuries. On land, the layer of permanently frozen ground underlying tundra vegetation is protected from melting by the insulating effect of the vegetative cover. Vehicles, sometimes even in winter, can destroy this cover, causing the permafrost to thaw and erode leaving deep gullies and wide ravines. Zeev Wolfson, a harsh critic of Soviet environmental practices, describes the damage done by oil and gas extraction to the Urengoy tundra,

> Flying over these places in summer, one can see thousands of square kilometers criss-crossed by yellow gashes, the tracks of the cross-country vehicles hollowed out by water. The following year, the cross-country vehicles can no longer use the same track and therefore a new one appears parallel to the old track. The processes of erosion are increased many times over in this way. Oil-drilling sites are linked by 'roads' a kilometer or more wide.[171]

Fig. 15. (b) Refuse, western Alaska.
Source: photo. by G. Osherenko.

(3) Large concentrations of animal populations heighten vulnerability to catastrophes (see Figure 16). It is well known that plant and animal diversity declines with an increase in latitude. Though the Arctic contains relatively few species, those species may occur in extremely high concentrations. For example, sixty-five to seventy percent of the world's population of northern fur seals breed on two small islands 40 miles apart in the Bering Sea. In many years, the Bering Sea pollock fishery is the largest single species fishery (by volume of catch) in the world. And the George River caribou herd in northern Quebec and Labrador now numbers between 600 and 900 thousand animals. But the flora and fauna are not uniformly distributed across this vast region. For reasons of protection from predators (especially during birthing and migration), access to food supplies, and, in the case of marine mammals, access to air to breath, mammal populations gather in large numbers. Over twenty thousand caribou from the George River herd drowned in the Caniapiscau River in northern Quebec in September 1984 while Hydro-Quebec released water from a reservoir during the caribou migration.[172] Several endangered species of whales migrate through a few passages in the Aleutian island chain in spring and fall.[173] Vast colonies of seabirds breed on the cliffs of a few Arctic islands including St George Island in the Bering Sea and Bylot Island in Landcaster Sound. A million birds may take flight when startled by the noise of a single helicopter or low-flying airplane knocking eggs off the cliffs and exposing chicks to predatory gulls

Fig. 16. (a) Portion of the Porcupine caribou herd,
Alaska National Wildlife Refuge.
Source: U.S. Fish and Wildlife Service.

and foxes.[174] Sea mammals congregate at polynyas, open water areas, in winter for a ready supply of oxygen and for access to particularly abundant food supplies. And on land, the Arctic 'desert' contains numerous 'thermal oases', small areas that are warmer and more moist than much of the Arctic landscape. These usually lie in the lee of high ground in areas where dry winds have warmed the air and helped to dissipate the persistent deck of stratus cloud that characterizes most of the Arctic adjacent to bodies of water. In summer, these thermal oases may receive five or six times as much radiation as the surrounding land, fostering higher productivity in plant and animal life.[175]

(4) Marine areas are particularly important in the Arctic in comparison with other regions of the globe. Food is concentrated in the sea where nutrients are continually available due to the convergence and mixing of warm and cold ocean currents that bring nutrients to the surface to sustain enormous quantities of plankton.[176] In winter, some mammals that live on land depend on the sea. Seals are a staple in the diet of Arctic foxes and many humans (Inuit) in winter and of polar bears year round. The coastal edge is particularly important in the Arctic. Marine mammals and seabirds select rookeries with protection from predators and ready access to food from the sea. Thus, environmental, fishery, and Native interest

Fig. 16. (b) Caribou drowned in the Caniapiscau River,
northern Quebec, 1984.
Source: photo. by H. Hill, *Caribou News*.

groups focus particular attention on protecting rich renewable resources offshore.

(5) Climatic conditions are likely to produce a more pronounced CO_2-induced warming trend in the Arctic than in temperate regions and are already leading to high concentrations of air pollutants that threaten vegetation as well as human and animal health. The Arctic is often called a polar desert. In winter, temperatures too cold to permit much precipitation coupled with a low stationary Arctic air mass combine to allow air pollutants transported from the temperate zones to accumulate in the atmosphere producing what is known as 'Arctic haze'. Visible from the 1950s, this brownish haze contains sulphur and heavy metals largely, but not entirely, from industrial sources far to the South.[177] Scientists studying 'the greenhouse effect' predict that the expected warming will be considerably more pronounced in the Arctic (during winter) than in the mid-latitudes.

> In the Arctic, feedback between radiation and highly reflective ice and snow surfaces, as well as the presence of a strong, surface-based temperature inversion, cause energy to be trapped near the surface. As a result, [A]rctic warming would not only be higher than at lower latitudes, but also seasonally dependent.[178]

The warming could be two and a half times greater and faster during winter in the Arctic than the global averages. Arctic vegetation is specially adapted to climate conditions such as low precipitation, strong winds, low temperatures, and a short growing season. Changes in climate due to a CO_2-induced warming will alter the vegetation, especially in the transition zone between tundra and forest.[179]

(6) Severe weather and ice dynamics make environmental protection and cleanup extremely difficult. The occasional occurrence of a massive overriding ice sheet, called 'ivu' by the Inupiat, in Arctic coastal areas dramatically illustrates the unpredictability and enormity of threats and the challenges faced by engineers designing offshore oil rigs and coastal industrial facilities for the Arctic.[180] Military and industrial interests must contend with nearshore ice movement, especially large, old ice flows, pressure ridges, unpredictable ocean currents, and strong winds. Severe climate conditions, moreover, impede clean up and rescue efforts in the event of an accident.

Combinations of these Arctic conditions intensified by several phenomena peculiar to the region make Arctic ecosystems extremely vulnerable to physical and chemical disturbance. For example, oil spilled at sea tends to concentrate under and between ice cover at the sea ice edges and in ice-free polynyas where phytoplankton, zooplankton, fish, and marine mammals are most abundant. Temperature inversions produce smog and ice fog in larger Arctic communities like Fairbanks or Yakutsk and contribute to the concentration of pollutants. In Fairbanks during winter, a shallow inversion layer sandwiches pollutants in a layer often only 10 meters thick. Thus, while the quantity of pollutants is smaller than in smoggy Los Angeles, the Arctic conditions in Fairbanks provide far less dispersion than the air above southern California where the inversion layer is apt to be 400 vertical meters. Fairbanks consistently ranks among the ten American cities most polluted by carbon monoxide.[181] High acidity of spring precipitation combines with the stagnancy of acid meltwater to damage fish because the spring thaw coincides with the stage of greatest vulnerability when as young fry, fish are least able to cope with acidity. Furthermore, the sensitivity of lichens and other vegetation to sulfur dioxide and other pollutants further complicates ecological problems.

5.2   The players: conservationists, environmentalists, and preservationists

We swap these three terms in our daily conversation as though they were interchangeable, naively lumping all environmental groups together as if they shared a common agenda. Even the members and contributors to an environmental group will refer to themselves as preservationists in one breath and conservationists in the next. But the three terms are different in origin and definition. Those involved in Arctic controversies would do well to understand the three distinct, but overlapping, schools of thought regarding natural resources and the environment – the preservation school, the environmental school, and the conservation school – so that they can identify the underlying philosophy, values, and interests at stake in a particular controversy.

Conservation, or progressive conservation as it was called in the United States in its heyday from 1890 to 1920, arose as a utilitarian response to the destructive use of natural resources.[182] The conservation movement was a reaction to short-sighted, profit-maximizing exploitation and a realization that the frontier was not unlimited. Originally linked with the Populist movement, conservationists argued that natural resources must be developed and preserved for the benefit of the many and not merely for the profit of the few. Multiple use and maximum sustainable yield became its buzzwords. The conservation ethic is anthropocentric; resources should be managed to provide for the needs of the human population of this and future generations. Hunters, trappers, and fishers follow the conservation ethic, and though there are frequent conflicts between Native and sport hunters, they share a desire to maximize the sustainable yield from certain wildlife populations.

Most university courses in natural resource and wildlife management are guided by this philosophy, though wrapped in a cloak of scientific methods to create the impression of objectivity. Wildlife managers working for government agencies follow its precepts. Conservation principles were mandated by the Convention for the Protection of North Pacific Fur Seals (which lapsed in 1984 when preservationists in the United States objected to a protocol to extend the treaty).[183] And major national laws regulating natural resources, such as national forests in the U.S., are based, at least in part, on maximizing sustainable yields.[184]

At the center of the spectrum of natural resource philosophies is the environmental school or the 'biosphere' school as Soviet specialists have called it.[185] This school of thought approaches environmental problems in a unified way emphasizing the interrelationships of air, water, and land. Its followers view the world's biomass as a dynamic life support system necessary to sustain human life. They regard humans as a part of nature, not separate from it or superior.

Informed by ecology, environmentalists seek optimum sustainable populations of wildlife (a concept not driven by high yields for hunters), maximum biological productivity, and biological diversity regardless of commercial value. Their concerns tend to be broader geographically and functionally than the groups guided by conservationist or preservationist philosophies. Their issues encompass global problems, urban issues, air and water pollution, nuclear weapons, nuclear radiation, and hazardous and toxic wastes. They neither oppose nor encourage hunting, but fight for protection of endangered or threatened species and their habitat. They will criticize multiple use but approve a zonal division allowing carefully planned industrial facilities to be sited away from protected areas. They seek to mitigate environmental impacts and minimize damage, but they are not romantics who oppose all development.

At the other end of the spectrum is preservation, an outlook that developed in the late 19th century in conjunction with transcendentalism. Writers such as Henry David Thoreau and John Muir looked to nature to transcend the discordant urban industrial society. Unlike the human-centered philosophy of the conservationists, preservationists would accord animals and plants rights comparable to the rights of humans.

The most radical proponents of preservation seek to end all consumptive use of wild animals or banish any human activity that would leave its imprint on lands designated as wilderness. The preservationist philosophy underlies the animal protectionist movement which campaigns to end the 'slaughter' of seals, ban the leghold trap, and halt commercial whaling.[186] A similar ethic regarding terrestrial and marine areas motivates groups whose charter is to protect special wild places through legal designations such as wilderness, wild and scenic rivers, and marine sanctuaries. In a few cases, preservationists have successfully embedded their preference for nonconsumptive use in the law. In the U.S., for example, the Marine Mammal Protection Act (MMPA) forbids hunting, harassing, and virtually any harm to marine mammals with the exception of non-commercial, subsistence hunting by Alaska Natives, taking for scientific purposes and public display, and killing incidental to fishing operations.[187]

In practice, it is not always easy to place organizations neatly into one of the three schools, but for an effort to categorize them along a spectrum, see Figure 17. Internal struggles within an organization may indicate that a group is shifting from one philosophy toward another or has internal inconsistencies in its positions. Still, these underlying philosophies do help to explain why certain organizations dealing with Arctic issues choose to champion specific causes, and why, frequently, natural resource protection groups are found on opposite sides of Arctic issues.

Few of the organizations concerned with such issues are headquartered in the Arctic or headed by Arctic residents. Most are part of the core/periphery configuration we discussed in previous chapters.[188] With the exception of local and regional organizations like the Northern Alaska Environmental Center in Fairbanks and the Yukon Conservation Society in Whitehorse, natural resource organizations operate from bases far to the south of the Arctic. Their staffs, boards, and members seldom include Arctic residents. Perhaps most estranged from the indigenous population of the Arctic are the relatively affluent, urban people living a life cut off from the land who lead the anti-harvesting, animal protection organizations such as the International Fund for Animal Welfare (IFAW), the Fund for Animals, and Friends of Animals. But all the national and international preservation, conservation, and environmental organizations operate with financial support, staff, and headquarters located in the South. Though some make a point of expressing concern for indigenous people's needs in the Arctic, they are often perceived by northern residents as another intrusive influence from the South.[189]

Two of the largest environmental organizations concerned with Arctic issues, the World Wildlife Fund (WWF) and the International Union for the Conservation of Nature and Natural Resources (IUCN), generally occupy the middle ground between environmentalists and conservationists. WWF has a long history in the business of preserving endangered

Fig. 17. Philosophical orientation of North American organizations active on Arctic issues. *Source*: prepared for this book by the authors.

Preservation School	Environmental School	Conservation School
• ARK II	• National Audubon Society	• Canadian Arctic Resources Committee
• Friends of Animals	• Sierra Club	
• Fund for Animals	• Sierra Club Legal Defense Fund	• International Union for the Conservation of Nature and Natural Resources (IUCN)
• Greenpeace		• World Wildlife Fund
• Humane Society of America (U.S.)	• Canadian Nature Federation	
		• National Wildlife Federation
• I KARE	• Friends of the Earth	• Canadian Wildlife Federation
• International Fund for Animal Welfare	• Natural Resources Defense Council	
• World Society for the Protection of Animals	• Northern Alaska Environmental Center	• Ducks Unlimited
	• Trustees for Alaska	
• Wilderness Society		

and threatened species, though not necessarily for the purpose of improving hunting. WWF (Canada), in a cooperative venture with Environment Canada, is supporting scientific toxicology studies to determine the effects of pollutants on polar bears and other northern species. While many of WWF's supporters avidly oppose hunting, the organization's leaders have distanced themselves from the animal rights advocates. IUCN and WWF share a vision of sustainable development through the use of renewable resources and appropriate technology. IUCN prepared an influential blueprint for development based on environmental information as an alternative to industrial society's usual method of planning development projects before considering environmental impacts. The blueprint, known as the World Conservation Strategy, has been adopted by the Inuit Circumpolar Conference as a model for creating an Inuit Regional Conservation Strategy, which will be the first regional transboundary conservation strategy and the first prepared by an indigenous organization.[190]

Groups interested in Arctic ecosystems in Nordic nations generally espouse an environmentalist philosophy. The Norwegian Union for Nature Protection, for example, although it concentrated on protection of wildlife species and land protection in the 1960s, shifted its focus to pollution control and resource management in the 1970s. The Soviet Union's burgeoning environmental advocacy movement, as well as the All-Russian Society for Conservation which operates on a government charter and had a membership of twenty-two million in 1973, focuses much attention on pollution problems.[191] Scientists and scientific organizations are often the chief critics of environmentally destructive government policies, and an acceptance of concepts drawn from ecology now dominates Soviet literature on the environment.[192]

A number of Native organizations take an active interest in Arctic environmental issues. These groups often espouse the conservation ethic, though the origin of Native interests in protecting the land and natural resources predates the birth of the conservation movement by centuries. The earliest records of northern lands being placed off limits to hunting were areas set aside by the hunters themselves. Chukchi, for example, traditionally banned hunting at several walrus hauling grounds on the coast of Chukotka. The Khanty and Mansi considered numerous places sacred, a practice that played a major role in protecting the sable and river beaver. Indigenous peoples throughout the North 'let the land rest' in places where they perceive a need to allow wildlife populations to recover from hunting pressure. The purpose of these 'reserves', as well as modern game preserves, sanctuaries, and wildlife refuges, is frequently in line with the conservationist ethic oriented toward providing habitat for migratory birds, brown bear, beaver, and other game species. Rapid population growth in northern Native communities has also impelled Native leaders to seek ways to protect and expand the renewable resources upon which the resident populations depend. And recognition of the need to protect the resource base against external threats has contributed to environmental activism on the part of Native leaders.[193] Makivik Corporation in northern Quebec, for example, has conducted research on the feasibility of re-establishing a cod fishery, increasing salmon runs, and enhancing eider duck populations in order to create an eider down garment industry.

Close analysis of the underlying philosophy as well as the economic and noneconomic interests of each organization enable us to comprehend changing alliances among Native, environmental, preservation, and conservation organizations. We can better understand how allies in one conflict become opponents in another controversy. For example, environmental groups are allied with some (but not all) indigenous organizations (primarily Dene groups of interior Alaska and the Yukon) in opposition to the opening of the Arctic National Wildlife Refuge to oil exploration which threatens the Porcupine caribou herd. But some of the same environmental groups oppose Native interests in using all terrain vehicles (ATVs) in national parks and preserves. Assessing the values and principles followed by an organization clarifies the common interests of Natives and conservation groups as well as the disparities between Native groups and animals protection organizations.

5.3   Arctic environmental problems

We have divided the issues posing the greatest threat to the Arctic environment or most likely to trigger serious clashes among Arctic players into three broad categories: long range transport of pollutants, habitat disturbance, and wildlife protection.

Long range transport of pollutants

The Congress finds and declares that…industrial pollution not originating in the Arctic region collects in the polar air mass, has the potential to disrupt global weather patterns, and must be controlled through international cooperation and consultation.

U.S. Arctic Research and
Policy Act of 1984, Section 102

The pristine Arctic is no longer pristine. Polar bears may be toxic and reindeer radioactive. Wind currents blow carbon dioxide (CO_2), sulphate compounds, soot, sulphur dioxide (SO_2), chlorofluorocarbons, and pesticides from mid-latitude sources to the Arctic where they produce Arctic haze, acid deposition, ozone depletion, and climatic warming. In addition to these recurrent pollutants, which are the by-products of normal industrial, commercial, and agricultural activities, nuclear and industrial accidents may disrupt Arctic ecosystems.

For those who would solve Arctic environmental problems, the long range transport of pollutants (LRTP) presents a particular challenge socially, economically, and politically. As pollutants travel across political boundaries, the coordination of monitoring, communication, notification of danger, response to crisis, cleanup, and containment becomes more complex. When the impacts of pollution are felt hundreds or even thousands of miles away, frequently in another nation, incentives to reduce pollution at its source decline. The United States government has not responded to the pleas of its friendly neighbour to reduce emissions from coal-fired power plants destroying life in Canada's lakes and killing its trees. How much more difficult will it be for the Soviet Union, European nations, and the U.S.A. to agree to reduce pollution casting a pall over most of the Arctic each year from January through April?

Arctic haze is an environmental DEW line – an early warning system signaling danger from distant sources. Visible air pollution in the Arctic or Arctic haze is suspended particulate matter that scatters solar radiation. It can reduce visibility from 125 miles (200 kilometers) to as little as 18 miles (30 kilometers). Sulphur dioxide (SO_2) produced by burning fossil fuels and smelting sulphide ores accounts for approximately 30% of the Arctic haze particles. Natural sources except for occasional volcanoes produce little of the Arctic haze. Initially, scientists blamed Arctic haze on industrial installations in the Far North, in particular the Soviet Union's copper and nickel smelting complex at Noril'sk. More recent research has revealed that, while pollutants from Noril'sk occasionally end up in the air above Barrow, Alaska, most Arctic air pollution originates much further south in the western Soviet Union and Europe. Ice cores from Greenland confirm that from 1952 to 1977 while SO_2 emissions in Europe doubled, Arctic pollution increased approximately 75 percent. The pollution sources of eastern North America are smaller, and prevailing winds in winter carry pollutants over the north Atlantic where storms cleanse the air. Sources of pollution in Eurasia, by contrast, travel northeast in winter over snow and ice in a path four times less likely to encounter precipitation. Pollutants reaching the Arctic during winter and early spring stay in the atmosphere because of the low precipitation and stable air mass. (See Figure 18).[194]

The hazards attributable to Arctic air pollution are not yet clear. Acid deposition, now recognized as a major problem in eastern Canada and parts of Scandinavia, is not yet as great a concern in the Arctic. Pollutants that wash out of the atmosphere en route to the polar region fall most heavily in Subarctic regions, acidifying soil and water and killing fish. When particulates do fall to earth in the Arctic, they leave carbon ash, heavy metals, SO_2, NO_x, and pesticides. Due to the low temperatures, pollutants are slow to break down and may be more damaging than at lower latitudes. Pesticides, such as lindane observed on Ellesmere Island,

Fig. 18. Arctic haze map. *Source*: *Arctic Haze Sheet*, Ottawa: Environment Canada, 1984.

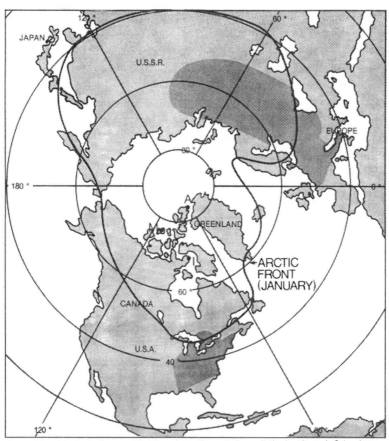

The position of the Arctic air mass at that time of year (January) when pollution is at its peak. Colored area shows pollutant source areas. A characteristic of the Arctic air mass is that in winter pollutants persist much longer than in summer.

Canadian air quality monitoring stations

M — Mould Bay, Northwest Territories
A — Alert, Northwest Territories
I — Igloolik, Northwest Territories

chlordane at Mould Bay, Canada, toxaphene in the Mackenzie River, and pesticides in the Norwegian Arctic, confirm the contribution of mid-latitude pollutants to the Arctic. Scientists studying toxicity of Arctic fish and mammals are just beginning to assess the damage to Arctic ecosystems.

The biggest threat associated with Arctic haze is its contribution to long-range climatic change. Gases, including CO_2, from mid-latitude combustion of fossil fuels arrive in winter and early spring along with the solid and liquid particles that make up Arctic haze. The various gases concentrate because they are not removed by precipitation. Some of the CO_2 is removed either as a result of uptake by vegetation in the course of photosynthesis or by dissolution into ice-free waters. Over frozen areas, however, CO_2 becomes more concentrated in the stationary air mass. Carbon dioxide and water vapour, and to a lesser extent methane, nitrous oxide, and chlorofluorocarbons, allow short-wavelength sunlight to enter the atmosphere relatively unimpeded. However, they absorb much of the long-wave radiation emitted by the earth's surface and reradiate it downward to warm the earth. At the same time, soot or black aerosols (components of Arctic haze) suspended over the white surface increase the solar radiation trapped in the troposphere. Computer models predict a slight warming of Arctic air during March, April, and May that could affect weather patterns in the Northern Hemisphere.[195] When deposited on the snowpack, the soot causes a decrease in the albedo. In turn, the darkening of the surface increases absorption of solar energy and hastens snowmelt. Scientists predict that fall and winter temperatures may rise 8 to 12 degrees centigrade in the Arctic within the next 100 years (assuming a global doubling of carbon dioxide). Summer temperatures are likely to increase 1 to 2 degrees centigrade. There is great uncertainty about the ultimate effects of this warming trend. Scientists project that it will dramatically increase snowfall in the Arctic which, some believe, could trigger the onset of an ice age. Most scientists agree that drastic climatic change in the Arctic will cause massive climatic imbalance, not only in the Arctic but in the temperate zones as well.[196]

Because of the greenhouse effect, biologists predict that tundra areas will shrink and forests will creep north along coasts, up mountain slopes, and into former tundra areas. They anticipate that higher CO_2 levels will increase photosynthesis, decomposition, and the nutrient cycling process. Coupled with a longer growing season, these processes would change the composition of plant and animal communities. Migration patterns of terrestrial and marine mammals as well as altered ice conditions would certainly affect the economy of subsistence-based communities. Cod, anchovy, and other northern fish, known to swim thousands of kilometers in response to changes of one or two degrees in ocean temperatures, might migrate with disastrous results for fisheries in several Arctic rim nations. Conflicts between nations intent on protecting the interests of their own fishing fleets may erupt when fish migrate across politically established economic or fishery conservation zones.

The warming trend also has major implications for human activities in the Arctic. Offshore oil drilling, conducted primarily in winter using sea ice to support convoys of heavy machinery to well sites, could be severely hampered by shorter winters and less stable ice. In time, however, complete disappearance of multi-year ice may make less expensive drilling technology usable in the Arctic. Melting permafrost could pose problems for engineers constructing pipelines and buildings. Ice-free Arctic summers and the absence of multi-year ice, however, could make Arctic shipping easier except in cases where increased icebergs clog channels. And spring floods would be greater changing the water budgets of hydroelectric power projects.[197]

Chlorofluorocarbons (CFCs), caused by propellants in aerosol spray cans and coolants in air conditioners and refrigerators, contribute one-sixth of the warming effect despite their relatively small concentrations in the atmosphere. In addition, they damage the ozone shield that blocks ultraviolet radiation. Scientists have documented a thinning of the ozone layer in the Arctic that is more pronounced than the general global decline of ozone, but not yet as dramatic as the huge hole in the ozone occurring over Halley Bay, Antarctica in winter.

Environmental advocates urge both governments and individuals to cut emissions drastically, conserve energy, and increase energy efficiency in home appliances and industry. They demand better pollution controls on coal-fired power plants, conversion to natural gas, and redesign of automobile air conditioners and other consumer products using CFCs. While the sources of Arctic pollution cannot be precisely pinpointed, nor the effects of climate disruption and ozone depletion definitively described, the probability of dramatic and disruptive consequences is sufficiently high to convince many that immediate action to curb pollutants is warranted.

After Chernobyl The cloud of radiation spawned by the accident at the Chernobyl nuclear power plant in the Soviet Ukraine on 26 April 1986 passed over Europe and spread high levels of radioactive iodine and cesium over the core reindeer herding lands of the south Sami in Sweden. The government of Sweden, using its network of devices to detect radioactive fallout from atomic bomb tests, determined that 100,000 reindeer were likely to be contaminated. The meat from ninety-seven percent of the first 1,000 reindeer slaughtered in 1986 exceeded the 300 bequerals per kilogram limit, in many cases by as much as a factor of ten. In order to buffer the Sami herding economy, which is linked to a gourmet food export business, the government allowed the meat to be sold to the region's mink and fox fur farms where it would not enter the human food chain (and where it sold for less than seven cents per kilogram) (see Figure 19).[198] But the danger will not end with the 100,000 reindeer caught under the cloud of radiation.

Lichen, the winter staple of reindeer, soaks up cesium 137, which has a half-life of 30 years, insuring perpetuation of the poison for decades. Swedes were warned not to eat local fish and cloud berries. Elk shot by hunters and killed in traffic accidents registered contamination above the legal limit.[199] As a result, hunters shot fewer elk and forest ecologists anticipate increased forest damage due to overgrazing. The Sami, who previously feared loss of their land and culture by encroaching urbanization, must face every day after Chernobyl the perils of nuclear pollution. And environmental advocates worldwide now recognize a danger many thought improbable prior to Chernobyl.[200]

Chernobyl is likely to produce serious secondary socioeconomic and

Fig. 19. Carcasses of reindeer contaminated by fallout from the Chernobyl accident make headlines in *Samefolket*. Source: *Samefolket*, photo. by M. Mattsson.

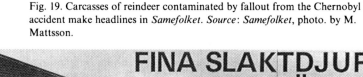

FINA SLAKTDJUR BLIR MINKFÖDA!

environmental effects in Sweden. Sami now recognize the extreme vulnerability of reliance on reindeer herding as an economic base and fewer young Sami are likely to choose this traditional way of life that depends on careful stewardship of pastureland. Additionally, Sweden, a country that is heavily dependent on nuclear power, now must come to terms with increased public pressure to accelerate the phase-out of nuclear power plants (currently scheduled for 2010) and to replace the lost power supplies by damming more northern rivers to generate electric power.[201] Biologists are also concerned about the effects on migratory birds that normally feed in areas clearly affected by the radiation, especially habitat located near Chernobyl.

Habitat disturbance

Agriculture, the leading cause of habitat disturbance throughout the world, barely exists in the Arctic. The cultivation of crops is an infant industry in the region, relegated to the cover of greenhouses and cold frames with an occasional potato or vegetable patch and the raising of honey bees. Nevertheless, habitat disturbance is a major environmental problem in the Arctic. Natural resource extraction and hydroelectric power projects are the chief causes. Transportation, tourism, human settlement, and a growing military presence contribute. Chapters 2 and 3 describe the current extent and future prospects of military and industrial activities in the Arctic. In this section, we touch briefly on the actual and potential environmental impacts of these activities.

Offshore oil and gas activities Oil spills could lead to widespread damage to marine habitat. In addition, chronic discharges of oil and wastes occurring during both exploratory and production drilling could have significant deleterious effects on localized populations of marine organisms, depending on the amount, duration, and toxicity of the contaminants. Diesel spills as well as discarded and misplaced equipment can kill marine mammals and seabirds in addition to damaging fishing nets and gear. Critical habitats, such as warm estuarine waters where beluga (white) whales calve, areas near seabird cliffs, or polynyas (areas of open water surrounded by ice) where subadult ringed seals and bearded seals overwinter, polar bears prey, and seabirds and whales feed during migration, are particularly vulnerable.

Noise from exploration, production, and tanker traffic may cause significant problems. During exploration, seismic charges may kill fish, a problem that can be minimized by using advanced acoustic and sound-generating equipment. Inuit, who have long depended on and closely observed whales, say the bowhead is highly sensitive to noise. Recent studies indicate that an icebreaker pushing ice out of the way to protect a drill ship in the Beaufort Sea produces enough noise to cause 50 percent of the whales in the area to move away in a zone that is 16–22 miles in diameter. Under 'quiet' environmental background conditions, the 'zone of response' around a drillship expands to about 34 miles in diameter.[202] Scientists know too little about marine mammal communication, echo-location processes, and responses to sound of various magnitudes to answer key questions regarding marine mammal disturbance resulting from hydrocarbon production and transportation.

In northern Norway and Scotland, fish breeding grounds have been damaged by massive trenching, earthmoving, and the dredging of large quantities of sand and gravel for construction. In order to drill offshore in the Arctic, oil companies build ice roads, causeways, and gravel islands, all of which alter the marine environment and have the potential to disturb spawning grounds and disrupt migration patterns.

The onshore effects of offshore hydrocarbon development are greatest during production when drilling and service activities require creation of new settlements or rapid expansion of existing communities. For example, the population of St Paul, a community of 550 people on the Pribilof Islands, could be swelled by 827 oil-related workers in the event of a commercial oil strike nearby.

Onshore hydrocarbon development Onshore, oil and gas extraction has already left deep scars on the Arctic. As Rostankowski says of the Soviet North,

> Clearly visible on this false color image [satelite pictures taken from a height of more than 900 km] of the area around Surgut is the fact that the Siberian tayga has been grubbed out and torn up over vast areas, polluted by waste water, criss-crossed by sand embankments and cut up by wide cleared swaths. The vegetation cover of northern Western Siberia, which regenerates only slowly due especially to the short growing season, is being damaged by oil and gas extraction... [203]

Nor is this Soviet case an isolated example. Similar criticisms have been launched at American and Canadian activities. In 1988, two environmental groups released a report detailing environmental problems at Prudhoe Bay and charging industry with numerous violations of environmental regulations. The report highlighted air and water pollution, problems of hazardous and other waste disposal, and habitat alteration on

Alaska's North Slope.[204] In December 1987, the U.S. Fish and Wildlife
Service reported serious discrepancies between actual environmental
impacts from onshore oil development and impacts predicted in a 1972
environmental impact statement before construction of production
facilities on the North Slope.[204a] A comparison of the Prudhoe Bay and
Kuparuk oil fields on the North Slope of Alaska illustrates that heightened
concern for the environment can reduce but not eliminate environmental
harm. Native development corporations, interested in employment and
economic gains as well as environmental protection, won the contract to
construct and operate the Kuparuk Industrial Complex (KIC), an all-
purpose facility including offices, housing, and entertainment for Kuparuk
oil field workers. As a result of negotiations with the oil companies, KIC
consolidated the infrastructure of all production operations at Kuparuk
into a single complex minimizing road construction and vehicular use at the
site. And the agreement between the North Slope Borough and the oil
companies calls for continued study and environmental monitoring.

The competition for land, the network of roads, air and water pollution,
and acidification of soil have diminished habitat for domestic and wild
reindeer in the Soviet North and contributed to local and regional
pollution problems. In North America, the onshore area with the greatest
potential for a major oil strike, located in the coastal plain of the Alaska
National Wildlife Refuge (ANWR), coincides with the calving grounds of
the Porcupine caribou herd. A major battle is brewing in Congress
between advocates of wilderness designation for the coastal plain of the
ANWR and those who favor oil exploration there (an unlikely coalition
including oil companies, the North Slope Borough, and a group of Alaska
Native corporations). Several national and regional environmental groups
(for example, The Wilderness Society, Trustees for Alaska, the Natural
Resources Defense Council, and the National Wildlife Federation) have
made protection of ANWR a top priority and are redirecting existing
funds as well as aggressively fundraising to support their efforts to resist
opening the area for hydrocarbon development.

Mineral extraction and processing

> The extraction of minerals inevitably entails the construction of
> approach roads, the granting of leases, the excavation of shafts
> and quarries, and the appearance of enormous dumps. The
> natural vegetation is destroyed, which in permafrost regions
> results in disturbance of the thermal balance and the development
> of denudation, erosion, and thermokarst. In addition, river beds
> widen and deepen, and lakes dry up. The direction of permanent

water courses and their rate of flow are altered, the turbidity of the water increases, channels silt up, the sandy gravel, in which fish deposit their eggs, is either buried or carried away. Aquatic and terrestrial ecosystems are polluted by toxic substances contained in dirt or washed out and carried away from mining regions. The acidity of water bodies increases. Changes in the chemical composition of soil, ground and surface water lead to corresponding changes in the soil microflora, fauna, and hydrobionts, the accumulation of chemical elements in organisms, as well as the environmental pollution described above.[205]

This description, written not by a private environmental advocacy group but by researchers in the Central Environmental Protection Laboratory of the Ministry of Agriculture of the U.S.S.R., canvasses the range of environmental problems encountered in mining coal, iron, lead, zinc, nickel, copper, apatite, gold, tin, diamonds, and other minerals as well as sand and gravel in the Arctic. The size and scope of mining operations coupled with the character of environmental safeguards in design, construction, and operation determine the number and significance of environmental problems. Pollutants from Noril'sk, the major copper and nickel production and processing center in the Soviet Union, reach the Arctic Ocean via the northward flowing Yenisei River. But much smaller operations such as the placer gold mine on the Tuluksak River in southwestern Alaska can pollute critical spawning streams causing extensive local damage.[206] Where smelting and refining processes accompany mining, air pollution occurs. The Soviets have made strides in reducing pollutants by developing and installing closed cycle technology at metallurgical works at Noril'sk.[207]

Hydroelectric power plants and water diversion schemes Massive dams and strings of smaller dams have destroyed large acreages of prime wildlife habitat and life support systems important to some northern communities. Reindeer calve in the early spring near meltwaters of streams and lakes where high quality grasses provide essential food for newborn calves. Dams replace natural rivers with large lakes that take longer to thaw. The new lakeshores are ill-suited for calving, exposed to cold mountain winds, and devoid of critical vegetation. Northern dams have flooded woodlands and destroyed prime fishing grounds. Cree Indians in the James Bay region of northern Quebec were relocated from their traditional hunting grounds and trap lines in preparation for the James Bay hydroelectric project, and Sami reindeer herders have had to change their spring and autumn camps numerous times as their traditional campsites were overtaken by hydropower development. Lake levels behind hydropower dams may fluctuate by several meters. In temperate regions, reservoirs are controlled to allow for spring spawning. In the North, where important species of salmon and white-fish spawn in the autumn, problems occur. As the level of the ice-covered lake drops, ice in the shallow spawning grounds settles to the bottom killing the spawned roe.[208] When hydroelectric power plants are accompanied by industrial facilities, as is common in the Soviet Union, the combination can be devastating to wildlife and traditional lifestyles.

More complex environmental problems may result from massive hydropower projects too. Scientists have measured dangerously high levels of mercury in fish and some animal species in the James Bay region which they attribute to the leaching of natural mercury from the soil into the newly created lakes. High levels of mercury, in turn, are a health hazard to humans dependent on the contaminated species.[209] Erosion of acidic soil into the lakes as well as decomposition of forests drowned by the reservoirs may also increase the water's acidity. Local climate changes may occur in tandem with large-scale hydroelectric power projects, and siltation reduces the life expectancy of the dams.

Drastic environmental problems could also arise from efforts to divert northern waters south. In the Soviet Union, plans to reverse major northward-flowing rivers to irrigate croplands and supply cities in the mid-latitudes were finally shelved during the 27th Party Congress of the Communist Party of the Soviet Union in 1986.[210] Even as that water resource scheme evaporated, another gained new vitality as the political architect of the James Bay project, Robert Bourassa, reemerged as Premier of Quebec in 1985 with plans to divert the waters of Hudson Bay south to serve the water-thirsty areas in middle America.[211] These massive water diversion projects raise enormous environmental questions that have received considerable attention from serious scholars.[212]

Transportation: TAPS to ATVs Transportation, from all terrain vehicles (ATVs) to tankers and pipelines, is a major source of habitat disturbance in the Arctic. Transportation of oil and gas out of the Arctic has led to numerous conflicts. Controversy surrounding the Trans-Alaska Pipeline System (TAPS), the hot oil pipeline carrying oil from Prudhoe Bay south to the port of Valdez, subsided after engineers redesigned the project with safeguards to avoid melting the permafrost. But environmentalists still question its long-term effects on migratory species and oppose opening the adjacent 'haul road' to the general public. The fear of a rupture in the pipeline leading to a massive oil spill, though diminished by technical advances in engineering, remains. Numerous pipelines deliver gas from the Soviet North to population centers to the south and west, further scarring the terrain. Plans to construct a natural gas pipeline from the Canadian Beaufort Sea south through the Mackenzie Valley caused considerable controversy before being shelved for a decade to allow Canada to settle Native land claims.

The other pathways from North American Arctic oil and gas fields lead east and west through the Arctic Archipelago. A consortium of Canadian companies led by Petro-Canada proposed during the late 1970s to lift liquified natural gas (LNG) in tankers from Melville Island in the high Arctic to a receiving port 3200 miles to the south in Quebec or Nova Scotia. This Arctic Pilot Project (APP) died for economic reasons in 1982 leaving many questions regarding its probable effects on marine ecosystems unanswered.

The greatest problems in tankering oil or gas involve accidental spills, noise, and ice disturbance. While an LNG accident can trigger an explosion and fire, the long-term effects are unlikely to be as damaging as an oil tanker accident leaving oil and toxins. Ships transiting ice-infested waters encounter greater risks than elsewhere. Thirty cargo vessels sustained damage, one ship was lost, and the entire Soviet fleet of Arctic icebreakers came to the aid of the convoy stuck in the eastern sector of the Northern Sea Route in 1983 when the shipping season ended both prematurely and abruptly in September. Oil spills, offshore or onshore, could have Arctic-wide effects due to land drainage patterns and ocean currents. Fifty-one percent of the Soviet Union's territory drains into the Arctic Ocean, as does much of the land in the North American Arctic.

Low-flying aircraft carrying biologists, geologists, tourists, hunters, and even wildlife managers scare birds from their nests and disrupt feeding and migration of mammals. Some observers believe that small planes ferrying hikers into Gates of the Arctic National Park in Alaska disturb wildlife more than snowmobiles.[213] A U.S. federal court decision that scuttled plans to use St Matthew Island in the Bering Sea as a support base for hydrocarbon exploration activities in the Navarin Basin drew particular attention to the detrimental environmental effects of air traffic on the five million seabirds that nest on the island. Summarizing information from a draft environmental impact statement, the opinion states that,

[n]ear flying aircraft inhibit breeding and initiate panic flights, potentially causing entire colonies to take to the air, knocking eggs and chicks into the ocean or leaving them vulnerable to

predators. Continued disruption may cause reproduction failure, and, in the worst case, colonies may be totally abandoned.[214]

The U.S. Fish and Wildlife Service requires aircraft to stay at least three (and sometimes twelve) miles offshore from the island, which is designated as both a wildlife refuge and wilderness area.

The growth of human populations centered in northern towns far from traditional hunting grounds initiated a transition to motorized transport – snowmobiles, motor boats, even helicopters – to continue subsistence activities. While some of these activities may be relatively benign, others trigger environmental battles. The U.S. National Park Service encountered stiff opposition by Native Alaskan hunters when it attempted to restrict ATVs to narrow corridors in Gates of the Arctic National Park and Preserve, thereby limiting access to hunting grounds. The Park Service argues that ATVs in use during summer and fall tear up the terrain, leaving permanent scars, unlike snowmobiles which are used only on snow and ice and cause little damage.

Human settlements Other than picturesque fishing villages in northern Scandinavia, southern Greenland, and Iceland, which benefit from warmer ocean currents, cities and towns in the far North are seldom pretty. The treeless lands of the Arctic are difficult to beautify by landscaping. A walk around Barrow, Kotzebue, or Pond Inlet in summer jolts most first-time visitors to Arctic communities.[215]

There is no Frank Lloyd Wright of Arctic architecture. Dwellings that blended into the tundra died out along with the sod underground houses of an earlier era. Construction is costly and seldom well-suited to the environment. Some suburban style houses perch on plots a fraction of the size of a suburban lot in the temperate regions, and poorly insulated 'matchbox' houses remain tucked between newer apartment complexes equally ill-adapted to the terrain or lifestyle. There are no laws banning disposable bottles and few, if any, zoning ordinances addressing aesthetics. It is impossible to conceal garbage on the tundra, and it cannot be buried in permafrost. One Native northern environmentalist commented, 'The ugliness is a blessing in disguise. It reminds us of the fragility of the Arctic'.[216]

Water supplies and waste disposal systems are costly. Many small communities have no sewage disposal system. In large communities, older sections may not be connected to sewer and water systems, and many residents (in the Alaskan Arctic) cannot afford connections to systems that do exist. Recycled oil drums and other containers of frozen human waste pile up throughout the winter until they can be dumped into the bays. Before the days of pop bottles, tin cans, and plastic packaging, litter was less of a problem. Modern day middens in the Arctic remain a monument to technology's failure to deal with cold climates. Ground water is limited in permafrost areas, and pure water may need to be piped or ice blocks cut and sledged from miles away. Cities in the Soviet North find some waters in the northward flowing rivers too polluted by southern sources to be used for drinking supplies.

Larger cities in the North, such as Yakutsk or Fairbanks, and industrial centers, like Noril'sk and Magadan, create their own microclimates which are warmer than the surrounding wilderness. Soviet biologists have suggested planting broadleaf trees in northern cities to absorb air pollutants and provide greenbelts.[217] When temperatures are below about −35 degrees centigrade, an unpleasant and unhealthy ice fog settles on Fairbanks and, presumably, other towns and industrial centers in the Arctic that are sheltered from wind. Finally, human occupation is frequently accompanied by fires that have converted spongy tundra plains into lifeless swamps.

Tourism is no picnic Tourists attracted to the Arctic often come to see polar bears more than people, to visit wild places and photograph seal rookeries, icebergs, whales, and bird cliffs. They come to climb glaciers and hike where they hope other humans will not have left a mark. Some arrive to hunt polar bears, caribou, or musk oxen or to fish for salmon and Arctic char. In short, they travel to the most remote and untouched places where their activities, however limited, may disturb wildlife as they cruise beneath bird cliffs or surround confused polar bears in their rubber motor boats. Tourism in the Arctic is still limited. The tour ships and hikers usually are careful not to disturb wildlife or leave trash behind. As tourism increases, however, the environmentally sensitive may be joined by hordes of less cautious pleasure and adventure seekers. Frequently, tourists cause disturbance by their mode of arrival and departure.

Military activities While radical groups call for a nuclear-free Arctic, more realistic environmentalists seek to identify ecologically sensitive areas where military activities should be excluded. Native communities demand efforts to clean up abandoned military sites and equipment and oppose plans to establish a NATO Tactical Fighter and Weapons Training Center at Goose Bay, Labrador, multiplying low-level overflights by jet fighters which already disturb Arctic wildlife. Plans to upgrade forward operating bases in Canada's North for the use of AWACs and jet fighters, the conduct of missile tests, and increasing submarine activity in the Arctic pose added threats. Accidental submarine sinkings could be hazardous to navigation and marine ecosystems. Four mishaps in recent years highlight these threats. On December 28, 1984, a Soviet cruise missile being used for target practice during naval exercises in the Barents Sea strayed across Norway and crashed in Finland, and in August 1986, a Soviet missile fired from a Delta 2 submarine in the Barents Sea misfired, landing in northeastern China more than 1,500 miles off course of its target, which was a testing range on the Kamchatka Peninsula in Siberia. In February 1986, an American cruise missile dropped into the Beaufort Sea offshore from Tuktoyaktuk.[218] And the Soviet satellite *Cosmos* 954 spread thousands of radioactive fragments over the Canadian North in 1978 when it re-entered the atmosphere.[219] Environmental activists seek more information about unmanned nuclear plants possibly under construction to power the North Warning Systems, a chain of radar stations running across Alaska and Canada. Military activities are a source of enormous skepticism throughout the Arctic as little environmental information is made available to the public and a pattern of government 'misinformation' has muddled answers to legitimate concerns.

5.4   Wildlife protection

The killing of wildlife engenders many of the hottest controversies in the Arctic. Deliberate killing or harvesting for subsistence, recreational, commercial, and scientific uses triggers conflicts within individual user groups and among different user groups as well as between consumptive users and those opposed to killing wildlife for moral, ethical, or biological reasons. Indirect or incidental killing pits wildlife users and those concerned for the welfare of wildlife against the industries and individuals responsible. In this section, we present a few representative cases to illustrate the range of conflicts over wildlife killing.

Harvest conflicts among wildlife users There are many ways to cut a pie, and when stocks of wildlife are insufficient to satisfy the demand of all the users, wildlife managers must contrive systems of allocation to prevent depletion of the resource. When a first come, first served system of commercial fishing allocation theatened to deplete fish stocks, for instance, the State of Alaska instituted a limited entry system for commercial fishing, allowing only those fishers holding permits to fish particular stocks at specific times. The system is not flawless and has sparked new controversies, especially over the effects of limited entry on rural communities dependent on local fisheries. (These controversies are discussed further in Chapter 7.) Sport hunting versus subsistence hunting constitutes the classic case of conflict between user groups. Subsistence hunters resent the imposition of bag limits, closed seasons, gear restrictions, and hunter tags, devices originally designed to regulate sport hunters.[220] Sport hunters seek to open more National Park areas in Alaska, now restricted only to subsistence hunting.

A conflict between users of wild and domesticated or semi-domesticated reindeer is unique to the Soviet North.[221] As the wild herd in the Taimyr grew, competition for limited pastureland, shared by wild and domesticated reindeer, increased. Experts in reindeer husbandry blame the wild herd for damage to grazing areas, introduction of disease, and withdrawal of the domestic herds from feeding grounds during large-scale migration of the wild herds. Most of the 26 northern tribes in the U.S.S.R. engage in reindeer husbandry, hunt wild reindeer, or both. Therefore, reducing the size of a wild reindeer herd may help those engaged in reindeer husbandry but hurt those whose livelihood and culture depend on hunting wild reindeer.

Harvest conflicts between wildlife users and non-users

'A lady in Paris says we should be vegetarians.'
Greenlandic hunter in Thule

Conflicts over consumptive use of wild animals between users on the one hand and preservationists, environmentalists, or conservationists on the other focus on three concerns: (1) biological arguments regarding the viability of stocks or species and the causes of population declines, (2) humane treatment arguments, and (3) ethical or moral arguments regarding the right of humans to kill wild animals.

Environmentalists and conservationists argue for limits on consumptive use for biological reasons, such as the need to protect endangered species or the desire to achieve maximum sustainable yield. Thus, a number of Arctic wildlife controversies center on questions concerning population sizes and causes of decline. For example, there are controversies over whether Alaska Native subsistence hunters shoot too many female bears with cubs and whether Norwegian whalers harvest too many minke whales in the northeastern Atlantic. Counting wildlife populations, especially in the case of marine species, however, is no simple matter. In 1977, the International Whaling Commission banned bowhead whale hunting in response to reports that the western Arctic stock might contain no more than 600 whales, a figure Inupiat whalers contested. After extensive research, biologists concluded that their earlier numbers were wrong. Scientists now believe the population numbers over 4,000.[222]

Some animal protection advocates seek to ensure that hunters and trappers use the most humane method of killing possible. But the line between advocates of humane treatment and opponents of all consumptive use blurs as we study animal protection controversies in the Arctic. Organized opposition to the baby harp seal harvest began in the mid-1950s with complaints by the New Brunswick S.P.C.A. regarding the methods of harvesting and the cruelty involved in killing the immature whitecoats while their mothers watched. Some animal rights advocates launched similar charges of cruelty at the conduct of the northern fur seal harvest on the Pribilof Islands. The anti-fur trapping campaign at first focused on opposition to use of the leg hold trap. But studies finding the prevalent methods of killing (such as clubbing the seal on its thin skull) to be the quickest and most humane, and even changes in harvest methods fail to quell the opposition.

Conflicts between consumptive users and animal protection organizations cannot be solved by biologists, better data, or more humane methods of harvest. Fundamentally, these are core value conflicts. Part of the Greenpeace philosophy states, 'As we feel for ourselves, we must feel for all forms of life – the whales, the seals, the forests, the seas'. Killing wild animals is unacceptable to many animal rights advocates. Some leaders of this movement do not believe that special exceptions should be made even for Native subsistence hunters. The fundraising brochures and advertisements of many animal protection organizations omit key facts about population levels and causes for population declines. The bottom line for the anti-harvest movement is total opposition to consumptive use of wild animals.[223]

Consumptive user groups such as the Canadian Sealers Association (CSA) and the Aboriginal Trappers Federation of Canada (ATFC) have been joined by a newly formed organization called Indigenous Survival International in efforts to counter the effects of the anti-harvesting campaign in the Far North. Environmental and conservation groups, such as the World Wildlife Fund (WWF), have moved to distance themselves from the preservationist groups, if not actively to support the Native hunters. One conservation group, the Canadian Arctic Resources Committee (CARC) based in Ottawa, actively joined Native efforts to counter the preservationists. The larger American conservation and environmental groups have usually steered clear of animal protection controversies in the Arctic.

Incidental kills Environmentalists are only beginning to direct attention to indirect or unintentional killing of fish and wildlife in the Arctic although fisheries enforcement officers have wrestled with the 'incidental catch' of prohibited fish and marine mammal species for years. Commercial fishers can employ a variety of precautions to avoid catching larger quantities of a particular species than quotas permit. Nevertheless, compliance with fishing regulations is not perfect, and enforcement of conservation measures is sporadic.

The fishing industry is also implicated in incidental killing of marine mammals and seabirds. For example, trawlers fishing at night too close to sea lion rookeries have trapped sea lions in their nets, suffocating several hundred marine mammals in a single catch. Discarded and lost nets and fishing gear kill fish, seabirds, seals, and sea lions. Fishing debris and household plastics attract marine mammals, especially the young, who either eat the objects or become entangled. The entrapped fur seal or sea lion expends extra energy to drag the foreign object, and the plastic netting often cuts through its skin, blubber, and muscle further weakening the animal. Diving seabirds also become victims of litter at sea. Monofilament fishing line used by sport and commercial fishers, which lasts indefinitely after being lost or discarded, entangles crabs near boat harbors and docks. On the coastal beaches, observers find foxes, birds, rabbits, and even reindeer decorated with discarded objects.

Some scientists believe debris is at the root of recent declines (4–8 % per year) in the northern fur seal population. They note that increased mortality of young fur seals coincided with a rise in observed entanglement and was followed five or six years later by a decline in the number of pups born. Biologists are far from reaching consensus on the reasons for this striking decline of northern fur seals on the Pribilof Islands. Some animal preservationists blamed the annual commercial harvest of young male fur seals on St Paul Island for the decline. But the population of fur seals on neighbouring St George Island, where there has been no commercial harvest since 1972, is declining at the same rate, and fully protected sea lion populations have suffered similar rates of decline. Recent studies, moreover, indicate that large-scale declines in the biomass of the Bering Sea have reduced food supplies available to support fur seals as well as fish and other species and may, therefore, be a significant factor in declining fur seal populations.[224]

5.5   Conclusion

The myth of a pristine wilderness in the Arctic is rapidly vanishing as environmental interest groups focus attention on increasing pollution, habitat disturbance, and destruction of wildlife in the Far North. These groups are no more homogeneous than are the industrial, military, and Native interests active in the region. Their causes vary dramatically. Some abhor killing wild animals, others seek to protect wildlife in order to ensure the availability of 'country food' for human consumption. Some seek total preservation of wilderness, others accept creative compromise to enable industrial and military development to coexist in a manner least destructive to Arctic ecosystems. This review of the philosophical underpinnings of groups engaged in Arctic environmental issues together with a roster of current Arctic environmental issues sets the stage for later chapters in which we explore methods of managing and resolving natural resource conflicts in the Arctic.

Notes to Part 2

1. Pierre Gallois, 'The Kola Peninsula and Its Strategic Importance', *Defense and Diplomacy*, 4 (September 1986), 38–41.
2. See also the essays in R. B. Byers & Michael Slack, eds., *Strategy and the Arctic*, Toronto: Canadian Institute of Strategic Studies, 1986 and Claude Basset, ed., *L'Arctique: Espace Stratégique Vital Pour Les Grandes Puissances*, Quebec City: Centre quebecois de relations internationales, 1986.
3. On the uncertain future of land-based missiles see Peter Grier, 'Hazy future for US missiles', *Christian Science Monitor*, 16 May 1986, 1, 36.
4. See Charles R. Babcock, 'Soviets Push Sub Detection Research', *The Burlington Free Press*, 28 September 1986, 6A.
5. For a detailed account consult Helge Ole Bergesen, Arild Moe, and Willy Ostreng, *Soviet Oil and Security Interests in the Barents Sea*, London: Pinter, 1987.
6. Note, however, that neither side could count on being able to move submarines between the Arctic and the North Pacific during time of war. Both the United States and the Soviet Union are capable of mining the narrow and relatively shallow Bering Strait effectively.
7. Fourth Report of The Standing Committee on External Affairs and National Defense, Parliament of Canada, February 14, 1986, at page 47.
8. This is not to say that air defense designed to counter manned bombers carrying cruise missiles is impossible. There is already talk in some American circles, for example, of an Air Defense Initiative (ADI) to complement SDI.
9. See also David G. Haglund, 'Soviet Air-Launched Cruise Missiles and the Geopolitics of North American Air Defense: The Canadian North in Changing Perspective', Centre for International Relations Occasional Paper no. 16, Queen's University, April 1987.
10. Military planners are likely to be attracted to the option of using a number of northern air routes simultaneously in this connection. In general, however, the geography of the Arctic Basin is favorable to the operation of manned bombers carrying ALCMs.
11. There is some indication that the location of the magnetic pole may cause greater problems for western OTH-B radar systems operating in the North American Arctic than for comparable Soviet systems operating in the Soviet Arctic.
12. W. Harriet Critchley, 'Polar deployment of Soviet submarines', *International Journal*, vol. xxxix, 1984. 857.

13. Peter Grier, '"Silent service" eyes deadlier attack sub', *Christian Science Monitor*, 9 July 1986, 3, 6.
14. Standing Committee on External Affairs and National Defense, *op. cit.*, at page 52.
15. Ron Purver, 'Security and arms control at the poles', *International Journal*, xxxix, 1984, 897.
16. One well-informed observer writes that 'Aside from the Strategic Defense Initiative, which is thus far only in its chrysalis stage, the maritime strategy represents *the* major change made in United States war planning by the Reagan Administration' (Jack Beatty, 'In Harm's Way', *The Atlantic Monthly*, May 1987, 37.
17. James D. Watkins, 'The Maritime Strategy', in *The Maritime Strategy*, Supplement to the U.S. Naval Institute *Proceedings*, January 1986.
18. The strategic merit of the maritime strategy is a subject of considerable controversy. For a vigorous criticism see John J. Mearsheimer, 'A Strategic Misstep', *International Security*, 11 (Fall 1986). A spirited defense of the maritime strategy appears in Bradford Dismukes, 'Strategic ASW and the Conventional Defense of Europe', Center for Naval Analyses Working Paper, 17 December 1986.
19. G. Leonard Johnson, David Bradley & Robert S. Winokur, 'United States Security Interests in the Arctic', in William E. Westermeyer & Kurt M. Shusterich, eds., *United States Arctic Interests: The 1980s and 1990s*, New York: Springer-Verlag, 1984, 289.
20. See Eugene J. Carroll Jr., 'The 131st bomber won't be the most popular aircraft', *Christian Science Monitor*, 5 June 1986, 20.
21. See Michael R. Gordon, 'Non-nuclear War Might Start Raids on Soviet Arms', *New York Times*, 7 January 1986, A1, A14.
22. For a good discussion of current Soviet military doctrine see Michael McGwire, 'Soviet Military Objectives', *World Policy Journal*, Vol. III, 1986, 667–95.
23. For an illustrated history see Stan Cohen, *The Forgotten War*, Missoula: Pictorial Histories Publishing Company, 1981.
24. While Finland and Sweden are also Arctic states, they are neutral countries that do not have any alliance ties with the United States.
25. Because the modernization of the BMEWS site at Thule involves the replacement of an earlier generation of radars with large phased-array systems, some observers regard this development as incompatible with the Anti-Ballistic Missile Treaty of 1972. See Peter Grier, 'Updating radars violates treaty', *Christian Science Monitor*, 3 September 1986, 3.
26. Specifically, Canada did not insist on the reinstatement of a clause prohibiting any steps that would violate the Anti-Ballistic Missile Treaty of 1972. See Christopher S. Wren, 'Canada to Renew Air Defense Pact', *The New York Times*, 19 March 1986, A7.
27. In January 1988, Canada and the United States signed an agreement on Arctic cooperation under which the United States undertakes to seek Canadian consent before sending American icebreakers (but not other vessels) through the Northwest Passage, while the two countries agree to disagree regarding Canadian claims to the waters of the Arctic archipelago as internal waters of Canada.
28. John Kirton, 'Beyond Bilateralism: United States-Canadian Cooperation in the Arctic', in Westermeyer & Shusterich, eds., *op. cit.*, 296.
29. Christopher S. Wren, 'Weinberger Remark Adds Fuel to Canada Debate', *The New York Times*, 19 March 1985, A12.

30. See Douglas Ross, 'Canada, the Arctic, and SDI', a paper presented at the Conference on Sovereignty, Security, and the Arctic, Toronto, 8–9 May 1986.

31. Department of National Defense, *Challenge and Commitment*, Canadian White Paper on Defense, Ottawa: Government of Canada, June 1987.

32. Nils Orvik, 'Greenland: the politics of a new northern nation', *International Journal*, Vol. xxxix, 1984, 959–60.

33. For some interesting Canadian observations on the militarization of the Arctic consult the essays in the Fall 1986 edition of *Information North*, a quarterly newsletter published by the Arctic Institute of North America in Calgary.

34. Kirton, *op. cit.*, 308.

35. The recent Simard-Hockin Report clearly recognizes the need for a coherent northern dimension in Canada's foreign policy. See *Interdependence and Internationalism*, Report of the Special Joint Committee on Canada's International Relations (Ottawa 1986).

36. Franklyn Griffiths, 'A Northern Foreign Policy', *Wellesley Papers* 7, Canadian Institute of International Affairs, 1979.

37. See Paul Buteux, 'The Arctic and the NATO Alliance', paper presented at the Conference on Sovereignty, Security and the Arctic, Toronto, 8–9 May 1986.

38. Kurt M. Shusterich, 'International Jurisdictional Issues in the Arctic Ocean', in Westermeyer & Shusterich, eds., *op. cit.*, 240–67.

39. On 26 August 1983, Canada and Denmark signed an agreement for cooperation relating to the marine environment of Baffin Bay and the Davis Strait. There remains a minor disagreement between the two countries over the status of Hans Island located in the Nares Strait between Greenland and Ellesmere Island. But this is not likely to constitute an obstacle to cooperation on other matters.

40. See Gordon, *op. cit.* This article summarizes the views of Adm. James Watkins, the American chief of naval operations, on the forward maritime strategy.

41. The importance of the Arctic in national security terms is stressed heavily in the U.S. Arctic Research and Policy Act of 1984 (PL 98-373, 98 Stat. 1242).

42. Kevin O'Reilly & Leslie Treseder, 'A Northern Perspective', *Information North*, Fall 1986, 3–4, 8.

43. For a more detailed discussion see Chapter 3 *infra*.

44. In Canada, for example, the Dene Nation and the Inuit Tapirisat of Canada have publicly declared their opposition to the testing and deployment of nuclear weapons in the Far North.

45. For an expression of this concern see George Erasmus, 'Militarization of the North: Cultural Survival Threatened', *Information North*, Fall 1986, 1, 12–13.

46. On this unfortunate episode, see D. K. Jones, *A Century of Servitude: Pribilof Aleuts under U.S. Rule*, Washington: University Press of America, 1980.

47. Christopher S. Wren, 'Eskimos View Radar Stations as Blots, Not Blips', *The New York Times*, 17 August 1985, 2.

48. For a detailed account of the bases of opposition to the proposed NATO Tactical Fighter and Weapons Training Centre in Goose Bay see the fact sheets on 'NATO in Nitassinan' that Operation Dismantle and the North Atlantic Peace Organization distribute.

49. For the perspectives of the environmental community on the importance of the Arctic National Wildlife Refuge see the Fall 1986 issue of *Wilderness*, which contains a collection of articles on this topic.

50. Project Chariot was a plan sponsored by the U.S. Atomic Energy Agency to

use a nuclear explosion to excavate a deep-water port in northwest Alaska. Though the Agency ultimately scrapped the plan, it remains a symbol of inappropriate ideas about the use of nuclear energy in the Arctic.

51. Greenpeace International is currently giving serious thought to initiating a project entitled 'Militarization in the Circumpolar Arctic'.

52. For an early vision of the Arctic as a future center of human industry and commerce see Vilhjalmur Stefansson, *The Northward Course of Empire*, New York: Harcourt, Brace, 1922.

53. For an expansive account of Arctic energy development based on this image see 'The Great Arctic Energy Rush', *Business Week*, 24 January 1983, 52–6.

54. For a more general account of energy development in the Soviet Union consult Ed. A. Hewett, *Energy Economics and Foreign Policy in the Soviet Union*, Washington: Brookings, 1984.

55. See John Hannigan, 'Oil and Gas Development in the Soviet North: Exploration, Production, Transportation', paper prepared for the Circumpolar Affairs Division of the Department of Indian Affairs and Northern Development, Ottawa, December 1986.

56. For Bourassa's own blueprint for the future see Robert Bourassa, *Power from the North*, Scarborough: Prentice-Hall, 1985.

57. Plans for such river diversion projects were shelved at the 27th Party Congress meeting in 1986. But ideas along these lines may well reemerge at some future time.

58. Lawson W. Brigham, 'New Developments in Soviet Nuclear Arctic Ships', *Proceedings of the U.S. Naval Institute*, December 1985, 131–3 and Lawson W. Brigham, 'Arctic Icebreakers – U.S., Canadian, Soviet', *Oceanus*, 29 (1986), 47–58.

59. Lee Dye, 'Visionary Sees Network of Highways Across Arctic Cap', *Burlington Free Press*, 14 September 1986, 10A.

60. For extensive accounts of Native interests and environmental interests in the Arctic see Chapters 4 and 5 *infra*.

61. Gulf Canada, for example, has been hesitant to initiate full-scale production in the Canadian Beaufort Sea, even though its Amauligak find has proven reserves of 700–800 million barrels. See David R. Francis, 'Canadian oil plans shelved by price fall', *Christian Science Monitor*, 29 August 1986, 19–20.

62. Douglas Martin, 'Distress Signs in the Yukon', *New York Times*, 7 January 1983, D1 and D4.

63. Philip Shabecoff, 'Alaskan Wildlife Refuge is Eyed by Oil Industry', *New York Times*, 1 August 1986, A6.

64. Jim Erickson, 'Oil price slump puts brakes on Alaskan economy', *Christian Science Monitor*, 1 August 1986, 3 and 5.

65. 'Canadian Arctic production prospects brighten', *Oil and Gas Journal*, 5 August 1985, 57–60.

66. For a general account of Soviet Siberian development consult Theodore Shabad and Victor L. Mote, *Gateway to Siberian Resources*, New York: John Wiley, 1977, esp. Ch. 1.

67. Clara Germani, 'Businesses say it's US, not Japan, that limits West Coast exports', *Christian Science Monitor*, 30 April 1985, 7.

68. Victor L. Mote, 'Environmental Constraints to the Economic Development of Siberia', in Robert G. Jensen, Theodore Shabad, & Arthur W. Wright, eds., *Soviet Natural Resources in the World Economy*, Chicago: University of Chicago Press, 1983, 15–16.

69. W. R. Mead, *The Scandinavian Northlands*, London: Oxford University Press, 1974, 20.

70. For a particularly influential account of the concept of internal colonialism consult Michael Hechter, *Internal Colonialism*, Berkeley: University of California Press, 1975.

71. Arvin D. Jellis, 'The Loss of Economic Rents', in Mel Watkins, ed., *Dene Nation: The Colony Within*, Toronto: University of Toronto Press, 1977, 67–8.

72. Northern communities may also benefit indirectly through various programs involving transfer payments mounted by federal, state or provincial governments. The issues raised by such programs are discussed below.

73. Arlon R. Tussing, 'Alaska's Petroleum-Based Economy', in Thomas A. Morehouse, ed., *Alaskan Resources Development: Issues of the 1980s*, Boulder: Westview Press, 1984, 51–78.

74. For an account of the experience of the North Slope Borough consult Gerald A. McBeath, *North Slope Borough Government and Policymaking*, Man in the Arctic Program Monograph No. 3, Anchorage: Institute of Social and Economic Research, 1981.

75. The block grant currently amounts to about two billion Danish kroner a year (approximately $250 million) or something like half the budget of the Home Rule government. See also Philip Lauritzen, *Oil and Amulets*, St. John's: Breakwater Books, 1983, 220–32 and Jens Dahl, 'Greenland: Political Structure and Self-Government', *Arctic Anthropology*, 23 (1986), 315–24.

76. Careful design may make it possible to mitigate this negative feature of transfer payments. For an interesting example see I. LaRusic, *Income Security for Subsistence Hunters: A Review of the First Five Years of Operation of the Income Security Programme for Cree Hunters and Trappers*, Ottawa: DIAND, 1982.

77. For a sophisticated account of Greenlandic politics see Nils Orvik, 'Greenland: the politics of a new northern nation', *International Journal*, xxxix (1984), 932–61.

78. In 1985, the per capita income in Alaska was $18,187. This compares with a per capita income of $13,867 for the United States as a whole. See *Alaska Economic Trends*, Juneau: Alaska Department of Labor, November 1986.

79. Tussing, *op. cit.*

80. 'Alaska Faces $900 Million Revenue Shortage', *New York Times*, 13 March 1986, A14.

81. The state government has authority over inshore fisheries and oil and gas development (that is, activities occurring within three miles of the baselines used to measure the inner boundary of the territorial sea).

82. James Fallows, 'Alaska: Nigeria of the North', *The Atlantic*, 254 (August 1984), 18–22.

83. Germani, *op. cit.*

84. Tussing, *op. cit.*, 53.

85. David R. Francis, 'How Ottawa perked up energy', *Christian Science Monitor*, 15 January 1986, 19–20.

86. *Loc. cit.*

87. 'Canada Backs Dome Merger', *New York Times*, 22 December 1987, D4.

88. Matthew L. Wald, 'Canadian Power Will Lower Northeast's Bills', *New York Times*, 14 September 1984, A1 and B2.

89. T. C. Pullen, 'Arctic Outlet', An Address to the Canada-Japan Trade Council, Ottawa, 25 March 1981.

90. Robert G. Jensen, Theodore Shabad & Arthur W. Wright, 'The Implications of Soviet Raw Materials for the World Economy', in Jensen, Shabad & Wright, eds., *op. cit.*, 679.

91. A consideration that may affect these percentages somewhat is the recent

decision of the Norwegian government to develop the natural gas of the Troll and Sleipner fields for export to Western Europe. See John Tagliabue, 'West Europe to Buy Norway Gas, Cutting Reliance on Soviet Supply', *New York Times*, 3 June 1986, 1 and D4.

92. See Helge Ole Bergesen, Arild Moe & Willy Ostreng, *Soviet Oil and Security Interests in the Barents Sea*, New York: St. Martin's Press, 1987, especially Ch. 2.
93. Allen S. Whiting, *Siberian Development and East Asia: Threat or Promise?* Stanford: Stanford University Press, 1981, 134–45.
94. *Ibid.*, 137.
95. *Ibid.*, 213.
96. See also John Kirton, 'Beyond Bilateralism: United States-Canadian Cooperation in the Arctic', in William E. Westermeyer & Kurt M. Shusterich, eds., *United States Arctic Interests: The 1980s and 1990s*, New York: Springer-Verlag, 1984, 295–318.
97. The phrase 'a country in reserve' comes from Boris Komarov (Zeev Wilson), *The Destruction of Nature in the Soviet Union*, White Plains: M. E. Sharpe, 1980.
98. Terence Armstrong, 'Soviet Northern Development, With Some Alaskan Parallels and Contrasts', ISEGR Occasional Paper No. 2, Fairbanks: University of Alaska, 1970, 4.
99. Terence Armstrong, 'The "Shift Method" in the Arctic', *Polar Record*, 18 (1976), 279–81.
100. For an interesting account of an effort to overcome these problems in connection with an income security program for Cree hunters and trappers see LaRusic, *op. cit.* And for a more general (and quite optimistic) analysis of recent developments among the Cree consult Richard F. Salisbury, *A Homeland for the Cree*, Kingston and Montreal: McGill-Queen's University Press, 1986.
101. Arctic issues arising from these values are discussed at length in Chapters 4 and 5 *infra*.
102. For relevant background consult Tom G. Svensson, 'Industrial Developments and the Sami – Ethnopolitical Response to Ecological Crisis in the North', paper presented to the Canadian Ethnology Society Meeting, Montreal, 1984 and Tom G. Svensson, 'Patterns of Transformation and Local Self-determination: Ethnopower and the Larger Society in the North, The Sámi Case', in Gurston Dacks and Ken Coates, eds., *Northern Communities: Prospects for Empowerment*, Boreal Institute Occasional Publication no. 25, Edmonton, 1988.
103. Thomas R. Berger, *Village Journey: The Report of the Alaska Native Review Commission*, New York: Hill and Wang, 1985, 176.
104. For a discussion of the underlying causes of such pathologies see Oran R. Young, 'The Politics of Pathology', paper presented at the Western Regional Science Association meetings, Napa, California, February 1988.
105. Literally, this means 'land of the Kallalit'. The Kallalit are a subdivision or tribe who entered Greenland about 1,000 A.D. They extend from Cape Farewell in the south to the Upernavik District in the north and are the dominant tribe after which the entire island is named.
106. Census figures from *Greenland in Numbers*, Ministry of Greenland, December 1986.
107. Philip Lauritzen, *Oil and Amulets*, St Johns: Breakwater Books, 1983, 225.
108. In the 1987 elections, a fourth party, backed by the fishermen and hunter's union, the Polar Party, won one seat in the Greenlandic parliament.

109. For a general account of the emerging political party structure of Greenland, see Nils Orvik, 'Greenland: The Politics of a New Northern Nation', *International Journal*, 39 (Autumn 1984), 943–944.

110. For an analysis of the Home Rule Government as well as background on events that led to its formation, see Jens Dahl, 'Greenland: Political Structure of Self-Government', *Arctic Anthropology*, 23 (1986), 315–24.

111. Alaska population figures are from the most recent 1980 census. The statewide population grew by nearly 130,000 between 1980 and 1987 largely due to an influx of non-Natives.

112. *Inupiat Community of the Arctic Slope* v. *Unites States* (*ICAS II*), 548 F. Supp. 182 (D. Ak. 1982), affirmed 746 F. 2d 570 (9th Cir. 1984), cert. denied 106 S.Ct. 68, 88 L.Ed.2d 56 (1985).

113. For an early critique of ANCSA, see Oran R. Young, *Natural Resources and the State*, Berkeley: University of California Press, 1981, chapter 2. For a recent discussion of the problems of ANCSA, see Berger, *op. cit.*

114. The general rule contained in the 1987 Amendments is that alienability restrictions continue until terminated by a majority vote of shareholders, but in no case before 18 December 1991. Shareholders of Native corporations may approve an amendment to allow shares to be recalled and reissued without restrictions by following specified 'opt-out' procedures. In the Bristol Bay and Aleut regions only, the default option may be reversed if the board of directors of a corporation in that region elects, within one year after enactment of the 1987 amendments, to use the alternative 'opt-in' procedures. In that case, alienability restrictions automatically terminate on 18 December 1991 unless extended by a vote of the shareholders. Shareholders may vote to continue restrictions on the sale of stock indefinitely or for a specified period (of 1 to 50 years). In no case is a vote to extend restrictions on sale of Native corporation stock irreversible. Under either opt-in or opt-out procedures, shareholders may, at some future time, reconsider the issue. Once restrictions are terminated, that action is conclusive. A third option, called the 'recapitalization' alternative, allows Native corporations to maintain alienability restrictions on their original stock, but sell additional unrestricted shares. Pub. L. 100–241 (enacted 3 February 1988), section 8, ANCSA section 37.

115. Pub. L. 100–241, section 11.

116. Pub. L. 100–241, section 4.

117. Previously, tribal government interests were promoted by United Tribes of Alaska, an organization that disbanded in the wake of serious financial and managerial problems.

118. These are the purposes of ANC as stated in the organization's first newsletter, *Village Government*, 1 (Anchorage: September 1986), 3.

119. Figures for Canada are based on the 1986 census. For the NWT, census figures were adjusted by the GNWT Bureau of Statistics. Because of the way population data are collected in Canada, it is impossible to be precise.

119a. Indian Register of population by sex and residence, Dept. of Indian Affairs and Northern Development, 1987.

120. *Calder et al.* v. *Attorney General of British Columbia*, SCR 313 (SCC 1973); affirming (on technical grounds) 13 DLR (3d) 64 (BCCA 1971); which affirmed 8 DLR (3d) 59 (BCSC 1969).

121. Task Force to Review Comprehensive Claims Policy, *Living Treaties: Lasting Agreements*, Ottawa: Department of Indian Affairs and Northern Development, 1985.

122. *The Western Arctic Claim: The Inuvialuit Final Agreement,* Ottawa: Department of Indian Affairs and Northern Development, 1985.

123. For a description of COPE and of the Kewaitin Inuit Association (KIA), see Lauritzen, *op. cit.,* 70, 122.

124. Soviet scholars include some additional ethnic groups among the northern peoples and divide the Near North from the Far North. Areas with an Arctic environment and permafrost extend well south of 60 degrees in Eastern Siberia, and some of the groups we list here also have populations south of what we would consider Arctic.

125. Many books in English translate this term poorly as 'small peoples' or 'lesser nationalities', translations with unfortunate connotations in English. For a wealth of information on indigenous Siberian peoples, consult M. G. Levin & L. P. Potapov, eds., *The Peoples of Siberia,* Chicago and London: University of Chicago Press, 1964.

126. See O. Igho Natufe, 'The Concept of Native Self-Government in the Soviet North', draft paper prepared for Department of Indian and Northern Affairs, Ottawa, (October 1979), 25.

127. Fyodor Abramov provides a lucid account of how central authorities dominated northern rural communities after the Second World War in his novel *Two Winters and Three Summers,* Ann Arbor, Michigan: Ardis, 1984, which tracks the lives of a family in a non-Native *kolkhoz* near Arkangel.

128. I. E. Bogdanov, 'Revewable Resources of North-East Siberia', Milton M. R. Freeman, ed., *Renewable Resources and the Economy of the North,* Ottawa: Association of Canadian Universities in Northern Studies, 1981, 133–7.

129. Gail A. Fondahl, 'Native Peoples of the Soviet North', *Northern Raven,* 5 (Summer 1985), 2.

130. Population counts range from 40,000 to 70,000 depending on the definition used and the method of counting.

131. See Eino Siuruainen and Pekka Aikio, *The Lapps in Finland,* Helsinki: Society for the Promotion of Lapp Culture, Series no. 39, 1977, 27, Table 3.

132. In 1584 and 1602, the Swedish crown issued 'letters of assurance' and 'protection' of Sami rights which are now the basis of Sami claims to 'aboriginal lands and rights' in Sweden and Finland. The crown levied 'Lapp taxes' between 1695 and 1924 and assured some protection from settlers until the 19th century when administrative control passed to the provinces. For a period, local courts (harad courts) with Sami magistrates decided conflicts between Swedish farmers and Lapp tax farmers. However, as colonization spread, provincial administrative authorities opposed the use of these local courts to decide financial matters between Sami and settlers. Administrative officials granted land owned by the Sami to settlers. Eventually, both the Sami magistrates and the tax lands disappeared. Prior exclusive Sami privileges to hunt, fish, and herd reindeer passed by transfer or inheritance to non-Sami. Today, Sami are attempting to reestablish their aboriginal right to land based on legal decrees (such as the codicil of 1751) and rights predating transfer of power to provincial authorities. Thus far, their efforts have been unsuccessful.

133. Contact with missionaries and settlers had begun by 1200 A.D. Although the Lutheran Church dominated religious life in Samiland, Greek Orthodox and Roman Catholic missionaries brought Christianity to some communities.

134. For maps of Finland's changing boundaries and maps comparing Sami-inhabited areas at 0 A.D. and today, see Nils-Aslak Valkeapaa, *Greetings from Lappland: the Sami – Europe's Forgotten People,* London: Zed Press, 1978, 30–1.

135. See Ludger Muller-Wille, 'The "Lappish Movement" and "Lappish Affairs"

in Finland and Their Relations to Nordic and International Ethnic Politics',
Arctic and Alpine Research, 9 (August 1977), 241.

136. See generally Tom G. Svensson, *Ethnicity and Mobilization in Sami Politics*,
Stockholm: University of Stockholm, 1976, 130–1. For discussion of the
creation and activities of the *Sami Institut'ta* see Muller-Wille, *op. cit.*, 1977,
242–3 and Israel Ruong, 'The Lapps: An Indigenous People in Fennoscandia',
draft paper, Ottawa: DIAND, October 1979, 99–104.

137. See Tom G. Svensson, 'The Sami and the Nation State: Some Comments on
Ethnopolitics in the Northern Fourth World', *Etudes Inuit Studies*, 8 (1984),
158–66.

138. Valkeapaa, *op. cit.*, 57, 58.

139. Among Kativik's first 30 teachers in training, by 1986 eleven had become
teachers, one a principal, several were researchers, some were administrators
and counselors. Interview with Doris Winkler, Kativik administrator,
November 1986.

140. Poul Thoe Nielsen, 'An Appraisal of National Languages among the North
Siberian Peoples', *Folk*, 14–15 (1972–1973), 223, 205–53. For a detailed
discussion of Soviet schooling in Native languages, see pages 229–46.

141. Natufe, *op. cit.*, 29, 30.

142. The greatest activity in promoting Native language education in Alaska has
occurred in the Yupik and Chupik speaking region.

143. Inupiaq University in Barrow operated in the 1970s, but is now defunct. In
1986, the North Slope Borough Higher Education Center opened in Barrow.
Although affiliated with the University of Alaska, it is controlled by a Board of
Directors with representatives from each community in the North Slope
Borough. Classes are held throughout the Borough.

144. For elaboration of this point see Barry Holstun Lopez, *Of Wolves and Men*,
New York: Scribner's 1978, 77–134, and the essays in Milton M. R. Freeman
and Ludwig N. Carbyn, eds., *Traditional Knowledge and Renewable Resource
Management in Northern Regions*, Edmonton: Boreal Institute for Northern
Studies, 1988.

145. For a brief account of this discovery see 'The Frozen Family of Utkiavik
Village', *The Arctic Policy Review* (April 1983), 7–10.

146. The term 'subsistence' as used by anthropologists studying northern
indigenous cultures and as we use it here differs substantially from the legal
definition of 'subsistence uses' in the Alaska National Interest Lands
Conservation Act, 16 U.S.C. section 3113, as well as in Alaska State law,
which includes non-Native as well as Native hunting, fishing, and trapping
activities that meet specific criteria.

147. V. D. Sapronov, 'Whaling and Nutritional Needs of the Aboriginal Population
of the Chukotka Peninsula', *Arctic Policy Review*, 3 (January 1985), 5.

148. *Tlingit and Haida Indians of Alaska* v. *U.S.*, 177 F. Supp. 452 (Ct. Cls. 1959)
and *Tlingit and Haida Indians of Alaska* v. *U.S.*, 389 F. 2d 778 (Ct. Cls. 1968).

149. JBNQA, *op. cit.*, section 24.5.

150. Terry Fenge, TFN, interview (15 Sept. 1988).

151. For a description and an analysis of the Taxed Mountains Case, see Tom G.
Svensson, 'Industrial Developments and the Sami – Ethnopolitical Response to
Ecological Crisis in the North', paper presented to the Canadian Ethnology
Society meetings, Montreal, 1984, and Svensson, 'The Sami and the Nation
State', *op. cit.* (1984).

152. The legal basis and the exact nature of Greenlandic territorial rights are a
subject of continual debate. See Jens Brosted 'Territorial rights in Greenland:
Some Preliminary Notes', *Arctic Anthropology* 23 (1986), 325–38.

153. For an argument that Native village corporation lands constitute Indian country within which tribal councils in Alaska may exercise jurisdiction over hunting and fishing see Heather Noble, 'Tribal Powers to Regulate Hunting in Alaska', *Alaska Law Review*, 4 (Fall 1987), 223, 246–56.

154. 18 U.S.C. section 1151 (1982).

155. ANCSA, section 39, added by Pub. L. 100–241, section 10.

156. For a discussion of the problem of dual systems of wildlife management (state systems and indigenous systems) operating in the Arctic, see Peter Usher, *The Devolution of Wildlife Management and the Prospects for Wildlife Conservation in the Northwest Territories*, Ottawa: Canadian Arctic Resources Committee (CARC), Policy Paper No. 3, July 1986 and Gail Osherenko, *Sharing Power with Native Users: Co-management Regimes for Arctic Wildlife*, Ottawa: CARC, Policy Paper No. 5, (February 1988).

157. Berger, *op. cit.*, 171.

158. For case studies of three of these co-management regimes, see Osherenko, 'Sharing Power with Native Users', *op. cit.*, and Osherenko, 'Can Comanagement Save Arctic Wildlife', *Environment* 30 (July/August 1988), pp. 6–13, 29–34.

159. The text of the Dene Declaration is printed in an appendix in Michael Asch, *Home and Native Land*, Toronto: Methuen, 1984.

160. See Maureen Davies, 'Aspects of Aboriginal Rights in International Law' and 'Aboriginal Rights in International Law: Human Rights', Bradford W. Morse, ed., *Aboriginal Peoples and the Law: Indian, Metis and Inuit Rights in Canada*, Ottawa: Carlton University Press, 1985, 16–47, 745–94, and Vine Deloria, Jr. and Clifford M. Lytle, *The Nations Within: The Past and Future of American Indian Sovereignty*, New York: Pantheon Books, 1984, 241, 242.

161. For a discussion of the role of international NGOs, see Margaret L. Clark & John S. Dryzek, 'The Inuit Circumpolar Conference as an International Nongovernmental Actor', Marianne Stenbaek, ed., *Arctic Policy: Papers presented at the Arctic Policy Conference, September 19–21, 1985*, Montreal: Centre for Northern Studies and Research, McGill University, 1986. This volume also contains papers by Inuit leaders and academic scholars relevant to the role of the ICC in shaping Arctic policy.

162. Berger, *op. cit.*, 28.

163. Haida Corp. emerged from bankruptcy in July 1988 with substantial assets after fully repaying its creditors. The corporation survived due to unique circumstances involving sale of its net operating losses and a congressionally approved land exchange. The Haida Land Exchange Act of 1986, Pub. L. 99–664, 100 Stat. 4808.

164. Jean-Pierre Rostaing, 'Native Regional Autonomy: The Initial Experience of the Kativik Regional Government', *Etude/Inuit/Studies*, 8 (1985), 3–40.

165. Pub. L. 100–241, section 2(8). Senator Stevens of Alaska, in his remarks on the floor of the Senate, stated:

> There is a great deal of controversy in Alaska over the issue of whether Alaska Native organizations may exercise some degree of governmental authority over lands or individuals. The controversy involves several complex questions – which Native groups might qualify as tribal organizations, what powers such organizations might possess, and whether there is Indian country in Alaska over which such organizations might exercise jurisdiction. The '1991' amendments are scrupulously neutral on this controversy.
>
> 100 *Congressional Record* S 18,699 (daily ed. Dec. 21, 1987).

166. For a brief history and description of the Nunavut proposal, see Michael S.

Whittington, 'Political and Constitutional Development in the N.W.T. and Yukon', M. S. Whittington coordinator, *The North*, Toronto: University of Toronto Press, 1985, 95–101. For a discussion of the politics involved in creating Nunavut, see Gordon Robertson, 'Northern Development within Canadian Federalism', *Ibid.*, 123–31.

167. Rice O'Dell, 'Alaska: A Frontier Divided', *Environment*, 28 (September 1986), 11.
168. Margaret Murie, 1956 writing about what is now part of the Arctic National Wildlife Refuge in Alaska, as quoted by Donald Dale Jackson, 'The Floor of Creation', in *Wilderness*, 50 (Fall 1986), 12.
169. Jackson, *ibid.* 19.
170. For a useful reference to understanding Arctic tundra ecosystems, see Yu. I. Chernov, *The Living Tundra*, Cambridge: Cambridge University Press, 1985.
171. The Environmental Risk of the Developing Oil and Gas Industry in Western Siberia', Research Paper No. 52, Jerusalem: The Soviet and East European Research Centre of the Hebrew University, October 1983, 8. Footnotes omitted. Wolfson's pen name before he immigrated to Israel from the U.S.S.R. was Boris Komarov.
172. For early accounts of the drownings see Douglas Martin, 'Thousands of Caribous Die in Quebec Rivers', *New York Times*, 4 October 1984, A1, A4 and 'Quebec Caribou Drownings', *Caribou News* 4 (December 1984), 1, 4.
173. To protect these species, a federal judge ordered restrictions on seismic exploration in the Bering Sea region as a condition of an oil and gas lease sale there. *Village of False Pass* v. *Watt*, 565 F. Supp. 1123 (D. Ak. 1983), reversed on appeal, *Village of False Pass* v. *Clark*, 733 F. 2d 605 (9th Cir. 1984).
174. This was one of the reasons a federal court prohibited the use of St Matthew Island as a supply base for oil exploration in the Navarin Basin west of the island. *National Audubon Society* v. *Hodel*, 606 F. Supp. 825, 843, 844 (D. Ak. 1984).
175. Interview with Dr Gerard M. Courtin, Department of Biology, Laurentian University (Wolcott, Vermont, January 1988). Information from unpublished research. See G. M. Courtin & C. L. Labine, 'High Arctic Microclimatological Data Analysis Study', prepared under contract no. OSU77–00309 for the Canadian Atmospheric Environment Service (April 1978). Dr Courtin's list of thermal oases include the Truelove, Skogen, and Sparbo Lowlands on the north shore of Devon Island, Alexandra Fjord on the east coast of Ellesmere, and the Fosheim Peninsula on the west side of Ellsmere north of Eureka.
176. *Polar Regions Atlas*, Washington, D.C.: Central Intelligence Agency, 1978, 20.
177. For detailed information on Arctic air pollution including Arctic haze see Bernard Stonehouse, ed., *Arctic Air Pollution*, Cambridge: Cambridge University Press, 1986.
178. Barrie Maxwell, 'Atmospheric and Climatic Change in the Canadian Arctic', *Northern Perspectives* 15 (December 1987), 2, 4.
179. For a discussion of the Arctic's role in the global energy balance, see D. James Baker, 'The Arctic's Role in Climate', *Oceanus* 29 (1986), 41–6.
180. See 'The Frozen Family of Utkiavik Village: Archeology Conference Points Up Ivu Danger', *The Arctic Policy Review*, (April 1983), 7–10.
181. *Christian Science Monitor*, 1 February 1985, 6.
182. For background on the rise of the conservation movement see Samuel P. Hays, 'Gifford Pinchot and the Conservation Movement', *The Living Wilderness*, 44 (June 1980), 4–9.
183. Interim Convention on Conservation of North Pacific Fur Seals, 9 February 1957, 8 U.S.T. 2283, T.I.A.S. No. 3948, 314 U.N.T.S. 105.

184. See, for example, the Multiple-Use Sustained-Yield Act of 1960, 16 U.S.C. sections 528–531.
185. Robert W. Clawson and William Kolarik, 'Soviet Resource Management: Political Aspects of Water Pollution Control,' W. A. Douglas Jackson, ed., *Soviet Resource Management and the Environment*, Ohio: Anchor Press 1978, 113–118. See especially note 65.
186. Some of the animal protectionist groups employ tactics that are as radical as their views. In November 1986, the Vancouver based Sea Shepherd Conservation Society sank two of Iceland's four whaling vessels in Reykjavik Harbor and sabotaged the country's only whale oil processing plant. Greenpeace groups also use direct, confrontational acts that grab headlines worldwide, but their actions are strictly non-violent. In 1983, Greenpeace's vessel, the Rainbow Warrior sailed into Soviet territorial waters to film a shore-based whaling operation on the Chukhotka Peninsula which the Soviets claim is limited to subsistence whaling. The Soviets arrested seven Greenpeace members triggering an international incident over their return. Greenpeace, usually perceived as a hardline preservationist group, has been fraught with internal conflicts. Recently, the organization's focus has shifted toward mainstream environmentalism as leaders of Greenpeace Canada seek to mend fences with the indigenous population and identify common causes such as limiting military activities in the Arctic. Nuclear war and peace issues have long occupied a prominent place on Greenpeace's agenda, beginning in 1970 with a voyage to protest American nuclear tests on Amchitka Island in the Aleutian chain.
187. Marine Mammal Protection Act, 16 U.S.C. Section 1361 *et seq.*, as amended.
188. See chapters 3 and 4 *supra.*
189. For a political analysis of the animal rights movements which includes discussion of controversies over northern fur seals, harp seals, bowhead whales, and fur trapping see Oran R. Young, 'The Politics of Animal Rights', paper presented at the Inuit Studies Assoc. meetings, Montreal, November 1986.
190. Canada is also preparing an Arctic Marine Conservation Strategy that will dovetail with the ICC project, as well as with conservation strategies undertaken by the governments of the Northwest Territories and Yukon. See Elizabeth Snider, 'The Arctic Marine Conservation Strategy', *Northern Perspectives* 15 (November 1987), 11.
191. For a discussion of environmental concerns in the Soviet North, see Terrence Armstrong, 'Environmental Control in Remote Areas: The Case of the Soviet Northlands, with an Alaskan Comparison', *Polar Record*, 20 (1981), 329–35.
192. Douglas R. Weiner divides nature protection in the Soviet Union into 3 categories that parallel those used here (preservation, ecology, and conservation schools). He labels them 'cultural-aesthetic-ethical', 'scientific', and 'utilitarian', *Models of Nature: Ecology Conservation and Cultural Revolution in Soviet Russia*', Bloomington, Indiana: Indiana University Press, 1988.
193. For a discussion of Native environmental leaders, see Gail Osherenko, 'Indigenous Peoples in Defense of a Northern Landscape', *Amicus Journal*, 8 (Fall 1986), 32–9.
194. For a summary and excellent bibliography on Arctic haze see Leonard A. Barrie, 'Arctic Air Pollution: An Overview of Current Knowledge', *Atmospheric Environment*, 20 (1986), 643–63.
195. Arctic Haze Fact Sheet, Ottawa: Environment Canada (1984).

196. Since the Arctic is a weather generator for the Northern Hemisphere, the pronounced warming trend occurring in the Arctic has global implications. Scientists have warned that oceans could rise six feet in the next hundred years eroding beaches, destroying coastal communities, flooding parts of Boston and Tokyo, eliminating essential estuarine ecosystems, and disrupting agriculture. For a series of articles on the implications of climate change in the Arctic see *Northern Perspectives*, 15 (December 1987).

197. More questions than answers remain. 'Should we not have considered the possibility of a salt water bay in the Yukon Valley bounded by the peninsulas of the Brooks and Alaska Ranges?' asked one humanist at a 1983 conference on carbon dioxide-induced climatic change in Alaska. Jenifer H. McBeath, *et al.*, eds., *Proceedings*, Fairbanks: University of Alaska, March 1984. Will movement of annual ice away from the shore lure seals and whales further offshore away from traditional hunting areas? Will gray whales and fur seals migrate further north? Which Arctic coastal communities and which walrus and seal rookeries will be inundated?

198. Unfortunately for the Sami, sales of reindeer meat plummeted by up to 80 percent following publicity about the damage although two-thirds of Sweden's reindeer and reindeer lichen were unaffected. For more information on the ecological and sociological effects of the Chernobyl disaster, see Tom G. Svensson, *op. cit.*, 1988.

199. At the time Sweden's legal limit of 300 bequerels per kilogram was considerably more cautious than the European Community's recommended 600 bq. or the United States' limit at 1,500 bq. Sweden raised its legal limit for reindeer meat to 1,500 bq/kg in May 1987.

200. There are few nuclear reactors in the Arctic. Two are located in the U.S.S.R. on the Kola Peninsula, one on the Chukotka Peninsula across the Bering Strait from Alaska.

201. This discussion of the primary and secondary effects of the Chernobyl accident benefited greatly from N. D. Broadbent, 'Chernobyl Radionuclide Contamination and Reindeer Herding in Sweden', *Collegium Anthropologicum*, 10 (1986), 231–42.

202. Thomas F. Albert, North Slope Borough Senior Scientist, Memorandum to Mayor George N. Ahmaogak, 7 December 1987. This memorandum is based on BBN Laboratories, Inc.'s study prepared for the U.S. Minerals Management Service (MMS), 'Prediction of drilling site-specific interaction of industrial stimuli and endangered whales in the Alaskan Beaufort Sea', OCS Study, MMS 87-0084.

203. Peter Rostankowski, 'The Decline of Agriculture and the Rise of Extractive Industry in the Soviet North', *Polar Geography and Geology*, 7 (October–December 1983), 289 at 296. For a harsh critique of the Soviet onshore oil and gas industry in Western Siberia, see Zeev Wolfson, *op. cit.*

204. Lisa Speer (NRDC) and Sue Libenson (Trustees for Alaska), *Oil in the Arctic*, New York: NRDC 1988.

204a. *Comparison of Actual and Predicted Impacts of the Trans-Alaska Pipeline System and Prudhoe Bay Oilfields on the North Slope of Alaska*, Fairbanks: USFWS, December 1988.

205. A. A. Kishchinskii & L. M. Ryabova, 'Nature Conservation in the North: an international problem', *Problems of the North*, No. 18 (1973), 39, translation of 'Problemy Severa' by National Research Council of Canada (1976).

206. See Osherenko (1986), *op. cit.*, 35. A case study of conflicts over a relatively small mining operation, the proposed Kiewit crushed rock quarry, in

conjunction with proposals to construct a port to support offshore
hydrocarbon development in the Beaufort Sea, appears in T. Fenge *et al.*, 'A
Proposed Port on the North Slope of Yukon: the Anatomy of Conflict', in
Barry Sadler, ed., *Environmental Protection and Resource Development:
Convergence for Today*, Calgary: University of Calgary Press, 1985

207. For a brief reference to the Nadezhdinskiy metallurgical works at Noril'sk and
a general discussion of environmental concerns in the Soviet North, see
Terence Armstrong, 'Environmental Control in Remote Areas: The Case of
the Soviet Northlands, with an Alaskan Comparison', *Polar Record*, 20 (1981),
329–35 at 332.

208. S. A. Strelkov & I. L. Friedin, 'Problems of Environmental Protection in the
Kola North', in *Problems of the North, op cit.*, 182.

209. For a general discussion of mercury contamination in connection with
northern hydroelectric power projects, see Robert E. Hecky, 'Methylmercury
Contamination in Northern Canada', *Northern Perspectives*, 15 (October 1987),
5.

210. 'Soviet Drops Diversion of River Flow to South', *New York Times*, 5 March
1986, A13.

211. Robert Bourassa, *Power from the North*, Scarborough, Ontario: Prentice-Hall
Canada, 1985. for a critique of the Grand Canal scheme, see Donald J.
Gamble, 'The GRAND Canal and the National Interest', *Northern
Perspectives*, 15 (October 1987), 2–7.

212. See Philip P. Micklin 'Large-Scale Interbasin River Diversions in the USSR:
Implications for the Future', in W. A. Douglas Jackson, ed., *op. cit.*, Philip P.
Micklin, 'Recent Developments in Large-Scale Water Transfers in the
U.S.S.R.', *Soviet Geography*, xxv (1984), 261–3, and Philip P. Micklin, 'The
Vast Diversion of Soviet Rivers', *Environment*, 27 (March 1985), 12.

213. For a discussion of air traffic in Alaska's national parks and
recommendations for regulation see Roderick Nash, 'Ideal and Reality in
'Ultimate' Wilderness; Aviation and Gates of the Arctic National Park',
Orion Nature Quarterly (Spring 1983), 4.

214. *National Audubon Society* v. *Hodel, op. cit.*, 843–4.

215. For a journalist's first impression of Barrow see Philip Lauritzen, *Oil and
Amulets*, St. Johns: Breakwater Books, 1983, 30–32.

216. Finn Lynge, interview with author, August 1986.

217. Kryuchkov & Shvetsov in *Problems of the North, op. cit.*

218. Accounts of each of these misfirings appear in the *New York Times*: 'Soviet
Cruise Missile Said to Stray Across Norway Into Finland', (3 Jan. 1985), A1,
A10 (follow up stories appeared on January 4 to 6), Richard L. Berke,
'A Soviet Missile Is Said to Misfire and Hit China', (16 Sept. 1986), A1, A8, and
'Cruise Missile Debris Sought', (27 Feb. 1986), A2.

219. Emmanuel Somers, 'Environmental hazards show no respect for national
boundaries', *Environment*, 29 (June 1987), 7, 8.

220. See Pete Schaeffer, Delano Barr & Greg Moore, *Kotzebue Fish and Game
Advisory Committee Regulation Review: A Review of Game Regulations
Affecting Northwest Alaska*, Kotzebue: Fish and Game Advisory Committee,
October 1986, and plaintiff's brief in *Bobby* v. *Alaska*, No. A84–544 (D. Ak.
filed 18 July 1985).

221. Because of comparatively lower numbers of both wild and domesticated
reindeer in Norway, problems of their interrelationship have not arisen. For
detailed information on the problem in the Soviet Union, see E. E.
Syroechkovskii, ed., *Wild Reindeer of the Soviet Union*, Moscow: Sovetskaya

Rossiya Publishers, 1975 (translation by Amerind Publishing Co. Pvt. Ltd., New Delhi, 1984).

222. Mark A. Fraker, *Balaena mysticetus: Whales, oil, and whaling in the Arctic*, Anchorage: SOHIO Alaska Petroleum Company and BP Alaska Exploration Inc., 1984.

223. See Brian Davies, *Savage Luxury: The Slaughter of the Baby Seals*, Toronto: Ryerson Press, 1970 and Robert Hunter, *Warriors of the Rainbow: A Chronical of the Greenpeace Movement*, New York: Rinehart and Winston, 1979. For a critical view of the animal rights movement, see Alan Herscovici, *Second Nature: The Animal-Rights Controversy*, Toronto: CBC Enterprises, 1985.

224. For a brief discussion of the most recent studies, see 'North Pacific Fur Seals – Pribilof Island Population: Designation as Depleted', Washington, D.C.: National Marine Fisheries Service, 52 Fed. Reg. 49450–49456 (31 December 1987).

Part 3
Handling Arctic conflicts

6

Arctic issues, Arctic conflicts

For centuries, the Arctic attracted outsiders, including explorers, missionaries, fur traders, whalers, and scientists, precisely because the region was relatively free of clashing interests or protracted confrontations among well-organized interest groups. While explorers sometimes found themselves locked in desperate struggles against the forces of nature in this vast region, they seldom encountered human opposition in their search for new Arctic lands or sea routes.[1] The region provided ample scope for a remarkable collection of missionary groups to stake out Arctic domains without running afoul of each other's operations. Fur traders and whalers usually succeeded in eliciting cooperative responses from the indigenous inhabitants of the region and generally found the Arctic's natural resources plentiful enough to accommodate them all without serious clashes. Scientists were able to pursue their quest for knowledge in the Arctic unhindered by human barriers or sensitivities regarding the military or industrial applications of the insights they obtained. For their part, public authorities located in far away capitals typically reacted by paying little heed to the activities of these groups and seldom made any concerted effort to resolve overlapping or incompatible jurisdictional claims in the Arctic. Instead, they assumed attitudes of benign neglect toward the region, adopting *laissez faire* Arctic policies that allowed individuals and groups to pursue their interests throughout the Arctic region with little interference and few demands for accountability.[2]

Today, all this has changed. The Arctic has become a locus of extensive human activities as well as a focus of intense interest for a variety of well-organized and influential interest groups. As the preceding chapters show, the principal parties with stakes in the region are not only organizing to pursue their Arctic interests effectively, they are also developing profoundly divergent perspectives on the Arctic. Those concerned with national security have come to regard the Arctic as an attractive theater for military operations involving key elements of strategic forces. Industrial interests as well as policymakers endeavoring to meet the demands of affluent populations in the temperate zones for energy and raw materials see the Far North as a resource frontier available for development in an atmosphere of relative physical security and political certainty. The Arctic region contains many of the most dramatic unspoiled natural environments on the planet together with important populations of marine and terrestrial mammals, a fact that has prompted environmentalists to place top priority on the struggle to protect huge areas of the Far North.[3] At the same time, the indigenous peoples of the Arctic are experiencing a remarkable rise in political consciousness and sophistication, a transformation producing a surging tide of well-directed claims focusing on the rights of these peoples to land, subsistence resources, and self-determination.

It is predictable, therefore, that those with significant stakes in the Arctic will clash repeatedly over an array of specific issues arising in the region. Already, we are witnessing sharp conflicts over issues like the opening of Arctic waters for oil and gas development, the damming of northern rivers to generate hydroelectric power, the consumptive use of wild animals on the part of indigenous peoples, and the designation of large tracts of land in the Arctic as wilderness areas. These clashes will inevitably become more pervasive as the level of human activities in the Arctic continues to rise and the region looms larger and larger in the calculations of numerous articulate and powerful interest groups. Not surprisingly, these developments have begun to stimulate public authorities to abandon their attitudes of benign neglect toward the region in favor of efforts to regulate the activities of diverse groups in the Arctic and to devise procedures for handling contemporary Arctic issues. So far, however, none of the Arctic rim states has succeeded in putting in place sophisticated Arctic policies or working out effective mechanisms to handle Arctic conflicts.

This chapter identifies the principal types of issues now surfacing in the Arctic, analyzes several features of these issues which make them hard to handle, and provides a preliminary account of current efforts to come to terms with the resultant conflicts. In the process, the chapter exposes the limits of conventional responses to conflict as applied to contemporary Arctic issues. In so doing, it documents the need to develop improved capabilities to handle Arctic conflicts. This sets the stage for the chapters to follow. Each of these chapters examines new approaches to Arctic conflicts and suggests ways to enhance our ability to settle these conflicts constructively in the future.

6.1   The landscape of Arctic conflict

Conflict occurs whenever two or more active and autonomous parties (individuals or collective entities like corporations, interest groups, or nation states) whose interests clash in the context of a specific issue must act collectively or in an interdependent manner rather than going their separate ways.[4]

Each element of this definition is important. Conflict is a social phenomenon; it involves relationships between or among parties rather than the behavior of individual parties. Thus, we speak of a conflict between the United States and Canada over the status of the Northwest Passage. Animal rights advocates and Native groups are engaged in a series of conflicts focusing on the killing or consumptive use of wild animals.[5] (See Figure 20.) Oil companies clash repeatedly with environmental groups and Native groups as well as those involved in the fishing industry over the opening of outer continental shelf areas for oil and gas exploration. We do not attribute any of these conflicts to the attitudes or actions of one or another of the interested parties. Rather, we treat each conflict as a facet of the relationship between or among the parties.

Similarly, conflict involves interests that clash in the sense that they cannot be fulfilled simultaneously or that the pursuit of one impedes or interferes with the pursuit of others. Often, we focus on the details of specific issues in describing conflicts. But it is important to bear in mind that it is the clash of interests in the context of these issues that engenders conflict. So, for example, we say that ARCO and the Audubon Society had a conflict over the use of St Matthew Island in the Bering Sea in the early 1980s because ARCO's interest in building a staging facility on the island to support oil and gas exploration in the Navarin Basin clashed with the Audubon Society's interest in maintaining the island as a wilderness area dedicated to the protection of seabirds. The Government of Norway and various Sami groups have engaged in a protracted conflict over the proposed Alta Dam because the interest of the government in increasing the production of hydroelectric power is incompatible with the interest of the Sami in protecting habitat required for reindeer herding. In the same way, the Soviet Union and Norway have a conflict over the status of the outer continental shelf adjacent to the Svalbard Archipelago because the Soviet interest in guaranteed access to the resources of this area clashes with the Norwegian interest in maximizing control over human activities in the area.[6] While the issues involved in Arctic conflicts vary greatly, therefore, a common thread running through all of them is the clash of interests between or among parties holding significant stakes in the region.

When parties can pursue their own interests or go their separate ways without affecting each other's welfare, conflict does not occur even though the interests of the parties may differ drastically. The fact that Able likes loud music while Baker prefers peace and quiet need not give rise to a conflict if the two live in different neighborhoods and do not come into contact with each other. The operation of tankers in the waters of the Canadian Arctic is of little concern from the point of view of the Sami of

Fig. 20. Residents of Uummannaq, Greenland, protest against the anti-harvest campaign during a meeting between representatives of Indigenous Survival International and Greenpeace International, 1985. *Source*: photo. by C. Kenny-Gilday.

Fennoscandia attempting to protect reindeer habitat threatened by proposed hydroelectric projects. As we suggested in the introduction to this chapter, such conditions prevailed throughout most of the Arctic until recently. Whenever parties are interdependent in the sense that the activities of each impinge on the welfare of the other(s), however, conflict is possible. The National Park Service and the Inupiat residents of Anaktuvuk Pass in northern Alaska, for instance, have a conflict over the use of all terrain vehicles (ATVs) in Gates of the Arctic National Park because the use of ATVs can be disruptive to the ecosystems of the Park while a prohibition on the use of these vehicles can significantly disrupt the subsistence activities of the Natives. Similarly, conflicts have begun to arise between military interests and environmental groups in the Arctic because military operations can threaten ecologically sensitive areas in the Arctic while restrictions on military operations to protect such areas may interfere with the efforts of military planners to enhance national security. In short, conflict arises when those who are interdependent in the sense that their actions affect each other's welfare find their interests clashing over specific issues.

As the preceding chapters suggest, the specific issues now giving rise to conflict in the Arctic are numerous and varied. Nonetheless, there are recurrent themes running through this array of issues which can serve as the basis for a simple taxonomy of Arctic conflicts.[7] Consider, in this connection, the following categories of conflicts currently unfolding in the Arctic.

Allocative issues

Many Arctic conflicts revolve around the allocation of resources among competing or incompatible uses. They focus, in essence, on the question of how society should allocate its resources (economists call them factors of production) among alternative uses that cannot be pursued simultaneously. Sometimes these conflicts are direct in the sense that the use of a specific resource for one purpose (for instance, hardrock mining) precludes or severely limits its use for another purpose (for instance, wilderness). In other cases, the conflicts are more indirect. This is the case when efforts to use one resource produce side effects (economists call these effects externalities) that severely impinge on efforts to use other resources in the area in a productive manner. To illustrate, oil and gas production in the Beaufort Sea could damage bowhead whales or cause these whales to alter their migratory routes in such a way as to make them unavailable to Native groups currently dependent on the bowhead whale as a subsistence resource.

Direct conflicts of use in the Arctic typically focus on dichotomies like consumptive *vs.* nonconsumptive use, commercial *vs.* subsistence use, or present *vs.* future use. Natural resources used as a source of commodities are not available for use as amenities.[8] The killing of wild animals is incompatible with the preservation of these animals as a source of biological diversity, pleasure for hikers, or insights for scientists. Fish harvested commercially are not available to sustain the traditional lifestyle of indigenous peoples or other subsistence users. Oil and gas reserves exploited today cannot be set aside as an energy source to fulfill future needs.

Indirect conflicts of use, by contrast, generally involve externalities that interfere with the productive activities of others.[9] In the Arctic, these conflicts typically stem from byproducts associated with the exploitation of non-renewable resources to supply the demands of affluent societies in the temperate zones for raw materials which disrupt efforts to make use of renewable resources on a sustainable basis for a variety of purposes. On one side, there are hydrocarbon development, hardrock mining, and hydroelectric power production coupled with the transportation systems required to move these raw materials to southern markets. On the other side, there are fishing, the consumptive use of wild animals for commercial, recreational, or subsistence purposes, and the protection of natural environments as a source of amenity values. Conflicts arise when activities aimed at exploiting the non-renewable resources destroy habitat required by fish or wildlife, produce various wastes or pollutants harmful to living organisms, or lead to visual blight that detracts from the amenity values of unspoiled natural environments. The severity of these indirect conflicts of use not only varies from case to case, it is also a matter of considerable controversy in many instances. It is undeniable, however, that the landscape of Arctic conflict is now littered with issues of this type.

Distributive issues

A second class of Arctic conflicts encompasses those centering on the distribution of benefits (or burdens) among competing claimants. These conflicts focus, in essence, on the question of who gets what in the distribution of values among individuals and groups in society rather than on the allocation of resources or factors of production among competing uses.[10] These are the conflicts that analysts envision when they introduce the idea of a welfare or utility frontier in conceptualizing conflict and approach conflict resolution as a matter of reaching agreement on a settlement located at a specific point on such a frontier (that is, at an identifiable locus on a contract curve).[11] Conflicts of this type are attractive to theoretically minded students of conflict because they are tractable in analytic terms. But it is well to remember that they constitute only one of the important classes of Arctic conflicts today.

Some distributive conflicts center on the division of the proceeds (especially the economic returns or rents) accruing from the exploitation of Arctic resources. For instance, what constitutes an appropriate division of the economic returns or rents from oil and gas production in Alaska among the federal government (in the form of bonus bids, royalties, and corporate income taxes), the State of Alaska (in the form of royalties, severance taxes, and taxes on corporations), local entities like the North Slope Borough (in the form of property taxes), and even consumers (in the form of reduced prices)?[12] Should the federal government share any proceeds it derives from outer continental shelf oil and gas development with the state government or local entities? Should public authorities at any level endeavor to collect economic returns in connection with commercial fishing in Arctic waters? Should the indigenous peoples of Northern Quebec or other Arctic areas receive continuing support in the form of income security programmes for hunters and trappers in return for accepting the use of northern rivers for hydroelectric power production?[13]

A second group of distributive conflicts in the Arctic involves the division of finite supplies of valued objects which for one reason or another do not lend themselves to monetized transactions among groups of claimants. Who should get the jobs created in connection with industrial projects in the Arctic? Specifically, what provisions for local hire are appropriate and how should local hire be defined? How should permits for commercial fishing be divided when the number of those desiring permits exceeds the number of permits available?[14] How should finite supplies of harvestable animals be divided among commercial, recreational, and subsistence users? Is it appropriate to give subsistence users an absolute priority when available supplies are severely limited? How should annual quotas for bowhead whales in the Alaskan Arctic or polar bears in the eastern Canadian Arctic be divided among those communities wishing to hunt these animals? How should the subsurface estate be apportioned between Denmark and the Home Rule government in Greenland or among Native peoples, the state government, and the Federal government in Alaska? In all these cases, the problem is the same. Because demand for the relevant objects exceeds the supply, the interests of those seeking a share of the available supply inevitably conflict.

Jurisdictional issues

Whether the underlying problems are allocative or distributive, Arctic conflicts frequently take the form of clashes over the locus of authority to make binding decisions regarding human activities in the region. Here the essential question becomes who should have the authority to make choices rather than how should resources be allocated among competing uses or benefits distributed among competing claimants. Since different decision makers or decision-making processes respond to disparate interests and are therefore apt to reach divergent conclusions regarding both allocative and distributive issues, the importance attached to these jurisdictional issues is no cause for surprise. Much traditional thinking about jurisdiction focuses on spatial boundaries on the assumption that decision makers will exercise complete or exclusive authority within their geographical domains. Yet this is by no means the only approach to jurisdictional issues. Jurisdiction may be divided functionally so that each of several decision makers exercises authority over different activities occurring within the same geographical area. Today, there is also growing interest in arrangements featuring shared or concurrent jurisdiction. Under arrangements of this type, several decision makers (for instance, federal, state, and local governments) may share jurisdiction over the same activities (such as outer continental shelf oil and gas development) in the sense that such activities can only proceed with the approval of all participating entities or in conformity with the requirements laid down by each of the decision makers.[15]

Some jurisdictional conflicts in the Arctic arise at the international level. They may center on traditional spatial conceptions of jurisdiction as in the maritime boundary conflicts between Norway and the Soviet Union in the Barents Sea, Canada and the United States in the Beaufort Sea, or the United States and the Soviet Union in the Bering and Chukchi Seas.[16] In other cases, they involve clashes over the provisions of regimes covering specific areas or resources in the Arctic. Examples of this sort of issue include the conflict between Canada and the United States over the status of the Northwest Passage, the conflict between the Soviet Union and Norway over the application of the provisions of the Spitsbergen Treaty of 1920 to the outer contintental shelf adjacent to the Svalbard Archipelago, and the conflict between the United States and Japan over the management of salmon in the segment of the Bering Sea beyond the American Fishery Conservation Zone.[17] While many of these international jurisdictional conflicts have been around for some time, they typically lay fallow during the period of benign neglect regarding Arctic issues. Today, however, they loom larger and larger as the stakes of various interest groups in the Arctic continue to rise.

Another category of jurisdictional conflicts in the Arctic involves clashes over the allocation of authority between central governments and various state, provincial, territorial, or home-rule governments. The U.S.

Federal government and the State of Alaska have clashed repeatedly over the management of marine mammals in the waters adjacent to Alaska, hydrocarbon development on the continental shelves extending from Alaska, the use of renewable resources for subsistence purposes, and the designation of Alaska lands as wilderness areas.[18] The Canadian Federal government and the government of the Northwest Territories engage in repeated battles over land use planning, the exploitation of the subsurface state, and the management of wildlife in the Territories. Denmark and the Home Rule Government of Greenland have established a Joint Resources Committee in an effort to handle jurisdictional conflicts over the exploitation of non-renewable resources in Greenland through a system of shared authority.[19] But this has not led to any clearcut resolution of the conflict between Denmark and the Home Rule Government over the ownership of the subsurface state in Greenland. The picture of jurisdictional conflict in the Arctic becomes even more complex when we expand our scope to encompass the growing claims of local authorities to participate in decisions affecting their areas. Local authorities can and increasingly do enter into jurisdictional conflicts with both federal authorities and state or provincial authorities. The North Slope Borough wants an effective voice in land use planning, coastal zone management, offshore development, and activities affecting the sea ice of the Beaufort Sea. Individual villages, like Gambel or Stebbins, want a say in federal outer continental shelf leasing decisions. And numerous communities want a voice in decisions regarding education, wildlife management, and the construction of industrial or military installations in their areas. Most of these issues revolve around claims to shared authority or local participation. Local authorities seldom seek anything approaching exclusive authority in their own areas. But this only adds to the complexity of emerging jurisdictional arrangements in the Arctic.[20]

A special, but increasingly important, category of jurisdictional conflicts in the Arctic arises in connection with the tribal sovereignty movement now emerging in many parts of the region. In essence, calls for tribal sovereignty amount to a series of jurisdictional claims or efforts to assert authority on the part of Native groups.[21] For the most part, these claims focus on specific functional areas (for instance, wildlife management, education, certain types of crimes). They do not involve assertions of sovereignty in the sense of claims to comprehensive or undivided authority within geographically demarcated areas. Nonetheless, such claims generate sharp conflicts not only because many other parties have an aversion to establishing special authority systems for ethnically defined groups within society but also because the creation of effective tribal governments would detract from the authority of existing entities like municipal governments and state or provincial governments. There is a sense, therefore, in which these clashes over tribal sovereignty engender sharp distributive conflicts involving the division of authority itself among competing claimants.

6.2   Cross-cutting cleavages

The landscape of Arctic conflict emerging from this account constitutes a complex mosaic rather than a unidimensional pattern featuring a single dominant cleavage or axis of conflict. The interest groups holding significant stakes in the region do not line up on the same side of each and every issue. Rather, Arctic conflicts form a pattern that political analysts describe in terms of the concept of cross-cutting cleavages.[22] Those who oppose each other on any given Arctic issue regularly find themselves making common cause on other issues. In the Arctic, your opponent today may well turn out to be your ally or partner tomorrow.

To illustrate this theme, corporate interests and the interests of Native groups clash whenever industrial development threatens subsistence activities by disturbing animal populations, polluting key environments, or destroying habitat. But industrial interests and Native groups regularly join forces in sponsoring projects creating employment opportunities in the Far North (for example, the Red Dog lead/zinc mine north of Kotzebue), joint plans for the development of natural resources (for instance, the Jameson Land project in eastern Greenland), or mutually beneficial industrial developments (for example, the Kuparuk Industrial Complex adjacent to Prudhoe Bay). Similarly, Native groups and environmentalists find their interests dovetailing nicely in efforts to protect ecosystems (for example, the marine environments of the Beaufort Sea) or to limit military operations in sensitive parts of the Arctic. But the interests of these groups come into conflict repeatedly with regard to issues like the consumptive use of wild animals, the use of all-terrain vehicles or snow machines in wilderness areas, and the development of mines or other industrial installations designed to provide cash income for Native communities. In much the same way, industrial interests and military interests are complementary when it comes to maintaining freedom of access in the Arctic and opposing efforts to place large segments of the Arctic off limits to industrial and military activities by including them in marine sanctuaries or wilderness areas. Yet these interest groups, too, are likely to clash on specific issues since a leading attraction of the Arctic from an industrial point of view is the fact that the region is unlikely to become a battleground in future military confrontations. Even the United States and the Soviet Union, parties that usually line up on opposite sides of conflicts in today's world, find themselves drawn into the pattern of cross-cutting cleavages in the Arctic. While the superpowers have opposing interests regarding the delimitation of jurisdictional boundaries in the Bering and Chukchi Seas, for instance, the interests of the Soviet Union and the United States are largely complementary when it comes to the extension of the Svalbard regime to the adjacent continental shelf. In effect, each of the superpowers has an interest in applying the Svalbard regime to this shelf in order to preserve the option of searching for hydrocarbons in this area.[23]

Students of conflict generally view the existence of cross-cutting cleavages with favor, at least from the point of view of society as a whole. Such a pattern of conflict seems more stable than a unidimensional pattern in which all or even most of the members of society line up on opposite sides of a central axis of conflict (like the East-West divide or the North-South split). Any party whose opponent on one issue may turn out to be its ally or partner on the next issue will experience incentives to behave with restraint in connection with individual conflicts. The existence of cross-cutting cleavages, that is, makes it costly to alienate those who may prove valuable as allies with regard to other issues, no matter how much you disagree with them on some particular issue.

6.3   The character of Arctic conflict

The result is a certain moderation that generally helps to keep society as a whole on an even keel. But this does nothing to reduce the severity of individual Arctic conflicts or to ensure that these conflicts will be easy to settle. The severity of a conflict is a function of the degree to which the interests of the parties concerned with an issue are incompatible together with the magnitude of the stakes of the parties in the issue.[24] Parties whose interests are strictly opposed on a given issue (that is, their relationship is one of pure conflict or zero-sum conflict in the language of game theory) may not regard the resultant conflict as severe if their stakes are sufficiently low.[25] Most parlor games exemplify this point. By contrast, high stakes can generate severe conflict even among parties whose interests overlap to a considerable degree. This is true of most arms races, for instance, where the conflict is certainly severe even though the interests of the parties are by no means strictly opposed. Of course, the most severe conflicts occur in cases where parties possessing high stakes have sharply incompatible interests at the same time.

Arctic conflicts exhibit several features that complicate efforts to arrive at straightforward assessments of their severity in these terms:

(1) Many Arctic conflicts focus on developments expected to occur in the future rather than on events currently taking place. For instance, they involve the projected impact on marine ecosystems of tanker traffic in Arctic waters or the anticipated impact on terrestrial ecosystems of the damming of northern rivers to produce hydroelectric power. Depending upon one's choice of assumptions, it is comparatively easy to magnify or diminish the significance of such prospective developments in analyzing these issues.

(2) Arctic conflicts often center on events that are inherently probabilistic. Thus, the best we can do is to assign certain probabilities to occurrences like the discovery of recoverable reserves of oil in specific geologic structures, oil spills under unfavorable weather conditions or during whale migrations, and ice conditions likely to damage offshore platforms. This gives rise to complex problems of risk assessment, and it makes attitudes toward risk an important consideration in assessing the severity of many Arctic conflicts. Since there is seldom any basis for calculating objective probabilities for the relevant events, it also ensures that subjective probability estimates become major determinants of assessments of the severity of these Arctic conflicts.[26]

(3) Arctic conflicts regularly involve interactions between complex ecosystems and equally complex social systems. Conflicts over the bowhead whale, Arctic caribou herds, and various species of migratory birds, for example, revolve around the cultural significance of these resources to local human communities as well as disagreements regarding the ability of these communities to regulate their use of the resources effectively. In such cases, it is always hard to isolate the causal significance of specific actions or proposed actions that become focal points in conflicts among interest groups.[27] The fact that it is ordinarily impossible to conduct systematic field experiments, much less truly controlled experiments, on the affected systems only exacerbates this problem.

(4) There is no suitable metric or measuring system for calculating the full range of costs and benefits at stake in most Arctic conflicts. How can we compare the benefits of an increase in the security of energy supplies flowing to the affluent populations of the temperate zones, for instance, with the costs of environmental disruptions to the subsistence lifestyles of those residing in small Arctic communities? As a result, utilitarian procedures like benefit/cost analysis are of limited use in assessing the severity of Arctic conflicts.[28]

(5) The problems of arriving at intergroup comparisons (that is,

devising a common metric in terms of which to make meaningful comparisons of gains and losses accruing to different groups) in analyzing Arctic conflicts are even more complex than the well-known problems of making interpersonal comparisons often discussed in mainstream analyses of social or collective choice.[29] Is the welfare of small indigenous groups clinging to subsistence lifestyles, for example, more or less important than the welfare of large urban populations dependent on readily available energy sources to support their affluent lifestyles?

It follows that there are no simple answers to questions regarding the severity of Arctic conflicts. Yet the behavior of those engaged in these conflicts clearly licenses the conclusion that the parties themselves often perceive Arctic conflicts to be severe. Those concerned with Arctic issues regularly invest substantial resources in the promotion and protection of their interests in the resultant conflicts. Consider, for example, the behavior of parties like Sohio, the North Slope Borough, or the Alaska Coalition in this connection. The parties to Arctic conflicts typically exhibit extreme hesitancy about turning their conflicts over to conventional methods of settlement, like litigation or legislation, for fear that their interests will be compromised in an unacceptable fashion. The reluctance of both Canada and the United States to resort to the International Court of Justice for a settlement of their conflict over the status of the waters of the Northwest Passage exemplifies this behavior. When Arctic conflicts are submitted to conventional methods of settlement, moreover, the parties have repeatedly proven unwilling to accept the initial outcomes. The protracted litigation over offshore oil and gas development in the Beaufort and Bering Seas, involving both appeals of initial decisions and recurrent lawsuits raising the same fundamental issues, testifies to the reluctance of the parties to Arctic conflicts to accept the outcomes of conventional methods of settlement. Despite the methodological problems impeding efforts to assess the severity of Arctic conflicts, therefore, it seems safe to conclude that the parties to these conflicts generally believe not only that their interests clash sharply but also that the stakes in the Arctic are high. (See Figure 21.)

Quite apart from the question of severity, Arctic conflicts commonly exhibit one or more of the following characteristics that complicate efforts to settle them.

Cross-polity conflict

In many cases, the parties to conflicts arising in the Arctic belong to different political systems. This is obviously true of international conflicts like the clashes over Svalbard and the Northwest Passage. But a similar phenomenon occurs in many conflicts between Native groups, who regard themselves as sovereign tribes or nations, and interest groups or government agencies representing the mainstream of the encompassing society. It is by no means self-evident, for example, that the federal legislatures of the United States and Canada have the authority to enact legislation that is automatically binding on the Natives of Alaska or the Northwest Territories or that state or provincial agencies have un-questioned jurisdiction over many activities taking place in Native communities.[30] Cross-polity conflicts are difficult to settle in part because of the common lack of institutionalized and widely accepted procedures for handling conflicts involving parties belonging to different political systems. Partly, the problem stems from the occurrence of differences between applicable standards of public order (what lawyers refer to as conflicts of laws). When the Natives of Alaska's North Slope and the United States Federal government enter into a conflict over the status of the sea ice of the Beaufort Sea, for instance, whose principles of public order should apply? To make matters more complex, there are profound questions regarding the proper legal characterization of the Arctic for purposes of dealing with many cross-polity conflicts in the region. To illustrate, the sea ice of the Arctic Basin is fully capable of serving as a platform for a wide range of human activities that ordinarily occur on dry

Fig. 21. Saboteurs sink Icelandic whaling vessels, December 1986. (Photo: O. K. Magnússon, courtesy of *Morgunbladid*.)

land. Conversely, land underlain by permafrost is unsuitable for many human activities that are characteristic of normal terrestrial spaces. Under the circumstances, those engaged in Arctic conflicts frequently appeal to fundamentally different principles of public order (for example, the law of the sea *vs.* municipal systems of land law) in building their cases regarding the issues involved in the conflicts.

Cross-cultural conflicts

Impediments to settlement are also apt to arise when the parties to conflict belong to two or more distinct cultures. Of course, cross-polity conflicts often take the form of cross-cultural conflicts as well. But cross-cultural conflicts regularly arise even within a single political system. This will happen whenever a political system encompasses distinct cultural groups that have not been assimilated into the polity and that are unwilling to regard themselves as subordinate to the dominant culture of the society. Such conditions are widespread throughout the Arctic where groups of indigenous peoples have survived as cultural entities despite pressures emanating from the dominant cultures of the societies in which they are located. All over the Arctic, in fact, there are indications that consciousness of cultural distinctiveness is now on the rise among indigenous peoples. As the history of misunderstandings between representatives of the dominant culture and Native peoples throughout the Americas attests, it is difficult to achieve meaningful communication among the parties to cross-cultual conflicts much less to devise effective procedures for handling these conflicts. (See Figure 22.) When the actions of those belonging to one culture begin to threaten the cultural integrity of another culture, such problems become particularly acute. This condition, too, is much in evidence in Arctic conflicts involving such matters as consumptive use of wild animals, damming of northern rivers, construction of pipelines, and use of the sea ice. Internal colonialism with its emphasis on the systematic subordination of those located in the peripheries once served to mute (though not to resolve) these cross-cultural conflicts in the Arctic.[31] As both Native groups and non-Natives located in the Arctic peripheries achieve enhanced political sophistication, however, we must expect the cross-cultural character of many Arctic conflicts to become increasingly prominent.

Core value conflicts

Beyond this, it is hard to settle conflicts that involve core human values or what people regard as fundamental rights. Conflicts of this type often arise in cross-polity or cross-cultural settings. But there is nothing

Fig. 22. First Ministers' Conference on Aboriginal Constitutional Matters, 26–27 March 1987. (a) Prime Minister Mulroney and Native leader; (b) Assembly of First Nations delegates George Erasmus and Gary Potts. *Source*: Office of the Prime Minister, Canada.

uncommon about the occurrence of conflicts touching on core values or fundamental rights even within societies exhibiting a high degree of cultural uniformity. In such cases, the parties will not only be reluctant to submit issues to conventional procedures for settling conflicts of interest, they are also apt to reject outcomes generated by the operation of such procedures.

Problems of this sort are much in evidence with regard to Arctic conflicts at both the domestic level and the international level. Animal rights advocates are not likely to rest content so long as a subsistence harvest of bowhead whales or a commercial harvest of harp seals or fur seals continues. No one can expect the Native peoples of Alaska's North Slope to accept industrial development that is disruptive to their subsistence-based culture no matter how many lawsuits pertaining to this issue they lose. Environmental groups are hardly likely to abandon their quest to obtain wilderness designation for more and more Arctic areas even if their plans evoke substantial opposition. It is hard to imagine energy companies passively accepting decisions to place substantial segments of the Arctic off limits to oil and gas development on a permanent basis. When core values or fundamental rights are at stake, conventional procedures may play a role in containing conflicts of interest over the short run. But it is unrealistic to expect them to resolve conflicts definitively or to prevent them from re-emerging from time to time.

6.4 Settling Arctic conflicts

Turn now to a consideration of methods or procedures for handling Arctic conflicts. In examining specific methods, we want to consider the following questions:

(1) Is a given procedure for handling Arctic conflicts effective in the sense that it yields decisive or clearcut outcomes? Are these outcomes durable in the sense that they produce lasting settlements?

(2) How efficient are the various methods of handling Arctic conflicts? Are they capable of minimizing both the monetary costs and the non-monetary costs (measured in terms of time, energy, and disruption to the social fabric) of these conflicts?

(3) Will any of these procedures generate outcomes that are equitable in the sense that the outcomes conform to reasonable standards of fairness or justice? Will they serve to promote the broader common good in addition to satisfying the concerns of the parties directly involve in Arctic conflicts?

The prevailing approaches to conflict in the Arctic rim states include both private sector procedures (such as market mechanisms and private bargaining) and public sector procedures (such as negotiation, litigation, and legislation). They also encompass activities intended to eliminate or alleviate conflict. In this section, we argue that each of these approaches offers a response to conflict which may prove helpful in dealing with certain Arctic conflicts. But we also conclude that the prevailing approaches to handling conflict, treated as a collection of social tools, leave much to be desired in the search for solutions to the array of conflicts now arising in the Arctic region.

Minimizing conflict

A reasonable response to some Arctic conflicts is to search for ways to eliminate or ameliorate the problem provoking the clash without trampling on the interests of any of the parties.[32] Such efforts to minimize conflict by altering the underlying problem may take a number of forms.

(1) Research may yield new technologies capable of handling complex tasks without injuring the interests of others. It is undoubtedly true, for example, that engineering and design studies carried out in recent years have enhanced the ability of oil companies to operate safely in Arctic waters.

(2) Careful planning and coordination may make it possible to avoid or minimize many of the disruptive consequences of Arctic activities. The contrast between the carefully controlled Kuparuk Industrial Complex and the comparatively chaotic pattern of industrial development at nearby Prudhoe Bay illustrates this option.

(3) Moderate regulatory restrictions may protect ecosystems or social systems without imposing severe costs on those wishing to exploit Arctic resources. Seasonal drilling restrictions to protect bowhead whales during the spring and fall migrations exemplify this approach.

Minimizing techniques are clearly useful in handling Arctic conflicts as well as many other types of conflict. Such techniques often prove more efficient (in both monetary and non-monetary terms) than other approaches to conflict, and they are certainly likely to arouse less public controversy in specific cases.

Yet this approach to conflict has severe limitations as a response to many of the conflicts arising in the Arctic today. The issues giving rise to Arctic conflicts often involve matters of principle or irreducible value conflicts that cannot be avoided through research, planning, or the imposition of straightforward regulations. This is true, for example, of the emerging jurisdictional battles associated with the claims of indigenous peoples to self-government as well as the confrontations occasioned by the desire of animal rights activists to put an end to the consumptive use of wild animals. Nor is there any basis for the comforting belief that research and planning are neutral processes, designed merely to enhance the common good. In the context of proposals to exploit the non-renewable resources of the Arctic, for instance, these processes typically pose the following dilemma. Development-oriented activities can be suspended or slowed down while research or planning takes place, in which case the interests of corporations (and their stockholders or clients) will suffer. Alternatively, such activities can be allowed to proceed during the phase of research and development, in which case the interests of indigenous peoples and environmental groups are apt to suffer. What is more, there are frequently opportunities for powerful interest groups to manipulate research and planning efforts to promote their own ends. Partly, this is due to the fact that ecosystems and social systems are so complex that it is difficult to foresee, much less to control, many of the impacts of activities carried out in the Arctic. This makes it relatively easy for those who engage in research and planning (for example, industrial or environmental groups) to produce studies that appear to buttress their own pre-dispositions and preferences. In part, it stems from the fact that a search for technical measures to minimize or mitigate conflict will often seem attractive to powerful interest groups anxious to appear publicly concerned about the interests of others but equally determined to avoid raising deeper questions of principle or value embedded in Arctic conflicts. Industrial interests, for example, may find it quite attractive to conduct research or agree to an array of technical regulations if this serves to suppress nagging questions about the preservation of biological diversity under Arctic conditions or the rights of the indigenous peoples of the Far North.

Market mechanisms

Those impressed with the performance of free enterprise systems will be predisposed to reply on markets to handle many Arctic conflicts. Markets routinely operate to allocate resources among competing users and to resolve questions regarding the commercial attractiveness of investment opportunities.[33] They are therefore well suited to handling disagreements concerning such matters as the pace of development of the outer continental shelf in the Arctic and the relative merits of pipelines and tankers in transporting Arctic oil and gas to southern markets. In the process, markets also produce distributive outcomes, so that there is no need to develop separate procedures to handle distributive issues in free enterprise systems.[34] Even where markets have not arisen spontaneously, it may prove possible to establish markets or quasi-markets as a matter of public policy.[35] The American system of lease sales for outer continental shelf tracts exemplifies this option. There is at present considerable interest in making use of similar arrangements to regulate access to other natural resources as well.[36]

For all their attractions, market mechanisms have severe limitations as a method of handling contemporary Arctic conflicts. Markets are inappropriate for handling conflicts over the allocation of authority (for example, all the Arctic jurisdictional issues) or conflicts in which there is no common metric, such as a price system, in terms of which to weigh alternatives (for example, disagreements among commercial, recreational, and subsistence users of wildlife). Markets are also incapable of resolving conflicts that focus precisely on the extent to which markets are appropriate for handling certain types of collective choices. In the Arctic, the institutional prerequisites for the operation of markets, such as systems of private property rights or exclusive use rights, are often lacking.[37] It is hard to think of areas where such systems have made fewer inroads than in the Arctic. As our discussion of indirect conflicts of use in an earlier section of this chapter indicates, moreover, the scope for externalities or social costs associated with many Arctic activities is enormous. Any effort to rely on markets to handle Arctic conflicts would therefore produce pressures to create extensive regulatory arrangements that would themselves engender additional conflict. Interest groups involved in the Arctic frequently espouse values that override the utilitarian considerations reflected in the operation of market mechanisms. This is apparent in the positions of those who advocate oil and gas development in the Arctic as a means of achieving energy independence, those who oppose the consumptive use of wild animals in the Arctic on moral grounds, and those who favor public support for northern enterprises in order to create local employment opportunities in northern communities. Many of those holding stakes in the Arctic will also oppose the use of market mechanisms to handle Arctic conflicts on equity grounds. As economists freely admit, the distributive outcomes produced by markets are only as fair as the intitial distribution of resource endowments. And as the jurisdictional issues now arising in the Arctic attest, it is precisely the initial distribution of resource endowments that a variety of organized interest groups are currently contesting in the region. While none of this suggests that market mechanisms are useless in handling Arctic conflicts, these comments do license the conclusion that such mechanisms will not carry us very far in settling these conflicts.

Private bargaining

Even when markets are nonexistent or inappropriate, parties whose interests clash in the context of a specific issue may be able to resolve their differences through private bargaining. This is the fundamental insight associated with the work of analysts like Coase who regard public sector procedures as costly and intrusive and who see scope for mutually advantageous transactions whenever the damages sustained by the victims of a given activity exceed the gains to the beneficiaries, thereby creating a contract zone between or among the parties.[38] The typical application of this line of reasoning has been to the handling of externalities or social costs arising from industrial or commercial activities. But it would be perfectly possible to extend the argument to a variety of other issues giving rise to conflicts in the Arctic. Animal rights advocates, for instance, might consider compensating subsistence users to cease killing wild animals under certain circumstances. Or those concerned with the disruptive impact of shipping in Arctic waters could think about paying commercial concerns or navies to move their operations elsewhere.

Whatever the attractions of this procedure as a means of forcing interest groups to reveal their true preferences, it also has fundamental drawbacks as a response to the array of conflicts now arising in the Arctic.[39] For the most part, the necessary liability rules are unspecified.[40] Not only is it unclear whether the animal rights advocates should compensate the subsistence users or *vice versa*, Arctic issues, expressed in the terminology of rights, also commonly focus precisely on whose interests should take precedence in clashes of this type. In many cases, there will be no contract zone or zone of agreement, a necessary condition for the success of private bargaining.[41] For example, it is hard to imagine groups of indigenous peoples being able or willing to pay those interested in hydrocarbons, nonfuel minerals, or hydroelectric power enough to persuade them to alter their plans. But this is far more likely to trigger a move toward litigation, legislation, or coercive activities than an attitude of resignation on the part of parties disadvantaged by private bargaining.

Even when there is reason to believe that a contract zone exists, numerous bargaining impediments are likely to limit the use of private bargaining to settle Arctic conflicts. Some parties (for example, Native groups or environmental groups) will be composed of large groups that are costly to organize and that are afflicted by intra-party disagreements. Many Arctic conflicts involve a multiplicity of parties so that there is ample scope for the formation and reformation of coalitions. Rapid changes in the socioeconomic, political, and legal environments are apt to produce swings in the relative bargaining strength of the parties that leave one or more key parties with an incentive to hold out at any given time. Beyond all this, private bargaining is offensive from the perspective of many conceptions of fairness or justice. In addition to providing advantages to those favored by the initial distribution of resource endowments, it places a premium on the manipulation of political processes to control the specification of the applicable liability rules. It seems unlikely, therefore, that many of the key parties holding stakes in Arctic conflicts will settle for private bargaining as a satisfactory procedure for handling contemporary Arctic issues.

Public negotiation

While the role of private bargaining as a response to Arctic conflicts seems limited, public negotiation has become a prominent feature of efforts to settle many Arctic issues.[42] Sometimes this is because governments clash with each other in an environment in which there are few alternatives to public negotiation. International jurisdictional issues (for example, the maritime boundary conflicts in the Arctic) as well as many domestic jurisdictional issues (for example, the conflict between the Danish government and the Home Rule government of Greenland over the ownership of the subsurface estate of Greenland) typically exemplify this pattern. Sometimes it is because agencies within the same government confront each other regarding the use of the public domain or areas under a government's exclusive management authority in the Arctic. Consider, for instance, the negotiations that have been going on for years within the Canadian Federal government over various proposed uses of the Lancaster Sound area. In yet other cases, governments have entered into public negotiations with groups in the Arctic of a quasi-public nature (for example, tribal or other Native organizations). The comprehensive claims negotiations in the Canadian North offer a clear illustration of this response to Arctic conflicts.[43]

The fact that parties frequently resort to public negotiation in their efforts to handle Arctic conflicts, however, should not blind us to the limitations of this response to contemporary Arctic issues. Public negotiation is not a notably effective procedure for handling conflicts of the type now arising in the Arctic. Sometimes this may merely signify that the parties cannot identify a contract zone or zone of agreement in connection with specific conflicts. It is not easy, for example, to see any outcomes that both sides would prefer to the *status quo* in the case of a conflict like the Soviet/Norwegian dispute over the seabed and water column boundaries of the Barents Sea. But the ineffectiveness of public negotiation is often a function of bargaining impediments arising from the complexities of intra-party bargaining, the rapid turnover of personnel in key positions, coalitional politics, and shifts in the relative bargaining strength of the parties.[44] The Canadian Federal government and various aboriginal groups have been actively negotiating comprehensive claims since 1973, for instance, but they have ' ... produced only three agreements, while twenty-one claims are under, or await, negotiation '.[45] Nor is public negotiation notable for its efficiency. Economists, used to resolving conflicts as a byproduct of the operation of market mechanisms, generally regard all bargaining and negotiation as socially wasteful. But even those who accept the necessity of expending resources on bargaining and negotiation cannot avoid becoming concerned about the expense of efforts to settle Arctic conflicts through public negotiations. To continue the previous example, the effort to negotiate settlements for the comprehensive claims of indigenous peoples in Canada has consumed more than $100 million since 1973, not to mention uncounted resources measured in terms of time, energy, and the diversion of attention from other fundamental issues.[46] While there is a case to be made for the fairness of the results produced by public negotiations, there is no basis for simply assuming that this procedure offers an equitable response to Arctic conflicts. When some of the parties (for example, the Cree and Inuit of northern Quebec faced with the onset of the James Bay Project in the 1970s) must participate under the threat of impending changes of a highly destructive nature, in fact, there are grounds for raising profound questions about the degree to which public negotiations eventuate in equitable settlements. It should come as no surprise, therefore, that we are currently witnessing a rapid intensification of opposition to the idea that negotiated arrangements like the James Bay and Northern Quebec Agreement of 1975 or the Home Rule agreement of 1979 in Greenland constitute final settlements of the issues at stake in the Arctic.[47] Despite the frequency with which parties resort to public negotiation as a response to Arctic conflicts, then, there is certainly no basis for treating this procedure as a wholly satisfactory response to the array of conflicts now arising in the Arctic.

Litigation

Those holding stakes in Arctic issues, especially in the United States, have regularly resorted to litigation as a method of handling the resultant conflicts. Native groups sue to halt outer continental shelf development in areas that contain important subsistence resources. Environmental groups go to court in an effort to prevent the extraction of non-renewable resources in parks, wildlife refuges, and so forth.

Sportsmen's associations turn to the courts as a forum for the expression of their opposition to granting a preference to subsistence users of wild animals. And it would be easy to expand this list of examples in many directions. Litigation appeals to those who believe that they stand to gain by casting issues in terms of rights rather than in terms of utilitarian standards like benefit/cost calculations. Courts may prove more responsive than markets or legislatures to the concerns of small groups whose financial resources are limited and whose access to standard political arenas is narrow. For those who simply want to block others from initiating some activity (for example, outer continental shelf drilling) protracted litigation may seem attractive regardless of the ultimate outcomes of the lawsuits they file.

Yet litigation also has severe limitations as a method of settling the array of conflicts now arising in the Arctic.[48] In some cases, no suitable judicial forum exists. This is obviously true of many of the international conflicts (for instance, the Svalbard dispute), and it may well be true of some of the cross-cultural conflicts involving confrontations between indigenous peoples and elements of the dominant white societies. Even where courts do exist, the parties will sometimes disagree profoundly on the extent to which an issue is justiciable or on the appropriate system of legal principles to apply in settling a conflict (for example, the disputes between indigenous peoples and federal governments regarding jurisdiction over the sea ice in Arctic waters). Equally serious, litigation is subject to severe criticism on the grounds that it is often ineffective and almost always costly. Losers in specific lawsuits are frequently unwilling to accept the judgments of courts as resolving the underlying issues at stake. On the contrary, they may well return to the courts again and again, searching for specific cases that will serve as more effective vehicles for the promotion of their causes. The result, quite often, is a series of closely related lawsuits that fail to settle underlying problems in either a decisive or a lasting manner. The continuing stream of litigation relating to outer continental shelf development in the Beaufort, Chukchi, and Bering Seas exemplifies this pattern. Of course, protracted litigation is expensive in purely monetary terms. But litigation is costly in non-monetary terms as well. It typically polarizes the parties to a conflict, forcing them to adopt a win/lose mentality and to abandon efforts at problem solving or integrative bargaining. Beyond this, it is far from self-evident that the results of litigation are defensible in terms of equity. It is true that litigation may sometimes prove helpful to those who lack the financial resources to profit from the operation of markets or the votes to achieve their goals in legislative arenas. As indigenous peoples in the Far North (for example, the Sami in Sweden or the Cree and Inuit in northern Quebec) have discovered, however, the courts cannot be counted on to protect the rights of minorities from pervasive encroachments on the part of dominant societies.[49] Nor is it apparent that those seeking to protect their rights have fared better in systems like contemporary American society where litigation is relied on extensively, than in systems like contemporary Danish society where various forms of negotiation and legislation are more prominent than litigation.

Legislation

Yet another response to Arctic conflicts is to turn to legislative arenas for settlements. While legislatures may not be able to come up with substantive solutions that satisfy all parties to conflicts, they do provide authoritative outcomes subject to enforcement by the apparatus of the state. The purpose of the Alaska Native Claims Settlement Act of 1971 was to resolve outstanding conflicts over the ownership of land in Alaska between indigenous peoples and the United States government. The Alaska National Interest Lands Conservation Act of 1980 was a response to the tangled mass of conflicting interests relating to the designation of portions of the public domain in Alaska for management as parks, refuges, national forests, and wilderness areas. Nor is legislation limited to the settlement of conflicts over such broad or generic issues as these. Those involved in much more limited issues, like the construction of an access road to the Red Dog mine site in northwest Alaska or the reorganization of an insolvent Native corporation, frequently turn to legislative arenas in search of a settlement of the clashing interests embodied in these issues.

Like the other approaches canvassed in this section, legislation has serious drawbacks as a response to the array of conflicts now arising in the Arctic. No suitable legislative arena exists for international conflicts, such as the Canadian/American dispute over the status of the waters of the Northwest Passage or the Soviet/American dispute over the status of the sector of the Bering Sea known as the Navarin Basin. In other cases, the parties disagree over the suitability of different legislative arenas, knowing full well that the choice of an arena may well determine the way in which a specific conflict is handled. The recurrent disputes regarding the extent to which subsistence issues should be handled by the U.S. Congress or the Alaska state legislature exemplify this problem. Beyond this, legislatures are often slow and indecisive mechanisms for the settlement of conflicts like those now arising in the Arctic. As the examples of Native claims and national interest lands in Alaska suggest, it commonly takes years to craft a solution to a complex issue that can win passage in the relevant legislative arena. And the enactment of a statute intended to resolve such an issue constitutes no guarantee that the settlement will stick. Those dissatisfied with the outcome are apt to waste no time in turning to the administrative agencies charged with implementing statutes in the hope of influencing the implementation process or to the courts in the hope of altering the effective outcome through judicial interpretation. As students of legislative politics have demonstrated repeatedly, moreover, it is naive to associate the outcomes produced by legislatures with the will of the majority in any simple sense. Legislatures offer great scope for exercises in the 'art of political manipulation', a fact that not only gives pause to those contemplating legislation as a method of settling conflicts but also raises questions about the legitimacy of the outcomes legislatures produce.[50] Nor are these the only grounds for questioning the degree to which legislative solutions conform to reasonable standards of justice or fairness. Of particular importance for the settlement of Arctic conflicts in this regard is the fact that legislatures reflect (often unconsciously) the built-in biases of a society's dominant culture. The result is a pronounced tendency to impose inappropriate policies or institutions in the North, such as wildlife regulations of the type devised to handle recreational use in the American lower forty-eight or for-profit business corporations as vehicles for the settlement of Native claims.[51]

6.5   Future needs

Today, the Arctic has emerged as a high stakes arena in which a number of parties pursue their interests in an increasingly well-organized fashion. It is predictable, therefore, that conflict will be a prominent feature of the Arctic landscape for some time to come. What is more, many of the conflicts now emerging in the region have characteristics that make them particularly difficult to settle in a lasting, much less efficient or equitable, manner. They are international in the sense that the parties belong to the different political systems, or they involve problems of communication in cross-cultural settings, or they focus on rights and core values that those involved treat as principles they cannot compromise. It follows that any effort to settle the array of conflicts now emerging in the Arctic will constitute a formidable challenge.

While the prevailing approaches to conflict in the Arctic rim states are certainly of some value in this context, they leave a great deal to be desired in the search for solutions to the range of conflicts now arising in the Arctic region. At a minimum, there is a need for improved gatekeeping capabilities designed to allocate individual conflicts to those procedures most likely to yield effective, efficient, and equitable settlements under the circumstances at hand. But there is also a clear need to invest energy in the development of improved methods of handling Arctic conflicts both in the private sector and in the public sector. The next three chapters address these needs. Chapter 7 presents an analysis of present and future prospects for handling Arctic conflicts within the private sector. Chapter 8 directs attention toward the public sector, critiquing existing governmental capabilities for handling Arctic issues and offering suggestions for the future. Chapter 9 adopts an international perspective, examining the prospects for devising regional arrangements to deal with the growing range of Arctic issues that transcend national boundaries.

7

Private initiatives: Arctic problem solving

We often think of conflict resolution as a function of the public sector. Governments regularly engage in efforts to manage or resolve the conflicting interests of private and public actors through legislation, adjudication, and administrative decision making. Yet private individuals, industry, and non-governmental organizations also endeavor to resolve and manage conflicts without resorting to governmental procedures.

Two trends have enhanced the role of private actors in resolving Arctic conflicts: an increase in private property interests in land and natural resources in the far North and a growing interest in alternatives to public sector dispute resolution. The first section of this chapter explains how devolution of northern lands from public to private ownership has changed the contours of Arctic conflict resolution, increasing the use of private bargaining and market transactions to resolve conflicts. The chapter then turns to alternative dispute resolution (ADR), a phrase that encompasses various forms of voluntary, third party assisted negotiation which often prove more efficient and equitable as methods of resolving disputes than public sector advocacy processes or legislation.[52] The use of ADR has naturally spread north. In addition to assisted negotiations, private actors increasingly engage in 'policy dialoguing' and consensus building activities that employ a variety of 'problem solving' approaches to deal with conflicts before they emerge on the public policy agenda.[53] The final section of the chapter reviews serveral northern cases in which private actors have attempted to reduce the likelihood of future national and international conflicts through problem solving activities.

Since the role of private actors is much reduced in social welfare states, like Denmark/Greenland and the other Scandinavian nations, and even more limited in the Soviet Union, this chapter focuses on the United States and Canada where the role of non-governmental organizations and industry in managing major Arctic conflicts is more pronounced. Private individuals, organizations, and corporations are not dormant in the area of conflict resolution elsewhere in the Arctic. For purposes of examining the already extensive role of private actors and exploring future prospects for the private sector, however, the North American Arctic provides a richer array of material.

7.1   Private ownership and market forces

Prior to the 1970s, the scope for market processes and private bargaining in the Arctic was extremely limited due to pervasive government ownership and control. But land claims settlements and changes in government policy in the 1970s and 1980s have enlarged opportunities for markets to operate and for private negotiations to occur.

Property transfers: full title

Private property was a rarity in Alaska prior to the Alaska Native Claims Settlement Act (ANCSA) of 1971, and it took construction of a massive hydroelectric project in Northern Quebec to secure relatively small enclaves of private property in the Canadian Arctic. ANCSA resulted in Native regional and village corporations owning 11·6% of Alaska's land. Less than 1% of the rest of Alaska is in private hands. The James Bay and Northern Quebec Agreement of 1975 (JBNQA) created a land regime that gave aboriginal peoples effective control (if not fee simple title) to over 5,403 square miles (primarily the settlement sites)[54] and exclusive hunting, fishing, and trapping rights in an additional 58,500 square miles. While the JBNQA fell short of the large-scale privatization mandated by ANCSA, it enabled aboriginal groups to offer property as security for loans and spawned development corporations that now negotiate with outside industry regarding economic development projects.[55] The Inuvialuit Final Agreement,[56] the only comprehensive land claim settled in the Canadian Arctic since the JBNQA, transferrred title to approximately 91,000 square kilometers of land (11,000 square kilometers of which includes both surface and subsurface rights) to the aboriginal peoples living in the northwestern corner of the Northwest Territories (NWT).[57] This leaves the bulk of northern lands in public hands, owned predominantly by federal governments,[58] although the State of Alaska holds title to roughly 28% of Alaska's land.

In addition to transferring title to land, in 1983 the Canadian federal government adopted a policy of privatizing government operations by selling a number of government owned businesses to individuals and small businesses and contracting with the private sector for some services previously provided by the government. This policy aimed to foster economic development throughout Canada, turn businesses losing money into profitable ventures, and create more jobs. As applied in the North, the policy resulted in the sale of the Northern Transportation Company, Ltd. (NTCL), the primary shipper of supplies to the Northwest Territories with over 200 vessels, to two Native corporations, Nunasi Development Corporation and Inuvialuit Development Corporation (IDC).[59] By 1985, Native northern companies were considering taking over or purchasing a craft shop and a fish plant in Rankin Inlet, sewing centers in Whale Cove and Baker Lake, and maintenance and janitorial services for numerous government buildings.[60] While most of these businesses are small and provide few jobs, they are significant in the context of a small, remote community's economy.

In terms of conflict management, the results of privatization are mixed. Land claims settlements (or the expectation of settlement) and creation of Native corporations has strengthened the Native bargaining position. Privatization has reduced core value conflicts between industry and Native corporations who now share an interest in developing resources to produce profits for their companies and shareholders. Native corporations in Alaska and Canada join with outside industries in joint venture fishing, oil exploration, oil field operations, construction, banking, and other enterprises. For example, the Denendeh Development Corporation (DDC) and the Metis Development Corporation have entered into a joint venture with Esso Resources which operates drill rigs in the Mackenzie Valley. And IDC participates in a joint enterprise that provides oil spill response services in the Beaufort Sea region.[61] This has reduced intergroup conflicts between many Native corporations and certain industry interests, but it has increased conflict between Native corporations and environmental organizations. And it has led to shifting coalitions.[62]

The clarification of title through land claims settlements has also enabled non-Native corporations to identify and deal with counterpart private (Native) businesses in the North. (See Figure 23.) Native corporate executives and outside industry executives now engage in integrative bargaining over Native hiring and training, environmental protection, the location and pace of development, provision of community services, and other issues that might well have resulted in protracted conflicts prior to ANCSA. Disputes that could have impeded development of the world-class Red Dog lead/zinc mine in northwest Alaska a decade ago were ironed out with remarkable speed once the NANA Corporation (a Native regional corporation) became the owner of the mine site. Operating as a joint venture, NANA and Cominco (a major mining company) were able

to clear numerous governmental hurdles including Congressional authorization of a land exchange between NANA and the National Park Service
and formation of a new state-chartered regional government (the
Northwest Arctic Borough). Similarly, private Native development
companies on Alaska's north slope bargained directly with ARCO and
other oil companies to obtain contracts for the construction and
operation of the Kuparuk Industrial Complex (KIC) that includes
housing and service areas for the Kuparuk oil field adjacent to Prudhoe
Bay. And Native corporations as well as regional governments now
exercise their considerable capacity to protect the environment, especially
subsistence resources.

This cooperation between Native enterprise and non-renewable
resource industries is evident in Canada too. For example, Esso Resources
Canada, Ltd. leased over a thousand square miles of land from the
Inuvialuit Regional Corporation for oil and gas exploration on the
Tuktoyaktuk Peninsula. In the early 1980s, the Nunasi Corporation
invested $22·8 million (Canadian), borrowed from a private bank, in the
Cullaton Lake Gold Mines. Through creative financing, Nunasi leveraged
a $5·5 million (Canadian) loan guarantee backed by expected revenue
from a future land claims settlement into a $3·9 million profit.
Negotiations with Cullaton also resulted in a manpower agreement that

Fig. 23. Red Dog port site located on the shores of the Chukchi Sea will be
the storage area for the over 750,000 tons of zinc and lead concentrate
produced annually from the Red Dog mine. *Source*: Cominco, Ltd.

produced jobs for over 70 Inuit in the Keewatin region. At the termination of the joint venture, Inuit labor at the gold mine dropped from a high of 48 percent to 17 percent.[63] Thus, as a result of increased ownership of resources and land by Native entities in the North, multi-party integrative bargaining is on the rise and is producing expansive and creative deals.

Yet privatization has also increased intragroup conflict by causing a split between the interests of small Native villages and large regional corporations. One of the classic arguments of opponents of privatization is that it leads to repression and exploitation by ruling classes. No one has closely examined the question of class conflict in relation to ANCSA, though a few commentators have noted that ANCSA (in particular its corporate structure) has made Native society more hierarchical and promoted class consciousness. Negotiators for Native interests in Canada have avoided ANCSA's corporate model, in part for this reason. They have sought to create political as well as economic institutions to implement their settlements which would cause less disruption of the social and cultural order of northern communities.[64] Dissatisfaction with the corporate system as a means to safeguard traditional lands for future generations has strengthened the tribal sovereignty movement in Alaska and kindled clashes within the Native community in Alaska as well as between the proponents of tribal sovereignty and the state government.[65]

Property transfers: lesser property interests

Offshore oil and gas leasing, mineral leasing, and the creation of marketable fishing permits by government comprise a separate category of property transfers. Federal and state governments have leased tracts of the outer continental shelf (OCS) for hydrocarbon exploration and development. Through the Alaska limited entry system, the state has issued permits to fish in specific fisheries.[66] The permits are transferable and have become valuable. Although limited in acreage and scope, the transfer to private parties of property interests in OCS lands and the creation of new private property interests through the limited entry system have, as in the case of transfers of full title, reduced some conflicts and heightened others. America's OCS leasing system, spelled out in the Outer Continental Shelf Lands Act (OCSLA), provides a way to allocate scarce resources among competing exploration and development companies, and it is designed to allow coastal communities and environmental groups to participate in the decision-making process. Nevertheless, the OCSLA leasing system has not emerged as an effective method of resolving clashes pitting government and industry against environmental groups and coastal communities in disputes over the location, extent, and timing of offshore development.

Alaska's limited entry law introduces a market mechanism to allocate scarce resources (total allowable catches of fish) among competing commercial fishers. By restricting the number of permits in each of 33 fisheries, the limited entry program has reduced conflicts among fishing interests. It has also reduced the fears of environmental and fishing interests who argued that unchecked competition would exhaust fish stocks, decrease earnings of those already fishing, and drive local fishers out of the industry. The system resolved some conflicts; however, it triggered others.[67] One of the major concerns is that the system disrupts the cultural and economic patterns of rural Alaskan communities. In Native communities culturally and economically dependent on fishing, patterns of influence, sex roles, status rankings, and individual identities were shaped by fishing.[68] The limited entry system increases the status of those few who own permits but blocks entry into the profession by new entrants, including offspring who would have traditionally chosen to follow the path of their parents. Though the system has not significantly reduced the number of commercial fishing vessels, it has effectively placed a ceiling on new entrants. And it is extremely difficult for rural residents to purchase a permit and necessary gear. Although the state has provided loan programs to enable state residents to purchase entry permits and new vessels, few rural Alaskans have benefited from these programs, in part because of poor credit ratings and in part because, as a group, they are the least financially literate and the least sophisticated about dealing with bankers and lawyers. Now, only one individual can inherit a fishery permit owned by a parent (if the parent chooses to pass it to the next generation). Those who do not own permits may serve as crew, but this too changes social relations within the community. With expanding populations, more and more locals must turn to non-traditional methods of participating in the cash economy. Statewide, permits held by Alaska rural local residents declined over 12 percent from 1975–1985.[69] Although the rate of decline slowed in 1984 and 1985, the limited entry system heightens feelings of frustration on the part of those who are economically excluded or disadvantaged by the high cost of entry into the commercial fishing business.[70]

Even if the system were restructured to place more permits into the hands of rural local owners, some commentators argue that rural locals would continue to sell their permits because of the demand for permits outside of rural areas and outside of Alaska, lower than average incomes produced by local rural fishers, and the need for cash that can be satisfied in the short term by selling a permit. (The same problems would have arisen if Native corporation stock were recalled in 1991 and reissued with no restrictions on alienation as ANCSA required prior to the 1987 amendments.)[71] While greater access to capital might remedy the problem, another solution would be to create a new class of fishing permits which would not be transferable outside the community or to which title would be held communally, a solution that removes some permits from the open market system.[72] This solution, however, would result in a separate class of permits less valuable monetarily than those traded on the open market, a solution that commercial fishers, who have organized a powerful lobby to protect their interests, would probably oppose.

While new property interests in permits to fish commercially or to explore for offshore hydrocarbons offer ways to allocate limited resources, they have proved to be continual sources of conflict. This is due in part to the difficulty of representing environmental values or the value of subsistence activities to an indigenous community in the utilitarian terms required to give them exchange value in market transactions.

Future prospects for private ownership and market solutions

In the Canadian North, we can anticipate sizable additional transfers of public land and money to aboriginal groups through the comprehensive land claims process. When ongoing comprehensive claims of the Dene/Metis, Council of Yukon Indians, Labrador Inuit Association, and Tungavik Federation of Nunavut are settled, existing development corporations will have ready access to both land and capital and will make even greater use of private bargaining and market forces to deal with conflicts over development, job opportunities, and environmental and social issues.

As in Alaska, new Native elites are emerging, and conflict between these elites and other village residents occasionally flare. However, the agreements are designed to avoid some of the major conflicts caused by ANCSA. The Canadian Native development corporations do not have individual shareholders; land is held as communal property by a landholding corporation that must act on behalf of all the 'members' of the region; membership in the region is continually open to Natives born after the settlement and is connected to long-term residency in the region, and separate investment corporations are responsible for protecting the compensation funds by looking for safe, low risk investments that provide a good profit. This last provision is an attempt to insulate the principal and some of the profits from loss through higher risk ventures aimed to stimulate economic development in the region. For example, the Inuvialuit Regional Corporation (IRC), the parent corporation run by directors elected from each of six subregions, determines major policy and allocates funds among three subsidiary corporations, each of which has different goals: one holds title to the settlement lands, one functions as a trust fund to protect a portion of the compensation funds, and a third is charged with economic development.[73] Ideally, the Native development corporations will not spend the principal of the settlement funds or put the corporate lands at risk, but will use only a portion of the income from the investment corporation, government grants and loans, and profits to invest in risky ventures to stimulate regional and local economic growth. If the system is successful, some of the conflicts that have arisen in Alaska between corporate leaders and proponents of tribal sovereignty may be avoided.

In Alaska, while there is little likelihood of major new transfers of public property to private hands, transfers of lesser property interests in the form of leases to explore for hydrocarbons and minerals are probable. One proposed transfer of subsurface rights in the Arctic National Wildlife Refuge (ANWR) is generating considerable controversy in Congress. In 1987, a group of Native corporations offered to exchange 891,000 acres of land within or adjacent to seven national wildlife refuges for hydrocarbon leases (mineral rights) to 65 whole tracts and 8 partial tracts in the ANWR covering 11 percent of the federally owned coastal plain.[74] Additionally, the state is likely to offer to sell land on favorable terms to attract new industrial development. For example, the state has offered a private energy corporation an option to purchase a site in Valdez for a future oil refinery.[75]

While proponents of tribal sovereignty seek to shift title to lands now held by many Native corporations (the private sector) to tribal governments (a form of public sector ownership), this is unlikely to become a widespread occurrence in the short term. Under the 1987 Amendments to ANCSA, stock in Native regional and village corporations will remain inalienable until the shareholders or the Directors with shareholder approval vote to remove the restrictions on the sale of their stock.[76] In all likelihood, the Cook Inlet Regional Corporation (CIRI) will ask shareholders to approve removal of the restrictions on alienation, and a few other corporations may follow suit. Some fear take-over of Native corporations, not by non-Native interests, but by a small Native elite that has acquired a sophisticated understanding of the corporate world and that is able, often in the role of corporate directors, to amass the capital to buy out low-income shareholders who will be pressed by personal economic circumstances to sell their stock. This would lead to even deeper divisions within Native communities and fuel the tribal sovereignty fight.

The likely future for limited entry fisheries is one in which Native individuals and communities will face increasing erosion of their economic base as permits pass into the hands of non-locals. This can only lead to larger disparities in income between urban and rural Alaskans, and between Native and non-Native residents, disparities likely to increase the frequency of anomie, alcoholism, suicide, and family violence which follow in the footsteps of a crumbling economy and the disruption of traditional economic and social activities.

Though recent declines in world oil prices have reduced interest in Arctic OCS leasing and development, and consequently reduced conflicts over exploration activities, the U.S. Secretary of the Interior still plans substantial lease sales offshore of Alaska as well as the opening of a portion of the coastal plain of the ANWR for oil and gas exploration. In the long run, both hydrocarbon and mineral exploration will engender conflict across the Arctic. While the current leasing arrangements are adequate to manage conflicts over allocation among competing industry interests, the OCS and mineral leasing systems do not resolve conflicts over fundamental issues of where, when, and how development should occur. Hence, these leasing programs are likely to continue to produce litigation and legislative battles. These conflicts, however, may be resolved in the private sector through the use of alternative methods of dispute resolution, an option discussed in the next section.

One area in which property interests could be expanded in the Arctic with dramatic effects on the handling of conflict involves the management of fish and wildlife. Nowhere in the far North has a proprietary interest in fish and wildlife been acknowledged in the law. But two prominent Canadian northern scholars have suggested that courts should recognize a proprietary interest of aboriginal peoples in fur, fish, and game resources. Banks and Usher argue that the Canadian legal right known as a 'profit à prendre', closely approximates the relationship Natives have with wildlife. The 'profit à prendre' accords its holders rights to compensation from third parties for damages to their interest. If Natives were accorded such a property interest in fish, fur, and game, they could resolve conflicts with holders of mining licences and other development permits through direct negotiations, and the courts would guarantee them compensation for damage to their 'profit' interest in accord with established rules of law.[77] Arguably, some treaty Indians in Canada and the lower 48 already have a similar property interest (a usufructuary right) in fish and wildlife under the terms of their treaties with federal governments. Judge Boldt's well-known decision, in Washington State, for example, accorded Indians a right to fifty percent of the fish caught in state waters, a decision that triggered further litigation over the issue of whether those treaty rights include the right to protection from third party damages to fish stocks as well as the right to an equal share of the allowable catch.[78] The bargaining position of Native peoples would be strengthened by this form of privatization, and established methods of private bargaining as well as market mechanisms could operate to resolve conflicts between subsistence users and extractive resource developers.

Privatization in the far North has undoubtedly led to more conflict resolution through private bargaining and the operation of market mechanisms. The increase in private ownership of land has created new alliances between Native interests and industry, while provoking new lines of conflict within the Native community between native corporate interests and village interests. Still, there is no structure of private property (or other transferable) rights associated with many Arctic resources (most of the land areas and offshore waters as well as all wildlife) due to the prevalence of public ownership or exclusive management authority throughout the Circumpolar North. Prevailing private sector procedures, like market-based exchange and private bargaining, therefore offer responses to a limited, though important, range of conflicts in the Arctic.

7.2   Alternative dispute resolution

Today, alternatives to conventional methods of conflict resolution, such as litigation, legislation, and direct negotiation, are flourishing. We have divided these alternatives into two broad categories: negotiation with the assistance of third parties and problem solving activities that address issues before they emerge as full-blown conflicts on the policy agenda. There is growing interest in developing constructive roles for third parties and employing creative problem-solving techniques, like simulation exercises, role playing, and future imaging. Problem solving describes an approach to conflict resolution in which parties break out of rigid formulations of the issues and reconceptualize them as joint or common problems requiring efforts to accommodate the legitimate interests of all parties. Such activities focus on maximizing joint benefits and avoiding mutual losses.[79]

Assisted negotiation: the case of the Bering Sea

In assisted negotiations, one or more third parties, whose roles may range from convener or go-between to conciliator and mediator, assist stakeholders to settle a specific conflict or set of conflicts. In 1985–1986, for example, representatives of oil companies, environmental groups, Native organizations, and fishing interests negotiated a joint position on offshore hydrocarbon leasing in the Bering Sea with the assistance of intermediaries. This is one of the few cases of assisted negotiation involving natural resources in the Arctic.[80] By examining the Bering Sea case in some detail, we can address a number of questions regarding potential roles for third parties in Arctic resource conflicts.

In May 1986, seven oil companies, six national and three Alaskan environmental groups (as well as a coalition of environmental groups that focus on coastal issues), two Alaskan commercial fishing organizations, eleven traditional Alaska Native villages, an Alaska Native environmental organization operating in the Yukon-Kushokwim Delta, and the regional coastal management agency representing villages of that region presented the U.S. Secretary of the Interior with a joint position on Interior's proposed Five-Year Oil and Gas Leasing Program for Mid-1987 to Mid-1992.[81] The joint proposal would have put all but 48 of the roughly 240 million acres in the Bering Sea (excluding Bristol Bay) off limits to the oil industry for the next five years. The agreement also created an ongoing process for resolving continuing issues of offshore development in the Bering Sea. The negotiations leading to this agreement involved the assistance of the Institute for Resource Management (IRM), a private non-profit organization founded by actor Robert Redford and based in Salt Lake City.[82]

Offshore oil and gas lease sales in Alaska have sparked numerous lawsuits – and Congressional battles – at great cost to environmental and Native plaintiffs and industry and government defendants. Generally, conflict arises because Native, environmental, and fishing interests want to prevent exploration in environmentally sensitive areas while the oil industry wants to maximize the area available for lease selection and potential drilling. While these interests appear to be diametrically opposed, the parties also have some common interests. In an adversarial process, all parties risk a total or at least substantial loss, face considerable expenses or costly delays, and often obtain a result that does not end the controversy. All parties to those controversies have a stake in finding more enduring and efficient ways of resolving them. The Bering Sea negotiation began as an attempt to get industry leaders together with environmental leaders to search for better ways to deal with offshore leasing issues throughout the United States.

At the outset, Redford invited a few environmental and industry leaders to meet in Washington, D.C. and asked IRM Board member, Congressman Philip Sharp, to chair the meeting. Sharp is Chair of the Subcommittee on Energy and Power (of the House Energy and Commerce Committee) and third ranking member of the Subcommittee on Energy and the Environment (of the House Interior and Insular Affairs Committee), making him extremely powerful regarding U.S. energy policy. This group (the initial steering committee) planned a larger meeting of environmental, fishing, and oil industry executives. The steering committee agreed to let each side choose its own participants, despite the reluctance of some participants to sit down at the table with certain other individuals or organizations. Industry eventually brought chief operating officers, exploration and production executives familiar with the issues, rather than the chief executive officers of the giant parent corporations. Environmentalists invited the chief executive officers of major national and regional environmental groups most involved in offshore leasing issues and key staff members concerned with offshore development. The participants came from a high enough level in their respective organizations to make binding decisions during negotiations. As the process evolved, Alaskan Natives and commercial fishing interests joined the environmental team. Four meetings with groups of about 30 participants (roughly 15 from each side) followed.

Redford invited the chosen participants to Morro Bay, California, in August 1985. Attracted by his name and reputation as well as the scenic coastal setting and, especially, intrigued by the prospects of settling major differences in a new way, executives of environmental organizations and oil companies agreed to attend. Most were skeptical that any agreement would emerge from the effort. The initial icebreaker, a dinner cruise along the shoreline, broke more ice than planned when nine foot seas left opponents 'clutching each other and getting seasick'.[83] The opening working session was even rockier as both sides engaged in what conflict theorists call ventilation and participants called 'chest-thumping'.

Despite, or because of, the rough beginning, participants agreed to a process that eventually produced a signed agreement. Selecting the Bering Sea offshore of Alaska as a test case, the parties agreed to produce two composite maps showing the areas of their greatest concern (limited to 30% of the total planning area). To preserve the confidentiality of proprietary information, companies were invited to submit selections to the accounting firm of Price-Waterhouse which compiled a composite map of industry interests. Price-Waterhouse requested the companies to rank their selections in three categories: 'IA' (highest priorities, limited to 5,000 tracts), 'IB' (medium high priorities, limited to 2,800 tracts), and 'II' (the remaining 20% or 15,600 tracts).

The environmentalists followed a similar ranking to compile a map of tracts they most wanted deleted from the five-year plan. Following the decision to use the Bering Sea as a test case, IRM provided the one Alaskan who had attended the Morro Bay meeting (David Benton, a private consultant to environmental and Native organizations) with travel funds that enabled him to meet with Native and environmental organizations along the Bering Sea coast from the Aleutian chain to Nome. A contingent of Alaskan representatives (including three Natives who played an active role in future negotiations) arrived at the next meeting with a composite map representing the interests of commercial fishers, Natives, and environmentalists.

When the maps resulting from this process were revealed at Headlands (near San Francisco) in November 1985, many participants initially thought the conflicts would be insurmountable. Both sides had identified most of the North Aleutian Basin (the Bristol Bay area) as a category I priority, and there were pockets of conflict elsewhere as well, especially along parts of the continental shelf break (an area that is extremely productive biologically) which coincided with a geological fault of interest to industry. At the time, litigation over Bristol Bay appeared imminent.

To avoid the problem of too many people at the negotiating table, the parties agreed to select smaller negotiating teams enpowered to make deals for their respective sides. In order to end continuing unproductive disputes, they agreed not to question the reasons behind particular tracts shown on each side's map and not to debate the risks involved in oil exploration and development.[84] When the smaller negotiating teams met, with the assistance of moderator Philip Sharp, they agreed to postpone negotiations over Bristol Bay.[85] This significantly reduced the areas of conflict. Participants estimated that the remaining overlap shown on the two maps covered less than five percent of the Bering Sea. The negotiating teams then engaged in a familiar bargaining process, swapping concessions to reach agreement in principle on a unified map. But the hard work of producing a detailed map, drafting stipulations regarding operations on tracts to be leased, and agreeing on a joint letter to the Secretary remained to be done. The parties aimed to complete the negotiations within a month.

The agreement almost fell apart before the next meeting at Sundance, Utah on December 20. Although the steering committee (which now included members of the small negotiating teams) worked continually to prepare for that meeting, the larger group would not sign the deal. Industry participants thought the environmental stipulations regarding operations were too restrictive. The meeting broke down in acrimony, a breakdown that might have been avoided had participants not been rushed. But some representatives could only spare one day for the negotiations at that time of year.

Media coverage added to the strained relations at the Sundance meeting. IRM had carefully selected one reporter to admit to the Morro

Bay meeting, Ken Wells of the *Wall Street Journal*. Industry participants demanded that Wells be excluded from the Headlands meeting while environmentalists wanted him there and trusted that he would not file a report without prior agreement of the participants. Despite being excluded, Wells obtained information and published a story that caused some problems at Sundance.[86]

IRM played its most active role at and after the Sundance meeting, first coaxing the parties to give the process another week and then preparing a 'white paper' that bought more time and, when refined, became the basis of the final agreement. Two IRM facilitators attended every joint negotiating session of the full group and provided occasional substantive ideas as well as frequent encouragement to the parties to stick with the process. Their back seat presence in negotiations prior to Sundance enabled them to understand and communicate with the parties in the month following the Sundance meeting when they talked intensively with both sides. With this assistance and push from the intermediaries, the steering committee worked out the final map and accompanying language.

The resulting agreement, finally signed in Houston in April 1986 and submitted to the Secretary of the Interior in May, proposed (1) a map indicating areas recommended for inclusion in and exclusion from the Five-Year Leasing Program (see Figure 24a and b), and (2) establishment of a committee to study and make recommendations to the Secretary regarding specific stipulations in the Bering Sea (subsequently named the Bering Sea Resource Association, BSRA). The three page document accompanying the map also contained principles and guidelines for stipulations to be developed by this more technical advisory committee. Recommendations for specific lease sale restrictions were left for future negotiations of the BSRA.

Selling the recommendations to the Department of the Interior (DOI), however, proved harder than reaching agreement. The Secretary's Final 5-Year Leasing Program for Mid-1987 to Mid-1992 released on July 2, 1987 contained all the 48 million acres that the joint agreement would have allowed to be leased. But the Secretary added 32 million acres encompassing 187 tracts environmentalists had identified as Category I priorities. Interior 'highlighted' the additional tracts for special presale consideration.[87] Only 2·4 percent (135 tracts) of the highlighted area had been identified on the industry map as industry priorities. And the area Interior added only increased the oil and gas potential by 1 to 2 percent.[88] Most of those who signed the final agreement were extremely disappointed by the Secretary's response.

Environmentalists who participated in the negotiation share the strong

Fig. 24. (a) Map showing Department of Interior's planning areas for leasing offshore of Alaska. *Source*: U.S. Dept. of the Interior, Minerals Management Service, '5-Year Leasing Program Mid-1987 to Mid-1992', April 1987.

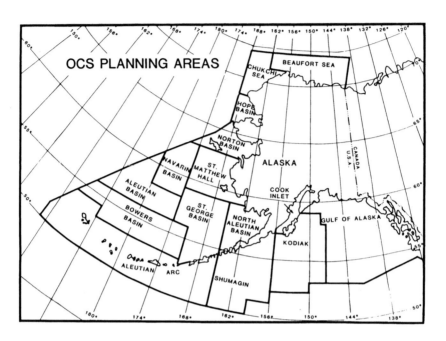

feeling that Interior based its decision in no small measure on hurt feelings over being excluded from the process and not being responsible itself for an obvious success. An Interior spokesperson, in fact, stated explicitly that the Minerals Management Service (MMS) and the State of Alaska, key parties in the formal decision process, should have been included in the negotiations.[89]

MMS officials viewed their final program not as a rejection of the joint agreement but as partial acceptance. They pointed out that the Plan includes all the tracts that would have been included under the joint agreement. This view, of course, ignores the fact that the parties reached agreement on the inclusion of these tracts only through hard bargaining over the elimination of other tracts that the DOI plan added. MMS also noted that the Secretary, by law, must consider comments from government, the Governor of Alaska, other industry representatives not present at the IRM meetings, and the general public, and that his decision must be guided by principles and goals set forth in the Outer Continental Shelf Lands Act. Signatories to the agreement argued that the Secretary's legal obligations were all addressed by the agreement and that the joint

Fig. 24. (b) Joint recommendations of signatories to the Bering Sea Agreement regarding areas for inclusion and exclusion from 5 year leasing program. *Source*: Institute for Resource Management.

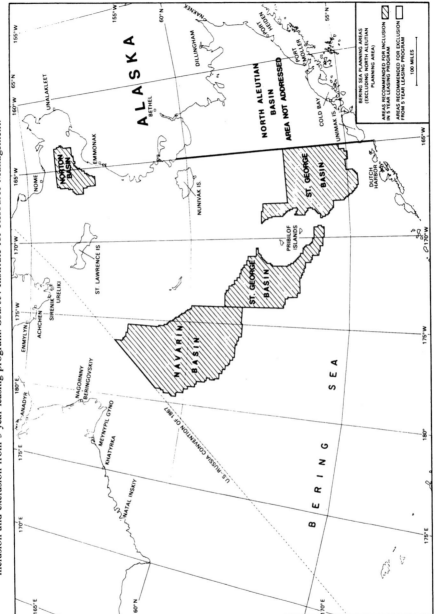

proposal presented DOI with a compromise politically acceptable to all sides, thus avoiding the usual political efforts to persuade Congress to place a moratorium on certain tracts and avoiding litigation over this part of the five-year plan and over future lease sales under the plan in the Bering Sea.

The Administration took the view that potential lease sale areas should not be narrowed until the final stage, when individual lease sales cover particular basins within the Bering Sea. This view is shared by at least one major oil company that submitted data for the map but did not participate in the negotiations. The Administration also argued that companies do not formulate their actual decisions until later in the process when new economic, geologic, and environmental data are available to influence their choice of tracts in a particular lease sale. This argument assumes that by chopping areas out of one five-year leasing program, it becomes more difficult to add those areas to future programs. Yet, this was a risk that oil company participants in the negotiation were willing to take in order to resolve conflicts, avoid litigation and legislative battles, and gain certainty for planning purposes.

Some industry participants believe that DOI will adopt the negotiated map at the lease sale stage, dropping the 'highlighted' tracts when it announces specific lease sales. But the overall objective of reaching a negotiated settlement has not been achieved. The parties hoped to avoid administrative and legislative battles as well as litigation over the size and location of each Bering Sea lease sale for the next five years. Instead, they will be occupied by these issues at each lease sale.

Participants in the negotiation are reluctant to devote time and resources to similar efforts in other areas without assurance that the Department of the Interior will implement any resulting agreement. Following the agreement over the Bering Sea and prior to the Secretary's final decision on the five-year plan, environmental and industry representatives (including some of the individuals who participated in the Bering Sea negotiation) began negotiating over leasing on Georges Bank in the North Atlantic offshore of New England. Shortly after negotiations began, however, the Secretary released his five-year plan, and the principal environmental organization opposing leasing there withdrew, refusing to return to the table unless the Secretary implements the Bering Sea agreement. Nevertheless, some participants believe that negotiated agreements are possible for other offshore areas, such as the eastern portion of the Gulf of Mexico and the North Atlantic.

The Bering Sea negotiation has resulted in improved relations and increased contacts among the principals. The Bering Sea Resource

Association met in October 1987. Some participants reported that new contacts made during the process enabled them to discuss other issues and avoid potential conflicts. The steering committee continues to converse regularly (by telephone) on OCS issues. Unfortunately, a number of the industry participants retired or were transferred during and after the negotiations, reducing the potential positive benefits that might have accrued from the building of new relationships among environmental, Native, fishing, and oil industry leaders.[90]

This case demonstrates that alternative dispute resolution processes can enable conflicting parties to identify and set aside areas of pure conflict and concentrate on the more tractable elements of a conflict. Positions regarding Bristol Bay had hardened even before negotiations began, and the maps confirmed the nearly total conflict of interests in this area. Accordingly, the parties agreed to set aside this zone of pure conflict and reached a negotiated settlement covering the remaining area of less severe, though still considerable, conflict.

Overall, this case convinced some participants of the positive benefits of private sector alternative dispute resolution. The parties certainly have a better idea of which conflicts are resolvable through assisted negotiations. However, they are not likely to use this process where the battle lines are already clearly drawn and positions fixed, nor are they willing to expend substantial human and monetary resources in the absence of encouragement from government.

Problem-solving activities

Efforts to deal with conflicts of interest before they precipitate crises or require specific policy decisions are more prevalent than assisted negotiations in the Arctic region. Private non-profit organizations, some oriented toward academic pursuits and others toward advocacy, are entering the arena of Arctic conflict resolution. While not all symposia or conferences involve conflict resolution, a number of meetings have employed problem-solving techniques to reduce, resolve, or manage Arctic conflicts. The chief difference between these efforts and assisted negotiation is that these are attempts to deal with issues before they become fully defined conflicts on the front burner of the policy-making process. Several examples of Arctic problem solving demonstrate the promise of this role of the private sector and raise questions about the organization of problem-solving activities in the future.

U.S.A.–Canada Arctic Policy Forum Twenty-six individuals from governments, groups representing industry, environmental, and Native interests, and académe gathered at the Banff Springs Hotel in October 1984 for a frank discussion of the potential for cooperation between the United States and Canada in the Arctic. This was no ordinary academic conference. Rather it was an attempt to provide, as the sponsors put it, 'a venue for "back-channel" negotiations'.[91] By drawing together some of the players and leading thinkers on Arctic problems (in roughly equal numbers from Canada and the U.S.A.), the sponsors hoped to explore a range of controversial Arctic issues, generate new approaches to Arctic policy, and provide an informal opportunity for stakeholders and policymakers to get to know their counterparts in a pleasant and private settting.

Unfortunately, both Native and environmental representatives were under-represented at the conference. The conveners might beneficially have included representatives of groups such as the Inuit Circumpolar Conference, the Inuvialuit (residents of the Canadian Beaufort Sea coast), the Coast Alliance (a coalition of U.S.A. environmental groups), the TFN (land claims negotiators for Inuit of the central and eastern Canadian Arctic), and the Canadian Arctic Resources Committee (CARC). While one forum participant, the science advisor to the North Slope Borough, raised issues relevant to environmental and Native groups, he could not fill the sizable gap left by the absence of leaders of such private sector organizations. Government officials and private consultants discussed and identified the interests of these groups, but their comments lacked the force and passion (as well as the ability to decide priorities of interests) that only stakeholders can provide.

The sponsors of this three-day event excluded media and promised the participants anonymity in publications stemming from the meetings in order to avoid hardening of each nation's position while generating new ideas that could gain the acceptance of policymakers on both sides of the border.[92] The isolated setting coupled with opportunities for participants to meet more informally at meal times and in the evening further advanced the sponsors' objectives.

This Forum differed markedly from the Bering Sea lease sale negotiations in which stakeholders bargained over a single, specific (though complex) controversy. The goals of the Arctic Policy Forum were more diverse and the subject matter far broader. The organizers hoped to identify transboundary Arctic problems that could be resolved through bilateral cooperation between the U.S. and Canada. The Forum entered the process at an earlier stage as participants were asked to pinpoint issues that could cause friction in the future and discuss ways to avoid crises through cooperation. The Forum can therefore be characterized more as an exercise in conflict prevention than in conflict resolution. While the problems discussed are real, they were not then on the front burner of the public policy agenda. In Canada, the new Mulroney government was still filling key posts and had yet to focus on the Arctic, much less to announce an Arctic policy. American policymakers, as usual, were not thinking much about the Arctic at all.

The first formal session of the Forum began with a presentation of papers. Participants then divided into country 'caucuses'. While the Canadians used their caucus to prepare a statement of their *interests*, the Americans bypassed this step and spent the morning mulling over an opening *position*. Thus, the conveners ignored one of the most basic precepts of ADR and problem solving; they allowed the participants to stake out positions before determining their interests, foregoing a crucial step necessary to determining where opposing parties' interests actually converge.

Gradually, the Forum produced an agenda for further exploration. From the broader realm of Arctic cooperation, participants identified the Beaufort Sea as an area ripe for transboundary cooperation, especially with regard to exploitation of natural resources, environmental management, and marine transportation. Conferees agreed that the jurisdictional disputes over the Northwest Passage and Arctic waters and the Beaufort Sea boundary would be much more difficult to tackle. Conference sponsors are currently seeking funding for two additional sessions of the Arctic Policy Forum to explore in detail ways of cooperating to solve U.S./Canadian conflicts in the Beaufort Sea area before positions on either side harden or provoke crises.

At this writing, it would be hard to attribute any direct results to the Arctic Policy Forum. Three American officials who participated have since retired or moved to other positions unconcerned with the Arctic. The U.S. has yet to articulate any new intiatives towards Arctic cooperation.[93] Conflict between the U.S. and Canada over opening the Arctic National Wildlife Refuge to oil and gas exploration is brewing. Gulf Canada has tankered oil from the Beaufort westward through the American Arctic despite protests by Native residents of the North Slope of Alaska. Continued meetings of the Arctic Policy Forum could improve communication over these conflicts and set the stage for creation of a transboundary regime for marine transport and environmental protection in the Beaufort. After the United States Coast Guard icebreaker, *Polar Sea*, transited the Northwest Passage in August 1985, Canadian and American positions on jurisdictional issues in the high Arctic hardened.[94] The Arctic Policy Forum could help to diffuse this conflict and pave the way to cooperative arrangements that serve the interests of both nations.

CARC's 'National Symposium on the North in the 1980s' In 1986 and 1987, the Canadian Arctic Resources Committee (CARC) hosted six public seminars on emerging northern issues with varying success. Three of these seminars offer particularly useful lessons for private actors interested in problem-solving activities.[95] Two of the seminars (one on Canada's sovereignty and international Arctic interests and one on Canada's land claims policy) dealt with issues just beginning to emerge on the policy agenda. The third (on Native harvesting and commercialization of northern wildlife) dealt with a full-blown controversy in which opposing sides have strong fixed positions.

(1) Symposium on Canada's Sovereignty and International Arctic Interests. A shift in emphasis from assertions of Canadian sovereignty in Arctic waters to discussion of mutual interests and possibilities for international cooperation in the Arctic would help resolve conflicts between Canada and her northern neighbors. CARC selected this topic to contribute to rethinking Canada's Arctic interests and policy on sovereignty. Arctic sovereignty generates considerable passion on the part of Canadians, but at this symposium, there were only a few moments when the chauvanistic tendencies of both Americans and Canadians flared.

Regarding participants, the most noticeable absence was a speaker from External Affairs. External sent representatives to listen and report to headquarters, but instructed them not to participate in 'broad ranging discussions of a speculative nature'.[96] The Department of National Defence, on the other hand, provided a panelist who had mastered the bureaucratic art of nondisclosure. And no U.S. government officials participated. The forum focused on Canadian policy, and understandably on Canadian views, but a spokesperson for the U.S. Department of State could have articulated the interests of a key party essential to reformulation of the sovereignty conflict as a common problem. Since the assembled audience did not hear from those directly responsible for international interests in the Canadian Arctic, the dialogue was confined to non-governmental experts, stakeholders representing Native and environmental interests, reporters, and interested onlookers.

CARC selected a generic conference room on the top floor of a Toronto hotel to hold the meeting. Government representatives, academics, a retired general, Native spokespersons, and advocacy groups presented their views on emerging international issues to a small, respectful audience who asked questions, commented, and went their separate ways when the formal symposium was not in session. While meetings in major cities offer ease of access, they also provide distractions and a means of escape, reducing the likelihood of future cooperation.

Despite these drawbacks, the meeting may have achieved one of its objectives; putting the North on the policy agenda of those dealing with international relations and defence. Two months later, in December 1986, the Secretary of State for External Affairs, Joe Clark, publicly acknowledged the need for a 'northern foreign policy' in remarks responding to a report of a Special Joint Committee of Parliament on Canadian International Relations. That report, *Internationalism and Interdependence* (better known as the Simard-Hockin report) devoted a chapter specifically to northern foreign policy. The Government has not, to date, developed a northern foreign policy or even a process to create one. But the Defence White Paper issued in June 1987 called for purchase of ten to twelve nuclear-powered submarines capable of operating in Arctic waters. This will force reconsideration of Canada's foreign policy in relation to the Arctic. As the papers and report from this CARC forum become available, they will add to the body of thought on which policy makers can draw as they address an issue that the symposium may have helped move to the forefront of decision making.

(2) Symposium on Land Claims Policy. In April 1986, private stakeholders (Native and industry leaders) in a controversy over the federal government's comprehensive aboriginal land claims policy assembled around a square table in Yellowknife, NWT, to discuss the report of the Federal Task Force on Native Claims Policy (also called the Coolican Report after Task Force chair, Murray Coolican). That report, released only a month earlier, recommended substantial changes in the scope and approach of Canada's land claims negotiations. Most notably, the report suggested that government abandon the practice of extinguishing all aboriginal rights and title through the claims process, and instead acknowledge and define those rights. Additionally, the report recommended greater flexibility in the process and less finality in the settlements.

At the time of the CARC symposium, the Minister of Indian and Northern Affairs had promised to revamp his Department's policy on comprehensive land claims and submit the new policy to Parliament within six weeks. At the same time, Native leaders had formed a Comprehensive Claims Coalition to lobby for acceptance of many recommendations in the Coolican report. Unlike the other symposia in the series, only invited participants were included in much of the discussion. Observers, including senior government officials, were asked to hold their comments until the end of the session. While some invitees used the event to pontificate on their positions, most engaged in a frank exchange that served to clarify the areas where conflicting parties' perspectives converged. The meeting was punctuated with direct, candid, and friendly exchanges between Native leaders and petroleum industry executives. The symposium helped these often opposing groups to identify and emphasize shared interests regarding land claims issues. The symposium demonstrated to senior policy makers and the public that a consensus opposing broad extinguishment of aboriginal rights had emerged among stakeholders (especially the Native organizations that had united in a strong coalition). The symposium may have helped to convince the public and policymakers that extinguishment characteristic of earlier land claims settlements is not only offensive to Natives but also unnecessary.

The meeting had numerous virtues from the standpoint of conflict resolution which set it apart from other CARC symposia and the Arctic Policy Forum. In particular, the timing, choice of participants, and structure of the meeting worked to produce non-confrontational communication between stakeholders and consensus on some key issues. Three factors especially contributed to success:

(1) the symposium dealt with a specific policy issue at a key moment in the decision-making process (after release of the Coolican report and before the federal government had responded (perhaps even before the parties had hardened their positions);

(2) high level representatives of the key players in the controversy participated; and

(3) conveners provided a workshop setting conducive to discussion among the stakeholders rather than a panel of paper presenters followed by general audience response.

It would be naive to credit this symposium with a determinate role in achieving agreement regarding the long-standing controversy over comprehensive land claims policy and procedures. As it turned out, Minister Crombie did not submit a new policy to Parliament in July. Instead, Prime Minister Mulroney shuffled his Cabinet replacing Crombie with Bill McKnight, who brought a new style and approach to the issues. There was a period in which some expected the Government to shelve the Coolican report without making policy changes. The Native coalition pushed hard to keep land claims policy on the agenda. In October, George Erasmus, National Chief of the Assembly of First Nations, met with Mulroney and pressed him to adopt a new policy based on the Task Force recommendations before the 1987 constitutional conference on aboriginal rights (scheduled for February 1987). Finally, in December, the

Government unveiled its new policy demonstrating partial acceptance of some of the broad principles of the Coolican report, especially with regard to sharing resource revenues with the aboriginal peoples and not extinguishing all aboriginal rights.[97]

While the CARC Yellowknife symposium may not have played a critical role in resolving the ongoing conflict over land claims policy in Canada, it served an important function as the only public meeting on the subject occurring between release of the Coolican Report and adoption of a new Government policy on comprehensive land claims. CARC played a useful role in providing neutral facilitation and a forum for discussion of an Arctic conflict at a crucial juncture in a controversy that is not settled yet.

(3) Symposium on Native Harvesting and Commercialization of Northern Wildlife. A different lesson may be drawn from the Montreal meeting in January 1987 on the topic, 'Native Wildlife Management, the Anti-harvest Movement and the Commercialization of Northern Wildlife'. Organizers invited Native leaders (from Indigenous Survival International and other organizations) to debate leaders of the animal rights and animal welfare movement in a highly publicized evening meeting. Supporters of each side (who grouped themselves in blocs, *pro* and *con*) packed a windowless auditorium exceeding the 250 seat capacity. The audience booed and cheered the speakers. Several times voices of both speakers and audience 'questioners' cracked with anger. Unwittingly, the sponsors created an ideal environment for further hardening of positions, strengthening the win/lose mentality that has characterized the animal protection controversy. The balance of the meeting consisted of panels of presenters followed by questions and comments from the floor and some brief discussion among the panelists and those attending the two days of workshops. While these sessions were less fraught with overt hostility, little serious exchange could occur in the shadow of the posturing of the leaders of major groups who, unsheltered from their publics or the media, used the event for their own purposes.

The symposium highlighted the fact that disputes over consumptive use of wild animals stem from intensely felt core values. The parties themselves are unlikely to find common ground (a contract zone) for cooperation. At best, public policy makers may be able to manage, but not resolve, the conflict. The meeting demonstrated the degree to which the parties are polarized and positions fixed. If this symposium accomplished any end, it strengthened the resolve of each side to promote its own interests and served notice to each side that its opponents are not likely to cooperate or to abandon their causes.

A subsidiary lesson of the Montreal symposium concerns the utility of disinterested sponsors. Animal rights activists questioned the fairness of the Chair in light of the co-sponsorship and financial support by the fur industry. CARC's executive director, John Merritt, said afterwards that he would think twice before co-sponsoring a seminar in the future with the fur industry, not because it undercut fairness, but because such sponsorship 'deflects the issues at hand and allows people to go off on conspiracy fantasies'.[97a] CARC, though not itself neutral on the animal rights controversy, saw this symposium as an opportunity to clarify the stakes for each side, elucidate the issues, and allow the public to choose allegiances. Had the sponsors been searching for common ground between stakeholders, rather than sparking vigorous debate, the issue of sponsorship would have seriously set back their objectives.

In this case CARC made no attempt to distance itself from the current controversies and did not provide a solving forum for conflict management. Instead, the symposium highlighted the lines separating opposing parties. In all likelihood, these lines were already indelibly fixed, making reformulations of the issues extremely unlikely, if not impossible.

7.3   Lessons of ADR and problem solving

The Bering Sea negotiations, the Arctic Policy Forum, and the CARC symposia provide useful lessons regarding selection of participants, the role of government officials, the place of media, the process, and the role of third parties for those engaged in assisted negotiated or in problem solving and consensus building activities in the future.

Selection of participants

Meaningful consensus requires participation of the key interest groups. Facilitators in a negotiation undoubtedly recognize that they must have representatives of all the major players in a specific controversy in order to reach an agreement that will not be attacked immediately by parties excluded from the process. But organizers of problem-solving activities aimed at emerging conflicts sometimes proceed without participation of key stakeholders despite the fact that a forum lacking such players can easily degenerate into nothing but an academic conference.

In the Bering Sea case, seven oil companies signed the final agreement, and three additional major oil companies with current lease interests in the Bering Sea concurred in the map (although they opposed establishing a technical advisory committee). In all, between 55 and 76 percent of those already holding Bering Sea leases at the time approved the map.[98]

However, at least one key company dropped out of the process after the Headlands meeting, and a number participated only minimally in the negotiations. Seventeen companies supplied data used in the map compiled by Price-Waterhouse; fifteen attended one or more of the meetings. More of the oil companies interested in a region will have to participate throughout negotiations and sign a final agreement to win the support of government officials. Ironically, it will probably take government encouragement to bring more oil companies to the table. Fears that MMS would not implement the agreement and might retaliate against those companies that did participate may have influenced some companies' decisions not to negotiate or not to sign the final agreement.

Representatives selected to participate in alternative dispute resolution processes should be those with the appropriate expertise and the authority to make decisions for their company or organization as they were in the Bering Sea negotiations. And participants on all sides should be approximate equals. For example, the chief executive officer of an environmental organization rather than lower level staff should participate opposite the president of an oil production company. Conveners must balance the need for a small, workable number of participants with the need for adequate representation of interests and sufficient numbers to ensure sustained gains.

Major benefits flow from personal contacts made at a symposium or during a negotiation. Organizers of problem-solving fora need to invite participants who will be in key positions to *influence* if not to *make* government policy. One of the problems in identifying appropriate participants is the risk that any accomplishments may be nullified when key participants retire or change jobs. The most appropriate individual may not be the person currently holding a government post, but a consultant or highly respected expert who wields influence as a trusted advisor regardless of which party is in power.

The role of government

Determining the proper role of government officials in private problem-solving activities is always difficult. In the CARC Yellowknife meeting, the presence of senior officials (as observers) was essential. The meeting was staged for them to have an opportunity to see and hear the leaders of the groups most affected by policy decisions. Though invited to speak at the CARC forum on international issues, the key government agency, External Affairs, preferred the role of observer. And in negotiations over the Bering Sea lease sale, private participants agreed to exclude government representatives. But that exclusion played a significant role in the Secretary's reluctance to accept the resulting agreement. Informants indicated that industry would not have participated or could not have been candid in the presence of government decision makers. Understandably, participants would be inhibited by the prospect of having to engage in the usual advocacy process if no agreement were reached. Legally, the Department of the Interior could not have committed itself beforehand to implementation of a negotiated position, and yet Interior's refusal to accept the recommendations has discouraged other efforts by private actors to engage in similar conflict resolution processes. It should come as no surprise that both state and federal government officials view private negotiations like the Bering Sea process as an intrusion on their functions.

Despite the necessity of excluding government observers or participants in the Bering Sea negotiation, the IRM facilitators concluded that they should be more open with government officials at the federal and, especially, the state level in the future. IRM wrote a brief and 'cryptic' letter to the Secretary of the Interior and communicated verbally with the Governor's Office in Alaska after the Morro Bay meeting informing government officials only generally of the existence of the process.[99] But officials had heard about the meeting through prior leaks. In future negotiations, the intermediaries should cultivate receptivity by state and federal officials both in advance of and throughout the process. Third parties need to find creative ways to obtain the trust and blessing not only of the highest officials in the relevant government agencies but also among the resistant ranks of large bureaucracies unaccustomed to having opposing interest groups resolve their differences outside processes that governments manage.

The role of media

The presence of media in assisted negotiations and problem-solving processes may serve the interests of some parties more than others and encourage strategic behaviour in processes designed to maximize cooperation and joint gains. Usually, the presence of reporters and especially of cameras inhibits frank discussion and encourages posturing. In a negotiating process, facilitators should exclude media or at least obtain agreement of the parties before admitting any media observers.

There are occasions when problem-solving efforts benefit from the media's presence (such as the CARC symposia). However, these occasions are designed to heighten public awareness and move issues onto the public policy agenda; they are not usually aimed at altering the positions of interest groups or obtaining consensus among divergent interests.

Unquestionably, the presence of media people reduces the candor of public officials invited to participate and usually stifles shifts in stakeholder positions that might occur behind closed doors.

Process and the role of third parties

Icebreaking is the first order of business. After the ice is broken, participants should expect some ventilation (chest-thumping and posturing). This is necessary to clear the air, but should not be allowed to permeate the whole process. Early on, participants should be asked to identify the interests of the key players to the conflicts. Mediation trainers emphasize the importance of interest identification preceding issue identification or position statements that tend to harden opposing views and suppress opportunities for mutual benefits. Though these few tips on process seemed especially pertinent to the cases of Arctic conflict resolution examined here, there are a variety of techniques in the tool kit of intermediaries to bring parties together, to determine if agreement is possible, and to develop creative solutions that maximize joint gains. Numerous commentators on conflict resolution have described and analyzed an array of techinques to forge agreement and reach closure.

A further evaluation of the role of the Institute for Resource Management (IRM) highlights some of the reasons that process succeeded in producing a map and agreement if not acceptance by Interior. IRM performed a range of third party functions in the negotiation. It served as a convener using the attraction of its founder and president, Robert Redford, and the political clout and reputation of Congressman Sharp, to bring parties together. The Institute identified and built a core group of individuals who were interested and could sell others on the idea of trying a new method of resolving conflicts over OCS leasing. IRM provided a disinterested moderator at meetings of the steering committee and the full group. As well, IRM provided two of its vice presidents (Jon Lear, an attorney with experience in politics and organizing, and Paul Parker, an environmental planner with experience in industry and government) as facilitators in the negotiations. Lear noted that he and Parker did not set the agenda or control the process. Rather, they encouraged the parties to create their own process in order to become invested in it. IRM also furnished extensive administrative, financial, organizational, and logistical support for the process. According to Redford, IRM 'provides a forum' for leaders of industry and environmental groups (and in some cases government) to discuss areas of conflict and 'serves as a catalyst for finding solutions born out of common ground'.[100]

The catalyst metaphor captures the essence of the IRM approach.

Without being involved itself in the controversies, IRM intermediaries triggered change in the relationships of opposing parties that resulted in resolution of the conflict. The IRM founder, moderator, and facilitators convinced industry, environmental, Native, and fishing leaders that their approach was at least as practical as current public sector procedures and regularly encouraged parties to trust the process and the other side. The facilitators served as sounding boards for each side to test its ideas, and they occasionally introduced ideas of their own. Finally, after the Sundance meeting, they increased their active involvement in the process in order to keep it from falling apart. They did not do the work for the parties, but they were essential in bringing about changes in the chemistry of relations among opposing parties necessary to resolve conflict.

7.4   Conclusion

Private sector dispute resolution is on the rise in the Arctic, enhanced by an increase in private ownership of land and natural resources and by the emergence of alternatives to public sector conflict resolution. Privatization of land has increased the bargaining strength of Native corporations and Native dominated regional governments, especially in negotiating a larger role in the modern economy. But changing ownership patterns have also intensified intragroup conflicts, particularly those pitting the new Native leadership at the helm of Native corporations and governments against Natives who perceive the corporate structure as a threat to cultural survival and to protection of lands and waters necessary for subsistence activities. Similarly, transfer of lesser property interests from public to private hands has stimulated the emergence of markets to resolve conflicts over allocation while sharpening conflicts over maintenance of environmental quality and village-based economies, since transactions occurring within markets for oil leases or fishing permits do not adequately reflect values that are difficult to represent in utilitarian terms.

In the 1980s, third party-assisted dispute resolution and problem-solving activities have emerged as viable alternatives to public sector dispute resolution. The Bering Sea negotiation showed that major players in the oil industry and in environmental, Native, and fishing industry organizations can, with the assistance of third parties, produce broad consensus in conflicts that government processes continually fail to resolve. In the wake of that case, private sector actors and politicians are likely to increase pressure on government agencies to welcome private efforts to tackle tough conflicts. The Bering Sea Resource Association could well serve as a demonstration of the willingness of a number of major players in the Arctic to work together to provide early warnings of emerging conflicts, weigh the relative merits of different approaches to their resolution, and help parties to devise responses that accommodate several sets of interests at the same time.

Today, private actors also play a growing role in dealing with international conflicts. Powerful individuals have long acted as go betweens or assumed self-appointed roles as conciliators between conflicting nations. The life of Armand Hammer provides numerous examples of an influential entrepreneur helping to break down barriers between governments.[101] But, increasingly, private organizations orchestrate efforts to avert or alleviate international frictions. In September 1987, for example, the non-governmental Finnish Institute of International Affairs brought representatives of public and private organizations from each of the smaller Arctic rim states together to explore prospects for arms control, confidence-building measures, and regional cooperation in the Arctic. More unusual are the recent efforts of the Natural Resources Defence Council (NRDC), a non-profit environmental law firm, in cooperation with the Soviet Academy of Sciences to demonstrate the feasibility of verifying a comprehensive ban on nuclear testing.[102] Scientists from several American institutes operating under the auspices of NRDC have tested seismic monitoring equipment near nuclear test ranges in both countries to improve the technology available for recording the size of explosions and to demonstrate the feasibility of verifying a comprehensive test ban.[103] Along with the cases of private sector involvement in international conflict resolution discussed in the body of this chapter, these examples suggest that roles for private actors are expanding in the realm of international, as well as domestic, Arctic conflict resolution.

8

Public initiatives: the United States in the Age of the Arctic

Governments dominate events in the Arctic to a degree that seems almost incomprehensible (and often inappropriate) to those more familiar with conditions prevailing in other regions of the world. For the most part, however, public authorities have demonstrated little capacity to mount coherent Arctic policies or to devise effective methods to deal with issues arising in their Arctic domains. Rather, they have characteristically adopted postures of benign neglect toward the Arctic, reacting to Arctic events only when the interests of powerful groups in society have clashed in a manner that threatens to become disruptive and therefore could not be ignored. In this chapter, we explore the sources of this state of affairs and consider the prospects for more active and constructive postures on the part of governments toward the issues arising in the Arctic today. To make the discussion concrete, we focus on the case of the United States. But similar concerns arise in connection with the Arctic policies and programs of other states as well.

8.1   Governments in the Arctic

The governments of the various Arctic rim states literally own most of the land and associated natural resources located in the Arctic. The case of Alaska, where the United States federal government and the State of Alaska together own about 86 % of the land, actually falls at the lower end of the scale in these terms. The Canadian federal government owns about 90 % of the land located in the Yukon and Northwest Territories. The Norwegian government holds title to 99 % of the land area of its three northern counties. There is no concept of private ownership of land in Greenland, a condition that allows the government of Denmark and the Home Rule government in Greenland to exercise effective control over Greenland's land base and natural resources.[104]

And, of course, the Soviet government owns just about everything in the Soviet North. It is hard to find any parallels to the resultant situation. Surely, there are no other areas of comparable size which are securely integrated into the sovereign jurisdictions of states and in which government control is so pervasive.[105]

A somewhat similar picture emerges from an examination of the marine areas of the Arctic, at least in *de facto* terms. Though governments do not actually hold title to the marine segments of the Arctic region, the advent of exclusive economic zones (EEZs) has provided them with the authority as well as the responsibility to exercise control over most offshore activities in the Arctic.[106] When the boundaries of the exclusive economic zones of the Arctic rim states are finally delimited, the areas remaining outside the jurisdiction of the governments of the Arctic rim states will be confined to a comparatively small section of the central Arctic Basin and an even smaller section of the central Bering Sea. In the Arctic region, moreover, the authority granted to governments under the general rubric of exclusive economic zones is augmented by the provisions pertaining to ice-covered areas of Article 234 of the 1982 Law of the Sea Convention. This Article specifies that

> Coastal states have the right to adopt and enforce non-discriminatory laws and regulations for the prevention, reduction and control of marine pollution from vessels in ice-covered areas within the limits of the exclusive economic zone, where particularly severe climatic conditions and the presence of ice covering such areas for most of the year create obstructions or exceptional hazards to navigation, and pollution of the marine environment could cause major harm to or irreversible disturbance of the ecological balance.

Admittedly, the Convention has not yet entered into force, the United States is not a signatory, and the terms of Article 234 are subject to a variety of interpretations. Still, the inclusion of this article is clearly indicative of a trend toward the entrenchment of the authority of the governments of Arctic rim states over human activities relating to Arctic waters.[107]

Taken together, these circumstances ensure that governments can and will play a central role in decisions regarding the human use of the Arctic's natural resources. Of course, private industry may display little interest in exploiting such resources even when governments offer to make them available on attractive terms. The sharp reductions in exploratory activities in the Beaufort and Bering Seas in the wake of the collapse of the world market price for oil in 1986 illustrates this prospect. Nonetheless, no Arctic resources can be developed without the active participation of governments as owners or managers, and governments are in a position to exert considerable influence over the incentives facing private industry in this realm by setting the terms on which they are prepared to make Arctic resources available for development. Among other things, these terms will include some specification of regulations designed to protect the integrity of the ecosystems and socio-economic systems of the Arctic, a fact that makes the actions of governments a matter of paramount concern to environmental groups and indigenous peoples interested in the Arctic. Beyond this, the growing use of the Arctic as a theater for the operations of major military systems is a matter wholly under the control of the governments of the Arctic rim states. As well, most of these governments continue to acknowledge some sort of trust responsibility toward the indigenous peoples of the Arctic region, though the extent and content of this responsibility are often difficult to determine in connection with specific issues.

What emerges from this discussion is that governments must play a central role in dealing with most clashes of interests arising in the Arctic today, whether they like it or not. What is less clear, however, is the extent to which governments are prepared to play this role in an informed and sensitive fashion. To evaluate the problems facing governments in this realm and to examine the prospects for enhancing the capacity of governments to handle Arctic issues, we turn at this point to a more detailed account of the circumstances facing the United States as an emerging Arctic nation.

8.2   United States Arctic interests

The combined effects of the emerging role of the Arctic as a theater of operations for major military systems, the growing importance of the region as a source of raw materials, and the resultant awareness of the Arctic as a distinctive region in political, economic and cultural as well as ecological terms are transforming the national interests of the United States in the region.[108] As a result, the United States is undergoing a rapid transition from the posture of a marginal Arctic rim state with parochial interests restricted to developments in and around Alaska to the role of a true Arctic nation with critical national interests extending to events occurring throughout the Arctic region. So far, however, the government of the United States has failed to respond to this transformation with any substantial enhancement of its capacity to handle Arctic issues. For the most part, American officials have been content to maintain their traditional policy of benign neglect toward the Arctic, making vague statements about the importance of the region from time to time but doing little to flesh out these statements or to upgrade American expertise regarding Arctic issues. Sometimes the consequences are merely embarrassing (as in the case of the transit of the Coast Guard icebreaker *Polar Sea* through the Northwest Passage in 1985).[109] But increasingly the consequences are politically dangerous (as in the case of growing Canadian distress over plans for air and aerospace defense of North America under the terms of the Strategic Defense Architecture 2000 program).[110] It follows that there is a need to initiate steps to rectify this situation.

Any serious consideration of the prospects for enhancing the capacity of the United States to handle Arctic issues must begin with some observations regarding the nature of the emerging American national interests in the region. Without doubt, the fact that the Arctic has acquired a vital role as a theater of operations for major military systems of both the United States and the Soviet Union has done more than anything else to awaken American national interests throughout the region.[111] As the federal government now puts it, '... the United States has unique and critical interests in the [A]rctic region'.[112] More specifically, the United States has embarked on a course of expanding its military presence in the Arctic as well as its capability to engage in Arctic warfare. The Navy regards the Arctic Ocean as '... the new frontier for possible warfare with the Soviet Union'.[113] Similarly, the Arctic figures prominently in Air Force planning not only because of its attractions as an arena for the operations of ALCMs but also because it is an increasingly important link in the comprehensive air and aerospace defense network contemplated under the Strategic Defense Architecture 2000 program.[114] It follows, among other things, that the United States will insist on preserving '... the principle of freedom of the seas and superjacent airspace' in the Arctic region,[115] regardless of the concerns of other Arctic rim states. Restrictions on freedom of access to a strategic arena of growing significance would be intolerable, quite apart from the unfortunate precedent such restrictions might set for freedom of access in other parts of the world. Unlike the Soviet Union, moreover, the United States now finds itself with heightened interests in tying its northern allies closely into its expanded security arrangements in the Arctic. This means that important allies, like Canada, will experience increased pressure during the foreseeable future to fall into line with American plans for the defense of North America against threats emanating from the Arctic region.[116]

The 1986 collapse of the world market price for oil has dampened the enthusiasm of private corporations regarding the development of high-cost Arctic hydrocarbons. All the major companies (with the partial exception of Gulf Canada Ltd.) have temporarily shut down their operations in the Canadian Beaufort Sea, and there have been sharp reductions in exploratory budgets for offshore work in northern Alaska.[117] But this should not be allowed to divert our attention from the significance of the raw materials of the Arctic in terms of the national interests of the United States. American dependence on imported oil is, once again, rising rapidly, and it is predictable that foreign supplies will be subject to disruption as a result of domestic or regional turmoil in the Middle East coupled with the market power of the principal oil producing states. Even now, pressures are building on the federal government to initiate action to mitigate this situation by taking steps to stimulate domestic exploration and development.[118] In the meantime, some influential policymakers advocate exporting a portion of the Arctic's raw materials to Japan or Korea, thereby helping to alleviate the massive trade deficits that the United States has run up in recent years. It follows that the raw materials of the Arctic will play a prominent role in calculations of American national interests during the foreseeable future, even if the high costs of producing and transporting these resources make it necessary for governments to intervene to alter the incentives facing private actors in this realm. It should come as no surprise, therefore, that the United States has officially gone on record as supporting '...sound and rational development in the [A]rctic region'.[119]

Increasingly, environmental concerns intersect with other issues to form an integral part of the mosaic of expanding American national interests in the Arctic region. Powerful environmental groups now seek to block oil and gas development by establishing large wilderness areas in the Arctic, restrict military operations that might prove destructive to ecologically sensitive areas in the Arctic, and eliminate the consumptive use of wild animals in the Far North.[120] Even more striking is the fact that environmental concerns can no longer be confined within traditional political boundaries in the Arctic region. Many wild animals migrate through several jurisdictions. Polluted water can spread throughout the Arctic Basin over a period of years. Problems involving the long-range transport of air pollution are already a fact of life in the Arctic in such forms as Arctic haze, which recurs on an annual basis, and radioactive fallout, which occurs more episodically. And the significance of the Arctic with regard to climate change in the northern hemisphere is increasingly evident. It is perfectly possible that developments originating in the mid-latitudes, like the CO_2 buildup, will produce a profound impact on the

Arctic which will, in turn, trigger a chain of events leading to far-reaching consequences for the industrial societies of the northern hemisphere's temperate zones.[121] Under the circumstances, it is no exaggeration to assert that environmental concerns have come to play a key role in the transition of the United States to the status of a true Arctic nation.

It is easy to overlook the role of the Arctic's indigenous inhabitants in thinking about the evolution of American national interests in the region. Since their numbers are small, they do not constitute a powerful bloc in voting terms. And their material resources are certainly limited by comparison with those available to military, industry, or even environmental groups. Nonetheless, it would be a mistake to underestimate the impact of Native peoples in assessing the evolution of American Arctic interests. The Native peoples of the Arctic own (or control) large areas in the Far North, and they still retain legitimate claims to some of the rest.[122] Throughout the Arctic, indigenous peoples have learned how to make good use of litigation, negotiating techniques, and other forms of political pressure in advancing their interests. Increasingly, they have succeeded in building bridges to powerful environmental groups (like the International Union for the Conservation of Nature and Natural Resources and the World Wildlife Fund) endeavoring to protect the Arctic's ecosystems.[123] And they have moved vigorously to create and then, to assert, leadership within a worldwide movement of indigenous peoples which is rapidly becoming a force to be reckoned with in connection with a number of issues.[124] Additionally, the indigenous inhabitants of the Arctic can count on garnering considerable support for their cause in southern societies because their lifestyle has a certain romantic appeal to urban dwellers who fall under the spell of the Arctic sublime and also because some southerners feel a sense of guilt about the treatment of Native peoples, including the permanent residents of the Arctic. In the final analysis, therefore, the concerns of the Native peoples of the Arctic are becoming a significant factor in shaping American national interests in the region. Since these peoples customarily think of the Arctic as a distinctive homeland and regularly strive to expand contacts across national boundaries in the region, it should come as no surprise that they have begun to play an important role in extending the reach of American interests throughout the Arctic region.[125]

8.3   American Arctic policy

Faced with these facts regarding the expansion of American national interests in the Arctic, many commentators react by concluding that there is a compelling need for the United States to articulate a coherent and comprehensive Arctic policy. Without doubt, this was a driving force behind the efforts of those who instigated the legislative initiative that eventuated in passage of the Arctic Research and Policy Act of 1984.[126] Nor is this concern confined to the United States. The 1986 Report of the Special Joint Committee on Canada's International Relations, for example, concluded that '...Canada's huge stake in [the Arctic] region requires the development of a coherent [A]rctic policy'.[127] And the Inuit Circumpolar Conference (ICC) has been hard at work on the development of a comprehensive Arctic policy for some years, a project that culminated in the adoption of an elaborate Arctic policy statement at the triennial General Assembly of the ICC in Kotzebue in 1986.[128]

In fact, the United States federal government, operating through the National Security Council, has made several efforts to formulate an American Arctic policy. National Security Decision Memorandum (NSDM) 144 of 22 December 1971 states that it is the policy of the United States to[129]

> '...support the sound and rational development of the Arctic, guided by the principle of minimizing any adverse effects on the environment; ...promote mutually beneficial international co-operation in the Arctic; and...at the same time provide for the protection of essential security interests in the Arctic; including preservation of the principle of freedom of the seas and superjacent airspace'.

NSDM 202, adopted in 1973, reaffirmed the 1971 policy statement and added the goal of promoting international cooperation in the field of scientific research.[130] The Reagan Administration, following a review of more recent experience in the realm of Arctic policy, restated American Arctic policy on 14 April 1983 in National Security Decision Directive (NSDD) 90.[131] The most striking feature of this statement is that it contains a formulation of American Arctic policy that is virtually identical to the formulation articulated in NSDM 144 and NSDM 202. The latest development of note in this realm is the adoption of an Arctic Research Policy by the Interagency Arctic Research Policy Committee at its meeting on 3 February 1985. The resultant document relies explicitly on the general statement of American Arctic policy contained in NSDD 90.[132]

Combined with the 1983 assertion to the effect that '...the United States has unique and critical interests in the [A]rctic region related directly to national defense, resource and energy development, scientific enquiry, and environmental protection',[133] these formulas might seem at first to fulfill the need for a coherent and comprehensive American Arctic policy. In fact, however, they do not provide much guidance for those charged with handling Arctic issues on a day-to-day basis. All the formulas are vague and loosely textured. What, for instance, are the essential security interests of the United States in the Arctic? And what would constitute sound and rational development in the Arctic region? To be more specific, does this formula justify opening large offshore areas to oil and gas development or providing public assistance to projects aimed at the exploitation of non-renewable resources in the Arctic? What would constitute mutually beneficial international cooperation in the Arctic, and should the United States initiate a vigorous campaign to achieve such cooperation rather than simply reacting favorably to the initiatives of others?[134] In short, the formulas of NSDM 144, NSDM 202, and NSDD 90 are not specific enough to provide real guidance to decision makers struggling to cope with concrete issues arising in the Arctic.

As well, though these formulas tell us something about the range of interests of the United States in the Arctic, they offer little direction for those who must deal with situations where individual interests conflict so that trade-offs become necessary. What should decision makers do, for example, when activities that seem desirable in security terms, like the construction of radar sites or the use of Arctic areas for low level training flights, prove disruptive to the environment? What trade-offs are acceptable in cases where activities associated with large-scale non-renewable resource development have adverse impacts on renewable resources of critical importance to the subsistence lifeways of the Arctic's permanent residents? Is it worth clinging to the doctrine of the freedom of the seas in specific cases (for example, the waters of the Northwest Passage), if this means alienating important northern allies like Canada? In actuality, most real-world situations involve such conflicts among different interests, and it is often hard to measure or to compare the costs and benefits involved in these trade-offs. It follows that any set of policy formulas that does not offer direction to those who must confront such trade-offs will be of little value as aids to decision making on a day-to-day basis.

The similarities among the formulas set forth in NSDM 144, NSDM 202, and NSDD 90 are also striking. As Westermeyer has observed, this '...suggests that little new thought has been given to the articulation of United States Arctic policy'.[135] Yet, as the previous section makes clear, recent developments in a number of fields have initiated a rapid transition in American national interests from those of a somewhat marginal Arctic rim state toward those of a true Arctic nation.[136] Under the circumstances, this continuity in the content of policy statements is hardly what one might reasonably expect from a government seriously committed to the proposition that the United States '...has unique and critical interests in the [A]rctic region'.[137] Rather, it suggests a policy of benign neglect in which general formulas that provide little guidance in coping with day-to-day decisions are offered as substitutes for clearcut policy statements based on careful assessment of evolving American interests in the Arctic region.

There is, in our judgment, a relatively straightforward explanation for these problems afflicting recent efforts to articulate a coherent American Arctic policy. Part of the explanation lies in the erosion over the last generation of traditional American attitudes toward the Arctic, which were characterized by an assumption that Arctic resources were there for the taking by agents of industrial society, a faith in assimilation as the preferred future for the indigenous inhabitants of the Arctic, and a general unwillingness to recognize the Arctic as an increasingly important region in international terms. What exists today, by contrast, is an intellectual vacuum. The old attitudes are demonstrably inadequate and cannot be resurrected. The concerns of revitalized indigenous cultures, powerful environmental groups, and other Arctic rim states are too insistent to permit this. Even so, the old attitudes were based on a world view that was part and parcel of American social thought at the time. No new world view has arisen to provide an alternative set of attitudes. Today, therefore, the United States lacks the intellectual capital to create a new vision of the Arctic capable of sustaining a coherent policy.

Another part of the explanation lies in the fact that the Arctic has become an arena for sharp confrontations among an array of powerful interest groups.[138] Environmental groups seek to advance their preference for pristine wilderness against the development plans of industry and even against the subsistence practices of Native groups. Animal rights advocates confront the preferences of consumptive users (commercial, recreational, and subsistence) over many issues pertaining to wildlife. Native groups oppose industry plans for large-scale non-renewable resource projects which would threaten the subsistence lifeways of the permanent residents of the Arctic. The activities of the military in the Arctic often evoke serious concern among both environmental groups worried about their impact on fragile ecosystems and among Native groups concerned about the consequences of the militarization of their homeland. More often than not, governments find themselves caught in the crossfire associated with these clashes. As one perceptive observer has recently put it, '[g]overnments would like to make everyone happy and, since this is impossible, react to current pressures, needs and the public's real or imagined concerns'.[139] This hardly constitutes an environment in which it is easy to articulate clearcut policies that are specific enough to provide guidance to decision makers grappling with concrete Arctic issues on a day-to-day basis. While the need for public leadership regarding Arctic policy is apparent, therefore, the task of articulating a coherent Arctic policy is daunting, especially in the absence of any new intellectual capital that could be brought to bear on this subject.

Before we rush to unduly negative judgments regarding this state of affairs, however, it is well to remind ourselves that there is nothing unique about the Arctic in terms of policy making. Undoubtedly, comparable discussions of American policy toward Africa, Asia, the Middle East, or Latin America would reveal similar shortcomings in the articulation of coherent and comprehensive policies directed toward these geographical regions. And there is a much longer history of efforts to devise policies covering these areas, all of which have been recognized as internationally significant regions for some time. This suggests that there are inherent limitations on efforts to articulate coherent and comprehensive policies covering large and complex international regions, at least in an era in which it is impossible to ignore the concerns of numerous influential interest groups possessing divergent goals and espousing conflicting courses of action. This is not to say that it is impossible to formulate policies covering specific functional areas, like wildlife management, self-determination for indigenous peoples, or scientific research, for a region such as the Arctic. But it would be naive to expect serious progress toward the articulation of a coherent and comprehensive American Arctic policy under the conditions prevailing in the region today.

8.4   Handling Arctic issues

These limitations on efforts to develop an American Arctic policy must not be allowed to divert our attention from the growing importance of the Arctic region to the national interests of the United States. What is more, there are steps that the federal government could take to enhance its capacity to handle Arctic issues in an informed and sensitive manner, even in the absence of a coherent and comprehensive Arctic policy. This is where the real opportunities for constructive public initiatives relating to the Arctic lie today. Accordingly, this section identifies and discusses a series of initiatives that would provide the United States with a capacity to handle Arctic issues commensurate with its evolving stature as an Arctic nation.

Cognitive maps

For starters, it would help to make a concerted effort to break out of the intellectual straitjacket imposed on our thinking about the Arctic by habitual use of the Mercator projection. Consider, in this connection, the contrast between the vision embedded in Figure 25, which represents the typical American world view, and Figure 26, which depicts an outlook widespread among residents of northern countries like the Soviet Union and Canada. Several pertinent observations emerge directly from such a contrast. In the American vision, the Arctic is both peripheral and truncated. The Mercator projection encourages East/West perspectives and stimulates planners to develop ideas involving an Atlantic Community or a Pacific Basin arena; it makes it almost impossible to envision the Arctic Basin as the focal point of an internationally important region. The polar projection, by contrast, not only highlights the central position of the Arctic but also makes it clear that the United States, Canada, and the Soviet Union are close neighbors in geopolitical terms. It takes little imagination, from this perspective, to understand the role of the Arctic as a transportation corridor between North America (and even Japan) and Europe or to comprehend the sense of common bonds so evident in the feelings of the indigenous peoples of the Arctic region toward each other.

The iron grip of the Mercator projection also helps to explain a number of more specific problems that afflict American efforts to handle Arctic issues. It is easy enough to see, for instance, how Alaska can be treated as little more than a northwestward extension of the lower forty-eight by those indoctrinated with this world view. A polar projection, however, makes it clear that Alaska and, in a sense, all of North America are actually components of the Arctic rim. Similarly, the strength of this world view helps to account for the peculiar definition of the Arctic region set forth in Section 112 of the Arctic Research and Policy Act of 1984.[140] This definition focuses on the Arctic Circle, a geographical boundary that has little policy relevance, except in Alaska, where it makes use of a boundary that can only be understood as the product of a political compromise. Anyone familiar with the vision of the world suggested by the polar projection would surely have come up with a different definition of the Arctic in connection with legislation of this type.

Similarly, the power of the Mercator projection has forced the Department of State into some extraordinary geographical contortions. Perhaps the most extreme is the lumping of Canada together with the European countries for diplomatic purposes.[141] But there are others, such as the handling of Greenlandic, Icelandic, and even Soviet affairs entirely within the Bureau of European and Canadian Affairs. The problem here,

Fig. 25. Mercator projection map. *Source: A Strategic Atlas*, G. Chaliand & J.-P. Rageau, New York: Harper & Row, 1985.

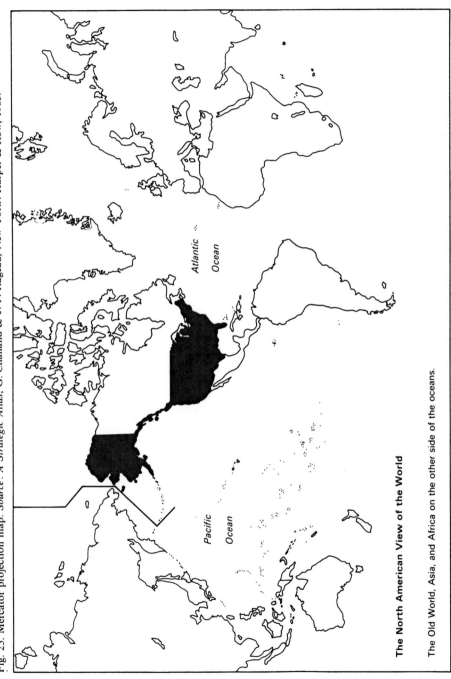

Atlantic Ocean

Pacific Ocean

The North American View of the World

The Old World, Asia, and Africa on the other side of the oceans.

Fig. 26. Polar perspective map. *A Strategic Atlas*, G. Chaliand & J.-P. Rageau, New York: Harper & Row, 1985.

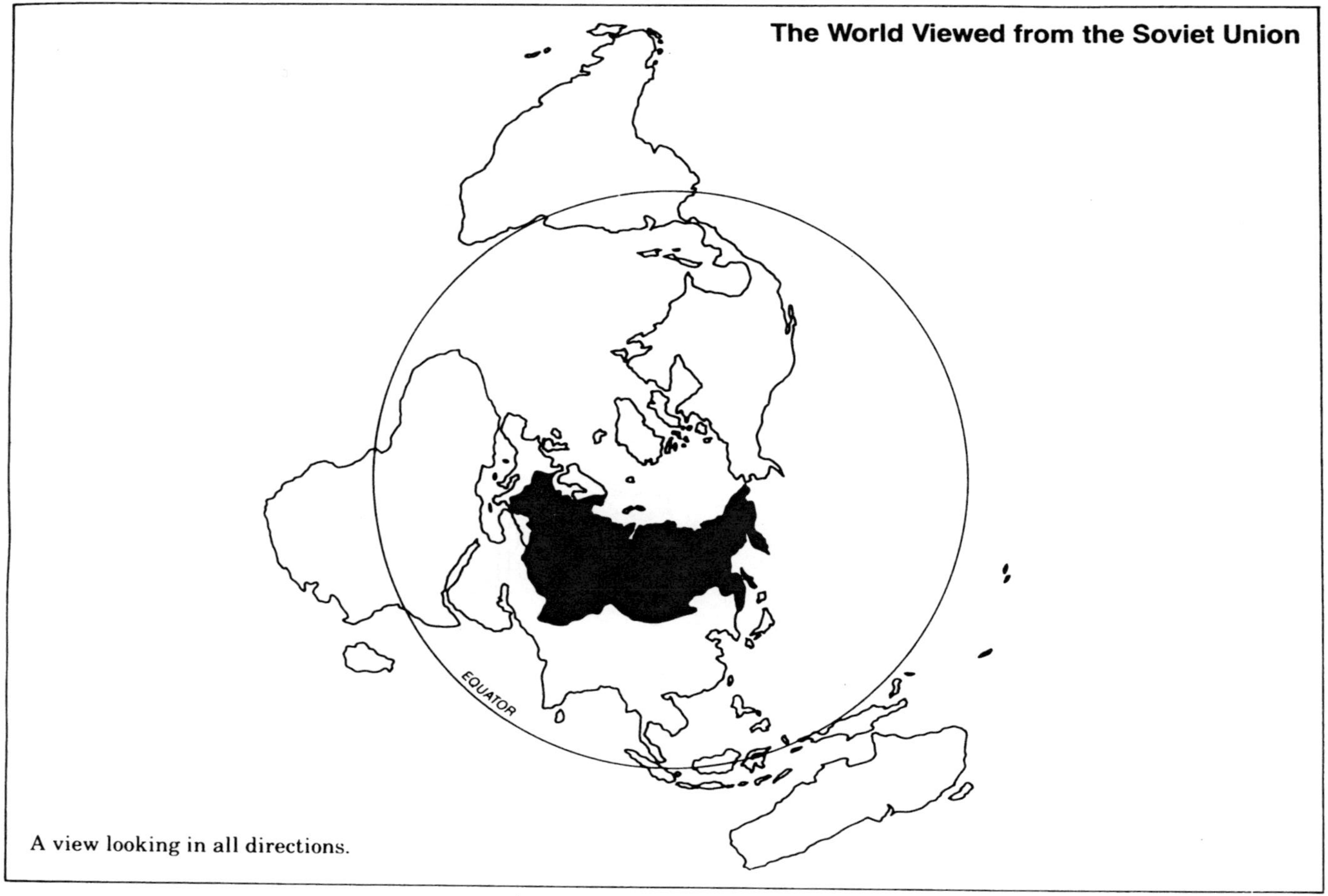

The World Viewed from the Soviet Union

EQUATOR

A view looking in all directions.

as in the previous examples, is the absence of any understanding of the Arctic as an internationally important region. Those who are able to think comfortably in terms of the polar projection, by contrast, will realize immediately that Canada, Greenland, Iceland, and the Soviet Union are all Arctic countries and that the Arctic rim states form a meaningful cluster in the realm of international affairs. It may not be easy to break out of the intellectual straightjacket imposed by the Mercator projection. This vision is, after all, instilled in the minds of most Americans from childhood on through their years of formal education. But breaking the iron grip of this vision alone would constitute a major step forward in the capacity of the United States to handle the Arctic issues arising today.

Structure

To make matters worse, the United States federal government is poorly organized to handle Arctic issues. Consider the situation at the Department of State, which should occupy a position of leadership in bringing the United States into the age of the Arctic in policy terms. Whereas African, Asian, European, and even Middle Eastern issues are handled by large regional bureaus, Arctic issues are of real interest only to the Office of Oceans and Polar Affairs (OPA), a subunit of the Bureau of Oceans and International Environmental and Scientific Affairs (OES). OPA is a small office that allocates the bulk of the resources it can devote to polar affairs to Antarctic issues.[142] It is staffed by relatively junior officials who usually do not regard polar affairs as an exciting or important assignment. And because it is located in OES, the Office has little reason to make a concerted effort to develop expertise regarding the economic, political, and security issues that are increasingly moving to center stage in the Arctic region. The result is that American responses to Arctic issues are driven more and more by the imperatives of the Department of Defense, where the Navy is concerned about the operation of submarines in the Arctic and the Air Force is concerned about the operation of high-endurance bombers and revamped air defense systems.[143] While there is nothing inappropriate about these concerns, they hardly reflect the full range of American national interests in the Arctic at the present time. It follows that the country is in danger of finding itself with a distorted presence in the Arctic because it lacks organizational arrangements competent to deal with the full range of issues now emerging in the Arctic in a balanced fashion.[144]

There are, as well, structural problems arising from the fact that at least a dozen major agencies of the federal government possess mandates extending to the Arctic and desire to retain an effective voice regarding a wide range of Arctic issues. Nor is there any obvious lead agency in this realm, such as the Environmental Protection Agency in connection with environmental issues, the National Aeronautics and Space Administration with regard to space, or the Department of Health and Human Services in the area of health. The result is an ongoing process of interagency jockeying that makes it difficult to achieve agreement on many federal actions affecting the Arctic. In recognition of this problem, the federal government has created an Interagency Arctic Policy Group (IAPG), a coordinating body located in the National Security Council and chaired by the Department of State, under the provisions of NSDM 144 (reconfirmed under the terms of NSDD 90).[145] But the experience of the IAPG in the years since 1971 is hardly reassuring. The Group has met sporadically, sometimes failing to convene even in connection with major Arctic issues.[146] To illustrate, the IAPG has not stepped forward to play an effective role in coordinating the American response to the call for international cooperation on Arctic matters articulated in Gorbachev's Murmansk speech of 1 October 1987, despite widespread concern about this matter among individuals interested in Arctic issues in the federal government. The member agencies frequently disagree regarding issues before the IAPG and sometimes even object to the operation of the Group at all. The Department of the Interior, for example, '... has questioned both the need for a coordinated United States Arctic Policy and the role of the IAPG'.[147] And in general, the Group has found it difficult to identify common ground between those agencies, like Interior, whose concerns are largely domestic and Alaska-oriented and other agencies, like State and Defense, whose concerns extend explicitly to international issues arising in the Arctic. Additionally, the IAPG has generally lacked the political clout to force entrenched agencies to take the problem of coordinating their responses to Arctic issues seriously.[148] Of course, there is nothing peculiar about fragmentation in the world of public policy. It is undoubtedly the rule rather than the exception in complex modern governments.[149] But the problem of fragmentation afflicting the efforts of the United States federal government to address a range of increasingly important Arctic issues is extraordinary even by these standards.

Beyond this, the federal government has exhibited little imagination in responding to challenges involving intergovernmental relations posed by the emergence of the Arctic region as a major policy arena. With regard to issues involving land use, wildlife management, and offshore resource development, for example, the federal government finds itself at loggerheads with the State of Alaska over and over again. With distressing frequency, the two governments end up litigating these issues, a process that comes to an end only when the federal government imposes some outcome through legislative action.[150] The federal government has hardly begun to address the rapidly expanding array of issues involving the claims of northern Native peoples to share management authority relating to wildlife and to exercise various forms of self-government within their traditional spheres of interest.[151] While this set of issues is certain to become more pressing over the foreseeable future, the federal government appears to operate on the naive hope that a policy of benign neglect will constitute an adequate response. Nor has the federal government initiated any serious steps to develop strong links to other governments or organized groups operating in the Arctic. It is apparent, for example, that the United States federal government has contented itself with a program of desultory and *ad hoc* consultations with Canada regarding Arctic issues, a procedure that undoubtedly helps to account for the widening gulf between the views of the two countries in this realm.[152] And the federal government did not even bother to send an official representative to the triennial General Assembly of the Inuit Circumpolar Conference in 1986, despite the facts that the ICC represents a large segment of the Arctic's permanent residents and that the top priority of the meetings was a series of detailed discussions focusing on Arctic policy.[153] It is easy enough to understand these failings as an outgrowth of the traditional posture of benign neglect that has characterized American attitudes toward the Arctic. But the current performance in these areas is not adequate to meet American needs as the United States becomes a true Arctic nation. Even if a coherent and comprehensive American Arctic policy is not likely to emerge during the foreseeable future, there is no reason not to revamp and strengthen structural arrangements at the federal level for addressing Arctic issues.

Political innovation

Despite the growing importance of the Arctic as an international region, American decision makers characteristically approach Arctic issues in a reactive mode, endeavoring to respond to the demands of persistent interest groups rather than to provide leadership in developing imaginative solutions to Arctic problems. Yet between them, as we have said, the federal government and the State of Alaska hold title to about 86% of Alaska. The two governments are also in a position to exercise effective control over large segments of the marine areas of the Arctic. As a result, governments can, for all practical purposes, determine the pace of non-renewable resource development and structure the use of renewable resources in the Arctic. Additionally, the federal government has a trust responsibility toward the indigenous peoples of the Arctic and it possesses the authority to respond to the demands of these peoples for self-determination at the local level. As well, the federal government is the principal player in all activities involving the use of the Arctic as a theater for the operations of major military systems.

Under the circumstances, a reactive approach to Arctic issues, issues that can be expected to become highly contentious if not addressed in an imaginative fashion soon, is wholly inadequate.[154] In the field of wildlife management, the most promising new ideas center on co-management schemes. (See Figure 27.) Yet many federal officials are still engaged in unimaginative efforts to force subsistence users to conform to management systems developed in connection with sport and recreational hunting.[155] With regard to self-determination, there is a pronounced tendency to man the barricades in opposition to the tribal sovereignty movement rather than to seize the opportunity to rethink the whole issue of self-government at the local level.[156] There are few signs that the advent of exclusive economic zones is being treated as an opportunity for a thoughtful reassessment of the unwieldy maze of existing jurisdictional arrangements covering fish, marine mammals, seabirds, and offshore hydrocarbons in the Arctic. Though the emergence of transnational organizations representing the interests of indigenous peoples (such as the Inuit

Fig. 27. A wildlife biologist (left) and a Yupik elder (right) together with an interpreter inspect goose nests under provisions of the Yukon Kuskokwim Delta goose management regime in western Alaska. *Source*: photo. by P. Paniyak, Yukon Delta National Wildlife Refuge, courtesy of *Environment*.

Circumpolar Conference) constitutes one of the most interesting and intriguing contemporary developments in the Arctic, federal officials are only dimly aware of this development and have yet to make any systematic effort to achieve good working relations with such organizations. There is little apparent awareness of the widening gap between Canada and the United States with respect to issues of sovereignty and security in the Arctic, much less any coherent plan for dealing with this problem.[157]

It follows that we must take steps to stimulate innovative thinking within the federal government in connection with an array of contemporary Arctic issues. A necessary condition for making progress toward this goal is a drastic upgrading of the importance attached to Arctic issues on the part of senior federal officials. Yet even this step is unlikely to be sufficient to ensure innovative thinking in this realm. This will almost certainly require the establishment of a planning staff for the Arctic, free from day-to-day operational responsibilities, backed by senior officials, and charged with the task of coming up with imaginative responses to increasingly pressing Arctic issues.[158]

Arctic problem solving

Until recently the Arctic was a remote region of little interest to public decision makers. Those active in the Arctic, like missionaries, scientists, and businessmen, simply went their own ways with little interference on the part of distant public authorities.[159] But the rapid growth of organized human activities in the Arctic has dramatically altered this situation. Today, well-organized groups possess major stakes in the region, and the interests of these groups clash sharply over an array of specific issues.

A particularly striking current example of these conflicts of interest involves the clash over the fate of the coastal plain of the Arctic National Wildlife Refuge (ANWR) in the northeastern corner of Alaska (the Section 1002 area of the Alaska National Interest Lands Conservation Act of 1980).[160] Some observers, in fact, have begun to characterize this battle as one of the pre-eminent environmental policy issues of the 1980s. The energy industry, envisioning the coastal plain as the best remaining onshore prospect for the discovery of sizeable recoverable reserves of hydrocarbons in the United States, wants the area opened for oil and gas development (that is, exploration and production) on favorable terms in the immediate future. Environmental groups, concerned about the fragile ecosystems of the area and desiring to maintain Alaska's pristine wilderness, oppose the opening of the coastal plain on any terms. For their part, the Native peoples of the area are divided on the issue, with some groups supporting development as a potential source of jobs and cash income and other groups opposing development as a threat to their subsistence lifestyle. Because the area is used as a calving ground by the Porcupine caribou herd, a herd which migrates annually back and forth across the Canadian/American boundary, the issue has even produced considerable international friction, with many Canadians not only expressing concern about the likely impact of oil and gas development in the ANWR on the caribou herd but also feeling chagrined about the apparent reluctance of American decision makers to consult Canada on the issue.

Nor is there anything unique or even particularly uncommon about this case. As we have stressed throughout this book, military, industrial, environmental, and Native interests now clash sharply over an array of Arctic issues. To be sure, it is tempting for public decision makers to treat many of these clashes as private matters, leaving the parties to work out their differences on their own. But this is not an adequate response to most of the conflicts now arising in the Arctic. In part, this is because the parties regularly turn to public forums, like courts or legislatures, as they pursue their interests in specific cases. Partly, however, it is because the role of government is so pervasive in the Far North that public officials cannot avoid becoming deeply involved in Arctic conflicts. The federal government, for example, owns the ANWR and exercises exclusive management authority over the bulk of the outer continental shelf adjacent to Alaska. Between them, federal and state authorities are responsible for the management of both marine and terrestrial wildlife in the North. And the federal government cannot simply ignore its general trust responsibility (not to mention its statutory responsibility) to protect the subsistence lifestyles of northern peoples even as it acts to provide secure supplies of energy for the rest of the nation. What is more, many Arctic conflicts raise issues concerning intergovernmental relations which cannot be resolved through the interactions of private parties.[161] What, for instance, is the proper allocation of management authority over wildlife between the federal government and the State of Alaska? Should the state government have veto power over the inclusion of specific tracts on the outer continental shelf in federal lease sales? How should the federal and state governments respond to Native claims to self-determination, claims that would give tribal entities some authority over wildlife and other natural resources? Should the government of the United States agree to seek permission from the Canadian government before allowing American vessels to enter the waters of the Northwest Passage?[162]

As we argued in Chapter 6, moreover, the conventional methods of handling disputes leave much to be desired in settling these Arctic conflicts. It follows that we face today a growing need to re-examine existing procedures and to devise new methods of problem solving to handle the array of conflicts presently arising in the Arctic. What is required, above all, is new intellectual capital to cope with these issues in an efficient, equitable, and ecologically sound fashion in contrast to additional efforts to recruit new members to swell the ranks of the various interest groups engaged in the struggles. While private initiatives are certainly valuable in this connection,[163] the dominant role of governments in the Arctic makes it clear that federal and state agencies must become leaders in efforts to respond to this need.

Arctic research policy

During the 1980s, the federal government initiated a serious re-examination of its Arctic research policy, with an eye toward strengthening the links between scientific research and public decision making with regard to this important international region.[164] The Arctic Research and Policy Act of 1984 not only calls for the formulation of '... national policy, priorities, and goals ... for basic and applied scientific research with respect to the Arctic',[165] it also establishes an Interagency Arctic Research Policy Committee to coordinate federal efforts in this realm and a presidentially-appointed Arctic Research Commission to examine broader issues relating to Arctic research. (See Figure 28.) What is more, these

Fig. 28. U.S. Arctic Research Commission meeting. Left to right: then Commission Chair, Dr. James Zumberge, a witness, and Commission members Oliver Leavitt and Elmer Rasmuson. *Source*: courtesy of U.S. Arctic Research Commission.

entities have been working vigorously during the years since the passage of the Act. Among other things, this has resulted in the formulation of a 5-year *United States Arctic Research Plan* which identifies federal research needs and priorities with respect to the Arctic and which is intended to heighten public awareness of the growing need for scientific knowledge regarding Arctic topics.[166] Additionally, it seems fair to say that the resultant process has helped to strengthen the bonds of community among those engaged in scientific research on Arctic topics.

These achievements are by no means trivial; far from it. Yet they constitute no more than a beginning in the effort to develop a constructive relationship between science and public decision making with regard to the Arctic. In part, the remaining problems lie in obstacles to the design of broadly conceived programs of research formulated in terms that are likely to yield policy-relevant results rather than findings that are of interest only to the scientific community or to lower-level administrators. Some agencies, like the Department of State, often seem to adopt the view that research would not be useful since departmental officials are already well-informed about Arctic issues and many of these issues are, in any case, too sensitive to be investigated by outside researchers. Other agencies, like the National Park Service and the National Marine Fisheries Service, are frequently so preoccupied with mission-specific activities that they find it difficult to gain the perspective required to develop an interest in broader issues, such as alternative approaches to wildlife management or land use planning in the Arctic. Still others, like the National Science Foundation, must cope with structural barriers to the development of a broadly conceived program of Arctic research.[167]

Partly, the remaining problems in strengthening the relationship between science and public decision making with regard to the Arctic lie in impediments to the injection of the findings of scientific research into the process of public decision making in a constructive manner. Above all, we must strive to overcome a severe two cultures problem in this realm.[168] Public decision making is an adversarial process in which interested parties endeavor to make the case for their preferred outcomes, even if this requires a highly selective (and sometimes openly manipulative) approach to existing knowledge.[169] Scientific research, by contrast, is a process that typically produces no more than probabilistic propositions and that generally points to the complexity of issues and the need for additional investigation rather than yielding confident conclusions about the relative merits of policy alternatives. There is, of course, nothing unique about the Arctic in this regard; such problems are pervasive in many realms. Whether we focus on the population dynamics of the northern fur seal, the impact of oil and gas development on indigenous lifeways, or the consequences of the militarization of the Arctic for the global strategic balance, however, the importance of bringing systematic knowledge to bear in guiding public decision making is hard to exaggerate. There is a compelling case, therefore, for working vigorously toward the development of a constructive relationship between science and policy with regard to this increasingly important region of the world.

Education/training

Numerous observers have recently directed attention to the dangers arising from the insular character of American society. Americans make comparatively little effort to learn foreign languages, and the lack of comprehension of other countries and cultures by Americans has been amply documented. Even so, there are well-established centers for European studies, Asian studies, African studies, and so forth located at many institutions of higher learning in the United States. By contrast, the country has no broadly conceived and properly supported program of Arctic studies. The Institute of Arctic and Alpine Research at the University of Colorado and the Institute of Polar Studies at Ohio State University mount programs of research on certain natural systems of the Arctic. The University of Alaska at Fairbanks offers a variety of individual courses on northern topics as well as several programs oriented toward meeting the needs of Native students, but it does not have a coherent Arctic Studies Program. A group of schools in the northeast (including Bowdoin, the Center for Northern Studies, Dartmouth, McGill, Middlebury, and the University of Vermont) have taken some steps toward establishing a College Consortium for Research and Education in Northern Studies. Yet there is no institution in the United States where a student can obtain a sophisticated grasp of issues pertaining to resource management in the Arctic, the political and socio-economic conditions of the region's indigenous inhabitants, the role of the region as a source of raw materials, or the evolution of Arctic international politics.[170] And members of the general public are forced to rely on the accounts of journalists who have virtually no comprehension of emerging Arctic issues for what little information they receive about the Arctic region.

No doubt, we need to develop a multifaceted approach to this problem of education regarding Arctic affairs. At the outset, however, it would help to establish one or more serious centers of Arctic studies to address the national need to develop a group of broadly trained experts who have a good grasp of contemporary developments in this region. The Senate Committee on Labor and Human Resources has recognized this need in its report on the Higher Education Amendments of 1986 and called for the establishment of a northern studies center under the terms of Title VI (International Education Programmes) of the Act.[171] This modest initiative would not, of course, bring the United States into the age of the Arctic in policy terms overnight. But it would be a step in the right direction because it would help to build intellectual capital for Arctic policymaking over the next generation and also because it would produce a group of well-informed and sophisticated individuals who could contribute to our efforts to grapple with increasingly complex Arctic issues during the foreseeable future.

8.5   Conclusion

With the emergence of the Arctic as a significant international region, all the Arctic rim states face a growing need to enhance their capacity to handle complex Arctic issues. Nowhere is this more apparent than in the United States. Recent developments have transformed the United States into a true Arctic nation in terms of the range and importance of its national interests in the region. But the United States has so far failed to respond by upgrading its capacity to handle Arctic issues. The result is a gap between national needs and national capabilities that has already produced politically embarrassing consequences and that is now beginning to produce outcomes that are politically dangerous as well.

Accordingly, there is a compelling need to take steps to strengthen the capacity of the United States to handle a growing array of Arctic issues in an informed and sensitive manner. There is, in the first instance, a need to broaden prevailing cognitive maps by adding the insights derivable from the polar projection to the traditional perspectives grounded in the Mercator projection. Structural problems that currently block efforts to address Arctic issues in a serious and sustained manner must be solved. We must overcome the natural tendency to approach Arctic issues in a reactive mode in order to develop innovative solutions to pressing Arctic problems. We must also recognize the array of serious conflicts now arising in the Arctic and take steps to devise methods of handling these conflicts which are well-suited to the conditions prevailing in the Arctic region. The character of the issues on the Arctic agenda today makes it particularly important to strive for a more constructive relationship between science and public decision making in this realm. And there is a growing national need to make provisions for the education of a group of experts possessing a sophisticated grasp of contemporary military, political, socio-economic, and cultural developments unfolding throughout the Arctic region. None of this would guarantee the articulation of a coherent and comprehensive American Arctic policy, a goal that is probably not realizable under contemporary conditions. Taken together, however, these steps would go far toward moving the United States fully into the Age of the Arctic in policy terms.

Because these steps would involve significant reorganizations in some existing governmental structures, it is likely that they could only be accomplished on the basis of explicit directives from the President. And the President, in turn, would benefit greatly from an authoritative set of recommendations to guide his actions in this realm. Accordingly, it would be desirable at this stage for the President to appoint an Arctic Policy Review Commission, composed of prominent Americans with experience in the Arctic and charged with formulating a series of recommendations designed to enhance the capacity of the United States to handle Arctic issues within a reasonable period of time.

9

International initiatives: building Arctic regimes

Speaking in the Arctic port city of Murmansk on 1 October 1987, Mikhail Gorbachev issued a ringing declaration of Soviet support for international cooperation in the Arctic. He stressed the 'Soviet Union's deep and undoubted interest in ensuring that the north of the planet…never again become an arena of war', and he proposed a six point program designed to establish '…a genuine zone of peace and fruitful cooperation' among the Arctic rim states.[172] Surely, many astute observers in the other Arctic rim states would agree that there is a growing need for international cooperation in the Arctic to deal with issues arising from the rapid growth of human activities in the region.

Yet the expansion of human activities in the Arctic has also engendered numerous conflicts of interest in the region that cut across the boundaries of national jurisdictions. Most of the resultant issues, moreover, involve activities of an ongoing or continuing nature. The Arctic will certainly remain a major theater of operations for strategic weapons systems during the foreseeable future. The struggles of Native peoples to maintain the integrity of their cultures and to achieve a measure of self-determination will continue in the face of various forms of socio-economic development likely to occur in the Arctic. The impacts of non-renewable resource extraction on Arctic ecosystems will clearly require monitoring and regulation on a long-term basis.

It follows that we must search for arrangements capable of managing conflicts of interest arising in connection with international issues in the Arctic on a continuing basis, rather than thinking in terms of procedures designed to settle such conflicts once-and-for-all. Perhaps the most promising approach to these concerns is to think in terms of international regimes and to examine the prospects for regime formation in the Arctic.

Regimes are social institutions or, in other words, networks of rights and rules governing interactions among the occupants of well-defined roles.[173] As such, regimes serve to overcome collective action problems and to institutionalize cooperation in situations in which interacting parties have complex mixes of compatible as well as conflicting interests. Despite the anarchical character of international society, numerous regimes operate at the international level; some of these institutional arrangements have played important roles in coping with transboundary and commons issues of interest to significant groups of players in international society. At least three of these arrangements actually focus on northern or Arctic issues: the four-nation regime for the northern fur seal which originated in 1911, the five-nation regime for polar bears which was initiated in 1973, and the multilateral regime for the Svalbard Archipelago which emerged as an element in the peace settlement following World War I.[174]

As every well-informed social scientist knows, however, the mere existence of transboundary or commons problems hardly insures that affected parties will coordinate their actions or devise institutional arrangements to overcome the resultant collective action problems. Individual actors endeavoring to maximize their own payoffs frequently behave in ways that lead to socially suboptimal (sometimes highly destructive) outcomes.[175] This is commonplace in situations exhibiting the logical structure of the famous prisoner's dilemma (of which the 'tragedy of the commons' is a case in point). But it also occurs in connection with other collective action problems, like those exhibiting the logical structure of 'chicken' or 'battle of the sexes'.[176] Accordingly, any investigation of the prospects for devising new institutional arrangements to handle Arctic issues must address seriously the politics of regime formation.

We must recognize, as well, that there is no hegemonic (or dominant) actor in the realm of Arctic politics.[177] Any arrangements designed to cope with international or transnational issues in the Arctic region must, therefore, take the form of negotiated regimes. What is more, no state or combination of states is ideally positioned to provide effective leadership in connection with regime formation in the Arctic.[178] Neither the United States nor the Soviet Union could play this role alone. Any such initiative on the part of one of the superpowers would inevitably provoke opposition from the other. The United States and the Soviet Union together could exert effective pressure to establish Arctic regimes. But the two countries are not in the habit of operating in tandem for such purposes; they are much more likely to compete for military advantages in the Arctic as a newly emerging strategic arena than to collaborate in the development of international regimes for arms control or other emerging Arctic issues. This leaves the lesser Arctic states as the most probable locus of leadership for efforts to devise international regimes for the Arctic. In many ways, this is an appealing role for these states. Canada, in particular, may find such a role in the Arctic attractive.[179] Not only would this role fit nicely with the image that many Canadians hold regarding the place of Canada in international society and that has energized Canadian efforts in the fields of arms control and peacekeeping, it would also help to assuage Canadian fears about being sandwiched between the great powers in the Far north and about succumbing to American pressures regarding issues of sovereignty and security in the Arctic. Whether the lesser Arctic states have the ability to offer effective leadership in the search for Arctic regimes is certainly open to question. But there can be no doubt that the analysis of the prospects for international cooperation in the Arctic must be approached in terms of a study of institutional bargaining and the factors affecting the establishment of negotiated regimes rather than in terms of a study of hegemony and the politics of dominance.

9.1   The Antarctic analog

In thinking about regimes for the Arctic, there is a natural tendency to turn to the Antarctic as a source of insights. Not only have we grown accustomed to using the phrase 'polar politics',[180] a manner of speaking that suggests the existence of substantial parallels between the two polar regions, it is also well-known that the Antarctic Treaty of 1959 establishes an international regime for Antarctica which many students of international relations find intriguing and which some of those concerned with Arctic issues would like to emulate.[181] Article I of the Antarctic Treaty (coupled with the more specific provisions of Article V) reflects an agreement that the Antarctic region should remain completely demilitarized. Article IV sets forth a method of coping with conflicting claims regarding sovereignty and jurisdiction in Antarctica which seems highly attractive to many of those who must wrestle with similar problems arising in the Arctic region. And numerous provisions of the Antarctic Treaty strongly encourage scientific cooperation in the region, a fact that makes the regime attractive to the international scientific community and that has undoubtedly played a role in the impressive achievements of Antarctic science in recent decades.[182] What is more, the parties to the Antarctic regime have made impressive efforts to build on the framework of the 1959 Treaty to extend this regime into new functional areas. This has already resulted in the negotiation of the 1980 Convention on the Conservation of Antarctic Marine Living Resources, an arrangement that is notable for its emphasis on a whole ecosystems approach.[183] And negotiators have now reached agreement on the terms of a mineral resources regime for the Antarctic region.[184]

The more we reflect on the Antarctic experience, however, the more it becomes apparent that the differences between the two polar regions with regard to regime formation greatly exceed the parallels. In many respects, the Arctic and the Antarctic are antipodes in terms of regime formation as well as in geographical terms. In 1959, when the Antarctic Treaty was signed, the various parts of Antarctica were not fully integrated into the political systems of contiguous states. It is doubtful whether those states advancing territorial claims in Antarctica could even have met the standard of 'effective occupancy' in any serious test of their claims. By contrast, no one doubts the sovereignty of the Arctic rim states in the Arctic, though there are questions regarding the precise boundaries of their jurisdiction as well as the more extreme versions of claims to marine areas based on the sector principle. Unlike the circumstances prevailing in Antarctica, extensive interactions between Arctic peripheries and national cores to the South predominate in the Arctic. Similarly, the Antarctic region was already demilitarized in *de facto* terms in 1959 in the sense that there were no military operations taking place in the region, let alone military bases or facilities located there. Contrast this with the emergence of the Arctic as a region of vital strategic significance to both superpowers. Whatever the prospects for international cooperation in the region, Arctic demilitarization is improbable during the foreseeable future.

Then, too, there is the fact that no industrial or commercial activities of any kind were taking place in Antarctica at the time the Antarctic regime was negotiated (apart from some residual whaling operations in the surrounding marine area which were ignored in the 1959 negotiations). Many thoughtful observers doubt whether such activities will arise during the foreseeable future, a fact that certainly makes it easier to respond favorably to proposals for restrictive measures in connection with the emerging mineral resources regime for the Antarctic region. The contrast with the Arctic, which is already the scene of world-class industrial activities, is stark. Nor does Antarctica constitute a homeland for significant groups of indigenous peoples. Whereas the Native peoples of the Arctic regard the region as a cultural mediterranean and demand a meaningful voice in the development of Arctic regimes, it was comparatively easy for diplomats and scientists located in distant capitals to devise mutually acceptable institutional arrangements for Antarctica without having to concern themselves with local reactions to such arrangements.

As well, the Antarctic regime clearly grew out of the activities of the international scientific community and has served, in turn, to provide a mechanism that nurtures the cohesiveness of this community. It is hardly an accident that the Antarctic Treaty was formalized in the aftermath of the International Geophysical Year (IGY) of 1957–1958. And the Scientific Committee on Antarctic Research (SCAR), which operates under the auspices of the International Council of Scientific Unions (ICSU), has played a substantial role in promoting the idea that Antarctica should remain a continent dedicated to science.[185] Though we are witnessing today increasingly serious efforts to foster an international scientific community concerned with the Arctic, there is surely no comparison between the two polar regions in these terms.[186]

As a result, simplistic comparisons between the Arctic and the Antarctic do more to confuse the analysis of prospects for international cooperation in the Arctic region than to shed light on this topic. The simple fact that interested parties have achieved considerable success in establishing an international regime for one polar region does not entitle us to conclude that the other polar region is ripe for success in these terms. All the available evidence suggests, in fact, that there is no real prospect for the creation of a comprehensive arrangement for the Arctic, along the lines of the Antarctic Treaty System, during the foreseeable future.[187] Yet this should not lead us to dismiss out of hand the idea of devising more limited or functionally delineated arrangements to handle specific issues now emerging in the Arctic.[188] The international and transnational issues requiring conscious cooperation or at least *de facto* coordination in the Arctic are far more serious than those that provided the impetus for regime formation in the Antarctic. In one sense, this poses problems for regime formation in the Arctic. Since the stakes are higher in this region, the interested parties may well bargain harder over specific provisions to be incorporated in international regimes for the region. But the need for institutional arrangements to ensure international cooperation in the Arctic region is also greater. Under the circumstances, we must address the problems of regime formation in the Arctic seriously and systematically, while not losing sight of the problems facing this enterprise.

9.2   Arctic arms control

The growing strategic importance of the Arctic to both superpowers virtually rules out the demilitarization of the region during the foreseeable future. As we pointed out in Chapter 2, moreover, the militarization of the Arctic has certain attractions from the perspective of stabilizing the global strategic balance. Barring highly improbable breakthroughs in military technology, the Arctic may play a major role in the development of a system of mutual deterrence that is secure enough to encourage the United States and the Soviet Union to agree to deep reciprocal reductions in land-based strategic weapons systems. Yet there is no basis for complacency in contemplating the militarization of the Arctic. The margins for error are small in this region; Arctic command and control problems make it comparatively easy to imagine the occurrence of serious accidental or inadvertent clashes in the region, and the Arctic may well become an arena for the deployment of new and potentially destabilizing weapons systems (for example, advanced cruise missiles or new forms of anti-submarine warfare). As well, the increasing militarization of the Arctic will inevitably generate anxieties among leaders of the lesser Arctic rim states because of its political as well as strategic implications. Accordingly, there is much to be said for starting with a discussion of Arctic arms control in any investigation of the prospects for international cooperation in the Arctic region.[189]

Strategic stabilization

Consider first the possibility of devising effective codes of conduct designed to minimize first-strike incentives and reduce the dangers of accidental or inadvertent clashes in contrast to measures requiring actual arms reductions. A basic attraction of the Arctic as a theater for military operations is the comparative safety it affords for manned bombers carrying air-launched cruise missiles and SSBNs equipped with SLBMs. This suggests the possibility of an agreement, whether explicit or implicit, between the Soviet Union and the United States to avoid wasteful expenditures on Arctic countermeasures.[190] Such an arrangement would permit the deployment of monitoring or tracking devices, like the North Warning System or improved measures to detect nuclear submarines operating in the marginal ice zones. But it would prohibit the development of air defense systems capable of combatting manned bombers or ALCMs operating in the Arctic theater (for example, some of the arrangements proposed under the American Strategic Defense Architecture 2000 program) and of improved anti-submarine warfare (ASW) devices like attack submarines specially designed for Arctic operations (for example, the proposed American SSN-21 or Seawolf). Such an arrangement would also require a renunciation of plans, like those associated with the American maritime strategy, to attack SSBNs in the Arctic during the course of a conventional war in Europe.[191] There is considerable evidence that the air defense systems and the ASW devices in question are not apt to prove cost effective. They are unlikely to be able to hold their own against improved strategic offensive weapons designed for deployment in the Arctic. Even more important, an arrangement along these lines would help to alleviate growing fears about the stability of nuclear deterrence arising from the increased vulnerability of land-based missiles. It follows that an agreement to leave the Arctic as a safe zone for strategic weapons systems might substantially improve the prospects for a subsequent agreement on more or less drastic cuts in ICBMs deployed on the home territories of the superpowers.

The dangers of accidental or inadvertent clashes in the Arctic stem, essentially, from limited reaction times attributable to the geographical proximity of the superpowers in the region, problems of command and control associated with Arctic atmospheric conditions, and misunderstandings or miscalculations arising from military exercises or even deliberate testing behavior. In all these cases, there is room to minimize, though not to eliminate, the relevant dangers through the development of informal conventions or codes of conduct coupled with improved communications systems capable of clearing up ambiguous situations quickly.[192] A useful initial step in this connection would be to make provisions for a sizable increase in scientific exchanges regarding Arctic issues. This would not only serve to provide the Arctic states, and especially the superpowers, with a common pool of knowledge regarding Arctic phenomena relevant to the operation of military systems (for example, the behavior of the aurora borealis or various types of sea ice), it would also yield a network of individuals whose personal contacts would help each side to interpret correctly the other's behavior.

Additionally, it is well worth considering the prospect of setting up a jointly operated tracking and monitoring system for the Arctic. The recent agreement among the United States, the Soviet Union, and Japan to establish a joint radar tracking system for aircraft operating in the North Pacific region (an outgrowth of the destruction of KAL 007 in September 1983) is distinctly encouraging in this connection.[193] So too is the experience of recent years with the SARSAT/COSPAS system, a collaborative arrangement involving the use of satellites to support search and rescue operations.[194] Admittedly, a joint tracking and monitoring system designed to minimize the dangers of accidental or inadvertent military clashes in the Arctic would be considerably more ambitious. But it would serve the interests of both superpowers (not to mention the lesser Arctic states) to have such a system in place, especially as the military significance of the Arctic continues to grow.[195] As well, the parties could collaborate on such a mechanism with little fanfare, given the geographical remoteness of the region and the fact that the system would be little noticed by anyone other than the scientists and engineers responsible for its operation.

Arms limitations

Comparing the Arctic with other remote areas, it is easy to reach the conclusion that it would be both desirable and feasible simply to demilitarize the whole region. Article I of the Antarctic Treaty of 1959, after all, sets forth the broad proposition that 'Antarctica shall be used for peaceful purposes only'. Similarly, Article 4 of the Outer Space Treaty of 1967 specifies that the '...moon and other celestial bodies shall be used by all States parties to the treaty exclusively for peaceful purposes'. The Svalbard Convention of 1920 even offers a limited precedent for demilitarization in the Arctic region itself. Article 9 of that Convention establishes what is, in effect, a condition of demilitarization by prohibiting the construction of naval bases or fortifications in the archipelago and specifying that Svalbard shall '...never be used for warlike purposes'.[196]

As the analysis of Chapter 2 makes clear, however, simple demilitarization is not a realistic prospect for the Arctic region during the foreseeable future. The Arctic is no longer remote, at least in functional terms. The militarization of the region has already progressed too far to be rolled back in an agreement to establish an international regime of the type devised a generation ago for Antarctica. As well, the emergence of the Arctic as a major theater for military operations holds real attractions even for those concerned about the stability of the central strategic balance between the superpowers. Given an appropriate code of conduct, as outlined above, the Arctic could play a significant stabilizing role in strategic terms. For the foreseeable future, this is certainly a more realistic hope for the region than the articulation of naive proposals designed to insulate the Arctic from superpower competition through some form of demilitarization.[197]

Yet this pessimistic appraisal of the prospects for demilitarization in the Arctic should not be read as a general dismissal of arrangements for the Arctic involving arms limitations. In fact, proposals for some sort of Arctic nuclear-free zone strike a responsive chord in many circles.[198] Regional nuclear-free zones have proven politically attractive in several areas of the world. The Treaty of Tlatelolco of 1967, for example, creates a regime designed to denuclearize Latin America. In 1985, the South Pacific Forum nations adopted a treaty establishing a South Pacific Nuclear-Free Zone. Closer to the Arctic, proposals for a Nordic nuclear-free zone have surfaced repeatedly since the Soviets first introduced the idea in 1958. Though some of these proposals have certainly taken the form of manipulative ploys, it is undeniable that they have a genuine appeal for many Scandinavians wishing to opt out of the continuing contest for influence between the United States and the Soviet Union.[199] In the Arctic proper, the Inuit Circumpolar Conference (ICC) has persistently advocated the creation of an Arctic nuclear-free zone since its initial meeting in Barrow in 1977. The Home Rule government in Greenland has designated the island a nuclear-free zone. And the Legislative Assembly of the Northwest Territories passed a resolution in 1986 declaring the Northwest Territories a nuclear-free zone.[200] Admittedly, these initiatives do not involve powerful actors capable of compelling the Arctic rim states to accede to their policy preferences. But they do have a certain moral standing since they reflect the voice of the permanent, predominantly indigenous residents of the Arctic region. Overall, then, the idea of some sort of Arctic nuclear-free zone seems worthy of further consideration.

To address this idea in a meaningful fashion, we must recognize from the outset that the phrase 'nuclear-free zone' actually encompasses a broad family of possible arms limitation arrangements. Functionally, an Arctic nuclear-free zone might involve any of a number of restrictions on nuclear weapons or materials, including prohibitions on the manufacture or acquisition of nuclear weapons, on permanent basing or stationing of nuclear weapons (or delivery vehicles for nuclear weapons) in the region, on periodic deployment or movement of nuclear weapons or nuclear-powered ships through the area, on testing nuclear weapons or delivery systems, on peaceful uses of nuclear devices, and on the disposal of nuclear wastes. In geographical terms, a nuclear-free zone for the Arctic could encompass the entire region or only certain well-defined portions of the region. It might also involve different provisions for the seabed, the water column, the surface of marine areas, land surfaces, and Arctic airspace. As well, proposals for nuclear-free zones under real-world conditions may include security belts with external guarantees to provide reassurance to those agreeing to give up the use of nuclear weapons in specified areas. With respect to membership, such an arrangement might include all states with Arctic interests, all the Arctic rim states, or only some subset of these states. There might or might not be a role for other actors, such as the ICC, in a nuclear-free zone arrangement for the Arctic.

What all this suggests is that we must think in terms of a family of options in assessing proposals for an Arctic nuclear-free zone. While we cannot examine all these options exhaustively, it is possible to identify a few key considerations relating to any such proposal. There is virtually no chance that either the Soviet Union or the United States will agree to any plan significantly limiting its ability to deploy strategic weapons systems in the Arctic. The limits imposed by Soviet military deployment patterns are particularly severe in this connection. Over half the Soviet fleet of SSBNs is permanently stationed in the Arctic. The Soviets have constructed a number of forward staging bases for manned bombers in their northern territories. In the absence of agreement on a comprehensive nuclear test ban, the Soviet Union may well wish to conduct underground tests on Novaya Zemlya, an area which has been a major Soviet nuclear test site in the past. For geopolitical reasons, the United States has less need to station nuclear weapons at Arctic bases. But the United States will certainly want to retain the freedom to deploy nuclear weapons in the region on a regular basis, to operate nuclear-powered ships in the region, and to test delivery vehicles (for example, air-launched cruise missiles) in the Arctic. Any proposals for an Arctic nuclear-free zone that ignore these basic facts will stand little chance of being taken seriously. Though some parties may nonetheless find such proposals attractive as expressions of moral preferences or as devices intended to embarrass the superpowers (especially the Soviet Union) politically, they will not prove generally acceptable to the key Arctic rim states in practice.[201]

Those who have the most to gain from the creation of some sort of nuclear-free zone in the Arctic are the lesser Arctic rim states. While it is true that several of these states are allies of the United States, most of them already prohibit the stationing of nuclear weapons on their territory.[202] It would not, therefore, require radical departures from existing policies for states like Canada, Denmark, Iceland, and Norway to think seriously about proposals restricting the deployment of nuclear weapons in the marine areas or airspace of the Arctic region. Moreover, the development of proposals along these lines might serve as an attractive vehicle for the emergence of an effective bloc of lesser Arctic rim states endeavoring to protect themselves from superpower pressures arising from the militarization of the Arctic. This is particularly true in the case of Canada, an Arctic rim state that seeks to assert sovereign authority over a huge slice of the Far North but that has no '...combat aircraft based in the north, no ground combat units, no warships, and no missile installations'.[203]

The ultimate question then is whether the lesser Arctic rim states can devise a plan for a nuclear-free zone in the Arctic that the Soviet Union and the United States will not simply reject out of hand. Any such plan would have to involve a highly restricted arrangement in contrast to a comprehensive Arctic nuclear-free zone. The lesser Arctic rim states might, for instance, formally prohibit the deployment of nuclear weapons (or delivery vehicles capable of carrying nuclear weapons) on their territory or within the exclusive economic zones (EEZs) adjacent to their Arctic coasts. They might advocate the designation of marine sanctuaries encompassing certain ecologically sensitive areas or zones heavily used by indigenous peoples for subsistence purposes in which all Arctic rim states would agree not to station or deploy nuclear weapons. Following the precedent of the Antarctic Treaty, they might separate out the issue of nuclear waste disposal and propose an agreement (similar to that incorporated in Article V of the Antarctic Treaty) prohibiting the disposal of radioactive wastes in the Arctic. It is certainly legitimate to raise serious questions concerning the utility of such limited measures, given the growing militarization of the Arctic in more general terms. Yet even modest arms limitations can prove worthwhile when they signal a willingness on the part of the participants to impose some restraints on inherently dangerous military developments. As suggested above, more-over, the very process of developing even a limited nuclear-free zone in the Arctic might prove politically beneficial for the lesser Arctic rim states (and certain transnational interest groups) as they seek methods to protect their interests in the face of growing Soviet and American military operations in the region.

Peacetime impacts

Short of an actual military clash, some of the most pressing problems arising from the militarization of the Arctic involve the peacetime impacts of the use of the region by a number of states as a theater for military operations. Air bases, radar sites, and other military installations often prove disruptive to sensitive northern ecosystems, the subsistence practices of local residents, or the social fabric of indigenous communities.[204] The establishment of the American airbase at Thule, for instance, not only occurred in the absence of consultation with local residents, it also eventuated in the involuntary displacement of these residents from their existing community.[205] Similar comments are in order regarding the use of Barter Island in northeastern Alaska by the U.S. Air Force for military purposes.[206] The testing of weapons systems in the Arctic constitutes an unwelcome intrusion from the perspective of local residents and frequently heightens the desire of Native peoples to protect themselves through the assertion of sovereign rights. The American program of testing cruise missiles in the Canadian Arctic is a current case in point. Even more concretely, military exercises carried out in the Arctic are capable of producing serious disruptions in ecological terms, and they are indicative of an extraordinary disregard for the concerns of local residents as well. The use of the airspace over Labrador to conduct exercises involving low-flying jet aircraft from West Germany, the United Kingdom, and Belgium offers a striking recent illustration. Labrador was selected as a site for these exercises because influential groups in Western Europe opposed the continuation of such exercises in European airspace and because military planners regarded Labrador as a remote area of little political consequence. Yet it appears that no one thought to make a study of the impact of jet aircraft flying at altitudes as low as 30 meters on animal populations, such as the George River caribou herd, in the region or to enquire about the reasonable concerns of the indigenous residents of the area.

Without in any way banning military operations in the Arctic, much could be done internationally as well as domestically to avoid or limit these peacetime impacts attributable to the militarization of the Arctic region. Reliance on unattended or minimally attended radars in connection with the North Warning System is a constructive step in this connection. But there is no persuasive reason for the failure of most of the Arctic states to conduct serious environmental and socio-economic impact studies in connection with projects like the North Warning System, the plan to upgrade the Ballistic Missile Early Warning (BMEWs) facility at Thule, or the construction of military installations on the Kola Peninsula. The Arctic rim states could create international sanctuaries (perhaps under the provisions of the Man and the Biosphere Program) in ecologically sensitive areas or areas heavily used by indigenous residents for subsistence purposes in which military operations would be prohibited during part of the year or even permanently banned. Similarly, military planners could consciously avoid construction or maintenance programs offering local residents employment opportunities that pay well for a time but that require lengthy absences from home communities and that provide no prospect of permanent employment. Regardless of the attractions of the Arctic as a theater for military operations, in short, there is no excuse for disregarding the peacetime impacts of military operations in the region. The Arctic is no longer a remote area of little concern to anyone but a small band of Native people and a handful of explorers or scientists. It is a region of great importance in both ecological and human terms which deserves as much protection as any other region of the world. It may well be that influential individuals in all the Arctic rim states can join forces in endeavoring to promote values of this kind.

9.3   Arctic industry and commerce

The industrialization of the Arctic has given rise to a growing network of transnational economic links in the region. Norway's decision to go ahead with the development of the Troll Field off its northern coast stems, in considerable measure, from European demands for additional sources of natural gas. Canadian industrialists have already begun to export crude oil produced in the Beaufort Sea to Japanese markets. Japanese corporations enter into joint venture agreements to process fish caught by Americans in the Bering Sea. Even the Soviets have indicated a growing interest in what they call joint enterprises as a mechanism for the exploitation of the natural resources of the Soviet North.[207]

Partly, these transnational links in the Arctic are an outgrowth of straightforward economic calculations. The Arctic has large deposits of natural resources but almost no local markets for such products. Given the geography of the region, it is perfectly natural for raw materials extracted in the Arctic to find their way to European and Japanese markets. As well, the scale and complexity of Arctic development pose extensive requirements for capital and advanced technology, a fact that opens up opportunities for foreign investors. In purely economic terms, therefore, the Arctic constitutes an attractive arena for the establishment of transnational partnerships for development. A variety of political considerations simply reinforce these economic rationales for forging transnational links in the exploitation of Arctic resources. The desire of several western European countries to limit their dependence on the Soviet Union as a supplier of natural gas, for example, undoubtedly played a role in the negotiations leading to the agreement with the Norwegians covering the development of the Troll Field. By the same token, the Soviet interest in the creation of joint enterprises for Arctic development is fueled in part by a desire to obtain advanced western technologies and to establish secure sources of foreign exchange in hard currencies. And the growing interest of the Home Rule leaders in Greenland in transnational economic links certainly owes much to the concern of these leaders about the political consequences of their government's continuing financial dependence on Danish grants.[208]

There is every reason to expect incentives of this sort to continue to operate in the future and to eventuate in an increasingly dense network of transnational economic links in the Arctic. Yet it is not apparent that this trend will generate any need for specialized international regimes in the Arctic. For the most part, the links in question involve straightforward contractual relationships among private corporations or those governments concerned with specific projects. American, Canadian, Japanese, and European corporations are all accustomed to negotiating agreements involving various types of joint ventures and direct investment arrangements. And it is also clear that western and Japanese corporations experience no difficulty in negotiating joint venture agreements with Soviet agencies whenever both sides perceive prospects for gains from such agreements.[209] In this connection, the existing structure of private international law covering matters like contracts, loans, technology transfers, insurance arrangements, and so forth seems entirely adequate to cover transnational relationships in the Arctic. While the Arctic is undoubtedly unique in other respects, therefore, the growth of transnational economic links in the region does not pose any problems that cannot be solved within the framework of existing international economic institutions.

A somewhat different picture emerges when we turn to a consideration of Arctic commerce. The industrialization of the Arctic has given rise to growing needs for facilities to move people, goods, and services between Arctic sites, like oil and gas fields, mines, and construction projects, and outside markets or sources of supply. Sometimes the resultant pipelines, power lines, shipping routes, and air corridors lie entirely within individual states and pose no need for international coordination. No one denies the authority of the Soviet Union, for example, to regulate its own shipping along the Northern Sea Route. Nor is there any question about the authority of the United States to make decisions regarding the Trans-Alaska Pipeline. Increasingly, however, Arctic commerce cuts across the boundaries of national jurisdictions, exploits the Arctic commons, or produces environmental impacts that are transboundary in scope. Canadian tankers or barges moving Beaufort Sea oil westward to Japan, for instance, will inevitably pass through the exclusive economic zone (EEZ) of the United States as well as any pollution control zones that the United States creates under the provisions of Article 234 of the 1982 Convention on the Law of the Sea. Pipelines designed to move natural gas from northwestern Siberia to Europe require coordination at the international level. Transmission lines constructed to ship power generated at the hydroelectric facilities of northern Quebec to markets in the northeastern part of the United States call for understandings that transcend national boundaries. And these examples constitute only a taste of things to come. Because the Arctic is a resource-rich region with few local markets, the development of Arctic resources is bound to produce extensive requirements for increasingly sophisticated transportation systems. Many of the resultant shipments will involve the movement of people, goods, and services across jurisdictional boundaries, so that the need for international coordination is destined to grow.

What is more, there are good reasons to establish specialized regimes to deal with Arctic commerce. In some cases, the incentives arise from the need for uniform standards. It is well and good, for example, for the Canadians to regulate navigation in the Canadian Arctic under the terms of the Arctic Waters Pollution Prevention Act of 1971. But the promulgation of a different regulatory regime in the American Arctic could pose severe problems for those wanting to ship crude oil by tanker from the Canadian Beaufort Sea westward to Japan. The obvious solution to this problem is to negotiate a common regulatory regime establishing uniform standards for all shipping using the waters of the North American Arctic (including Baffin Bay and the Davis Strait).[210] Any other response would yield highly inefficient results and might make otherwise attractive projects economically infeasible. Similarly, there is much to be said for devising international arrangements to provide important services for Arctic commerce. Ice forecasting and search and rescue services, for instance, can both be handled most efficiently through the use of commercial satellites. In this connection, coordination at the international level can not only eliminate duplication but also increase coverage, thereby improving the quality of the services. The environmental impacts of Arctic commerce will often assume transboundary proportions providing yet another reason to create international regimes in this realm.[211] Highly migratory animals, like bowhead whales, can be injured by commercial activities affecting any segment of their migratory routes. And the configuration of the Arctic gyre renders it certain that water pollution associated with marine transportation originating anywhere in the Arctic Basin can spread throughout the region. As commerce increases in the Arctic, therefore, incentives to devise international regulatory regimes covering Arctic commerce will grow as well.

9.4   Arctic culture and science

The most extensive networks of transnational relationships in the Arctic today involve the region's indigenous peoples. Perhaps this is understandable given the fact that the permanent residents of the Arctic have long perceived the region as a cultural mediterranean and regarded the political boundaries that have hardened during the twentieth century as highly artificial. Still, it is remarkable how effective these people have been in maintaining and even cultivating transnational links in the Arctic. The Inuit, now operating through the Inuit Circumpolar Conference (ICC), have moved vigorously to solidify their common culture throughout the North American Arctic. (See Figure 29.) They have even taken the lead in bringing pressure to bear on the Arctic states to give serious consideration to the development of common Arctic policies.[212] The Sami, working through the Sami Nordic Council, have emerged as a significant transnational interest group in Scandinavia. And there are signs that the indigenous peoples of the Arctic are interested in taking steps to coordinate their efforts on a broader, circumpolar basis. Sometimes this interest arises from concrete concerns like the problem posed by the anti-harvesting movement, a problem which has led to the creation of a transnational organization known as Indigenous Survival International (ISI).[213] In other cases, the permanent residents of the Arctic have sought to make common cause within the larger context offered by the emerging Fourth World movement. This has led them to seek leadership roles in organizations like the World Council of Indigenous Peoples (WCIP) and the Working Group on Indigenous Peoples established under the auspices of the Commission on Minorities of the United Nations Economic and Social Council (ECOSOC).

What are the implications of this cultural transnationalism for the development of international regimes in the Arctic? It is possible, of course, that this phenomenon will trigger a spillover process leading to various forms of economic and political integration in the Arctic. On the whole, however, this prospect seems unlikely. Today, nation states are more concerned with solidifying and extending their jurisdictions in the Arctic than with fostering functional integration in the region. The days when human beings could pursue their individual or group interests in the Arctic without any regard to political boundaries are long gone. Under contemporary conditions, for example, it is hard to imagine traders casually moving back and forth between the east and west coasts of the Bering Sea, or explorers, like Sverdrup, singlehandedly staking claims to large areas of the Canadian Arctic Archipelago.[214] On the contrary, we now find ourselves wrestling with questions like the precise location of the boundary between Soviet jurisdiction and American jurisdiction in the Navarin Basin[215] or the persuasiveness of Canadian assertions to the effect that the waters of the Arctic Archipelago are internal waters and therefore subject to Canadian control just as if they were land.[216] In the face of this transition, it is hard to foresee any dramatic move toward regional integration in the Arctic, despite the remarkable vitality of cultural transnationalism on the part of the region's permanent residents.

At the same time, the transnational activities of the indigenous peoples of the Arctic may well stimulate the development of international Arctic regimes designed to regulate interactions among the indigenous peoples of the region. To deal with issues arising from the annual movement of Sami

Fig. 29. (a) The 1986 General Assembly of the Inuit Circumpolar Conference, Kotzebue, Alaska. Members of the Executive Committee, left to right, are Oscar Kawagley (Alaska), Jimmy Stotts (Alaska), Mary Simon (Canada, incoming President), Hans Pavia Rosing (Greenland, outgoing President), Aqqaluk Lynge (Greenland), Mark R. Gordon (Canada), Rhoda Inukshuk (Canada). (b) A Greenlander models a new sealskin coat. The fashion show was just a small part of the cultural sharing at the General Assembly. *Source*: photos. by G. Osherenko.

reindeer herders across their borders, for example, Norway and Sweden maintain a regulatory regime dating back to the nineteenth century.[217] Today, there is a growing need for somewhat similar international regimes on a much larger scale in the Arctic region. Inuit are displaying an intense desire to move freely throughout their traditional homelands, including parts of eastern Siberia. Sami strive to pursue their common interests not only in Norway and Sweden but also in Finland and even Karelia. More broadly, the indigenous peoples of the entire Circumpolar North are increasingly interested in exploring common concerns through a variety of mechanisms. Of course, nation states may react to these pressures apprehensively, seeking to obstruct the growth of cultural transnationalism in the Arctic. Yet there is a strong case for the creation of an international regime designed to facilitate the growth of this cultural transnationalism in the Arctic while allowing individual Natives to remain citizens in good standing of their respective nation states.[218] The costs of proceeding in this way in a remote region like the Arctic would not be great. And any other course runs the risk of stimulating the emergence of increasingly dissatisfied and potentially disloyal groups of individuals living in communities that are virtually impossible to control and that are located in a region of increasing importance in economic and strategic terms.

Another and potentially complementary force for transnationalism in the Arctic region is the scientific community. (See Figure 29.) By contrast with Antarctica, science has not become an effective mechanism for the achievement of international cooperation in the Arctic. The International Geophysical Year (IGY) of 1957–1958 did not trigger a powerful movement for the establishment of an international regime for the Arctic. There is no scientific committee for Arctic research capable of playing a coordinating role in the Arctic similar to that played by the Scientific Committee for Antarctic Research (SCAR). Above all, there is no institutional arrangement in the Arctic comparable to the Antarctic Treaty System, which not only guarantees that Antarctica will be open to scientists from all member states but also includes provisions that create effective incentives for scientific cooperation. In many ways, in fact, the International Polar Year of 1882–1883 constitutes the high point of international scientific cooperation in the Arctic.[219] While scientists have mounted specific cooperative ventures in the Arctic in more recent years, none of these projects can match the record of fourteen coordinated Arctic expeditions involving eleven separate nations compiled under the International Polar Year.[220]

As we have already said, the circumstances prevailing in the Arctic today differ sharply from those obtaining in Antarctica with respect to the opportunities for scientific research. The fact that the Arctic is of great importance in industrial and strategic terms certainly means that it would be naive to envision setting aside the Arctic as a region for science. As a result, those who caution that we cannot simply create a SCAR for the Arctic and get on with the business of building an international scientific network in the region are undoubtedly justified in their views.[221] Nonetheless, an extraordinary sense of enthusiasm for the creation of transnational linkages in Arctic research is percolating within the scientific community today. Given the rapid growth of human activities in the Arctic region, there is a sense of urgency about the need to improve our understanding of the biological and physical systems of the Arctic that is not present in the Antarctic. And many scientists interested in the Arctic believe that the political atmosphere surrounding international co-operation regarding scientific research in the Arctic is improving.[222] As a result, we can expect a variety of initiatives aimed at the stimulation of scientific transnationalism in the Arctic during the near future. Already, this dynamic has engendered or reinvigorated bilateral agreements regarding cooperation in Arctic science between Canada and the Soviet Union, Norway and the Soviet Union, and the United States and the Soviet Union. At the same time, enthusiasm has grown for the creation of a multilateral mechanism to facilitate scientific coordination and cooperation throughout the Arctic region. The prospects for early agreement on the establishment of such a mechanism, in the form of an International Arctic Science Committee, now seem excellent.[223]

To conclude this discussion, we would simply note that the prospects for success in forming cultural or scientific regimes may well hinge on the ability of the scientific community and the permanent residents of the Arctic to make common cause. The basic goals of scientific trans-nationalism and cultural transnationalism in the region are similar. Both groups seek to promote free and unhindered movement of people and ideas throughout the Arctic region. In effect, they wish to minimize political and juridical barriers to the pursuit of their common interests, promoting cooperative arrangements among the Arctic rim states in the process. What is more, the two groups need each other's support in these endeavours. Given the growing political sophistication and control of Native peoples in many parts of the Arctic, scientists can no longer expect to carry out meaningful research at Arctic sites without the cooperation of the region's indigenous population. On the other hand, it is increasingly evident that science can contribute greatly to the efforts of Native peoples to articulate and defend their interests not only in domestic arenas, like government agencies, but also in international arenas, like the International Whaling Commission or the biennial meetings of the parties to the Convention on International Trade in Endangered Species (CITES). The fact that leaders of both the Native community and the scientific community are now increasingly aware of their common interests in these terms augurs well for the prospects that these interest groups can work together and may constitute an effective basis for future international cooperation in the realms of Arctic culture and science.

9.5   Arctic environmental cooperation

Numerous observers have suggested the need for international mechanisms to cope with an array of newly emerging transboundary environmental problems in the Arctic. (See Figure 30.)[224] As we indicated in Chapter 5, the existence of such problems is easy enough to document. The fact that water moves back and forth across the Canadian/American boundary in the Beaufort Sea, for instance, takes on added significance in the light of serious exploration for oil in offshore areas on both sides of the boundary. The migratory paths of marine mammals, including endangered species like the bowhead whale, take the animals not only into areas used for offshore oil operations but also in and out of numerous

Fig. 30. Noel Brown, Director of North American Operations for the United Nations Environment Programme (on left) talks with Canadians Sam Omik, Peter Ernerk, and Titus Allooloo, during a break of the Environment Working Group, ICC meeting, Kotzebue, 1986. *Source*: photo. by G. Osherenko.

political jurisdictions. Tanker traffic in the Arctic, already emerging in connection with nonfuel minerals and (since 1985) oil, is bound to raise environmental issues of interest to groups located in several of the Arctic rim states. Even more troublesome are the implications of Arctic haze, a form of air pollution that spreads throughout the Arctic Basin during the winter and spring months without regard to jurisdictional boundaries.

Several deeper concerns lend a certain urgency to proposals for international cooperation to deal with these transboundary environmental problems in the Arctic. The ecosystems of the region are undeniably fragile in that limited biological productivity greatly extends the time required for recovery following disturbances and that low temperatures severely retard the breakdown of wastes or pollutants through processes of biodegradation. As well, there is a widespread expectation that the extent and intensity of human activities in the Arctic will continue to increase dramatically during the foreseeable future. While the notion advanced by Lamson and VanderZwaag of a developmental 'high pressure' system in the Arctic seems somewhat exaggerated,[225] few would disagree with the proposition that levels of human activity in the region will continue to rise during the foreseeable future. And these concerns are only heightened by the growing realization of the close connections between the Arctic and the temperate zones in environmental terms. To illustrate, the buildup of carbon dioxide, caused largely by developments in the temperate zones, is expected to produce considerably more warming in the polar regions than in lower latitudes. This, in turn, may have dramatic consequences for the temperate zones both because it could release large volumes of water currently locked in the pack ice of the Arctic Basin and in the Greenland icecap and because the Arctic is widely regarded as the 'weather kitchen' of the Northern Hemisphere.

None of these environmental problems can be solved in a satisfactory manner without coordination among some or all of the Arctic rim states. But is this sufficient to ensure success in negotiating international arrangements to cope with the environmental problems of the Arctic? To answer this question we must turn again to the politics of regime formation, this time with particular reference to the conditions governing environmental cooperation.

Political environment

The state of the broader political environment is a key determinant of the prospects for regime formation in specific issue areas. Sometimes the political environment is conducive to efforts at institution building; it may even provide a powerful impetus toward regime formation, regardless of the content or coherence of specific proposals. There is little doubt, for instance, that the spirit of cooperation engendered by the activities of the International Geophysical Year (IGY) of 1957–1958 played an important role in helping the twelve original Consultative Parties to negotiate the major provisions of the Antarctic Treaty of 1959.[225] By the same token, the broader political environment may impose severe constraints on regime building in specific issue areas. Any effort to negotiate a unitization arrangement for recoverable reserves of oil that may be discovered in the Navarin Basin, a comparatively simple problem in its own right, for example, would be bound to run afoul of problems arising from the frictions and sensitivities associated with the overall relationship between the Soviet Union and the United States.

Is the general climate of Arctic affairs today favorable to the negotiation of international regimes to handle the emerging transboundary environmental problems of the region? The essential consideration in this connection is the fact that we are now entering the Age of the Arctic, an era in which the Arctic is emerging as an international region of vital significance in economic and political terms.[227] As a result, those concerned with public policy will devote considerably more attention to the Arctic in the future than they have in the past.[228] This, in itself, may promote efforts to develop regimes to handle transboundary environmental problems in the region. At a minimum, proposals addressing these problems will be less likely to be met with ignorance and indifference as the importance of the Arctic becomes common knowledge. Yet this development may also pose serious problems for the creation of Arctic environmental regimes. The fact that the region is emerging as a major theater for military operations will heighten the sensitivities of the great powers to any constraints (real or imagined) associated with new institutional arrangements. And the pressures arising from efforts to exploit the raw materials of the region may have the effect of pushing aside concerns regarding the environmental and socio-economic impacts of Arctic development. The Arctic is still a relatively remote area in physical terms, and its residents carry little weight in national policy-making processes. Despite the presence of pristine environments in the Arctic and the fragility of the region's ecosystems, therefore, the Arctic could well come to seem attractive as a sacrifice zone from the point of view of one or more of the major Arctic states.[229]

Other aspects of the broader political environment may also play a role in affecting the prospects for devising cooperative arrangements to deal with transboundary environmental problems in the Arctic. Arctic politics have come increasingly to focus on jurisdictional issues, like the status of the Northwest Passage or the locus of the Norwegian/Soviet boundary in the Barents Sea. The resultant atmosphere of friction may obstruct efforts to devise cooperative arrangements to deal with transboundary environmental problems in the region. As the case of Antarctica suggests, however, such an atmosphere can also have the opposite effect when states find it attractive to cooperate in well-defined functional areas, like environmental protection, as a means of defusing their conflicts over jurisdictional matters. Additionally, the dramatic decline of the world market price for oil occurring during 1986 has taken the wind out of the idea of a 'great Arctic energy rush' and slowed what had begun to seem like a headlong rush toward Arctic industrialization in the early 1980s.[230] This may deflate the sense of urgency about environmental concerns in the Arctic, thereby reducing pressures to give serious consideration to international arrangements designed to cope with transboundary environmental problems in the region. Even so, the resultant lull may free interested parties from the pressures of fighting Arctic brushfires and allow them to engage in more systematic efforts to design coherent and mutually beneficial regimes to deal with environmental concerns in the Arctic. Then, too, there is the fact that most of the Arctic rim states are experiencing growing pressures to reexamine their Arctic policies and to reassess the basic premises underlying their activities in this region. In fact, several of the Arctic states, like Canada and Norway, appear to be searching for new northern roles, roles that would allow them to transcend the problem of feeling sandwiched between the superpowers in the Arctic in strategic terms.[231] Seizing the initiative with regard to the development of cooperative arrangements to cope with the emerging transboundary environmental problems of the region may seem quite attractive to leaders in these states.

Of course, the occurrence of one or more major environmental crises with transboundary implications in the Arctic would undoubtedly help to galvanize an effective international coalition to deal with the newly emerging environmental problems of the region. Anyone who studies the politics of regime formation cannot help being struck by the role of crises (real or imagined) in breaking logjams and persuading parties immobilized by the complexities of bargaining processes to accept new institutional arrangements. Cases in point involving northern problems like severe threats to fur seals, polar bears, and bowhead whales come readily to mind.[232] But what is the probability of crises of this sort occurring in the Arctic during the foreseeable future? Important as the newly emerging environmental problems of the region are, it is not apparent that any of them is likely to engender a major crisis soon. Threats to animal populations, like the Porcupine caribou herd, associated with non-renewable resource development are significant but not likely to prove overwhelming. A really large oil spill in Arctic waters is a possibility, though the probability of such an event in the near future is low. Arctic haze could become much worse and begin to produce truly severe environmental impacts within the region. Warming associated with the greenhouse effect could produce a dramatic increase in the activity of glaciers in the Arctic, causing mounting problems in heavily populated areas of the Northern Hemisphere. It is certainly predictable that a number of these Arctic environmental problems will become more pressing with the passage of time. But efforts to create international regimes to cope with environmental problems in the region may well have to plug along without the impetus sometimes provided to such efforts by a genuine atmosphere of crisis.

Bargaining dynamics

Those who assume that actors (including nation states) are coherent and rational decision makers are regularly surprised when parties fail to reach agreement despite the apparent existence of a contract zone or find it difficult even to initiate serious negotiations regarding common problems. Students of bargaining, by contrast, are seldom surprised by such occurrences.[233] As they know, the dynamics of bargaining often make it hard for those involved in negotiations to realize their common interests. It follows that we must consider the character of the relevant bargaining processes in examining the prospects for the formation of international regimes to handle the array of emerging transboundary environmental problems in the Arctic.

There is, at the outset, the matter of agreeing on the issues to be considered and the actors to be included as parties to any negotiations.[234] Is it preferable to tackle Arctic environmental problems narrowly to maximize the prospects of reaching agreements or in relatively broad terms to ensure that any agreements reached are effective in dealing with the relevant problems? Should we seek only to protect the bowhead whale during its migrations or should we adopt a broader ecosystem approach designed to maintain the stability of an array of marine systems in the Beaufort Sea? What are the relative merits of starting with localized issues like Canadian/American environmental concerns in the North American Arctic in contrast to considering the entire Arctic region from the beginning?[235] Should Arctic environmental issues be separated on the grounds that it is easier to solve the relevant problems piecemeal or joined together to form a package in the manner of the law of the sea negotiations? Is there any excuse for excluding Japan, a country that may eventually develop greater interests in commercial navigation in the Arctic than any of the Arctic rim states? Given the increasingly bitter criticism of the Antarctic Treaty System as an exclusive club, would the Arctic rim states be well advised to draw in other members of the international community at an early stage in their efforts to cope with environmental problems in the region?[236] It takes little insight to realize that these questions are serious enough to preclude any move to rush into negotiations aimed at creating one or more Arctic environmental regimes without serious preparation.

By its nature, bargaining is a mixed-motive activity. Those attempting to devise regimes to handle transboundary environmental problems (or any other problems) seldom, if ever, find themselves operating behind a Rawlsian veil of ignorance, cut off from specific information regarding the roles they occupy in international society.[237] Rather, each party strives to achieve outcomes as favorable to its own interests as possible, even while making an effort to move the outcome in the direction of the utility or welfare frontier.[238] In this connection, parties frequently fail to achieve a proper balance, placing too much emphasis on the distributive or conflictual aspect of bargaining and insufficient emphasis on the productive or integrative dimension of negotiation. There is every indication that this has occurred, for example, in the desultory efforts of Canada and the United States to reach mutually satisfactory arrangements regarding the waters of the North American Arctic in general and the waters of the Northwest Passage in particular.[239] What is needed in such cases is a good faith effort on both sides to engage in integrative bargaining with an eye toward expanding the relevant contract zone in contrast to the repetition of unilateral declarations based on rigid negotiating positions.[240]

In the absence of such an effort, bargaining can easily eventuate in a condition of deadlock or stalemate. Such outcomes typically occur when the parties to a negotiation commit themselves to rigid positions for bargaining purposes and find it difficult to back off from their commitments without losing face or compromising their credibility as effective bargainers. Something of this sort seems to have occurred between Norway and the Soviet Union with regard to the status of the continental shelf adjacent to the Svalbard Archipelago and between Canada and the United States with regard to the Northwest Passage in the wake of the 1985 transit of the *Polar Sea*. Yet decommitment is not impossible, with or without the aid of a third party.[241] An attractive device for breaking stalemates in certain situations, for instance, is to redefine the principal issue. It appears that there is considerable scope for making use of this approach in coming to terms with the Canadian/American dispute over the Northwest Passage. Instead of defining the issue as a jurisdictional question, an approach that is virtually bound to produce a winner and a loser, the two sides could agree to deal with the Northwest Passage or, for that matter, the waters of the entire North American Arctic as a matter of designing a cooperative management regime structured in such a way as to protect the Arctic environment while safeguarding the vital political and socio-economic interests of both parties.[242]

Those engaged in bargaining processes always keep one eye on the future, watching for any shifts in relative bargaining strength likely to occur with the passage of time. Parties anticipating gains in relative bargaining strength over time are apt to be reluctant to reach a negotiated settlement today, while parties expecting losses in relative bargaining strength will be anxious to conclude negotiations quickly. Given the current volatility of the Arctic, we must expect that all those interested in the emerging transboundary environmental problems of the region will be alert to this phenomenon. In a general way, it is probable that the relative bargaining strength of the superpowers regarding Arctic issues will rise during the foreseeable future. This is due to the growth in the effective presence of the United States and the Soviet Union in the region, especially in military terms. This trend will lead each of the superpowers to upgrade its Arctic interests, a development that is not likely to make either of them particularly accommodating when it comes to negotiating the provisions of regimes to handle transboundary environmental problems in the Arctic.[243] On the other hand, the same development may stimulate the lesser Arctic rim states to form an effective bloc to protect themselves against superpower pressures building up in the region. And such a bloc may seize on transboundary environmental issues, along with issues pertaining to arms control, as an attractive area in which to exercise leadership regarding Arctic matters.

Yet another problem associated with the dynamics of bargaining involves the fear of precedent. There is nothing uncommon about situations in which parties who would otherwise benefit from entering into some institutional arrangement refrain from doing so because they anticipate that the arrangements will be interpreted by others as a precedent or as an indicator of what they can expect in their own negotiations with one or another of the parties to the original arrangement. This is a particularly worrisome problem with respect to matters that are seen as belonging to some larger class of comparable issues. Thus, efforts to resolve disputes over the delimitation of maritime boundaries (for example, the Beaufort Sea boundary or the Barents Sea boundary) are tricky because numerous maritime boundaries around the world are in dispute. Similarly, shifts in the status of straits or potential straits (for example, the Northwest Passage) are sensitive at a time when there are actual or emerging controversies regarding many straits around the world. The way to solve such problems, of course, is to emphasize the unique features of specific cases, thereby breaking the force of any analogy between specific cases and other situations that seem superficially similar. Here, the conditions prevailing in the Arctic seem genuinely favorable to progress regarding the formation of international regimes to protect the region's environment. The Arctic is undeniably different, if not unique, in several important respects, including the virtual irrelevance of the traditional distinction between land and sea. This fact was sufficient to permit the inclusion of Article 234 in the Law of the Sea Convention of 1982, without undue concern about the creation of precedents. It ought to go a long way toward alleviating fears concerning the tendency of others to seize on specific institutional arrangements negotiated to cope with transboundary environmental problems in the Arctic as precedents in pursuing their interests in other regions.

Problems of implementation

Some regimes devised to solve transboundary problems remain dead letters. Others yield results that diverge dramatically from those anticipated at the time of their creation. Many of the institutional arrangements set up to stabilize international commodity markets (for example, the sugar and coffee agreements) or to prevent over-exploitation of fish stocks (for example, the international North Pacific fisheries agreement) illustrate these problems of implementation.[244] To what extent would similar problems plague efforts to devise international responses to the transboundary environmental problems now arising in the Arctic?

In some cases, the problems arise from the actions of free riders.[245] These are participants in regimes who seek to reap the benefits associated with institutional arrangements while avoiding contributions to the production of these benefits themselves. The member of OPEC which increases its own oil production even while benefiting from the higher world market price for oil resulting from the restraints of other members is a case in point. So too is the member of the international monetary regime which benefits from the existence of stable or orderly exchange rates at the international level even while making no attempt to control its own currency. Interestingly, there may be scope for avoiding such problems in connection with international regimes designed to cope with transboundary environmental concerns in the Arctic. This is so because it seems feasible to structure some of the relevant arrangements in such a way as to minimize opportunities to free ride rather than because Arctic players do not experience incentives to free ride. It would be hard for any individual party to reap the benefits of an arrangement to protect an endangered species like the bowhead whale, for example, without upholding its own end of the bargain. Much the same would be true of a coordinated arrangement to prevent pollution associated with commercial shipping in Arctic waters. It is possible that opportunities for free riding might arise in connection with arrangements to control Arctic air pollution (for example, the problem of Arctic haze). But in general, there appears to be considerable scope for designing international regimes to cope with transboundary environmental problems in the Arctic in such a way as to minimize opportunities for free riding.

A problem that may prove more serious in the case of the Arctic involves compliance in general and verification, monitoring, and enforcement in particular.[246] The critical issue here concerns the behavior of private actors (or in the case of the Soviet Union, lower-level bureaucratic agencies) rather than the actions of governments as such. Oil companies operating offshore in the Arctic might be asked to comply with stipulations regarding safe operating procedures or contingency plans for cleaning up oil spills. Shippers might be required to comply with regulations covering not only the construction of their vessels but also the operation of these vessels under Arctic conditions. Construction companies working on the development of Arctic facilities might be told to comply with explicit rules regarding the disposal of residuals or wastes that degrade at an extremely slow rate in the Arctic. And it would be easy to add many more examples to this list.

The central problem in this realm stems from the difficulties of monitoring the activities of various operators under Arctic conditions. Many of these activities take place in remote areas and under severe conditions with respect to which it is a complex and costly matter to carry out adequate monitoring. What is more, none of the Arctic rim states is currently in a position to take on expensive obligations regarding monitoring and enforcement in connection with new regimes to protect the Arctic environment. This is not to say that the resultant limits on the implementation of environmental regimes for the Arctic are insurmountable. It is probable, for example, that there is considerable scope for making use of sophisticated technologies, such as electronic transponders, to monitor certain Arctic activities on an unmanned basis.[247] Nonetheless, it would be a mistake to underestimate the significance of this range of constraints affecting efforts to implement international regimes designed to cope with the newly emerging transboundary environmental problems of the Arctic.

9.6　Conclusion

It is undeniable that many Arctic issues and the conflicts associated with them are international or transnational in scope. And there is ample reason to expect the resultant problems to become more severe as levels of human activity rise in the Arctic region during the foreseeable future. Yet it would be naive to expect a coherent collection of international regimes to cope with these problems to spring up effortlessly. Institutional arrangements in this realm will generally take the form of negotiated regimes, a fact that makes it imperative to examine the politics of regime formation in thinking about the development of international institutions in the Arctic region. Given the circumstances prevailing in the Arctic today, we should not expect the emergence of anything resembling the comprehensive regime for Antarctica set forth in the Antarctic Treaty of 1959. Even so, there are opportunities to devise functionally specific arrangements in the Arctic. Arms control arrangements designed to minimize the dangers of accidental or inadvertent clashes in the region look increasingly attractive. The Native peoples of the Arctic may achieve some success in forging international agreements aimed at protecting the integrity of the region's aboriginal cultures. Environmental arrangements, especially those directed toward a specific problem like protecting the Porcupine caribou herd or certain marine systems of the Beaufort Sea, may prove comparatively easy to negotiate. Additionally, it seems well worth examining carefully the potential for *de facto* coordination, in contrast to formal international cooperation, in the Arctic. Coordination occurs when each of several parties adopts policies or regulations to deal with an issue which are parallel or complementary in nature even though they are not embedded in a formal agreement. Such a response can solve specific problems, like the establishment of submarine safe zones in the Arctic Basin or the creation of compatible regulatory systems to govern commercial shipping in the Arctic, without raising some of the complex issues associated with the politics of regime formation. In the Arctic, today, there is considerable room for such coordinated solutions to emerging international problems in addition to the neater, but chancier, solutions associated with the establishment of formal regimes.

Notes to Part 3

1. For an overview see Barry Lopez, *Arctic Dreams*, New York: Charles Scribner's, 1986, Chapters 8 and 9.
2. William R. Hunt, *Arctic Passage*, New York: Charles Scribner's, 1975.
3. The current focus of this environmentalist quest is the Arctic National Wildlife Refuge located in the northeast corner of Alaska. For a ringing call to action see Alaska Coalition, *Arctic National Wildlife Refuge: Treasure of the North*, Washington, D.C., June 1987.
4. For an accessible account of modern approaches to the analysis of social conflict see Howard Raiffa, *The Art and Science of Negotiation*, Cambridge: Harvard University Press, 1982.
5. Shelagh Jane Woods, 'The Wolf at the Door', *Northern Perspectives*, 14 (March–April 1986), 1–8.
6. Willy Ostreng, 'Soviet-Norwegian relations in the Arctic', *International Journal*, xxxix (1984), 866–87.
7. Taxonomies are never objectively correct. All such classification systems rest on conceptual distinctions we devise and impose on the complexities of real-world phenomena to lend order to our thought. Even so, taxonomies are useful in generating insights and assisting us to make sense out of complex realities.
8. On the distinction between commodity values and amenity values see John V. Krutilla & Anthony C. Fisher, *The Economics of Natural Resources*, Baltimore: Johns Hopkins University Press, 1975.
9. For an account of the modern theory of externalities see Richard Cornes & Tod Sandler, *The Theory of Externalities, Public Goods, and Club Goods*, Cambridge: Cambridge University Press, 1986, Part II.
10. For a straightforward account of the distinction between allocative concerns and distributive concerns see Robert H. Haveman & Kenyon A. Knopf, *The Market System*, 3rd edn, Santa Barbara: John Wiley, 1978, 261–7.
11. Raiffa, *op. cit.*, Part II.
12. For a more general account of the issue of dividing the economic returns or rents arising from oil and gas development see J. W. Devanney III, *The OCS Petroleum Pie*, Report No. MITSG 75-10, Cambridge: Massachusetts Institute of Technology, 1975.
13. For a discussion of the income security programme devised for the Cree under the terms of the James Bay and Northern Quebec Agreement consult I. LaRusic, *Income Security for Subsistence Hunters: A Review of the First Five*

Years of Operation of the Income Security Programme for Cree Hunters and Trappers, Ottawa: DIAND, 1982.

14. See also the discussion in Stephen Langdon, 'Commercial Fisheries: Implications for Western Alaska Development', 3–26 in Theodore Lane, ed., *Developing America's Northern Frontier*, Lanham: University Press of America, 1987.

15. See also Oran R. Young, *Resource Regimes: Natural Resources and Social Institutions*, Berkeley: University of California Press, 1982.

16. For a survey of the outstanding international jurisdictional issues in the Arctic consult Kurt M. Shusterich, 'International Jurisdictional Issues in the Arctic Ocean', 268–94 in William E. Westermeyer & Kurt M. Shusterich, eds., *United States Arctic Interests: The 1980s and 1990s*, New York: Springer-Verlag, 1984.

17. Franklyn Griffiths, ed., *The Politics of the Northwest Passage*, Montreal: McGill-Queen's University Press, 1987 and Ostreng, *op. cit.* In January 1988, Canada and the United States signed an agreement concerning the use of the Northwest Passage by American icebreakers, while reserving their conflicting positions on the legal status of the waters of the Canadian Arctic Archipelago.

18. Ned Farquhar, 'Federal-State Natural Resource Issues in Arctic Alaska', 219–39 in Westermeyer & Shusterich, eds., *op. cit.*

19. Jens Dahl, 'Greenland: Political Structure of Self-Government', *Arctic Anthropology*, 23 (1986), 315–24.

20. Eugene Brower & James Stotts, 'Arctic Policy: The Local/Regional Perspective', 319–44 in Westermeyer & Shusterich, eds., *op. cit.*

21. On the legal foundation of such claims in Alaska consult David S. Case, *Alaska Natives and American Laws*, Fairbanks: University of Alaska Press, 1984, Chapters 8–10.

22. Robert Axelrod, *Conflict of Interest*, Chicago: Markham, 1970, Chapter 7.

23. For an extensive treatment of the background and history of the Svalbard regime see Willy Ostreng, *Politics in High Latitudes*, London: C. Hurst, 1977.

24. See also Axelrod, *op. cit.*, Part I.

25. Anatol Rapoport, *Two-Person Game Theory*, Ann Arbor: University of Michigan Press, 1966.

26. For an accessible account of the role of probabilities in such calculations see Anatol Rapoport, *Strategy and Conscience*, New York: Harper and Row, 1964, Chapters 3 and 10.

27. It is also important to bear in mind that most Arctic communities have experienced dramatic changes in the postwar era for reasons having little to do with the commercial development of natural resources. This makes it even harder to isolate the probable consequences of largescale resource development.

28. For a sophisticated effort to extend benefit/cost analysis to deal with such issues see Krutilla & Fisher, *op. cit.* And for an equally sophisticated critique of such efforts see Mark Sagoff, 'Economic Theory and Environmental Law', *Michigan Law Review*, 79 (1981), 1393–419.

29. Kenneth J. Arrow, *Social Choice and Individual Values*, 2nd edn, New York: John Wiley, 1963.

30. Case, *op. cit.*, Chapter 10.

31. For an influential account of internal colonialism generally see Michael Hechter, *Internal Colonialism*, Berkeley: University of California Press, 1975, especially Part I.

32. This line of thinking certainly played a role in the enactment of the Arctic Research and Policy Act of 1984 in the United States. See also David M.

Hickok, Gunter Weller, T. Neil Davis, Vera Alexander & Robert Elsner, 'United States Arctic Science Policy', Anchorage: Arctic Division, American Association for the Advancement of Science, February 1981.

33. Haveman & Knopf, *op. cit.* See also Kenneth J. Arrow, 'The Organization of Economic Activity: Issues Pertinent to the Choice of Market Versus Nonmarket Allocation', 67–81 in Robert H. Hoveman & Julius Margolis, eds., *Public Expenditure and Policy Analysis*, 2nd edn, Boston: Houghton Mifflin, 1977.

34. Haveman & Knopf, *op. cit.*, 261–7.

35. For a well-known account consult J. H. Dales, *Pollution, Property and Prices*, Toronto: University of Toronto Press, 1968.

36. Ideas of this kind are prominent in the thinking of those associated with the privatization movement. For a range of perspectives on this movement see the special issue of the *Journal of Policy Analysis and Management* on privatization, 6 (summer 1987).

37. In Alaska, the Federal government and the State government together hold title to about 86% of the state's land base. And the percentage of public ownership is generally higher in other parts of the Arctic.

38. R. H. Coase, 'The Problem of Social Cost', *Journal of Law and Economics*, 3 (1960), 1–44.

39. For a general critique see Alan Randall, 'Coasian Externality Theory in a Policy Context', *Natural Resources Journal*, 14 (1974), 35–54.

40. On the role of liability rules see Guido Calabresi & A. Douglas Melamed, 'Property Rules, Liability Rules, and Inalienability: One View of the Cathedral', *Harvard Law Review*, 85 (1972), 1089–128.

41. For a discussion of this condition consult Raiffa, *op. cit.*, Part II.

42. An interesting recent development involves the negotiation of partnerships between government agencies and actors in the private sector to handle Arctic issues. Across the North American Arctic, for example, government agencies charged with wildlife management are negotiating agreements with Native organizations establishing regimes calling for joint decision making in managing individual species, like beluga whales, caribou, and migratory geese, and, in a few cases, all wildlife in a region. Relationships between agencies and private actors are not always easy in these co-management arrangements. Government officials like to describe them as cooperative agreements rather than co-management arrangements, and they commonly resist any initiatives requiring a transfer of legal authority or jurisdiction. Even so, many wildlife managers now acknowledge that they cannot protect Arctic wildlife without the cooperation of Native users, a fact that makes them increasingly willing to consider hybrid public/private arrangements like co-management schemes. See also Gail Osherenko, 'Wildlife Management in the North American Arctic: The Case for Co-management', *CARC Policy Paper* No. 5, Ottawa: Canadian Arctic Resources Committee, 1988.

43. For a thoughtful review consult Task Force to Review Comprehensive Claims Policy, *Living Treaties: Lasting Agreements*, Ottawa: DIAND, December 1985.

44. For an account of the impact of these bargaining impediments at the international level see Oran R. Young, '"Arctic Waters": The Politics of Regime Formation', *Ocean Development and International Law*, 18 (1987), 101–14.

45. Task Force to Review Comprehensive Claims Policy, *op. cit.*, i. On 5 September 1988, the Canadian federal government signed an 'Agreement in Principle' covering the land claims of the Dene and Metis of the Northwest Territories. Similar agreements with the Indians of Yukon Territory and the Inuit of the Northwest Territories may soon follow. Nonetheless, the process

of translating such 'Agreements in Principle' into final settlements is always complex and sometimes protracted.

46. *Loc. cit.*
47. *Ibid.*, especially Chapter 5.
48. For a more general critique of litigation as a method of handling disputes under contemporary conditions see Derek C. Bok, 'A Flawed System', *Harvard Magazine*, 85 (May–June 1983), 38–45 and 70–1.
49. On the recent Sami experience with litigation see Tom G. Svensson, 'Litigations as Ethnopolitical Action: A Means of Attaining Improved Land Rights', unpublished paper, 1986.
50. For an intriguing account of some historical examples see William H. Riker, *The Art of Political Manipulation*, New Haven: Yale University Press, 1986.
51. Osherenko, *op. cit.* and Oran R. Young, *Natural Resources and the State*, Berkeley: University of California Press, 1981, Chapter 2.
52. For information regarding the evolving theory and practice of alternative dispute resolution, see Lawrence Susskind and Jeffrey Cruikshank, *Breaking the Impasse: Consensual Approaches to Resolving Public Disputes*, New York: Basic Books 1987, *Negotiation Journal*, published quarterly in cooperation with an inter-university Program on Negotiation based at Harvard Law School beginning in January 1985, and *BNA's Alternative Dispute Resolution Report*, a looseleaf reporter updated regularly which is published by the Bureau of National Affairs in Washington, D.C.
53. For a discussion on environmental alternative dispute resolution activities including policy dialogues, mediated negotiation, and problem solving, see Gail Bingham, *Resolving Environmental Disputes: A Decade of Experience*, Washington, D.C.: The Conservation Foundation 1986.
54. The federal government of Canada holds title to these Category I lands in trust for the beneficiaries of the JBNQA, the Native residents of the region.
55. For example, the Waskaganish Enterprise Development Corporation (WEDCO), a Cree owned company in northern Quebec, entered into a cooperative venture with Yamaha Japan to manufacture fiberglass reinforced plastic boats suitable for northern climates.
56. *The Western Arctic Claim: The Inuvialuit Final Agreement*, Ottawa: Department of Indian Affairs and Northern Development 1985.
57. See Chapter 4 for details of these land claims agreements.
58. Title to northern areas not covered by settlement agreements remains clouded by aboriginal title claims.
59. Verne Balding, 'The Inuvialuit Corporations', *Nunasi Report* 2 (Sept. 1985), 16.
60. 'GNWT Begins Privatization'. *Nunasi Report* 2 (Sept. 1985), 16.
61. See Michael S. Whittington, *Native Economic Development Corporations: Political and Economic Change in Canada's North*, Ottawa: Canadian Arctic Resources Committee, Policy Paper No. 4, July 1986, 55–60.
62. ANCSA and the Canadian land claims settlements have also led to creation of Native dominated regional governments such as the North Slope Borough in Alaska and Kativik Regional Government in northern Quebec. These regional governments have become major players in Arctic conflicts frequently shifting decision making from central governments in the south to the local arena and, in some cases, greatly facilitating conflict resolution. The North Slope Borough has particularly brought a shift in alliances since its revenue comes almost entirely from a capital improvement tax on oil producing property within its jurisdiction.
63. 'Cullaton Lake Deal Concluded Successfully', *Nunasi Report* 1 (Jan. 1984), 10, 11.

64. For example, the JBNQA is more than a transfer of land and money. It also defines relations among the Province of Quebec, the federal government, and new Native regional governments created under the Agreement (the Cree Regional Authority, Kativik Regional Government, the Kativik School Board). For descriptions of the regional Cree entities, see Richard F. Salisbury, *A Homeland for the Cree*, Kingston and Montreal: McGill-Queen's University Press 1986, 64–75.

65. Development of this split can be traced in numerous articles in the *Tundra Times*. For example, see Steve Pilkington & A. J. McClanaham, 'Murkowski's 1991 package sparks debate', and Willie Kasayulie, 'Kasayulie explains opposition to 1991 bill', (10 Aug. 1987), 1, 3.

66. A fishery is defined by species, location, and gear type.

67. For description and analysis of the limited entry system, see Oran R. Young, 'Fishing by Permit: Restricted Common Property in Practice', *Ocean Development and International Law Journal*, 13 (1983), 121–70. For an account which compares the British Columbia system with the Alaska system, consult Thomas A. Morehouse & George W. Rogers, *Limited Entry in the Alaska and British Columbia Salmon Fisheries*, Anchorage: Institute for Social and Economic Research, 1980.

68. See Young, *Ibid.*, 155–6. Also see Steven Langdon, 'Commercial Fisheries: Implications for Western Alaska Development', Theodore Lane, ed., *Developing America's Northern Frontier*, Maryland: University Press of America, 1987, 3–26.

69. The decline is considerably more pronounced in some fisheries than others. See E. Dinneford & B. Hart, *Changes in the Distribution of Permit Ownership in Alaska's Limited Fisheries 1975–1985*, Juneau: Alaska Commercial Fisheries Entry Commission Report No. 86-6, June 1986.

70. State representative Al Adams of Kotzebue said, 'What you'll see is an influx of outsiders. And then there will be tensions'. Quoted by Steve Pilkington, 'Rural Alaska loses limited entry permits', *Tundra Times* (20 July 1987), 1.

71. In December 1987, Congress amended ANCSA to avoid wholesale re-issuance of stock that may be traded on the open market. ANCSA now restricts such re-issuance to Native corporations whose shareholders vote to put the shares on the open market.

72. Canadian land claims negotiators have tried to solve the problem of Native land passing out of the hands of Natives in a similar fashion by creating a communal form of ownership in landholding corporations.

73. See Verne Balding, *op. cit.*

74. See *Oil and Gas Journal*, 85 (3 Aug. 1987), 22–3 and *Tundra Times* (27 July 1987) 1, 5. Although the Secretary of the Interior is authorized to approve transfers that meet certain legislatively defined criteria, in practice, major exchanges have been made only with Congressional authorization.

75. Personal communication with T. C. Campbell, CEO of Alaska Pacific Energy Corporation.

76. P. Law 100–241, section 8. See Chapter 4 for further description of the 1987 Amendments.

77. Peter J. Usher & N. D. Banks, *Property, The Basis of Inuit Hunting Rights – A New Approach*, Ottawa: Inuit Committee on National Issues, 1986.

78. A district court determined that the treaty fishing clause accorded Indians in the Pacific Northwest a right to have the fishery habitat protected from man-made despoilation, but the appelate court vacated this part of the decision. Sitting *en banc*, the Ninth Circuit Court of Appeals vacated the lower court decision on the environmental issue as 'contrary to the exercise of sound

judicial discretion'. Two of the judges, writing in dissent, would have upheld the lower court decision on the issue of a right to habitat protection. *U.S.* v. *Washington, Phase II*, 506 F.Supp. 187 (W.D. Wash. 1980), 197, 202, rehearing granted, opinion below affirmed in part, vacated in part 759 F.2d 1353 (9th Cir. 1985). For a discussion of this issue, see Fay G. Cohen, *Treaties on Trial: The Continuing Controversy over Northwest Indian Fishing Rights*, Seattle and London: University of Washington Press, 1986, 137–53.

79. For an early discussion of the generic idea of problem solving see James G. March & Herbert A. Simon, *Organizations*, New York: Wiley 1958, 177–82. On problem solving as an approach to conflict resolution at the international level, see John Burton, *Deviance, Terrorism, and War*, New York: St Martin's 1979.

80. In the lower 48 and southern Canada, the use of intermediaries, especially mediators, in settling natural resource disputes has increased over the last decade. For discussion of environmental dispute resolution in the U.S.A. and Canada, see Gail Bingham, *op. cit.*, and Barry Sadler, 'Environmental conflict resolution in Canada', *Resolve*, 18 (Washington, D. C.: The Conservation Foundation, 1986). For a case study of a mediated negotiation between oil companies and fishing interests over oil drilling operations off the California coast, see Gerald W. Cormick & Alana Knaster, 'Oil and Fishing Industries Negotiate: Mediation and Scientific Issues', *Environment* 28 (December 1986), 6.

81. Ken Wells called it an 'unprecedented accord', *Wall Streeet Journal* (7 May 1986), and a *New York Times* editorial termed it 'an unusual and promising privately negotiated accord', (30 May 1986).

82. For a description of IRM's objectives, philosophy, and activities, see Robert Redford, 'Search for the common ground', *Harvard Business Review* 65 (May–June 1987), 107–12.

83. Redford, *op. cit.*

84. In response to industry representatives' request for information explaining the environmental/Native/fishing interest selections, David Benton and Matthew Iya (representing the Eskimo Walrus Commisson) gave a short seminar on the ecology of the Bering Sea which was well received by the industry representatives.

85. Subsequently, the State of Alaska and environmental and Native groups filed lawsuits against the Secretary of the Interior over Bristol Bay. They obtained an injunction in Federal District Court in Alaska on March 15, 1988. The appellate court, however, lifted the injunction in October 1988. See *Tribal Village of Akutan* v. *Hodel*, 859 F.2d 651 and 859 F.2d 662 (9th Cir. 1988).

86. 'Environmentalists, Big Oil Talk Truce', *Wall Street Journal* (26 Nov. 1986), 6.

87. The 'highlighted' areas are to receive 'special mention in the Call for Information and Nominations and consideration ... as potential deferral alternatives in the EIS [environmental impact statement] scoping process'. *5-Year Leasing Program Mid-1987 to Mid-1992: Proposed Final* (Decision and Summary), Washinton D.C.: Department of the Interior, Minerals Management Service, April 1987, 19.

88. Report of the House Interior and Insular Affairs Subcommittee on General Oversight and Investigations on the June 25, 1987 Hearing on DOI's Plan to Allow Oil and Gas Exploration and Development on the Georges Bank Area of the Outer Continental Shelf (November 1987), 12, 13.

89. Telephone interview with Paul R. Stang, Chief of Branch of Program Development and Planning, MMS, DOI, Washinton, D.C., 18 December 1987. He was uncertain whether participation of MMS in such a negotiation would be legal under the terms of the Outer Continental Shelf Leasing Act of 1978 as amended.

90. In part, these retirements and replacements were caused by the downturn in oil prices (oil dropped from $30/barrel to about $10/barrel) during the course of negotiations.

91. Robert Freidheim, July 1987 proposal to the Donner Foundation for 2nd and 3rd fora. The University of Southern California's Institute for Marine and Coastal Studies and the School of International Relations and the University of Calgary's Arctic Political Studies Programme co-sponsored and co-chaired the meeting with financial support from the William H. Donner Foundation of New York.

92. While a record and report of the forum are available, statements and ideas in these are not attributed to any individual. Robert L. Friedheim, 'The U.S.– Canada Arctic Policy Forum: Impressions from the American Co-Chair', *Arctic* 39 (Dec. 1986), 360–7.

93. See Chapter 8 *infra* for a discussion of U.S. Arctic policy.

94. For essays analyzing Canada's response to the *Polar Sea* and earlier *Manhattan* passage, see Franklyn Griffiths ed., *Politics of the Northwest Passage*, Kingston and Montreal: McGill-Queen's University Press, 1987.

95. CARC described the National Symposium series in its promotional literature as, '…a forum where representatives of northern aboriginal organizations, community leaders, industrialists, government officials, and scholars can meet to consider the issues that constitute the new northern agenda, assess how these issues relate to current national policies for the North, and recommend decisions that will address these issues properly'. For CARC's record of five of the six seminars, see *Changing Times, Challenging Agendas: Economic and Political Issues in Canada's North*, Ottawa: CARC, 1988.

96. Letter from Under Secretary of State, Taylor, to CARC, declining CARC's invitation to participate on a panel.

97. For details of events leading to a change in Government policy and for a comparison of the Task Force recommendations and the eventual Government policy, see *Northern Perspectives*, 15 (Jan.–Apr. 1987). Our own discussion benefited from interviews with John Merritt, Executive Director of CARC, and Terry Fenge of TFN (August 1987).

97a. Merritt, Letter to authors, 5 May 1988.

98. MMS Memo on the IRM Proposal (October 22, 1986).

99. Immediately after the Headlands meeting, representatives met with the Governor and his staff and presented the negotiated map. Subsequently, participants from Alaska kept the Governor's office informed. (Telephone interviews with Jon Lear, 6 January 1987, and David Benton, 7 March 1988.) Some describe the official response of the State to the IRM process and negotiated agreement as 'lukewarm'.

100. Redford, *op. cit.*, 108.

101. Armand Hammer, *Hammer*, New York: Putnam, 1987.

102. Numerous press reports describe this unusual cooperative arrangement. See, for example, Joseph Palca, 'Private diplomacy emergent', *Nature* (12 June 1986), 638 and William J. Broad, 'American Scientists in Soviet Getting Ready to Monitor Atom Tests', *New York Times* (5 September 1987), A3.

103. Cooperation between NRDC and Soviet scientists and policymakers also led the Soviets to grant NRDC permission to visit a controversial radar site accompanied by three U.S. Congressmen. William J. Broad, 'Soviet Radar on Display', David K. Shipler, 'Americans Who Saw Soviet Radar Unsure If It Violates Pact', *New York Times* (9 September 1987), A1 and A6, and telephone communication with Jacob Scheer, NRDC, Washington, D.C., 5 October 1987.

104. For a discussion of the origins of this unusual situation see Jens Brosted,

'Territorial Rights in Greenland: Some Preliminary Notes', *Arctic Anthropology*, 23 (1986), 325–38.

105. Antarctica differs because the jurisdictional claims of some states are not accepted by others and are, in any case, set aside without prejudice under the terms of Article IV of the Antarctic Treaty of 1959. For a discussion of conditions prevailing in Antarctica see Philip W. Quigg, *A Pole Apart: The Emerging Issue of Antarctica*, New York: McGraw-Hill, 1984.

106. Note, however, that the management authority accorded to coastal states under the concept of exclusive economic zones does not extend to jurisdiction over shipping in these zones. There remains a need for interstate coordination, therefore, whenever the needs of those engaged in using natural resources come into conflict with the needs of shippers.

107. Canada was the prime mover behind the provisions that became Article 234 during the law of the sea negotiations. For Canadian perspectives on the origins and meaning of these provisions see D. M. McRae, 'The Negotiation of Article 234', 98–114 in Franklyn Griffiths, ed., *Politics of the Northwest Passage*, Kingston and Montreal: McGill-Queen's University Press, 1987 and D. M. McRae & D. J. Goundry, 'Environmental jurisdiction in Arctic waters: the extent of article 234', *University of British Columbia Law Review*, 16 (1982), 197–228.

108. Oran R. Young, 'The Age of the Arctic', *Foreign Policy*, 61 (1985–1986), 160–79 and Franklyn Griffiths, 'The Arctic as an International Political Region', 1–14 in Kari Möttölä, ed., *The Arctic Challenge*, Boulder: Westview Press, 1988. See also the collection of essays that appeared under the title 'Polar Politics' in *International Journal*, xxxix (Autumn 1984).

109. Even moderate Canadians were aroused by this incident. See, for example, Peter Burnet, 'Paper Sovereignty', *Northern Perspectives*, 13 (May–August 1985), 1–7.

110. On the growing gap between Canadian and American perspectives concerning Arctic security issues see Oran R. Young, 'Canada and the United States in the Arctic: Testing the "Special Relationship"', *Northern Perspectives*, 15 (May–June 1987), 2–6.

111. See R. B. Byers & Michael Slack, eds., *Strategy and the Arctic*, Toronto: Canadian Institute of Strategic Studies, 1986 and Claude Basset, ed., *L'Artique: Espace Stratégique Vital Pour Les Grandes Puissances*, Quebec: Le Centre quebecois de relations internationales, 1986.

112. This statement is from Department of State press release no. 161 of 9 May 1983 summarizing the contents of National Security Decision Directive 90.

113. Richard Halloran, 'Navy Frontier: Submarines Rendezvous at North Pole', *New York Times*, 16 December 1986, B15.

114. On the role of the Arctic in the emerging air and aerospace defense network for North America see Douglas Ross, 'Canada, The Arctic, and SDI', a paper delivered at the Conference on Sovereignty, Security and the Arctic, Toronto, May 1986.

115. This statement of American policy was articulated initially in National Security Decision Memorandum (NSDM) 144 of 22 December 1971. It has been reiterated on several occasions during the intervening years.

116. See Young, 'Canada and the United States in the Arctic', *op. cit.*

117. Neal Fried, Greg Huff & Judy Hallanger, 'The Oil Patch Slide – How Alaska's Economy Compares to Other Oil States', *Alaska Economic Trends*, Juneau: Alaska Department of Labor, December 1986, 1–10.

118. Robert D. Hershey Jr., 'U.S. Oil Shortages Seem Unavoidable to Many Analysts', *New York Times*, 17 February 1987, A1 and D5.

119. This statement also appears in NSDM 144 and its successors.

120. Perhaps the most dramatic current clash along these lines arises from proposals to open the coastal plain of the Arctic National Wildlife Refuge in northeastern Alaska to oil exploration and development. See Philip Shabecoff, 'Foes Clash on U.S. Plan to Drill for Oil in Arctic', *New York Times*, 10 January 1987, 33.

121. D. James Baker, 'The Arctic's Role in Climate', *Oceanus*, 29 (1986), 41–6.

122. In Alaska, for example, Native peoples own over 11% of the State including areas containing some of Alaska's most valuable natural resources. When negotiations are completed, Native peoples may own even larger segments of the Canadian North.

123. To illustrate, the Inuit Circumpolar Conference is currently developing an Inuit Regional Conservation Strategy with the active support of IUCN and WWF.

124. See also Thomas R. Berger, *Village Journey: The Report of the Alaska Native Review Commission*, New York: Hill and Wang, 1985.

125. As one prominent commentator noted in 1981, 'It is a mark of the times that the only continuing Arctic forum to date is a Circumpolar Conference of Alaskan, Canadian and Greenlander Inuit'. See Lincoln P. Bloomfield, 'The Arctic: Last Unmanaged Frontier', *Foreign Affairs*, 60 (1981), 90.

126. See David M. Hickok, Gunter Weller, T. Neil Davis, Vera Alexander & Robert Elsner, *United States Arctic Science Policy*, Anchorage: Alaska Division of the AAAS, 1981.

127. Special Joint Committee on Canada's International Relations, *Independence and Internationalism*, Ottawa: Queen's Printer, 1986, 127. See also Griffiths' earlier observation to the effect that 'Bits of policy, large and small, are floating about in the absence of a clear sense of purpose, much less a policy process to lend coherence to Canadian actions' – Franklyn Griffiths, 'A Northern Foreign Policy', *Wellesley Papers 7*, Toronto: Canadian Institute of International Affairs, 1979, 76.

128. The statement, entitled 'Principles for an Arctic Policy', is currently being prepared for circulation by the ICC.

129. For the full text of NSDM 144 see Brian D. Smith, 'United States Arctic Policy', *Oceans Policy Study* 1:1, Charlottesville: Center for Oceans Law and Policy, 1978, 39–40.

130. William E. Westermeyer, 'United States Arctic Interests: Background for Policy', in William E. Westermeyer & Kurt M. Shusterich, eds., *United States Arctic Policy: The 1980s and 1990s*, New York: Springer-Verlag, 1984, 14–18.

131. The substance of NSDD 90 is summarized in Department of State, press release no. 161 of 9 May 1983.

132. This document, entitled 'U.S. Arctic Research Policy', was approved by the Interagency Arctic Research Policy Committee on 3 February 1986. The text of the policy is included in the 5-Year Arctic Research Plan mandated under the Arctic Research and Policy Act of 1984.

133. Department of State, press release no. 161 of 9 May 1983.

134. This question has acquired special significance in the wake of General Secretary Gorbachev's striking appeal for international cooperation in the Arctic region in his Murmansk speech of 1 October 1987. For the full text of this speech see Foreign Broadcast Information Service (FBIS)-SOV-87-191, 2 October 1987.

135. Westermeyer, *op. cit.*, 15.

136. See also William E. Westermeyer, 'The Growing Significance of the Arctic: Opportunities for Transnational Cooperation', *International Studies Notes*, 11 (Spring 1985), 5–9.

137. Department of State, press release no. 161 of 9 May 1983.
138. See Oran R. Young & Gail Osherenko, 'Arctic Resource Conflicts: Sources and Solutions', in Westermeyer & Shusterich, eds., *op. cit.*, 199–218.
139. Fred Bruemmer, *The Arctic World*, San Francisco: Sierra Club Books, 1985, 143.
140. Section 112 of the Act defines the Arctic as '... all United States and foreign territory north of the Arctic Circle and all United States territory north and west of the boundary formed by the Porcupine, Yukon, and Kuskokwim Rivers; all contiguous seas, including the Arctic Ocean and the Beaufort, Bering, and Chukchi Seas; and the Aleutian chain'.
141. Details regarding the organization of the Department of State can be found in *United States Government Manual*, Washington: Government Printing Office, any edition.
142. Given the primary concern of the bureau with environmental and scientific affairs, this is perhaps understandable since the Antarctic Treaty regime focuses on such matters and since recent years have witnessed serious efforts to augment this regime in the areas of living resources and minerals. See also Lee Kimball, 'Whither Antarctica?' *International Studies Notes*, 11 (Spring 1985), 16–22.
143. To gain a sense of the contrast, note that the Department of Defense presently spends over $25 million a year on Arctic research while the Department of State spends just $20 thousand.
144. By contrast, Canada has an entire federal department, the Department of Indian Affairs and Northern Development, responsible for handling northern issues of interest to Canada. While most of those who work for the Department are located in line agencies with day-to-day administrative responsibilities, the Department does possess a Circumpolar Affairs Division which is, in effect, a small policy planning staff for Canadian Arctic policy.
145. NSDM 144 specifies that 'The Interagency Arctic Policy Group will be responsible for overseeing the implementation of U.S. Arctic policy and reviewing and coordinating U.S. activities and programs in the Arctic, with the exception of purely domestic Arctic-related matters internal to Alaska'.
146. Smith, *op. cit.* 34–35.
147. Westermeyer, 'United States Arctic Interests', *op. cit.*, 16.
148. It is interesting to compare and contrast the performance of the IAPG with that of a similar Canadian coordinating body, the Advisory Committee on Northern Development (ACND). While some observers found the ACND useful, others have been less impressed by the performance of this now defunct body. See also Griffiths, 'A Northern Foreign Policy', *op. cit.*, 72–88.
149. Robert L. Freidheim, 'The U.S.–Canada Arctic Policy forum', *Arctic*, 40 (1986), 363.
150. A dramatic case in point is the long feud over the management of federal lands in Alaska which eventuated in the passage of the Alaska National Interest Lands Conservation Act of 1980.
151. For a comprehensive review of existing regulatory regimes governing subsistence hunting and gathering see Steve J. Langdon, 'Alaskan Native Subsistence: Current Regulatory Regimes and Issues', a paper prepared for the Alaska Native Review Commission, October 1984.
152. Since 1976, Canadian and American officials have met annually on a relatively informal basis to exchange information on Beaufort Sea developments. As Freidheim (*op. cit.*) observes, however, these meetings have not been sufficient to cope with a number of issues arising in the Beaufort Sea area, much less to

provide a broader forum in which to address Canadian/American issues in the Arctic region.

153. By contrast, the Danish Minister for Greenland represented Denmark and a special assistant to the Minister of Indian Affairs and Northern Development represented Canada.

154. For some evidence suggesting that this concern is shared even in official circles consult Lisle A. Rose, 'Recent Trends in U.S. Arctic Affairs', *Arctic*, 35 (1982), 241–2 and R. Tucker Scully, 'Arctic Policy: Opportunities and Perspectives', 1–5 in *Proceedings of a Conference on Arctic Policy and Technology*, New York: Hemisphere Publishing Corporation, 1983.

155. On the reasons why it is important to form effective partnerships between government managers and representatives of user groups as well as on recent experience with such partnerships in the North American Arctic see Gail Osherenko, 'Sharing Power with Native Users: Co-Management Regimes for Arctic Wildlife', *CARC Policy Paper No. 5*, Ottawa: Canadian Arctic Resources Committee, 1988 and Langdon, *op. cit.* For useful background on comparable issues in the Canadian North consult Peter J. Usher, 'The Devolution of Wildlife Management and the Prospects for Wildlife Conservation in the Northwest Territories', *CARC Policy Paper No. 3*, Ottawa: Canadian Arctic Resources Committee, 1986.

156. For a good example of this defensive response to the tribal sovereignty movement see Governor's Task Force on Federal–State–Tribal Relations, *Report Submitted to Governor Bill Sheffield*, Juneau, 14 February 1986.

157. In January 1988, the two countries signed an agreement under which the United States will seek Canadian consent for American icebreaker operations in the waters of the Arctic Archipelago, while still refusing to acknowledge Canadian sovereignty over these waters. In effect, the two countries have agreed to disagree on the issue of sovereignty over the waters comprising the Northwest Passage. See David R. Francis, 'US and Canada break the ice on Arctic sovereignty issue', *Christian Science Monitor*, 14 January 1988, 10. For information on the broader background consult Young, 'Canada and the United States in the Arctic', *op. cit.*

158. While many informed Canadians regard it as inadequate, this is essentially the role of the Circumpolar Affairs Division in the Department of Indian Affairs and Northern Development.

159. For an account of the freewheeling activities of earlier times consult William R. Hunt, *Arctic Passage*, New York: Charles Scribner's, 1975.

160. For background information consult United States Department of the Interior, *Arctic National Wildlife Refuge, Alaska, Coastal Plain Resource Assessment*, Draft, Washington: USDOI, 1986. And for an analytic treatment of the issues involved see William E. Westermeyer, 'The Arctic National Wildlife Refuge and Competing National Interests', a paper presented at the Conference on the Polar Regions, Charlottesville, Virginia, March 1987.

161. Ned Farquhar, 'Federal-State Natural Resource Issues in Arctic Alaska', 219–39 in Westermeyer & Shusterich, eds., *op. cit.*

162. For discussions of the January 1988 agreement between the two countries regarding this matter see Francis, *op. cit.* and Jeff Bradley, 'U.S., Canada sign Arctic accord', *Burlington Free Press*, 12 January 1988, 1.

163. For an extended discussion of private initiatives in this connection see Chapter 7 *infra*.

164. James Zumberge, 'Introduction', *Oceanus*, 29 (1986), 2–8. This issue of *Oceanus* is devoted entirely to research initiatives and needs relating to the Arctic Ocean.

165. This language is from Section 102(b) of the Act.
166. The 5-Year *U.S. Arctic Research Plan*, which emerged from a lengthy consultative process among a wide range of groups, was submitted to the President in July 1987 and subsequently transmitted to Congress. Under the terms of the Arctic Research and Policy Act, the Plan must be revised and updated biennially. Note also that the National Science Board has recommended a substantial increase in funding for Arctic research under the auspices of the Division of Polar Programs of the National Science Foundation and that the National Academy of Sciences has established a Committee on Arctic Social Sciences under the auspices of the Polar Research Board to develop an agenda for policy-oriented research on Arctic topics.
167. To illustrate, while the National Science Foundation has a special Division of Polar Programs, it is located within the Geosciences Directorate, a fact that has prevented the Division from sponsoring research in the social and behavioral sciences.
168. We owe some of the following observations to a discussion with Stephen H. Schneider, a climatologist who is Deputy Director of the Advanced Study Program at the National Center for Atmospheric Research.
169. The recent debate concerning the ratification of a Protocol to extend the Interim Convention on the Conservation of the North Pacific Fur Seal, for example, was dominated by groups seeking to use existing knowledge selectively to buttress predetermined policy preferences.
170. Compare the situation prevailing in Canada where the Association of Canadian Universities for Northern Studies includes over 30 universities which mount a variety of programs addressing Arctic issues.
171. United States Senate Committee on Labor and Human Resources, Report No. 99-296, 13 May 1986, 38.
172. For the full text of Gorbachev's Murmansk speech consult Foreign Broadcast Information Service (FBIS)-SOV-87-191, 2 October 1987.
173. For a variety of perspectives on international regimes see Stephen D. Krasner, ed., *International Regimes*, Ithaca, Cornell University Press, 1983 and Oran R. Young, *International Cooperation: Building Regimes for Natural Resources and the Environment*, Ithaca: Cornell University Press, 1989.
174. See Oran R. Young, *Natural Resources and the State*, Berkeley: University of California Press, 1981, Ch. 3; Simon Lyster, *International Wildlife Law*, Cambridge: Grotius Publications, 1985, Ch. 3, and Willy Ostreng, *Politics in High Latitudes: The Svalbard Archipelago*, Montreal: McGill-Queen's University Press, 1978. At present, the northern fur seal regime is in limbo as a result of the failure of the United States to ratify a 1984 Protocol extending the life of the regime.
175. For a sophisticated review of such problems consult Russell Hardin, *Collective Action*, Baltimore: Johns Hopkins University Press, 1982.
176. Kenneth A. Oye, 'Explaining cooperation under Anarchy: Hypotheses and Strategies', 1–24 in Kenneth A. Oye, ed., *Cooperation Under Anarchy*, Princeton: Princeton University Press, 1986.
177. On the concept of hegemony see Robert O. Keohane, *After Hegemony: Cooperation and Discord in the World Political Economy*, Princeton: Princeton University Press, 1984, Ch. 3.
178. For a discussion of this type of leadership see Charles P. Kindleberger, 'Hierarchy versus inertial cooperation', *International Organization*, 40 (1986), 841–7.
179. Special Joint Committee on Canada's International Relations, *Independence and Internationalism: Report of the Special Joint Committee on Canada's International Relations*, Ottawa: Queen's Printer, Ch. 10.

180. See, for example, the special issue of *International Journal* entitled 'Polar Politics' (vol. xxxix, Autumn 1984) and the special issue of *International Studies Notes* entitled 'Polar Politics in the 1980s' (vol. 11, Spring 1985).
181. For a straightforward account of the Antarctic Treaty regime see Philip W. Quigg, *A Pole Apart: The Emerging Issue of Antarctica*, New York: McGraw-Hill, 1983.
182. Polar Research Board, *Antarctic Treaty System: An Assessment*, Washington: National Academy Press, 1986.
183. Lee Kimball, 'Whither Antarctica?' *International Studies Notes*, 11 (Spring 1985), 16–22 and James N. Barnes, 'Resources and Environment in Antarctica', paper presented at a Seminar on the Polar Regions, Charlottesville, Virginia, March 1987.
184. William E. Westermeyer, *The Politics of Mineral Development in Antarctica: Alternative Regimes for the Future*, Boulder: Westview Press, 1984.
185. James H. Zumberge, 'The Antarctic Treaty as a Scientific Mechanism – The Scientific Committee on Antarctic Research and the Antarctic Treaty System', 153–68 in Polar Research Board, *op. cit.*
186. On current plans to promote international cooperation in Arctic science see E. F. Roots, O. Rogne and J. Taagholt, 'International Communication and Co-operation for Arctic Science: A Proposal for Action', unpublished discussion paper, October 1987.
187. See also Lincoln P. Bloomfield, 'The Arctic: Last Unmanaged Frontier', *Foreign Affairs*, 60 (1981), 87–105.
188. For an application of this approach see Oran R. Young, *Resource Management at the International Level: The Case of the North Pacific*, London and New York: Pinter and Nichols, 1977.
189. For a review of earlier proposals for arms control in the Arctic region see Ronald G. Purver, *Arms Control in the North*, Kingston: Queen's University Centre for International Relations, 1981, and Ronald G. Purver, 'Arctic Arms Control: Constraints and Opportunities', *Occasional Papers* No. 3, Ottawa: Canadian Institute for International Peace and Security, 1988.
190. See Gorbachev's Murmansk speech *op. cit.* for a clear indication that Soviet policymakers have begun to think about the attractions of such an agreement.
191. On the maritime strategy see also Jack Beatty, 'In Harm's Way', *The Atlantic*, 259 (May 1987), 37–53.
192. The 1987 agreement between the Soviet Union and the United States to establish crisis control centers is encouraging in this connection.
193. The agreement, known as the Japan/US/USSR Air Traffic Control Agreement, was negotiated in 1985.
194. See Office of Technology Assessment, *U.S.–Soviet Cooperation in Space*, Washington: Government Printing Office, 1985, 109–13.
195. See Gorbachev's Murmansk speech *op. cit.* for an indication of Soviet awareness of the value of such arrangements.
196. For an extended account of the Svalbard regime see Ostreng, *op. cit.*
197. For a proposal stressing demilitarization in the Arctic, however, see Owen Wilkes, 'A Proposal for a Demilitarized Zone in the Arctic', Project Ploughshares Working Paper 84–4, Waterloo, Ontario (October 1984).
198. In addition to the comments in Gorbachev's Murmansk speech, see the essays in Kari Mottola, ed., *Nuclear Weapons and Northern Europe*, Helsinki: Finnish Institute of International Affairs, 1983 and Pertti Joenniemi, ed., *Nordic Security*, a special issue of *Current Research on Peace and Violence*, ix (1–2), 1986.
199. Consult, *inter alia*, the essays by Holst, Wiberg, and Apunen in Mottola, ed., *op. cit.*

200. It is also worth noting that two of Canada's national parties, the Liberals and the New Democrats, are currently interested in various nuclear-free arrangements for Canada.

201. For a case in point see Wilkes, *op. cit.*

202. While there is no formal ban on nuclear weapons at the Thule base in Greenland and the Keflavik base in Iceland, the Greenlandic Home Rule government has clearly indicated its opposition to nuclear weapons in Greenland, and it is understood that there is an informal agreement between Iceland and the U.S. prohibiting nuclear weapons at Keflavik.

203. G. Leonard Johnson, David Bradley & Robert S. Winokur, 'United States Security Interests in the Arctic', in William E. Westermeyer & Kurt M. Shusterich, eds., *United States Arctic Interests: The 1980s and 1990s*, New York: Springer-Verlag (1984), 282.

204. For a variety of examples see the essays in *Information North*, a publication of the Arctic Institute of North America, Fall 1986.

205. See Jens Brosted, 'Civil Aspects of Military Installations in Greenland', *Information North*, Winter 1986, 14–16.

206. Jon M. Nielson, 'Kaktovik, Alaska: An Overview of Relocations', North Slope Borough Commission on History and Culture, November 1977.

207. See Helge Ole Bergesen, Arild Moe & Willy Ostreng, *Soviet Oil and Security Interests in the Barents Sea*, New York: St Martin's, 1987.

208. Jens Dahl, 'Greenland: Political Structure of Self-Government', *Arctic Anthropology*, 23 (1986), 315–24.

209. For some specific examples see Allen S. Whiting, *Siberian Development and East Asia: Threat or Promise?*, Stanford: Stanford University Press, 1981.

210. William E. Westermeyer & Vinod Goyal, 'Jurisdiction and Management of Arctic Marine Transportation', *Arctic*, 39 (1986), 338–49.

211. Cynthia Lamson & David VanderZwaag, 'Arctic Waters: Needs and Options for Canadian-American Cooperation', *Ocean Development and International Law*, 18 (1987), 49–99.

212. The 1986 General Assembly of the ICC, for example, formally adopted a set of Arctic policies covering a wide range of issue areas.

213. See Shelagh Jane Woods, 'The Wolf at the Door', *Northern Perspectives*, 14(2), 1986, 1–8.

214. For an interesting history of such activities in the Bering Sea region see William R. Hunt, *Arctic Passage*, New York: Scribner's, 1975.

215. For a review of the jurisdictional issues now arising in the Arctic see Kurt M. Shusterich, 'International Jurisdictional Issues in the Arctic Ocean', 240–67 in Westermeyer & Shusterich, eds., *op. cit.*

216. D. M. McRae, 'Management of Arctic Marine Transportation: A Canadian Perspective', *Arctic*, 39 (1986), 350–9. In January 1988, the United States and Canada signed a bilateral agreement in which they pledged cooperation on Arctic maritime matters but agreed to disagree on the legal status of the waters of the Arctic Archipelago in general and the Northwest Passage in particular.

217. See Tom G. Svensson, *Ethnicity and Mobilization in Sami Politics*, Stockholm: University of Stockholm, 1976, esp. Ch. 7.

218. See Gorbachev's Murmansk speech *op. cit.* for a high level Soviet recognition of this point.

219. William Barr, *The Expeditions of the First International Polar Year, 1882–83*, Technical Paper No. 29, Arctic Institute of North America, Calgary: AINA, 1985.

220. For a survey see E. F. Roots, 'International and Regional Cooperation in Arctic Science: A Changing Situation', in *Rapport fra Nordisk Vitenskapelig*

Konferanse om Arktisk Forskning, Trondheim: Universitet i Trondheim Press, 1984.

221. E. F. Roots & O. Rogne, 'Some Points for Consideration in Discussions on The Need For, Feasibility, and Possible Role of an International Arctic Science Committee', unpublished discussion paper, 1987.

222. In his Murmansk speech, Gorbachev *op. cit.* specifically includes science in laying out a six point program for international cooperation in the Arctic.

223. For background on the effort to establish an International Arctic Science Committee see E. F. Roots, 'Cooperation in Arctic Science: Background and Prospects', keynote address to the meeting on International Cooperation in Arctic Science, Stockholm, 24–26 March 1988.

224. See, for example, Bloomfield, *op. cit.*; Lamson & VanderZwaag, *op. cit.*; Boleslaw Boczek, 'The Arctic Ocean: An International Legal Profile', *International Studies Notes*, 11 (Spring 1985), 10–15; J. Enno Harders, 'The Arctic Ocean: Environmental Protection and Circumpolar Cooperation', Westwater Research Centre, University of British Columbia, 1986, and Gerald S. Schatz, 'The Polar Regions and Human Welfare: Regimes for Environmental Protection', 465–78 in Edmund A. Schofield, ed., *Earthcare: Global Protection of Natural Areas*, Boulder: Westview Press, 1978.

225. David L. VanderZwaag & Cynthia Lamson, 'Ocean Development and Management in the Arctic: Issues in American and Canadian Relations', paper prepared for the U.S.–Canada Arctic Policy Forum, Banff, Alberta, 1984.

226. For a straightforward account see Quigg, *op. cit.*

227. Oran R. Young, 'The Age of the Arctic', *Foreign Policy*, 61 (Winter 1985–1986), 160–79.

228. Lisle A. Rose, 'Recent Trends in U.S. Arctic Affairs', *Arctic*, 35 (1982), 241–2.

229. For a discussion of the Soviet Union in these terms see Boris Komarov, *The Destruction of Nature in the Soviet Union*, White Plains: M. E. Sharpe, 1980, Ch. 9.

230. On the image of a great Arctic energy rush see 'The Great Arctic Energy Rush', *Business Week*, 24 January 1983, 52–6.

231. On the Canadian case see Special Joint Committee, *op. cit.*, Ch. 10.

232. On the case of whales, see George L. Small, *The Blue Whale*, New York: Columbia University Press, 1971, Ch. VII.

233. Thomas C. Schelling, *The Strategy of Conflict*, Cambridge: Harvard University Press, 1960 and Howard Raiffa, *The Art and Science of Negotiation*, Cambridge: Harvard University Press, 1982.

234. James K. Sebenius, 'Negotiation arithmetic: adding and subtracting issues and parties', *International Organization*, 37 (1983), 281–316.

235. For an account endorsing Canadian/American initiatives see Robert L. Friedheim, 'The U.S.–Canada Arctic Policy Forum: Impressions from the American Co-Chair', *Arctic*, 29 (1986), 360–7.

236. On the Antarctic case see Kimball, *op. cit.*

237. John Rawls, *A theory of Justice*, Cambridge: Harvard University Press, 1971.

238. For an extended account of bargaining in these terms see Schelling, *op. cit.*

239. Franklyn Griffiths, ed., *Politics of the Northwest Passage*, Kingston and Montreal: McGill-Queen's University Press, 1987. But note that the January 1988 agreement between the United States and Canada on Arctic waters constitutes a hopeful sign in this connection. While the agreement does not set forth a cooperative regime in this realm, it does lay the groundwork for such a development by setting aside the relevant jurisdictional issues without prejudice.

240. On integrative bargaining see Raiffa, *op. cit.*, Part III.

241. Thomas C. Schelling, *Arms and Influence*, New Haven: Yale University Press, 1966, Ch. 2.

242. Oran R. Young, 'Arctic Shipping: An American Perspective', 115–33 in Griffiths, ed., *op. cit.* It is worth noting in this connection that the January 1988 agreement between the United States and Canada speaks explicitly of the Arctic waters of both countries.

243. See also the essays collected in Westermeyer & Shusterich, eds., *op. cit.* Even so, the sentiments expressed in Gorbachev's Murmansk speech seem promising in this connection.

244. Mark W. Zacher, 'Trade gaps, analytical gaps: regime analysis and international commodity trade regulation', *International Organization*, 41 (Spring 1987), 173–202.

245. For a seminal account of the free-rider problem consult Mancur Olson Jr., *The Logic of Collective Action*, Cambridge: Harvard University Press, 1965.

246. See Oran R. Young, *Compliance and Public Authority, A Theory with International Applications*, Baltimore: Johns Hopkins University Press, 1979 and Roger Fisher, *Improving Compliance with Internation Law*, Charlottesville: University Press of Virginia, 1981.

247. For an analysis of the use of such technologies in connection with fisheries law enforcement see U.S. Coast Guard, *Study of Coast Guard Enforcement of 200-Mile Fishery Conservation Zone*, Washington, D.C., May 1976.

Epilogue: An Arctic update – May 1989

We are struck by mounting evidence that the Arctic is coming into its own as a focus of attention among policymakers and scholars alike. Proposals for international arrangements to protect the environment of the Arctic have surfaced recently in a number of quarters. An international conference on Arctic research, designed to promote cooperation among the Arctic states and hosted by the Soviet Academy of Sciences in Leningrad during December 1988, drew over 500 participants. Prominent private funding sources, like the MacArthur Foundation and the Ford Foundation in the United States, as well as publicly supported funding sources, like the Canadian Institute for International Peace and Security, have signaled a growing interest in the role of the Arctic in world affairs by making sizeable grants to those working on Arctic projects. And courses dealing with Arctic or polar politics have begun to show up in the curricula of major universities.

Arctic issues – Arctic conflicts

During the interval since completion of the main text of this book, a number of Arctic conflicts involving the interests of military establishments, major industries, Native groups, and environmentalists have surfaced or taken on new dimensions. Consider a few striking examples:

● On March 24, 1989, the supertanker *Exxon Valdez* ran aground 25 miles from the terminus of the Trans Alaska Pipeline spilling 10.1 million gallons of oil into Prince William Sound. The disaster exposed the inadequacy of existing accident prevention measures as well as containment and contingency plans to clean up a major spill. The accident undercut the credibility of oil industry arguments and strengthened the bargaining position of environmental groups in ongoing controversies.

Legislation to allow oil development in the Arctic National Wildlife Refuge has been put on hold while Congressional committees turn their attention to safety and clean-up measures. The accident has sharpened conflict between oil companies and environmental and rural community advocacy groups as the latter capitalize on the opportunity to advance their interests while the former retrench to defend their industry. Positions, at least for the moment, have hardened, and efforts to promote creative problem solving are on hold.

● Two weeks after the Prince William Sound spill, a Soviet nuclear-powered, Mike class attack submarine carrying two torpedos with nuclear warheads caught fire, exploded and sank in the Norwegian Sea north of Norway. Forty-two sailors died. Scientists placed equipment near the vessel to monitor radiation levels, and preliminary tests showed no radiation leakage from the submarine's reactor. Yet, the accident underscored the environmental and safety risks of increasing military activity in the Arctic.

● In Canada, the Mulroney government cancelled plans to acquire 10–12 nuclear-powered submarines capable of operating for extended periods under Arctic conditions.

● Encounters between Soviet Bear bombers and American interceptors off the north and west coasts of Alaska have increased.

● The anti-trapping movement launched a new offensive in the European Parliament in the fall of 1988, proposing legislation requiring labels on fur products caught in steel-jaw, leghold traps. Native organizations are attempting to counter this initiative which they see as a new assault on the economic and cultural security of northern communities.

● The Alaska Native Claims Settlement Act Amendments of 1987, designed, in part, to defuse the ardor of tribal sovereignty advocates, have instead intensified the debate. In October 1988, the annual conference of the Alaska Federation of Natives, centered on the theme 'We Are Sovereign', became a forum for expression of conflicting views on tribal sovereignty and self-determination.

● Environmental concerns are surfacing throughout the Soviet system. Fyodor Morgun, chairman of the new State Committee for the Protection of the Environment, has spoken openly about pollution problems in the USSR that have accumulated over the past three decades. And *glasnost* has brought a new candor, even in the presence of westerners, about the serious negative social and environmental impacts of gigantic gas complexes and other industrial developments in the North. In March 1989, the Government temporarily suspended plans for new gas production on the Yamal Peninsula declaring environmental studies insufficient. And simulation models designed to determine the direction of Arctic development helped to defeat a proposal to construct a super-icebreaker.

● The new openness has brought to light the need to raise the standard of living and provide meaningful jobs for Native peoples in the Soviet North. A battle between assimilationists and those advocating self-determination is brewing in the Soviet North as in other Arctic nations.

● Faced with a severe economic decline in its northern counties, Norway has begun to rethink its policies regarding them. Norway wants to maintain a strong national presence along its common border with the Soviet Union and to stabilize the oil and gas industries; therefore, the Government has taken steps to stimulate offshore exploration in the Barents Sea as well as scientific and economic activities in Svalbard. While Norway has become a prominent advocate of sustainable development worldwide, at home oil accounts for roughly 30 percent of the GNP and half of Norway's foreign exchange. Meanwhile the political and economic status of the Sami people residing in the northern counties has still to be resolved. Given these conflicting pressures, northern policy is likely to remain an important item on Norway's political agenda for some time to come.

These and other emerging issues do not represent a sharp change of course in Arctic affairs. In fact, they involve clashes among the interests and interest groups we describe in detail in the first half of this book. What is new, in our judgment, is the visibility of these Arctic issues and the public attention they have begun to draw. A number of factors have combined to enhance public awareness of Arctic issues. Despite the region's remoteness, informed publics have become aware of the dangers associated with the militarization of the Arctic. Evidence is mounting concerning the role of the Arctic in global climate change. The current leadership in the Soviet Union has not only allowed a vigorous debate regarding Arctic issues to surface in domestic forums, it has also taken steps to stimulate international cooperation in the Arctic.

Just as Arctic issues are coming into focus in the eyes of informed publics throughout the Circumpolar North, we also see evidence of many new initiatives aimed at settling Arctic conflicts. The resultant activities involve the private sector and the public sector; they aim at both international and predominately domestic concerns. In this brief update, we touch on some of the most striking initiatives, grouped into the categories employed in Chapters 7–9.

Private initiatives

In addition to the much publicized Polar Bridge Expedition (see Figure 31), a surprising number of privately sponsored initiatives aimed at resolving long-standing Arctic conflicts and spurring long-term co-operation among Arctic states are quietly unfolding. Some of these ventures explicitly address issues of peace and security; others seek to open channels of communication between East and West and are part of a rapidly growing network of contacts between individuals and organizations in the USSR and the other Arctic states. Many of these efforts, like the agreement on medical research between the University of Alaska and the Siberian Branch of the Soviet Academy of Sciences, are bilateral arrangements between private or quasi-governmental institutions. But a growing number represent multilateral attempts to address problems that cannot be resolved without the cooperation of several or all of the Arctic states.

A Working Group on Arctic International Relations, composed of individuals from all the Arctic states, met in Iceland in July 1988 and in Greenland in April 1989. Funded by the MacArthur Foundation, the

Fig. 31. Members of the Soviet–Canadian Transpolar Expedition at the North Pole on 26 April 1988, having skiied 980 kilometers from the USSR in 54 days. The expedition went on to complete the first ever crossing of the Arctic Ocean on skis, arriving at Canada's Ellesmere Island on 1 June 1988. *Source*: photo. by J. Major, courtesy of Polar Bridge Expedition.

Working Group is dedicated to the cause of international cooperation in the Arctic. The Group will continue to meet at approximately nine-month intervals. The Greenland session focused on the theme of sustainable development in the Arctic.

In October 1988, an International Conference on Arctic Cooperation, sponsored by Science for Peace and funded in large measure by the Canadian Institute of International Peace and Security, met for several days in Toronto. The Conference participants, individuals from all the Arctic states including an impressive contingent of northern Natives, explored opportunities for Arctic cooperation and generated a sense of optimism about cooperation in this region.

The Tampere Peace Research Institute, supported again by the MacArthur Foundation, has organized several meetings of a 'Workshop on Alternative Security and Development in the Arctic Regions'. In Ivalo, Finland, during November 1988 the Workshop focused on prospects for promoting peace through international economic cooperation and development. The group is planning additional meetings in Aberdeen, Scotland, and Lentiira, Finland, in 1989 to address such themes as arms control, demilitarization, Arctic regimes, and the status of indigenous peoples.

December 1988 brought a second Arctic Policy Conference at McGill University in Montreal (its predecessor took place in September 1985). This conference, an off-the-record session designed to prepare the ground for the Inuit Circumpolar Conference's General Assembly to be held in Sisimiut, Greenland, during July 1989, featured participation by political leaders of northern Alaska, the Northwest Territories and Nunivik (the new official name for the predominately Inuit region of Northern Quebec) in Canada, and Greenland. It was remarkable for the clarity and candor with which northern leaders voiced the concerns of the Arctic's permanent residents and sought to design strategies to protect Arctic residents from the impacts of southern economic imperatives and environmental problems.

The growing interest in multilateral cooperation in Arctic science is providing new opportunities for some existing organizations, like the Comité Arctique International based in Monaco, and revitalizing others, like the Northern Science Network established under UNESCO's Man and the Biosphere Program in 1982. During the fall of 1988, the Network's secretariat issued a new edition of its lapsed newsletter and offered the services of the Network as a coordinating mechanism for international scientific cooperation in the Arctic pending the establishment of the proposed International Arctic Science Committee (see discussion below).

On another plane but of equal interest are the efforts of the Native peoples of the Bering Sea region to reestablish regular contact on a circum-Bering Sea basis, opening the border between the United States and the Soviet Union to a variety of international exchanges in the process. This initiative has already borne its first fruit. In July 1988, Alaska Airlines took a planeload of Alaskans to the Soviet community of Provideniya on the Chukotka Peninsula. Shortly thereafter a boatload of Soviets paid a return visit, stopping at Saint Lawrence Island and calling at Nome. Efforts are now underway to expand this initial contact into a regular flow of people between Alaska and the Soviet Far East. Several months later, in September 1988, a joint Soviet/American exhibition on the cultures of the Bering Sea region, entitled 'Crossroads of Continents', opened in Washington, D.C. After touring in North America, the entire exhibition will move to the Soviet Union.

The year 1988 also witnessed a flowering of joint enterprises, opening up the prospect of substantial commercial ties linking various parts of the Circumpolar North. The Soviet Union, which has purchased icebreakers from Finland for many years, is now entering into joint ventures aimed at offshore hydrocarbon exploration, with Norwegian companies supplying advanced technology and engineering. And there is considerable talk about joint development zones in the Arctic of the type established to resolve the conflict between Norway and Iceland regarding the marine areas surrounding Jan Mayen. While joint enterprises represent a departure from past practice in the Far North, the scale of the investments required and the risks associated with developing renewable and non-renewable resources in the Arctic make the region a natural for increased joint venture activity. And as western business interests become more deeply involved in industrial development in the Soviet Union, we can expect them to become staunch supporters of amicable and stable relations between East and West.

Finally, non-governmental environmental organizations, following the lead of the World Commission on Environment and Development (the Brundtland Commission), are calling for an expansion of the concept of security and identifying environmental or ecological security as one of the most pressing problems of our era. The global agendas of these organizations have brought the Arctic into the limelight as scientists increasingly focus on this region to understand global weather patterns, heat exchange, and the depletion of stratospheric ozone.

Public policies

Throughout the Arctic, governments are establishing new structures to handle emerging Arctic issues and beginning the task of reexamining Arctic policies in the light of recent developments. In Chapter 8, we commented on the role of the Arctic Research Commission and the Interagency Arctic Research Policy Committee in the United States. But structural developments in other Arctic states are equally if not more impressive. On 1 January 1989, for instance, the Ministry for Greenland in the Danish government went out of existence; its functions either devolved to the Greenlandic Home Rule government or transferred to Denmark's newly created Polar Center. It is probable that the Canadian government will act during 1989 to establish a Canadian Polar Research Commission charged with the task of advising government agencies on polar matters as well as coordinating research dealing with Arctic concerns. And Sweden is on the verge of creating a Swedish Sami Parliament along lines that parallel the existing Finnish Sami Parliament.

Most impressive of all in structural terms, however, is the Soviet State Commission for Arctic Affairs established during 1988 and now beginning to function. Operating under the auspices of the Council of Ministers of the USSR and chaired by a first deputy prime minister, this Commission includes representatives of all major ministries and state committees in the Soviet government. In addition to serving as an interagency coordinating body on Arctic matters within the Soviet government, the Commission has been charged explicitly with the task of stimulating and managing cooperation between the Soviet Union and other Arctic states on matters of scientific research and environmental protection. To facilitate these efforts, the Commission has established under its auspices a Scientific and Technical Council. No other Arctic state has yet taken steps to establish such a high level mechanism to formulate and coordinate public policies on Arctic issues.

In several of the Arctic states, moreover, new policies regarding Arctic matters are beginning to emerge. The Greenland Home Rule government is committed to maintaining small communities. Though, by southern standards, their fishing fleets and small fish-processing plants are inefficient, the Home Rule authorities take the view that over the next century, their investment in the support of small, remote communities and settlements will prove wise.

An early assessment of the impact of the 1987 Amendments to the Alaska Native Claims Settlement Act, developed by our colleague Nicholas Flanders, suggests that this legislation heralds a notable shift in

American policy away from assimilationism for Alaska's Natives. In effect, the Amendments signal an abandonment of the view that the economic future for the Native peoples of Alaska lies largely in the development of non-renewable resources located on lands belonging to Native corporations. The Amendments automatically put all undeveloped land owned by Native corporations into a land bank that exempts the land from taxation and the claims of creditors. Coupled with provisions permitting the creation of settlement trusts and abrogating the requirement that stocks in Native corporations become alienable in 1991, the effect of the land bank is to encourage conservation and to promote sustainable development based on hunting, fishing, and trapping. While the debate over the passage of the 1987 Amendments stirred controversy between advocates of tribal sovereignty and those willing to live with modified corporate structures, the effect of this legislation in practice may be to alleviate conflict between environmentalists and advocates of industrial development.

In some ways, the most dramatic shift in Arctic policies has occurred in the Soviet Union. With Gorbachev's Arctic zone of peace initiative has come a dramatic increase in interest throughout the Soviet policy community in multilateral as well as bilateral approaches to Arctic international cooperation aimed at economic development, environmental protection, and reduction of tensions associated with militarization of the Arctic. With *glasnost*, moreover, has come an outpouring of concern for the environmental consequences of economic development in the North. This movement has even begun to slow hydrocarbon development in northwestern Siberia and to force a balancing of environmental and social effects with economic needs.

International cooperation

The year 1988 opened with a flurry of bilateral agreements between Arctic states. In January, Canada and the United States signed an Agreement on Arctic Cooperation under which the U.S. pledged to obtain Canadian consent for navigation of American icebreakers 'within waters claimed by Canada to be internal', even while agreeing to disagree regarding the legal status of the waters of the Arctic Archipelago. In October, the *Polar Star* transited the Passage from West to East under the terms of this agreement without incident and without provoking even a ripple of the angry response that followed the transit of its sister ship, the *Polar Sea*, in the summer of 1985.

Also in 1988, the Soviet Union signed a series of bilaterals with Norway, Sweden, and Finland pertaining to Arctic matters. One of the bilaterals with Norway provides a framework for cooperation regarding environmental protection and places particular emphasis on examining pollution of Barents Sea waters, countering oil spills in the Barents Sea, and resolving Soviet/Norwegian conflicts relating to air and water pollution emanating from the Kola Peninsula. Another initiates a program of scientific and technological cooperation on problems relating to the Arctic. A third establishes procedures for assisting each other in search and rescue operations in the Barents Sea. Yet a fourth calls for notification of nuclear accidents that could lead to radioactive contamination crossing from one country to the other. This agreement (and a similar agreement between the Soviet Union and Sweden) is motivated, in part, by Norwegian and Swedish concerns stemming from the proximity of a Soviet nuclear power plant on the Kola Peninsula. Soviet/Finnish bilateral agreements provide for an exchange of information regarding safety measures in nuclear power stations, establishment of rules designed to increase safety in such facilities, and cooperation to reduce transboundary air pollution.

The Soviet Union also increased activity under the terms of bilateral agreements with Canada and the United States in 1988. At the Moscow summit in the spring, a Soviet/American agreement on mutual fisheries relations was formalized. The agreement focuses particularly on conservation and management of Bering Sea fish stocks. And plans are nearing completion at this time for a Soviet/American oil spill contingency plan for the Bering and Chukchi Seas. The proposed bilateral Agreement on Arctic Cooperation between Canada and the Soviet Union, which has been widely discussed since 1987, remains to be formalized. But Canadian sources have indicated that the conclusion of such an agreement is probable during 1989.

Denmark and Norway have submitted their dispute over maritime boundaries between Jan Mayen and Greenland to international arbitration. Coupled with the 1981 arbitration that resolved a similar conflict between Iceland and Norway, this development may provide new impetus for proposals to initiate joint development zones (of the sort recommended in the 1981 decision) to manage the human use of the natural resources of the Arctic sector of the North Atlantic. Such a development could also breathe new life into earlier proposals for the establishment of similar zones to manage the use of the transboundary resources of the Bering and Beaufort Seas.

Even more striking than this proliferation of bilateral agreements is the growing recognition that many Arctic problems require multilateral responses and the consequent emergence of serious interest in multilateral regimes in the Arctic. In December 1988, representatives of the eight Arctic states prepared a set of 'founding articles' that they hope will lead to the establishment of an International Arctic Science Committee (IASC) in 1989. This plan, the product of four international meetings in 1988 and several years of discussions of proposals elaborated in background papers, will produce an ongoing organization to promote cooperative research on the Arctic and to link the concerns of Arctic scientists to the program of the global change movement emerging in connection with the International Geosphere-Biosphere Programme (IGBP). For the Soviets it may mean access to areas, like Greenland, which have been off limits for Soviet scientists. And western scientists anticipate access to areas of the Soviet Arctic previously closed to them. As negotiations relating to the proposed IASC progressed, significant concessions were made by all parties, with the Soviets making an important shift from a position favoring participation limited to the five states actually bordering on the Arctic Ocean to a position of accepting participation by Finland, Iceland, and Sweden as well and finally to a willingness to allow meaningful participation by scientists from other countries mounting active and continuing Arctic science programs. At this writing, plans are underway to launch a five-year scientific program (1992–1997) with freeze-in drifts in the Arctic commemorating the centennial of Fridtjof Nansen's polar drift during the 1890s and the fiftieth anniversary of the drift of the Soviet icebreaker *Sedov* (1937–1940). Scientists from the Federal Republic of Germany as well as Canada, Norway, the Soviet Union, and the United States are expected to participate in this program.

There are, in addition, indications that these new developments in international cooperation regarding Arctic science will spill over into other areas. The Government of Finland, for example, has launched an initiative which it hopes will lead to a comprehensive regime for protection of the Arctic environment. Finland has invited the other seven Arctic states to participate in an ambassadorial level conference later in 1989 to discuss protection of the marine and coastal environment, living resources, climate change, and the threat of radioactive contamination. To date, Sweden and the Soviet Union have indicated a willingness to participate in such talks and others have signaled receptivity to the idea more informally. At the December 1988 Leningrad Conference, moreover, there was much discussion of the need for multilateral responses to the environmental problems of the Arctic region. And on the practical level, all of the Arctic nations have provided Exxon with equipment to assist in the clean up of Prince William Sound. It appears to us, then, that 1989 may witness a broad movement toward multilateral arrangements dealing with environmental issues in the Arctic.

The recent flurry of activity regarding international cooperation in the Arctic bears witness to the emerging perception of the Arctic as a distinctive region of considerable importance in global terms. Whether cooperation regarding scientific, cultural, and environmental matters will slow the militarization of the Arctic or lead to Arctic arms control, however, remains to be seen. Many Soviets increasingly emphasize links between cooperation on civil matters and the issues of peace and security. The Soviets have become leaders in espousing the concept of environmental or ecological security and arguing that economic development and environmental protection are both, in considerable measure, contingent upon controlling or even reversing the arms race. In his speeches and writings, for example, Gorbachev has repeatedly called attention to the need to reduce military spending in order to devote more resources to restructuring the Soviet economy and protecting the global environment. Foreign policymakers in the West, on the other hand, have generally resisted this move to link civil and military issues. Many express skepticism about the usefulness of concepts like ecological security, and the western states have largely dismissed or rejected the arms control provisions in the Soviet Arctic zone of peace initiative, even while cautiously welcoming other elements of the initiative. Despite this difference in perspectives, however, it appears to us that the growth of an increasingly dense network of bilateral and multilateral arrangements encompassing both governmental and non-governmental participants is a hopeful sign with respect to the capacity of the Arctic states to cope with the growing array of conflicts in the region that transcend national boundaries.

Conclusion

Arctic issues pitting the interests of military establishments, corporations, Native groups, and environmentalists against each other have become more prominent in the months since we completed the main body of this book. Yet we are also witnessing a growth in public awareness of the Arctic as a distinctive region together with some initial steps toward increasing the capabilities of the Arctic states to deal with Arctic conflicts. Interestingly, the results are surfacing simultaneously in the form of private initiatives, public policies, and arrangements designed to facilitate international cooperation. Far from representing competing thrusts, we believe that these developments will serve to reinforce each other both by crystallizing the views of a number of constituencies regarding the value of approaching the Arctic as a distinctive region and by providing a growing collection of institutional tools that can be brought to bear to resolve specific issues pertaining to the Arctic.

Index

Printed in the United States
79102LV00003B/44